VISIBLE DEEDS OF MUSIC

VISIBLE DEEDS OF

MUSIC ART AND MUSIC FROM WAGNER TO CAGE

SIMON SHAW-MILLER

YALE UNIVERSITY PRESS

NEW HAVEN & LONDON

Small sections of Chapter 1 appeared in the review essay "Sounding Out," *Oxford Art Journal* 20, no. 1 (1997), 105–9. A section of Chapter 2 appeared as "Skriabin and Obukhov—*Mysterium* and *La Livre de vie:* The Concept of the Total Work of Art," in *Consciousness, Literature and the Arts* 1, no. 3 (December 2000; e-journal: www.aber.ac.uk/tfts/journal/december/skria.html). An earlier version of Chapter 3 appeared as "Instruments of Desire: Musical Morphology in the Early Work of Picasso," *Musical Quarterly* 76, no. 4 (Winter 1992), 442–64. An earlier version of Chapter 6 appeared as "Concerts of Everyday Living": Cage, Barthes and Fluxus: Interdisciplinarity and Inter-Media Events," in a special number of *Art History,* entitled *Image-Music-Text* 19, no. 1 (March 1996), 1–25. Music examples 5.3–5.8 were created by Robert Michael Weiss and first published in the catalogue *Josef Matthias Hauer, 80 Jahre Zwölftonmusik* (Kulturamt der Stadt Wiener Neustadt, 1999) for the J. M. Hauer exhibition in Wiener Neustadt, April 1999. They are reproduced by courtesy of Josef Matthias Hauer Studio Robert Michael Weiss, Vienna. Music example 5.12 was made for this publication by Robert Michael Weiss, transcribed from the first recording made by Victor Sokolowski on LP Phillips 6599 333 (1973).

Designed by Nancy Ovedovitz and set in Times Roman with Meta types by Tseng Information Systems, Inc. Printed in the United States of America by Edwards Brothers, Inc.

Library of Congress Cataloging-in-Publication Data
Miller, Simon, 1960–
Visible deeds of music : art and music from Wagner to Cage / Simon Shaw-Miller.
     p.   cm.
Includes bibliographical references and index.
ISBN 0-300-08374-2 (alk. paper)
1. Art and music—History—19th century.   2. Art and music—History—20th century.
I. Title.
ML3849 .S47 2002
780'.07—dc21   2001008006
A catalogue record for this book is available from the British Library.

The paper in this book meets the guidelines for permanence and durability of the Committee on Production Guidelines for Book Longevity of the Council on Library Resources.

10 9 8 7 6 5 4 3 2 1

Dedicated to a most harmonious sound:
"LA!"
(Lindsey and Aniella)
and a silence:
in memoriam
(John Raisin, 1938–1999)

CONTENTS

The absolute arts are a sad modern impertinence. Everything is falling apart.
There is no organization to foster all the arts together as Art.
—Friedrich Nietzsche

The relationships between music and visual art in the first half of the twentieth
century are the subject of this book. From Richard Wagner to John Cage, I explore a number of themes that emerge in the consideration of modernism on the
nexus of sight and sound, the spatial and the temporal. This work is not an attempt to cover all instances of art and music's interrelations in this extraordinary
period. Rather, it addresses the media bias of discussions of modernism through
consideration of a number of key moments—between c. 1860 and c. 1960, when
the purism of modernism (especially in the writings of Clement Greenberg and
Michael Fried), in terms of definition through media specificity, is contrasted
with the more hybrid and "theatrical" manifestations of practices that operate
under the "surface" of this paradigm of modernism.

Chapter 1 raises a number of issues in relation to interdisciplinary study and
aims to differentiate inter- from cross- and multidisciplinary research. It takes up
the philosopher Jerrold Levinson's discussion of hybridity (into the categories

"juxtaposition," "synthesis," and "transformation"). Through the filter of a number of discussions that use Gotthold Lessing's *Laocoön* and his differentiation of the arts on the basis of temporal and spatial characteristics, this chapter looks at ways that art and music have been historically separated from each other. The main argument can be summarized thus: (1) music operates as an exemplar of autonomy for the visual arts within the paradigm of modernism; or (2) music conversely operates as an exemplar of connection for art practices within the paradigm of postmodernism (and to an extent with premodern practice). In the first statement, music is to be understood as mere sound, what has been called "music alone."[1] In the second, music is to be understood as a field of activities, a discourse or discursive practice.

The contention is that notions of media purity in modernism are the historical exception. The conception of fluid boundaries between the sonoric and the visual (as indeed also between the textual) is a closer reflection of artistic practices throughout history, than the seeking out and patrolling of borders on the basis of time, space, or media alone.

Chapter 2 addresses Richard Wagner's music and ideas at the time of Charles Baudelaire's definition of modernity. Wagner argues that each separate art form tends to extend itself (its power) to its limits and cannot pass this limit without losing itself in incomprehension. This move to, or beyond, the ontological limits is the enterprise of modern art. The *Gesamtkunstwerk,* or art work of the future as he most often expresses it, is a means of containing excess and safeguarding meaning. Baudelaire's response to Wagner was to recognize that here was an art that truly threatened the long-affirmed supremacy of poetry: poetry becomes a form of protomusic. The Gesamtkunstwerk is positioned as the "end of art," in as much as it is the unification and synthesis of all the individual arts (under, however, the banner of music). It is the most modern in its lack of an antique model.

Greenberg's response to this same crisis was rather to build up each art's defensive barriers so that "each art would, to be sure, narrow its area of competence, but at the same time it would make its possession of this area all the more secure."[2]

For Greenberg, then, the conditions of representation are central to artistic practice, so that art becomes its own subject; this is not so much a stylistic shift as a paradigmatic transformation. Art does this in order to arrest the drift that Wagner identifies in the extension of the arts beyond their limits (into unintelligibility). This act of purification, ironically, moves painting toward music (as it conversely moves away from the sculptural and the literary). Although contrary to Wagner and the conception of the Gesamtkunstwerk, Greenberg's modernism pursues a strategy of exclusion. The influence of Wagner's aesthetic is briefly discussed in relation to Aleksandr Scriabin and Nikolay Obukhov, with a note on

Olivier Messiaen. Consideration of these figures shows that at the birth of modernity, one powerful strain of practices stands in antithesis to the purism of formalist modernism, in its pull to achieve unification.

Chapter 3 considers a central defining plank of the modernist canon: cubism, specifically the cubism of Pablo Picasso. Although for Greenberg, Edouard Manet was the first modernist, cubism marks a fundamental shift in the development of modern art. Greenberg discusses cubism in terms of formal innovation, and it has been seen by many to mark a fundamental shift in the history of art: from a perceptual to a conceptual emphasis. However, if we consider a contextual understanding, focusing on music, we can show conceptual contact with a wide range of cultural issues. Cubism's concern with traditional subject matter, as a vehicle for that formal innovation in technique, is important, but it is not the whole story. Music and musical instruments, in Picasso's cubist works, both signify Idea, rather than the visible particular (indeed its invisibility gives music its power), and through musical objects (instruments) other extravisual elements such as touch and hearing, and physical bodies, are played on within the rules of a complex game. The subject matter of these works is far from neutral. Such *corps sonores* resonate outside the confines of the frame.

Greenberg's ideas lead to (and from) abstraction, indeed were formulated in the 1940s within the context of abstraction's identification as avant-garde, and as such form the elite vehicle that maintains superiority over kitsch or academicism. Here music again acts as a powerful agent of meaning. Following Wagner, this is achieved not via the mind but via the feelings, through the instinct of the artist. It is apparent that music means something profound, but its significance lies in the subject rather than the object. In Chapter 4, the role of music in the work of František Kupka, a little discussed but important early abstract artist, is contrasted with that of Paul Klee. Music for Kupka is a transcendental signifier, a re-presentation of the will, the spirit, the idea. For Klee, music is to be understood as an organic, and already cultural, metaphor of growth, creation, and the forces of nature. For Klee music was principally seen as a way to emphasize the dimension of time, and therefore change, in visual art, as against Lessing's divisions. Klee's work does not pursue or reflect a simple teleology of modernism but is a more circular, essentially an experimental rubric.

The Austrian composer Josef Matthias Hauer is the main focus of Chapter 5. Like Klee, Hauer stands to one side of the modernist paradigm. Hauer's music and ideas have much in common with Greenbergian modernism, for example, in the attempt to develop a new metamusical language. Yet if we look in detail at his little discussed aesthetic, if we distinguish its specificity—in contrast to the more familiar tactic of describing it as an inferior form of serialism—we find not so much a minor modernist, but rather a challenging, somewhat anachronistic figure, a figure whose aesthetic, by virtue of its deviance from this paradigm, is conceptually close to minimalism, the first art movement to challenge Greenbergian ideology in the 1960s. This chapter necessarily contains a good deal of technical discussion due to the unfamiliarity of Hauer's ideas, especially for the English-language reader. The argument considers Hauer's ideas in relation to the developments from dodecaphony to Karlheinz Stockhausen's notion of *moment form* to minimalism, in both music and visual art. It relates Hauer's aesthetic to a concern with three basic categories, first employed by the musicologist Jonathan Bernard in relation to minimalism: (1) the avoidance of aleatoricism, (2) the emphasis on surface, and (3) the concern with disposition rather than composition.

The final chapter brings back the idea of the Gesamtkunstwerk, but in the context of John Cage's work, which is in many ways antithetical to the idea in its Wagnerian guise. Here the concern is with silence over amplification, coexistence over synthesis; music does not sublimate the other arts (nor, in Greenberg's terms, provide them with a "notion of purity derived from the example of music"). Volume does not drown out the other arts' voices. Rather, it is through Cage's aesthetic of silence that the other arts can be *seen* to be a part of the discourse of music—textual, visual, and theatrical. They are already part of the fabric of music, part of the chorus of voices that make up the concept "music." This allows us to relate back to the initial discussion of the separation of the arts and its emphasis in Greenbergian modernism. But in the face of a post-Cagian (postmodernist) culture, we are made more aware of the blurring of disciplinary boundaries and the necessity to rethink relationships.

ACKNOWLEDGMENTS

I should like to express my thanks to a number of individuals who have commented on the contents of this book in its various states of development (who are of course in no part responsible for its faults): Paul Binski, John Covach, Thomas Crow, Jonathan Impett, James Lawson, Richard Leppert, Donald Mitchell, Marcia Pointon, Antony Sellors, Peter Vergo. I also owe a debt of gratitude to Alessio Antonielli, whose calm and conscientious approach to the drudgery of bureaucracy saw the consolidation of the illustrative material through the later stages. Thank you. Also to Suzanne Reynolds of Honeychurch Associates for her care and interest. Sylvia Carlyle's way with the Web helped me tie up some last-minute bibliographic queries, for which I'm most grateful.

Any contemporary researcher on J. M. Hauer will at some point owe a considerable debit to Robert M. Weiß of the Joseph Matthias Hauer Konservatorium in Wiener Neustadt. I most certainly do, and I thank him for his help, patience (when the technical details of Hauer's approach took time to sink in), and generous friendship over the years.

To single out any of my colleagues in the School of History of Art at Birkbeck would be inappropriate, as all of them provide a most supportive and intellectually stimulating environment in which to work (not least the School's administrative and support staff).

As a dyslexic I am sensible of a second-hand relationship to language, that it has passed through others' minds on its way to me. I hope I have not misrepresented them in my attempts to refashion and reapply them. That my thoughts have achieved passable English is largely a result of a number of timely interventions. My wife, Lindsey, who is always my first editor, mainly instigated these, with patience and sympathy. She has shared my interests and in discussion helped to form them into clearer prose. My "second" editor, Harry Haskell at Yale, has likewise been most supportive and above all enthusiastic for this project since he solicited its embryonic (and rather different) synopsis. The diligent and sympathetic copyediting of Laura Jones Dooley saved me from many embarrassing errors. Thank you for your care and for providing me with (at least on paper) an American accent.

If I might borrow and rephrase the words of Michel Chion: this book might not be complete, nor immune to criticism, but at least it exists!

ONE
UT PICTURA MUSICA

INTERDISCIPLINARITY, ART, AND MUSIC

All art constantly aspires towards the condition of music. — Walter Pater

Comparing the resources of totally different arts, one art learning from another, can only be successful and victorious if not merely the externals, but also the principles are learned.
— Wassily Kandinsky

Novalis: "This is waking, that is a dream, this belongs to the body, that to the spirit, this belongs to space and distance, that to time and duration. But space spills over into time, as the body into the soul, so that one cannot be measured without the other. I want to exert myself to find a different kind of measurement."
— Penelope Fitzgerald, *The Blue Flower*

Our words for the practices of art and music have classical roots. The Greek word *technē* and the Latin *ars* both originally related closely to notions of skill. *Technē* included a specific form, *mousike technē*, which signified the "art of the Muses."

However, the word *technē* was often omitted in Greek usage, and *mousike* on its own stood for "art of the Muses." And although this is the root of our word *music,* it was first a concept signifying any art form over which the Muses presided: poetry, song, dance, astronomy.[1] *Mousike* did not, therefore, signify in a narrow sense what we might now think of as "music"; it is not used in Greek as a term for a solely auditory art form until at least the fourth century B.C.

The visual arts of painting, sculpture, and architecture, activities that can be distinguished in part by their devotion to aesthetic issues above utility and craft, appear not to have been thought of as a group before the fifth century B.C. Indeed, in antiquity it would be more accurate to designate all such "visual" cultural practices under the concept "craft" rather than art. Similarly, the artist had no social status above other artisans, until in the fifth century art was developed as a more distinct activity, although this was then a relatively subtle distinction. One of the definitive contentions that emerged at this time was the relationship of the arts to necessity and luxury. Painting and music were famously classified by Plato (against the more hedonistic views of some of his contemporaries) as luxuries, but with the proviso that elements of them could rise above this material status to provide benefit to the soul; a link is made between beauty and moral worth: "ugliness of form and bad rhythm and disharmony are akin to poor quality expression and character, and their opposites are akin to and represent good character and discipline."[2] This statement is part of a general discussion of education in which Plato is concerned to promote exposure only to the good. Both music and the graphic arts share rhythm and harmony as the means to produce beauty.

For Plato, central to the classification and purpose of the arts was the concept of imitation (*mimesis*), as this relates directly to his notion of the *eidos,* the realm of suprasensible reality, which is distinct from the *eidolon,* which is the impression of this reality based on likeness (*eikon*). The fact that the visual arts might be more than mere imitation is not of concern to Plato, and indeed for him, only certain types of music or musical modes (*harmoniai*) were acceptable or beneficial to the soul, and thus appropriate to education. In this it was important to distinguish the intellectual principles of harmony, for example, and not to surrender to their more sensuous elements. The close relationship between tone and word (in mousike)—the invariable length and pitch of Greek syllables from which the sound was related and developed—linked sound and meaning through the medium of the word. However, music gradually became more independent of the word. By the middle of the fifth century instrumental improvisations had developed, often based on imitations of natural sounds rather than words, and it was to this that Plato largely responded in his attempts to promote and prohibit certain types of aesthetic development. The relationship between music and the word is an issue we shall take up again in the next chapter.

For Aristotle, all arts are arts of imitation. He wrote in the *Poetics*: "Epic and tragic poetry, comedy too, dithyrambic poetry, and most music composed for the flute and lyre, can all be described in general terms as forms of imitation or representation." Here music is in service to the word and aims to represent "men's characters and feelings and actions."³ Music is seen to function as a natural sign system, one grounded in imitation. In *The Politics,* he characterizes rhythm and melody as aesthetic elements best able to produce imitations of such passions as anger, courage, and other qualities of character.

Neoclassical thinkers tended to think of music and imitation in narrower terms, more suited to the visual arts alone, as representations in a medium that shares properties in common with the thing represented. The medieval division of the arts into the seven "liberal" arts consisted of grammar, logic, rhetoric, arithmetic, geometry, astronomy, and music. In the fifteenth century the conceptual separation or combination of art and science as two different activities would not have been a part of the artist's project. For Leonardo da Vinci, "art" referred to something like skill and "science" meant something like knowledge.⁴

Until the seventeenth century "art" still included such varied activities as mathematics, medicine, and angling, but then it came to signify a more specialized group of skills that had not before been formally grouped together—namely, drawing, painting, engraving, and sculpture. Up to the eighteenth century it was common to discuss painting and sculpture, music and dance but not to speak of "art" as a general term.⁵

Indeed, our common use of "art" did not come into being until the nineteenth century, along with the distinction between art and craft, artist and artisan. Alexander Gottlieb Baumgarten (1714–62) coined the word *aesthetics* in *Reflections on Poetry* in 1735 and used the word slightly later as the title of his two-volume work *Aesthetica* (1750–58). But in the reconsideration of music's place in aesthetics that took place in the eighteenth century, Aristotle's terms of reference— music as the imitation of the passions or as the sonic signifier of the passions— again emerged as important elements in the debate. Principal among these terms was the notion of music as a natural sign system, as part of a general representational theory. Abbé Jean-Baptiste Dubos wrote early in the century: "Whereof as the painter imitates the strokes and colours of nature, in like manner the musician imitates the tones, accents, sighs, and inflexions of the voice; and in short all those sounds, by which nature herself expresses her sentiments and passions."⁶

The dominant tradition of aesthetics up to the eighteenth century was not one that aimed to pursue generic differences, seeking out and patrolling the borders between the arts. Rather, it was primarily concerned with the issue of resemblance, that which was shared by art forms, the "sister arts." Horace's (65– 8 B.C.) phrase "ut pictura poesis" (as is painting, so is poetry) derives from the

Ars poetica (361). It was attributed to Simonides (556–468 B.C.) by Plutarch in the form of "painting is mute poetry and poetry a speaking picture" (*Moralia*, 346). The analogy remained powerful, even when challenged, while the arts were thought of as essentially imitative. But with the romantics the arts were thought of more as expression than imitation, and this analogy was replaced by another, what we can call "ut pictura musica" (as is music, so is painting).

I do not intend to provide a historiography of the concepts of music and visual art. Here it is enough to stress that they are mutable concepts; not only have they changed their meaning on the verbal level, but such surface changes of meaning signify deeper underlying cultural movements and trends. For it is useful to consider the difference between music and the visual arts as a matter of *degree*, not of *kind*. In so doing we are forced to reflect on scholarly practice, to see the validity of traditional disciplinary premises as historical, ideological conventions, not as natural unequivocal boundaries. This is not the same as saying that there are no differences between art and music or that such distinctions are false. It is the very power of these distinctions, to construct ways of seeing, that we need to remember. The issue of difference is one of constant negotiation.

This might appear at first sight to be a rather ill-judged overstatement, but I take support from W. J. T. Mitchell's convincing arguments deployed against similar issues of difference in poetry and painting in his important work *Iconology: Image, Text, Ideology* (1986).[7]

The historical material I deal with in this book takes the form of a series of case studies within the period of history now commonly termed modernist (c. 1860–1960). The theoretical characterization of this phase of history was marked by an attempt to (re)establish the "essential" identity of each branch of cultural practice, each art form. But more than this, a strong sense of censure was (is) attached to the project: that through the "self evident truth" of the "natural" boundaries between the arts, the issue becomes as much a moral one—that the arts *should* only "concern themselves with certain formal characteristics"—as it was a merely neutral formal requirement—that they "can only express certain things within these essential borders." Yet as Mitchell points out, "There would be no need to say that the genres *should not* be mixed if they *could not* be mixed."[8] In other words, the definition of modernism was as much an ideological tendency as it was a "scientific" drawing of demarcation lines. Indeed, the very notion that a "scientific" method can be an appropriate explicatory model must be questioned. Rather, we should consider music and art relations to be a result of particular historical formations, dependent on relations of production, reproduction, and sociopolitical forces, which are transformed within history. I do not simply wish to oppose attempts at single unitary systems of thinking, such as certain notions of modernism, that attempt to account for all similarities and differences. And I cannot hope to explore all the ideological issues that underlie the approaches I discuss in these pages. Instead, in the following chapters, I argue that it is more appropriate to see attempts at systemization and demarcation in the arts as historically grounded, as part of a dialogue, one that questions at the level of both theory and practice. I provide a series of case studies that complicate the conception of modernist art practice as grounded in unique, practice-specific essences. In doing this I am aware that issues of class and gender, among others, could be developed from the discussion, issues bound up with the social history of art. My intention is to expose the intellectual basis of art and music relationships within notions of modernism—a level of theory that is diminished within social and political analysis—and to make sonoric concerns visible. In this way ideological notions can become apparent and open to question, even if all social ramifications cannot be exposed here.

So let us briefly explore the nature of the "essential" identity of music and visual art. I begin with the premise that there is no single essential or *sufficient* defining difference between them, although that is not to say that there are not *necessary* characteristics.

We have seen that in antiquity the boundaries between the arts were not as they now are. But one of the most famous accounts of demarcation, indeed perhaps the first extended attempt to define distinctive and "appropriate" spheres of action between art forms, a work that characterizes artistic medium and is the source for modernist assumptions of the uniqueness and autonomy of the individual arts, a work written in the eighteenth century but based on antique practices, is Gotthold Ephraim Lessing's *Laokoon: Oder, Über die Grenzen der Malerei und Poesie* (1766).⁹ Using the Late Hellenistic sculpture of Laocoön and his two sons being attacked by serpents, Lessing follows Johann Joachim Winckelmann in promoting the assertion that classical art is invariably tranquil and static, concerned with the presentation of flawless beauty (fig. 1.1).¹⁰ The display of strong emotion or impassioned movement would distort the purity of form, he argues, and in the visual arts formal considerations must always control expression. Poetry, by contrast, could display strong emotion without disrupting form. Virgil's evocation of the scream in his account of the death of Laocoön "has a powerful appeal to the ear, no matter what its effect on the eye."¹¹ Although the *Laocoön* is concerned with poetry and painting, Lessing's characterization of poetry as a temporal art and painting as a spatial art can be applied equally to music and painting (the ear and the eye). It was Lessing's intention in the planned second part of this work to consider music in relation to poetry, and in the third part the relation of dance to music and the different genres of poetry, one with the other. Both these further parts, however, remained incomplete at his death in 1781.

1.1 Hagesandros, Athenodoros, and Polydoros of Rhodes, *The Laocoön Group*, c. 175–150 B.C., height 242 cm. Museo Pio Clementino, Vatican. Monumenti Musei e Gallerie Pontificie, Rome

LAOCOÖN

Taking up the antique view that music is seen to function as a natural sign system, one grounded in imitation, a useful starting point for our discussion is the work of the philosopher Moses Mendelssohn (1729–86, grandfather of the composer Felix). He was a contemporary and close friend of Lessing, whose ideas had an impact (negative in the case of music) on Lessing's formulations. Mendelssohn's essay "Hauptgrundsätze der schönen Wissenschaften und Künste" (On the main principles of the fine arts and sciences) of 1757, revised in 1771, is in part an attempt to separate the arts on semiotic grounds.[12] What Lessing and Mendelssohn share is a particular conception of mimesis. In the case of painting, a highly mimetic art, there are certain physical properties, such as color and contour, which it shares with the original. However, for precisely this reason its efficacy is reduced, for it partakes of the physical nature of the original and therefore incurs the same restrictions as the original. A more effective mimesis, a representation to the imagination of ideas, would be one of ideas itself, where materiality is left behind. This is a major reason for the supersession of poetry and its use of metaphor over the visual arts: if painting adopts a similar strategy—allegory—it is merely an inferior form of poetry, what Lessing calls a "speaking picture."[13]

Both Lessing and Mendelssohn's work was part of a more general interest in systematizing the arts; their work aims to provide a theoretical structure of aesthetics as a hierarchy of rules. They tend toward a definition of the "essence" of each art form in order to make artistic communication more autonomous, more transparent. The purpose of art was characterized as the presentation to the imagination (or soul) of an intuitive representation of the object, to elicit pleasure. The arts can then be compared in terms of the means to this end, characterized in terms of the different semiotic media they employ. Music, for Mendelssohn, is a natural semiotic, as opposed to language, which is an arbitrary one:

> The signs by means of which an object is expressed can be either natural or arbitrary. They are natural if the combination of the sign with the subject matter signified is grounded in the very properties of what is designated. . . . Those signs, on the other hand, that by their very nature have nothing in common with the designated subject matter . . . are called arbitary. . . . The fine sciences [arts], by which poetry and rhetoric are understood, express objects by means of arbitrary signs, perceptible sounds, and letters.[14]

According to Mendelssohn, both the visual arts and music are natural symbols, or sign systems, as opposed to poetry, which employs arbitrary symbols. The arts are further distinguished by the sense organ to which they appeal, which separates music from the visual arts. In turn, the visual arts can be subdivided according to the arrangement of their parts—in time or space (the only temporal visual art for Mendelssohn is dance). This focus on media-based rules separates aesthetic experience, as we have seen, from other experiences aiming to facilitate transparency between aesthetic object and the subject.

The understanding of how the arts combine, having been separated by such a taxonomy, follows similar structural lines. Mendelssohn argues that there must always be a dominant partner, for if this were not the case a clash between "essences" could occur, causing confusion. For example, in song, music must always take second place to poetry; in opera, to drama. Wagner, as we shall see, took a rather different view.

According to the notes for the planned second volume of *Laocoön*, Lessing, while sharing many ideas with Mendelssohn, differed in his view of music. For these notes suggest that music is, at least in part, an arbitrary sign system, as it, too, frees the imagination.[15] This view, which allies music and poetry, was to become dominant by the end of the century.

Autonomous music, separated from poetry, was viewed at first as something of a loose cannon. The mimetic view of music was, throughout this time, progressively diminished, which led to music's assuming a different place within the aesthetic hierarchy. One of the clearest examples of this change, toward the end of the century, is to be found in British rather than German theorizing. The Scottish thinker Adam Smith sees music as a primarily expressive medium: "The effect of instrumental Music upon the mind has been called expression. . . . Whatever effect it produces is the immediate effect of that melody and harmony, and not of something else which is signified and suggested by them: they in fact signify and suggest nothing."[16]

For Smith there is a decided break between music as a signifier and its (natural) signified, although for him this is not necessarily a good thing. Moreover, seen in such terms there was an inherent (Platonic) danger: music free of the control of words was music free of morality. Legislation was needed to contain this influence. As Lessing put it in the *Laocoön:*

> We laugh when we hear that among the ancients even the arts were subject to the civil code. But we are not always right when we do so. Unquestionably, laws must not exercise any constraint on the sciences, for the ultimate goal of knowledge is truth. . . . But the ultimate goal of the arts is pleasure, and this pleasure is not indispensable. Hence it may be for the lawmaker to determine what kind of pleasure and how much of each kind he will permit.[17]

But not all eighteenth-century minds saw music in such Platonic terms. Some saw the origin of music in the divine (Orpheus, Apollo, or his biblical counterpart David), but whether music was seen as a nature-derived phenomenon or as a supernatural gift, both accounts were dependent on mimesis. The view that music was intimately related to the word or poetry, however, also underwent a further variation, which acknowledged a trace of the *Ursprache*. This is an idea that was later taken up and modified by Arthur Schopenhauer, Friedrich Nietzsche, and Richard Wagner. Here music is not so much a mimic of speech and natural sounds as an original or fundamental mode of communication that existed prior to language.[18]

As the imitative view of music underwent transformation, to a point where expressive theories replaced mimetic ones, music became an even more effective paradigm for the other arts. In Germany, with such writers as Jean Paul Richter, Ludwig Tieck, Wilhelm Wackenroder, and E. T. A. Hoffmann, within the emergent aesthetic of romanticism, instrumental music became fundamental precisely because of its arbitrary, suggestive nature. Music was seen now as the least imitative of the arts, and its status was raised to a point where all other arts were required to aspire to its imprecisely suggestive condition. But this again is a species of "sister arts" criticism, a focus on commonality, a drawing together of the arts, and it would be incorrect to give the impression that modernist criticism explicitly acknowledged such common ground. Rather, it sought difference, addressing itself to the "essential" nature of each medium. Here Lessing provided the ground rules. His essay is of seminal importance, for in a reworking of its central arguments by the American critic Clement Greenberg, in his essay "Towards a Newer Laocoon" (1940), the essence of modernist art is defined.[19] But here first is Lessing's initial discussion and its division of the arts on the basis of the categories of space and time:

> I reason thus: if it is true that in its imitations painting uses completely different means or signs than does poetry, namely figures [bodies] and colours in space rather than articulated sounds in time, and if these signs must indisputably bear a suitable relation to the thing signified, then signs existing in space can express only objects whose wholes or parts coexist, while signs that follow one another can express only objects whose wholes or parts are consecutive.
>
> Objects or parts of objects which exist in space are called bodies. Accordingly, bodies with their visible properties are the true subjects of painting.
>
> Objects or parts of objects which follow one another are called actions. Accordingly, actions are the true subjects of poetry.[20]

Interestingly, Lessing next acknowledges that such distinctions are not as cut-and-dried as this would lead us to believe. "However, bodies do not exist in space only, but also in time. . . . On the other hand, actions cannot exist independently, but must be joined to certain beings or things." What appears therefore to be an essential difference — differences of kind — turns out instead to be differences only of degree or focus.

The need to consider the fundamental differences between the arts, here poetry and painting,[21] is for the purpose of criticism and judgment. The fact that, in Lessing's view, followers of the ut pictura poesis tradition have failed to acknowledge the fundamental difference between art forms has led to a "mania for description" in poetry and "a mania for allegory" in painting, which attempts "to make the former a speaking picture, without actually knowing what it could and ought to paint, and the latter a silent poem, without having considered to what degree it is able to express general ideas without denying its true function and degenerating into a purely arbitrary means of expression."[22]

Lessing's project is to contain as much as it is to explain. He conflates, in other words, evaluative issues with ontological ones. From the nature of the medium springs the possibility of certain subjects; what can be expressed is intimately related to "how," the vehicle of expression. This assumption tends to think of the "how" as fixed, for a change in "how" could lead to a change of subject. The "how" of his particular historical moment leads Lessing to value poetry over painting: "poetry has a wider range . . . there are beauties at its command which painting is never able to attain," a valuation that, as Mitchell argues, is tied up with ideology, particularly at the level of gender. Painting as a silent, beautiful art, a natural sign system, made for the eye and from bodies in space — these are all qualities associated with femininity. Opposed to this is the eloquent, sublime discourse of poetry, an arbitrary sign system, addressed to the ear and mind in time — values associated with masculinity.[23] In fact, Lessing's analysis is implicitly binary, one that cannot help but become evaluative and hierarchical, privileging one side (poetry) over the other (painting). Value and restrictions are inferred from the spatiotemporal distinction. The border between art forms thus characterized must not be transgressed. Lessing condemns paintings that attempt to present the passage of time: "It is an intrusion of the painter into the domain of the poet, which good taste can never sanction, when the painter combines in one and the same picture two points necessarily separate in time,"[24] and likewise for the poet who transgresses this "natural" border, but in the opposite direction. There are many such examples throughout the *Laocoön,* developed from the root characterization and division of the arts on spatiotemporal lines, presenting the distinction as not only permanent and rightful but unassailable if value is to be maintained.

Before we return to the legacy of Lessing's *Laocoön,* it is worth exploring the issue of "essential" defining character in the arts, especially in music and the visual arts. The philosopher Jerrold Levinson's essay "Hybrid Art Forms" is a useful starting point in this endeavor.[25]

HYBRIDITY AND PURITY IN ART FORMS

As is implicit in the discussion above, and as Levinson argues in "Hybrid Art Forms," a hybrid is primarily a historical phenomenon that emerges out of existing artistic conventions and fields of activity. From antiquity different media and modes of communication have been in dialogue, conjoining and separating as the dictates of society and culture allow; mousike is a good early example. As Levinson argues, a hybrid art form should not be thought of as a structural category, not simply a medium-derived phenomenon. It is a consequence of history. From this he concludes that so-called pure (what he calls thoroughbred) art forms can only be so defined as a nonhybrid (nonessential): "two things are immediately evident. One, the notion of a thoroughbred art form is logically secondary to that of a hybrid. . . . Two, the ordinary categorization of an art form as thoroughbred or nonhybrid will usually be a relative or limited one, not positing an absolute purity reaching back to the dawn of Western art."[26]

He goes on to characterize hybrid art forms under three headings: (1) juxtaposition, (2) synthesis, and (3) transformation.

We can supplement this by using terms that describe appropriate forms of analysis, so that (1) would be multidisciplinary, (2) interdisciplinary, and (3) crossdisciplinary. To give examples:

Juxtaposition: Multidisciplinary

At its simplest, a juxtapositional hybrid art work would be where one art form is accompanied by another but where the elements can be perceived as distinct and do not merge into a third term. However, there are also more complex examples in what are sometimes called multimedia performances, where commonly more than two art forms are brought into play. Levinson mentions the example of Philip Glass and Robert Wilson's collaborations on *Einstein on the Beach* (1976), but a more radical example might be the American composer John Cage's "circuses," works that have their roots in Cage's early 1950s experiments at the Black Mountain College and that lead to the explosion of "Happenings" in the 1960s. The circus pieces, unlike happenings, are all on a large scale. Cage's first was presented at the University of Illinois Stock Pavilion, a large space used for showing cattle, on 17 November 1967 between 8:00 P.M. and 1:00 A.M. The performance was a culmination of a number of issues that Cage had been pursuing to that point, among them chance and indeterminance, performance ritual, the work of

Henry David Thoreau and Marshall McLuhan, collaboration, and simultaneity. No score was made and no instructions were given; instead, Cage invited various performers to participate. As he later described it himself,

> There were: the composer Salvatore Martirano, who, like the others, used a group of performers and gave a program of his own; Jocyde Olivera (Carvalho), who gave a piano recital including Ben Johnston's *Knocking Piece,* music by Morton Feldman, etc.; Lejaren Hiller; Herbert Brün; James Cuomo and his band; another jazz band; David Tudor and Gordon Mumma; Norma Marder giving voice recital sometimes accompanying a dancer, Ruth Emerson; mime Claude Kipnis, who responded with a whole sound environment; . . . In the center of the floor was a metallic construction [by Barney Childs] upon which the audience could make sounds. . . . No directions were given anyone. I connected contact mikes to the light switchboard, changing lights and, at the same time, producing sounds of switches. At either end of the Pavilion but beyond the screens, were places to buy apple cider and doughnuts, popcorn, etc. (A reference to Ives.) Ronald Nameth arranged the play of films and slides. And also obtained dark, light and large balloons. . . . The various musics each had a stage or platform near the bleachers so that the floor was free for use by the audience. The general sound was of a high volume, though not everything was amplified. Loudspeakers were high up around the perimeter. The general shape of the building is rectangular but with rounded ends.[27]

Approximately five thousand visitors participated in this free event, Cage's intention being that they did not hear *any*thing but, rather, that they hear *every*thing. No unique sonoric source or, for that matter, any aesthetic element was privileged over another. The audience members were free to move around in the space, encountering the parts in their own way, according to their own agendas, to make up an individual whole. Such an individualized encounter was part of Cage's interest in democratic, nonhierarchical art experiences: a loose aesthetic structure, with no primary focus, encouraging or requiring audience participation, that models a utopian social and political structure. His intention was not an overt critique of society at the level of politics, nor was it an attempt by art to solve social problems, so much as it was an attempt to make us aware of problems and issues, to alert us to circumstances beyond the "concert hall." However, such notions of an effect on society cannot, of course, be realized absent from the social and political conditions that would be required to maintain them.[28]

The use of dance, film, slides, lighting effects, and varied sound sources was not in any way coordinated, save that everything took place under one roof at approximately one time. Each element was therefore distinct and separable from the others, and the overall experience for each member of the audience varied tremendously. Cage's intention was not to merge or dissolve the differences between media, nor was it to control perimeters; his role was one of facilitator rather than author. Such works are not written, they are generated. In this way, at least to an extent, Cage's synthetic circus works escape Theodor Adorno's critique of the Wagnerian Gesamtkunstwerk, where Adorno argues that no individual can renounce the divisions of labor on which bourgeois identity is founded, nor can one individual possess all the specialist skill necessary to bring about a true Gesamtkunstwerk. Adorno quotes Wagner's own admission:

> No one can be better aware than myself, that the realization of this drama [the Gesamtkunstwerk] depends on conditions which do not lie within the will, nay, not even within the capability of the single individual—were this capability infinitely greater than my own—but only in the community, and in a mutual co-operation made possible thereby: whereas, at the present time, what prevails is the direct antithesis of both these factors.[29]

Although Wagner may have hoped that the historical development of the concept of the "Art Work of the Future" would eventually meet such conditions, in fact, these "factors" are no more present now than they were when Wagner wrote. However, Cage's aesthetic could be seen as having reconceived this project in at least more participatory, more democratic terms—the result being a juxtapositional rather than synthetic hybrid.

Cage organized a number of "circus" events. By their very nature, the works are hard to define as simply "music" or "theater" or "visual spectacle." They attempt to resist the scientific notions of cause and effect, and although at their best they are always more than the sum of their parts, they yet resist definition into anything other than multimedia events.[30]

Synthesis: Interdisciplinary

In many ways this form is the opposite of the juxtapositional hybrid art work, for here the elements are brought together in order to mix, so that they are submerged into a third term. The elements do not have a parallel existence in the same temporal-spatial environment; they are not, so to speak, sounded together but heard as separate. Once combined, their individual identities have been modified and forged into a new whole.

An obvious example, as Levinson mentions, is Wagner's conception of the Gesamtkunstwerk, at least in terms of the synthesis of song and drama. Yet Wagner explicitly saw his art work of the future in terms of synthesis (interdisciplinarity) rather than "mere" coexistence (juxtaposition or multidisciplinarity): "He who can only conceive the combination of all the arts into the Artwork as though one meant, for example, that in a picture gallery and amidst a row of statues a romance of Goethe's should be read aloud while a symphony of Beethoven's was being played, such a man does rightly enough to insist upon the *severance* of the arts."[31]

Wagner aimed to achieve sung drama, not a drama with songs. But it is debatable whether Wagner ever realized a full synthesis in the terms outlined above. For example, dance conceived of as a visible temporal art form ("the most realistic of all the arts")[32] is seldom fully integrated into Wagner's music dramas, and singers are not required to link vocal and gestural expression in a way that can be regarded as synthetic. Wagner argued that music and word are synthesized at the level of tone and that through rhythm and melody "ensouled by Tone, both Dance and Poetry regain their true essence."[33] In practice, while the melody and rhythm of the libretto can, at least in part, be seen to flow into melody, dance as an abstract form of gestural expression never flows successfully from the nature of the drama. Similarly, the integration of painting, and specifically landscape painting, is justified as a reproduction of nature, not "man" (which is the concern of sculpture), for following Lessing's characterization of painting as a spatial art, the living "man" is achievable more fully in the temporal art of drama. Painting then provides a natural backdrop to the unfolding action on stage and as such co-exists, shares the stage space, but is not synthesized in the way that musicality of speech fuses word and tone. The true integration of the visual arts is, however, implied by Wagner when he argues that art must appeal to the eye: "Without addressing the eye, all art remains unsatisfying, and thus itself unsatisfied, unfree. Be its utterance to the Ear, or merely to the combining and mediately compensating faculty of Thought, as perfect as it may—until it makes intelligible appeal likewise unto the Eye, it remains a thing that merely *wills,* yet never completely *can;* but Art must *can.*"[34]

This is an argument for the embodiment of art, seeing the body as a site of art. The nature and visible presence of the body in music making, for example, is explicitly a part of Cage's aesthetic—that the presentation of music is a priori visual (see Chapter 6)—but such a notion finds no effective, explicit vehicle in Wagner's work, in spite of such hints at the level of theory. This is obviously the case in Wagner's placing of the orchestra out of sight, in a pit, below the stage in his theater at Bayreuth. A fully integrated Gesamtkunstwerk was, however, attempted by Aleksandr Scriabin, which involved gesture, sound, word, sight, and even smells.

Another synthetic hybrid mentioned by Levinson is the shaped canvas. In the work of Frank Stella, for example, the boundaries between painting and sculpture are thrown into question. Such paintings draw attention to the literal boundaries of themselves as objects, and the frame, the dividing line between painting and the outside (wall), becomes a point of focus. Rather than aspiring to the state of a window, aiming at transparency, such works instead announce themselves as constructed objects. The work of English artist Jeremy Moon (1934–73) was in-

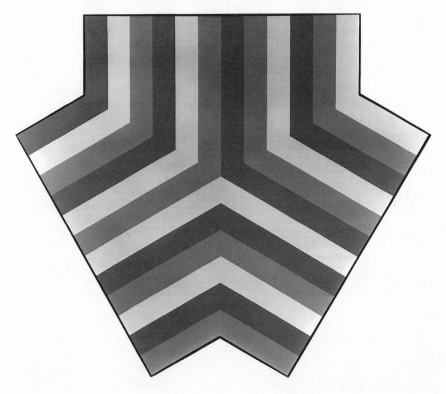

1.2 Jeremy Moon, *Blue Rose,* 1967, oil on canvas, 218 x 251 cm. Tate Gallery, London, 2000

fluenced by these developments in painting. The simple geometric patterning of his *Blue Rose* of 1967 (fig. 1.2) is the direct result of the overall shape of the canvas. The angles at the top right and left and center bottom of the canvas produce a series of chevrons that meet and thus form the center of the work. In this way, the work is addressed to its own "objecthood."[35] A later, more elaborate example of this hybridity is Stella's *Queequeg in His Coffin* of 1989 (fig. 1.3). The title is a literary reference to Herman Melville's novel *Moby-Dick*. In addition to the literary quotation, the painting "quotes" from modernist art by mixing gesture with the geometrically hard-edged forms of abstraction. As an object it explodes through the confines of its "frame" into sculpture. But because the relief elements are wall mounted, however, they resist simple definition as sculpture, and their anchoring inside the etiquette of the image, if anything, brings the work closer to an abstract bas relief.

Levinson also mentions collage and assemblage as examples of synthetic hybridization. In the work of Pablo Picasso, however, where diverse elements co-

1.3 Frank Stella, *Queequeg in His Coffin*, 1989, mixed media on magnesium and aluminum, 289 x 471 x 122 cm. Private collection. © ARS, New York, and DACS, London 2000

exist within the picture frame, there is often a deliberate play on their varied natures. In this way the elements tend to resist synthesis, calling attention to and contrasting the conventions they bring with them from their different sources. The integration of a range of image sources is an element of the works of Robert Rauschenberg, which make reference to collage without being papier collé compositions, more often using the techniques of silk-screen printing and homogenizing the images at the level of facture.

The case of collage is complex and is found in music and poetry as well as the visual arts.[36] Collage is deployed for diverse reasons and is best considered case by case in this context. In some musical instances, for example, particularly in contemporary practice, it would be better to think of musical collage as "style juxtaposition" (juxtapositional hybridity). This is the case in Cage's *William's Mix* of 1952 and *Fontana Mix* of 1958, which both employ recordings of street, country, electronic, manually produced, wind-produced, and small amplified sounds. One of his most elaborate examples is his "opera" *Europera* of 1988, which uses individual pages from standard-repertory operas chosen at random (the costumes, too, are chosen in a similar way). The use of collage in the work of the Russian composer Alfred Schnittke is entirely different. In Schnittke, musical elements may quote diverse musical sources (Antonio Vivaldi and Niccolò Paganini are two examples), but the parts are woven together to produce a homogeneous whole. I return to this point when we consider these categories in relation to the paradigms of modernity and postmodernity.

An example from the diverse work of the artist Robert Morris provides a final example of synthetic hybridization—an oeuvre that Rosalind Krauss has called "sculpture in the expanded field."[37] In 1961, Morris produced *Box with the Sounds of Its Own Making,* a cube-shaped box containing a tape recorder. It plays a tape loop of over three hours' duration of sounds recorded during the construction of the box, including the artist leaving the studio. The work explicitly takes to task Lessing's definition of visual art as spatial and nontemporal: duration and temporality are constituent elements of the art work. It refers the "viewer" beyond the space and time of their perception to the "present" history of the development (making) of the object. This history is sonorically present but visually absent; the labor of construction is not hidden in the crafting of the box but contained within it in the form of sound. Sculpture and sound are tangibly linked and interrelated. This might lead us to consider the piece under the heading "sound sculpture," but in fact, that is found under the final hybrid category Levinson proposes.

Transformation: Crossdisciplinary

This category of hybrid art form is characterized by an unstable relationship between its constituent elements. Unlike synthetic hybridization, where there is parity between elements, here there is a movement in the direction of one art, so that the identity of this element tends to overshadow its coparticipants. In this way it reminds us of Moses Mendelssohn's comparative semiotics of the arts in combination, where structural dominance must occur, where one art must define the priorities of compositional organization, in order for the essential nature of each individual art form not to lead to incoherence and illegibility. The relationship is always, therefore, one of dominant and subordinate, in any combination. If in a juxtapositional hybrid, the art forms share a temporal and spatial location but remain in other ways distinct, and if in a synthetic hybrid each art form moves to a middle ground somewhere between their respective individual positions, then in a transformational hybrid, one art form crosses over into the territory of the other(s).

The example Levinson gives is kinetic sculpture, which he defines as "ordinary sculpture modified in the direction of dance."[38] While retaining its identity as sculpture, kinetic sculpture incorporates characteristics of dance—movement in space and time—though not so much that it can be called a species of dance (although it might be metaphorically referred to in this way): it is terpsichorean

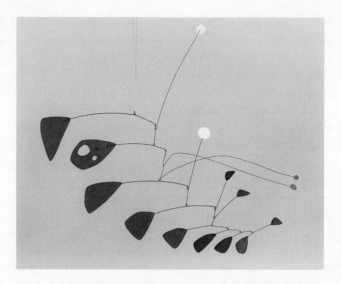

1.4 Alexander Calder, *Antennae with Red and Blue Dots,* 1960 (mobile) aluminum and steel wires, 111 x 128 x 128 cm. Tate Gallery, London. © ADAGP, Paris, and DACS, London 2000

sculpture, not sculptural dance. Of particular interest in such sculpture is that the formal elements are subject to constant change within a limited set of possibilities. Interaction and reconfiguration, dependent on ambient conditions beyond the artist's control, takes place within a precomposed whole. Each installation produces a subtly different "performance." Alexander Calder's mobile sculpture, developed in the 1930s, was a direct influence on a number of composers (fig. 1.4). Earle Brown wrote *Available Forms I* and *II* in the early 1960s because of his interest in Calder's kinetic art. *Available Forms II* is an "open-form" work for two groups, each with a conductor, in which the order and combination of elements is left to the conductors in performance, through hand signals. The score's notation involves a range of complex graphic elements, intended to stimulate improvisational responses in the performers (ex. 1.1). Such "graphic scores" can also be considered in this category of transformational hybrids.

Although all scores are the result of written textual activities, achieved in the process of visualization, graphic scores are a particular case. For example, transcription is much more difficult. Although they can be reproduced through photographic means (as a painting can), they do not allow simple transfer into another format (as conventional notation can be written out in another hand). The Western musical tradition has been predicated on, and developed through, notation: the creative reflection on sounds through a visual medium, in terms of both the

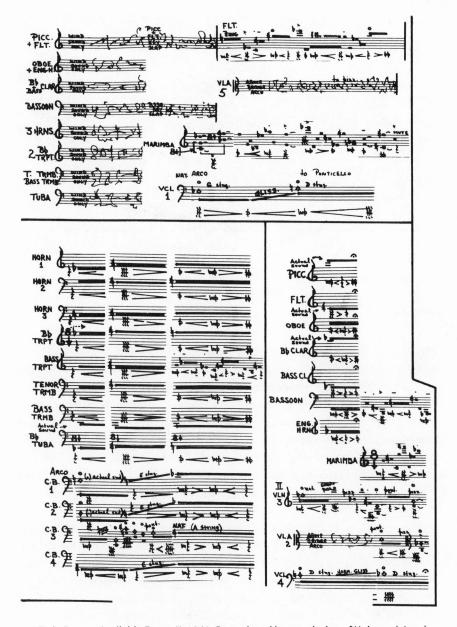

1.1 Earle Brown, *Available Forms II,* 1962. Reproduced by permission of Universal, London

1.5 Tom Phillips, *Last Notes from Endenich*, 1974, charcoal and conté on paper, 75 × 150 cm. Published by permission of the artist. © Tom Phillips 2000.

organization of the large and complex forces that make up orchestral and choral works in the processes of composition itself and the understanding of the tradition to which composers turn in order to effect their work in relation to history. Even improvisational practices that have developed within the Western tradition depend implicitly, if not explicitly, on written musical custom. If, for many, this scored tradition has become so commonplace as to appear "natural," or a transparent route to a composer's intentions, graphic scores remind us that all scoring is a code. Such scores explicitly make visible the processes (and problems) of communication and organization; script and score are not allowed to remain an "invisible" medium.

The artist Tom Phillips (b. 1937) has produced a number of graphic scores, among them his *Four Pieces for John Tilbury* and *Music for n Players* (both 1966). In addition, his already hybrid text-graphic book, *A Humument* (published in 1966 but continually reworked; the second revised edition was published in 1997) has been used to generate *Irma—An Opera* (1969). A later work, *Last Notes from Endenich* of 1974 (fig. 1.5), was "a score not intended for performance," but in collaboration with Jean-Yves Bosseur a performing version (with added transparencies) was developed. Cornelius Cardew's large work *Treatise* (1963–67) is a compendium of graphic indications but cannot quite escape the sequential stave elements of conventional scoring (ex. 1.2). The range of graphic pyrotechnics grows out of the stave structure and takes place above a constant countersubject in the form of a double-stave "accompaniment" (ex. 1.3). In the work of Syl-

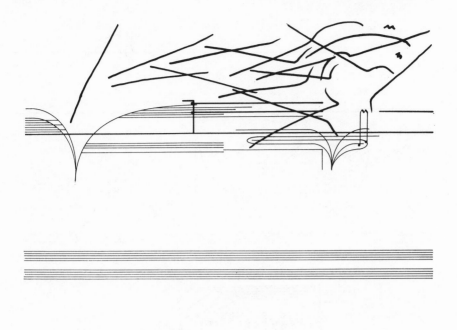

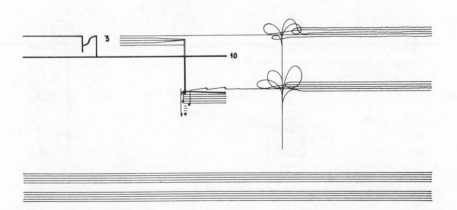

1.2 Cornelius Cardew, *Treatise,* 1967. © 1967 by Gallery Upstairs Press USA © 1970 assigned to Hinrichsen Edition, Peters Edition Limited, London. Reproduced by permission of the Publishers

vano Bussotti, his *Five Pieces for David Tudor* of 1959, for example, the elaborate use of graphic elements, distorting and overwhelming conventional musical symbols, reduces their role as signifiers of specific musical events (in pitch and time) and produces a set of more tenuous connections with improvisation—the score is then unbalanced in the direction of graphics and visual art (ex. 1.4). For Bussotti, musical results, whatever they may be, flow directly from the visual. The

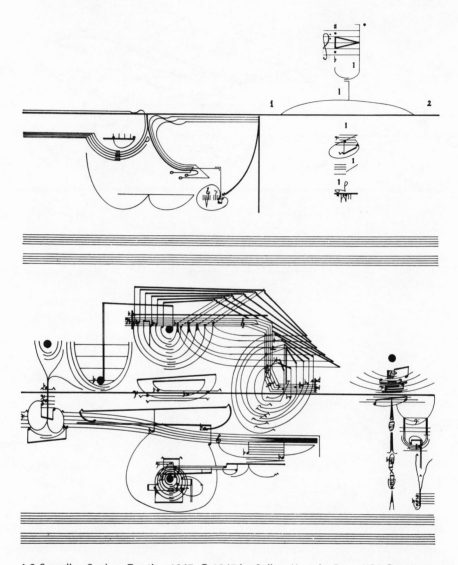

1.3 Cornelius Cardew, *Treatise,* 1967. © 1967 by Gallery Upstairs Press USA © 1970 assigned to Hinrichsen Edition, Peters Edition Limited, London. Reproduced by permission of the Publishers

ear plays no part until the work is performed. One final example from the period of greatest experimentation in this area, the 1950s and 1960s, is the wonderfully jokey and evocative score Roberto Zamarin drew for Cathy Berberian's *Stripsody* (1966).[39] This score is composed as a strip cartoon, a temporal arrangement of characters (Tarzan and Superman, among others) and onomatopoeic sounds in approximate pitch ("oink," "zzzzzz," "pwuitt," "bang," "uhu," "kerplunk,"

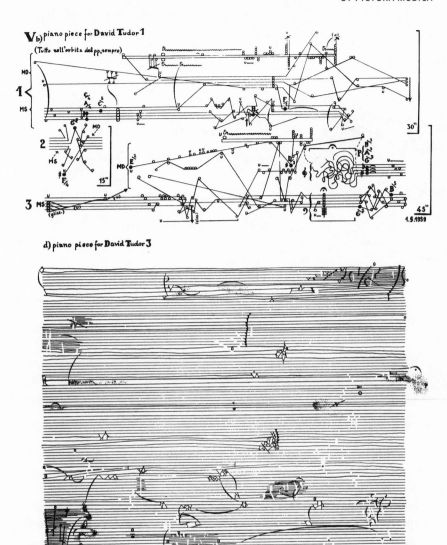

1.4 Sylvano Bussotti, *Five Pieces for David Tudor*, 1959. Reproduced by permission of Casa Ricordi, Italy

and so on), as a cue for Berberian's vocal gymnastics (timbre is an area that conventional notation systems have been less able to accommodate, often resorting to verbal instructions). Although the score forms a magnificent visual document for private consumption, the performance of the work is no less visually significant in public. The instructions to the performer explain, "The score should be performed as if [by] a radio sound man, without any props, who must provide all

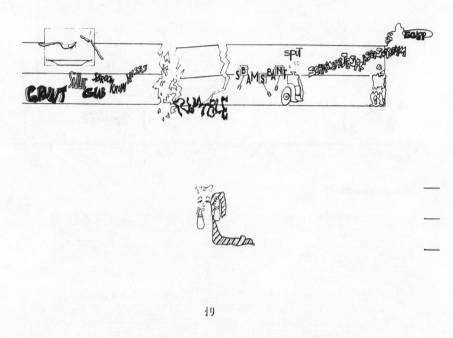

10

1.5 Cathy Berberian, *Stripsody*, 1966. Edition Peters no. 66164 © 1966 by C. F. Peters Corporation, New York. Reproduced by permission of Peters Edition Limited, London

the sound effects with his voice." In addition, certain "scenes" (in the score lines enclosed by bars) are to be acted out: "whenever possible, gestures and body movements should be simultaneous with the vocal gestures." The silence on page 10, for example, is represented by a drawing of a child with its thumb in its mouth (to silence the voice) and its hand cupped to its ear (to visualize or draw attention to the sound's absence), a pose that the performer is to emulate (ex. 1.5).

Other examples of transformational hybrids are what have been called sound sculpture and its twin concept, ambient music. Sound sculpture can be defined as the sonic exploration of objects, ambient music as the sonic exploration of spaces and environments. Although both objects and spaces are elements of conventional music (musical instruments and concert halls, for example), in sound sculpture and ambient music the emphasis is placed on the visual aesthetics of the objects and the specific nature of the site, rather than on the abstracted consideration of music as pure sound.

A practitioner who has executed work in related fields is Max Neuhaus.[40] After a successful career as a virtuoso percussionist, at the tender age of twenty-eight

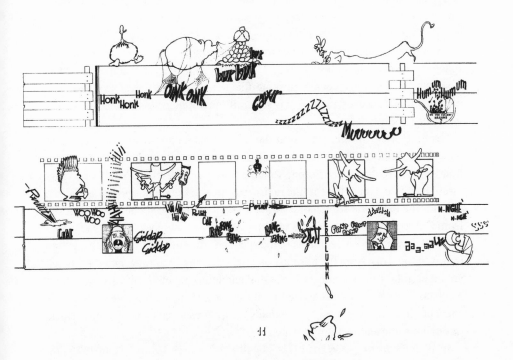

Neuhaus reconceived his identity as a sculptor, but one who works with sound rather than color and form. It is significant that he started out as a percussionist, because this range of instruments, perhaps more than any other, is diverse in material and scale. Percussion provides the greatest visual impact within a conventional symphonic environment, ranging from the very small Chinese bells to the very large bass drum, from the noise-producing cymbal to the polyphonic piano, and from the use of skin in the drum and wood in the block to strings in the piano and metal in the bells.

Neuhaus described his career shift as follows: "In terms of classification, I'd move the installations into the purview of the visual arts even though they have no visual component, because the visual arts, in a plastic sense, have dealt with space. Sculptors define and transform spaces, I create, transform, and change spaces by adding sound. That spatial concept is one which music doesn't include."[41]

Later he redefined his oeuvre as "sound works," his "broadcast works" as "networks," and his "installations" as "place works." The "networks," such as *Public Supply I–IV* of 1966–73 and *Radio Net* of 1974–77, are phone-in "pieces" in which he asked radio listeners to phone in sounds (whistles, for example). Neuhaus then altered these sounds electronically, mixed them, and broadcast them. These "network" pieces are very large-scale, audience-participation compositions. More relevant in our context, however, are Neuhaus's later "place works."

Even though Neuhaus's Lessing-inspired definition treats music as nonspatial, space is, and has always been, integral to all music. Space is the site of transmission from producer to receiver, most familiar to us in the science of acoustics. It is certainly true, however, that space is generally an implicit element that Neuhaus's work makes explicit.

His early work in this vein used the ubiquitous nature of the automobile in American society. In this piece, the car radio was the receiver of "wireless" sound transmitters Neuhaus set up along Lincoln Parkway in Buffalo, New York. Only through the receiver in the car (the radio) was the work audible, and it was audible only for the half-mile stretch of road set up to generate the sound. This work ran from October 1967 to April 1968 but existed for each member of the "audience" only whenever they passed through the space. Its duration of four months, which removed the work from the normal conventions of musical time, and its specific yet intangible siting soundly wove spatial and temporal elements together. Soon Neuhaus's siting of sounds shifted to allow for a more shared listening experience, but in these new works the sound's location was made tangible and plastic through his chosen medium of water.

In *Water Whistle I–XVII* of 1971–74 and *Underwater Music I–IV* of 1976–78, Neuhaus used water as a transmitting medium for sound. In *Water Whistle,* water was forced through whistles underwater to produce pitched sounds that could be heard by the audience only when they submerged themselves, or at least their ears. In *Underwater Music* he modified this technique by using specially designed underwater loudspeakers and electronically generated sounds, which were composed through a combination of scientific experiment and intuitive, creative decisions. Such compositions literally immersed Neuhaus in the medium—the sites were swimming pools—as he adjusted pitch perimeters and envelopes, in effect "coloring" the sound. They dramatized the spaces of sound, its limits, because the medium contained them.

Besides such focused sound events, Neuhaus is interested in what he has sometimes called "discoverables." These are long-term place works that are sited to allow people to "come across" them, displaying qualities of organized sound that subtly differentiate them from their settings. His best known is *Times Square,* of 1977–92.

It took Neuhaus four years to persuade the New York Metropolitan Transportation Authority to agree to the siting of this work—although it is important to point out that his works are site-specific and in no sense precomposed and then installed. Such transactions with public bodies, which are also an aspect of the work of Christo, draw attention to the complex interrelations and stages that characterize the juncture of artist, work, patrons, and public. In Neuhaus's case this is not an activity he relishes.[42] Negotiations are often more dramatic when the artist chooses to move outside the confines of socially defined artistic spaces—museums or concert halls.

Times Square was situated between 45th and 46th Streets, where Broadway and 7th Avenue begin to intersect. Beneath a thirty-foot-long, triangular subway grill, Neuhaus installed sound-generating equipment that emitted an organlike drone. The sound was not signaled visually in any way and was detectable only by careful aural focusing. This setup draws sound closer to the condition of sight, for it allows attention to it to be selective; like looking at or away from an object, you can aurally attend to the sound or not.

In producing and refining his work Neuhaus makes drawings and written statements. Some are alternative ways of approaching the same problems as the works themselves, and others are reflections, after execution, on the problems raised in disposition and perception. They are not scores, although some do provide delicate diagrams of the shape and location of the sounds (fig. 1.6). Conventional musical scores do not concern themselves with spatial factors, and it is this refocusing in Neuhaus's work that allows them to be categorized as transformational hybrids. While taking a central defining characteristic of music—organized sound—he modifies it to explicitly address notions of space, replacing interest in the conventional narrative of music in time.

In all hybrids, whether juxtapositional, synthetic, or transformational, the combining of music and the visual arts draws attention to points of similarity, difference, and contrast. These points of intersection are their most apparent elements of interest and are significant in how they reflect aspects of art's evolution. Rather than thinking of purity at all, it might be better to see hybridity as the more natural state for art, because purity is a historical contingency, whereas hybridity is part of the flux of creativity itself: the putting of things together.

Two further refinements conclude Levinson's argument, two opposing elements that are characteristic of hybrid art forms: integrative and disintegrative. The integrative effects a rich and complex whole, with individual elements cooperating toward a common goal. This type of heroic presentation, which tends to be the case in synthetic hybrids, is more obviously associated with modernity and the vestiges of a romantic sensibility: the power of the artist to weave different elements, to provide a distance from experience through analysis, an analysis confident in its ability to distinguish at the level of value. This type of aspiration is part of the self-image of modernism.

By contrast, although the disintegrative, too, is rich and complex, it tends to juxtaposition, not unity, and individual elements do not formally meld. Here no

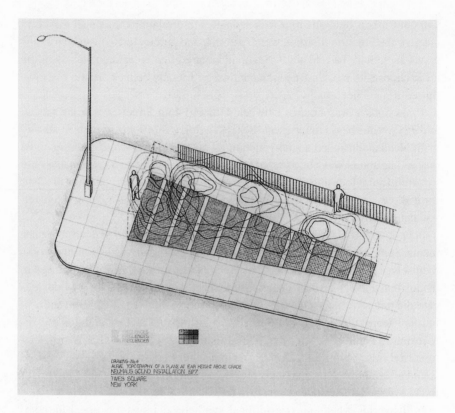

1.6 Max Neuhaus, drawing of aural typography of "Times Square," 1984, silk screen on paper, 61 x 73 cm. Collection of the artist

hierarchical value is assigned to the parts, and the value of the contributing elements is not addressed; rather, the parts are left as freestanding agents, often speaking different "languages," with no attempt to resolve them into a lingua franca. The defocusing and multifaceted nature of juxtapositional hybrids means that they will affect the audience in different ways depending on the observers' or listeners' individual orientations and experiences. More information is provided than any one observer can assimilate. The allusive nature of the psychological fragmentation to which such works relate is in this case more obviously associated with notions of postmodernism. We should remember, too, that technology, especially digital technology, can be used to homogenize diverse sources through the screen of the computer. All sources, visual, textual, and sonoric, can be translated into digital information to enable manipulation. The ramifications of this development lie outside the scope of this study. I have restricted myself to a brief description of analogue systems (as in describing Cage, above), but computers have and will continue to affect artistic production and enable control over a range of aesthetic perimeters, which cannot but promote hybridity at the expense of purist paradigms.

A NEWER LAOCOÖN

Lessing's project to differentiate artistic practice, and to propose criteria by which we might successfully patrol the borders between one art form and another, was taken up by the American humanist Irving Babbitt in 1910 in *The New Laokoon*.[43] Babbitt's intention was to take up the debate where Lessing left off, with notions of romanticism, "especially the attempts to get with words the effects of music and painting."[44] Again, this is not just a formal issue, no matter how explicitly Babbitt may have proclaimed it as his intention, for the issue of value is ideologically driven. In his discussion of the hybrid art form of program music, he argues that modern composers, in their concern with impression or expression, have lost sight of both structure and aim: "They have displayed the same intemperance in this respect as the romantic word-painters, and exposed themselves to the same criticism; they have dwelt too much in an outlying province of their art instead of at its centre. As Sainte-Beuve would say, they have transferred the capital of music from Rome to Byzantium; and when the capital of an empire is thus pushed over to its extreme frontier it is very close to the barbarians."[45]

Babbitt makes the association of hybridity with the abnormal and dangerous even more explicit in the following section on "color-audition," what he calls "hyperaesthesia" (or synesthesia, as we shall call it in the next chapter), which "is nearly always a sign of nervous disorder." He goes on, "But I have already said, color-audition has found literary expression only in those who belong to what we may term the neurotic school. It manifests itself in connection with the melomania of the German romanticists, their tendency not only to worship music, *but to reduce to music all the other arts*."[46] Thus, hybridity in art, a lack of purity, is linked to the barbarian (the Oriental) and is pathological; purity, by implication is linked to the civilized (the Occidental) and rational. Further, hybridity depends excessively on feeling and emotion, both values associated with the feminine that since romanticism have led art from the path of objectivity and truth: "if confusion has crept into the arts, it is merely a special aspect of a more general malady . . . from which, if my diagnosis is correct, the occidental world is now suffering."[47]

Babbitt is assured, following Lessing, that the arts have definite boundaries that are rightful and permanent, boundaries that must not be crossed, because to do so is not just to cause confusion on an aesthetic level but to endanger the whole of civilization and political life, in both personal and public spheres. The infection of the other (the Oriental, the feminine, the primitive and mentally unstable) causes standards to drop and rot to set in.

Thirty years later the baton was passed to Clement Greenberg, who wrote "Towards a Newer Laocoon" for the *Partisan Review* in 1940.[48] His aim was, like Babbitt's, to update Lessing's arguments concerning the defining limits between art forms and the issue of value within these boundaries. In this case Greenberg was primarily concerned with the status of abstract painting in the face of claims then being made for the concept of realism within figurative art. He wanted to demonstrate that abstract painting was the fulfillment of a teleology, one based on the specificity of medium. This definition of modernism in art is addressed at various points in the chapters that follow, and I am not reducing Greenberg's aesthetic to one text. My main task here is simply to consider the issue of purity and disciplinary demarcation as it relates to the foregoing arguments about hybrid art forms.

In his opening remarks on the purity of artistic integrity and confusion over the differences between the arts, Greenberg writes, "Purism is the terminus of a salutory reaction against the mistakes of painting and sculpture in the past several centuries which were due to such confusion."[49] His starting point is that such a thing as purity exists and therefore that any "confusion" between art forms is a mistake. He makes no attempt to locate the Arcadian site of such purity in history; instead, he addresses the "infection" of art by literature in the seventeenth century as the point of departure. Every age, he contends, has a dominant art form, and it is the fate of this single art to become the "prototype of all art: the others try to shed their proper characteristics and imitate its effects."[50] This is an important point, for whereas the dominance of literature is seen as corrupting, by the nineteenth century the dominant art form had become music, and Greenberg sees the influence of this art on painting as positive. This is because music becomes a model as a *method,* rather than as a kind of *effect,* at which point "the avant-garde [found] what it was looking for."[51] Cause and effect are thus separated, emphasis being placed on conception rather than reception. Throughout Greenberg's discussion music plays a central role. Ironically, despite the plea for exclusivity, it is to the condition of music, to use Walter Pater's cliché, that all art now constantly aspires.[52] This is acceptable, then, as long as the dependence is a formal, procedural one, rather than one born of results and effects: "Only by accepting the example of music and defining each of the other arts solely in the terms of the sense or faculty which perceived its effects and by excluding from each art whatever is intelligible in the terms of any other sense or faculty would the non-musical arts attain the 'purity' and self-sufficency which they desired."[53]

Through a brief note, Greenberg adopts much of Pater's reasoning, Greenberg in this text is largely pure Pater. For example, in the opening of his essay "The

School of Giorgione," Pater writes, "Each art, therefore, having its own peculiar and untranslatable sensuous charm, has its own special mode of reaching the
imagination, its own special responsibilities to its material. One of the functions
of aesthetic criticism is to define these limitations: to estimate the degree in which
a given work of art fulfils its responsibilities to its special material."[54] Pater then
argues that Lessing's analysis of the differences between poetry and the visual
arts are only a part of the story, because a full consideration would require an appreciation of a "whole system of art-casuistries." He then sketches this terrain,
concluding that art's appeal must be to "imaginative reason," a Kantian concept
that hovers somewhere between sensation and intellect. Art, Pater suggests, is
always inclined toward "ends in themselves"; this is what distinguishes it from
a concern with "mere intelligence." Form is linked to sensation and subject to
intelligence. The mission of art lies in finding a balance between these binary
poles: "Art, then, is thus always striving to be independent of the mere intelligence, to become a matter of pure perception, to get rid of its responsibilities to
its subject or material; . . . that the material or subject no longer strikes the intellect only; nor the form, the eye or ear only; but form and matter, in their union or
identity, present one single effect to the 'imaginative reason.'"[55] And for Pater,
as for Greenberg, it is the example of music that most completely realizes this
ambition: "Therefore, although each art has its incommunicable element . . . its
unique mode of reaching the 'imaginative reason,' yet the arts may be represented
as continually struggling after the law or principle of music, to a condition which
music alone completely realizes; and one of the chief functions of aesthetic criticism, dealing with the products of art, new or old, is to estimate the degree in
which each of those products approaches, in this sense, to musical law."[56]

Greenberg can be seen to take up this challenge, and in his summary of historical developments that have taken part and that have led to abstraction, he provides
a link between the new and the old, so that the avant-garde is seen as a continuation of art history, not a rejection of past achievements but a logical extension
of them. Guided by the "purity" of the example of music, painting has been led
to the point where, in order to distinguish it from its aesthetic neighbors, it has
sought solace through the accentuation of its material or mode, the nature of its
physical support.

The arts lie safe now, each within its "legitimate" boundaries, and free trade has
been replaced by autarchy. Purity in art consists in the willing acceptance, of the
limitations of the medium of the specific art. . . .
    The arts, then, have been hunted back to their mediums, and there they have been
isolated, concentrated and defined. It is by virtue of its medium that each art is unique
and strictly itself. To restore the identity of an art the opacity of its medium must be

emphasized. For the visual arts the medium is discovered to be physical; hence pure painting and pure sculpture seek above all else to affect the spectator physically.[57]

And later, "The history of avant-garde painting is that of a progressive surrender to the resistance of its medium; which resistance consists chiefly in the flat picture plane's denial of efforts to 'hole through' it for realistic perspectival space. In making this surrender, painting not only got rid of imitation—and with it, 'literature'—but also of realistic imitation's corollary confusion between painting and sculpture."[58]

The terms in which Greenberg expresses this characterization are worth pause, for the questions remain: Why should any art form seek its identity through "willing acceptance"? Why can it preserve its integrity only through "surrender"? Why is autocracy preferable to free trade? The combative terms suggest a war between artist, musician, and poet and between artist and medium, forms of expression that have resonance with the concept of the avant-garde itself. The fear of the other manifests itself in terms of assault.

Linked to this is the role of institutions in the formation of knowledge. This is a complex issue, and I do not intend to pursue it in historical detail. Yet a number of general points need to be made in regard to the present topic of artistic boundaries. The institutional structuring of academic departments, although challenged in recent years, has traditionally made it difficult to cross the borders of disciplines, from music to art history and back again, for example. The specialist nature of the separate fields (and discourses) mean that when discussion does take place, it is usually in terms of already accepted categories and demarcations formulated in relation to only one of the disciplines involved.[59] What W. J. T. Mitchell has done, in his two books *Iconology* and *Picture Theory,* is to show that the prevailing tropes of differentiation between verbal and visual representation are not the stable theoretical foundation they are commonly assumed to be. My intention is to add a supplement to this, pertaining to sonoric and visual modes of communication, to argue that here, too, distinctions are a matter of degree and historical process. Further, I submit that hybridity, as mentioned earlier, is perhaps the general condition of the arts. Purism then becomes the aberration, an attempt motivated by particular historical, social, and political forces to collapse art into arenas more easily demarcated and patrolled. These historical forces formed Greenberg's early Marxist characterization of modernist art practices against the grain of social and political reactionary forces—Stalinism, commercial mass markets, and kitsch, for example. In response to such definitions of modernism the academy has been an important player in the emergence of postmodernism as well as in debates about the relationship between diversity and uniformity through its commitment to multiplicity and relativity. There is still a question whether the academy accommodates or challenges, what Jürgen Habermas has called the "legitimation crisis."[60] I do not intend to get embroiled in this debate, but I do want to make a few points in relation to the discipline within which I work.

We could assert that art history as an academic practice, is, and always has been, by nature, interdisciplinary. In this regard, for example, Marcia Pointon has written, "Art history is polymatic and we have long recognised its debt to philosophy, all branches of historical analysis, literature, archaeology and other disciplines. What used to be perceived as a weakness (it was difficult to accommodate art history into a departmental system . . .) should now be acknowledged as a source of strength on political and academic grounds."[61] We could add that while the student of Renaissance art history needs familiarity with, among a host of other things, Roman Catholic theology, Classical writers, European social and political history, so the student of modern art is required to engage with semiotics, psychology, structuralism and poststructuralism, and so on. This is not so much a point about methodology (an issue for all scholars, whatever their subject or period) as it is simply that artists' work and the critical discourse that surrounds that work calls on, both implicitly and explicitly, ways of thinking that tend, jackdawlike, to move across several specialist idioms. What this means, at its most optimistic, is that art history has the potential to be a useful site for discussion of the work of figures who sit on the boundaries of artistic practice, particularly those associated with "performance art," for example. But if such debate is to be true to the tenor of such hybrid art practices, then it needs to do more than simply concern itself with issues of comparison. For the nature of certain types of hybridity results in more than simply two or more areas of practice coming together. Even in cases of juxtapositional hybridity, any critique needs to recognize that what has been produced is often more than the sum of its parts.

In 1977, Stephen Heath selected and translated a series of essays by Roland Barthes that were published under the title *Image-Music-Text*. One of the central conceptual strands of Heath's selection is the "constant movement from work to text," where "text" is taken to mean a methodological field and "work" a "fragment of substance," an object. In the essay of this title ("From Work to Text"),[62] Barthes begins with a discussion of the changing nature of the object of study:

What is new and which affects the idea of the work comes not necessarily from the internal recasting of each of these disciplines [amongst others, linguistics, anthropology, psychoanalysis — we might add art history], but rather from their encounter in relation to an object which traditionally is the province of none of them. It is indeed as though the *interdisciplinarity* which is today held up as a prime value in research cannot be accomplished by the simple confrontation of specialist branches of knowledge. Interdisciplinarity is not the calm of an easy security; it begins *effectively* . . . when the solidarity of the old disciplines breaks down . . . in the interests of a new object and a new language.[63]

This new object is, for Barthes, the *text*. This book, too, addresses itself to such issues of interdisciplinarity—to the hyphens, if you will, in the phrase image-music-text.

Before concluding this discussion I wish to return briefly to the issue of whether such essentializing terms, which have been used since Lessing to divide the arts, are correct or useful in the first place. This does not mean that I think there is no difference between art forms—merely that the differences that do exist are historically (not essentially) contingent, and that although it might be possible to arrive at a list of necessary conditions, such conditions should not be confused with sufficient ones. In the discussion of Lessing I stated that the distinctions between the arts along spatiotemporal lines are governed by degree or focus, not kind. Both music and the visual arts consist in the interplay between objects in space and comprehension in time; sound cannot be divorced from the means of its production or its consumption—actual bodies in space and history—any more than visual art can be understood apart from the notion of temporal action and comprehension. Greenberg and Pater see music as an exemplar of formal and aesthetic autonomy by defining it as a purely sonoric art. In Chapter 6, I consider Cage's concern with silence and the issues he raises about the elements of music that emerge when sound is "silenced." But metaphorically, silence is central to notions of genre and denotation, for in the process of definition something is always excluded or silenced, and what is excluded by conceiving of music as just sound is its identity as a discourse, one that is involved with institutions and practices and the mechanisms of ideology.

Music is visual as well as sonoric. Its performance is replete with modes and codes of presentation (those familiar with music videos will have no problem with this, where visual presentation, image, and style are at least as important as the sound of the music). There is often a textual element (scores and other forms of writing), and the theater of the concert occasion involves elaborate lighting and ritual (a semantics of expression and absorption). This theatricality is precisely what Michael Fried, in his development of Greenbergian ideas, wants to expunge from art. Indeed theater, as he defines it, is antithetical to art:

> A failure to register the enormous difference in quality between, say, the music of Carter and that of Cage or between the paintings of Louis and those of Rauschenberg means that the real distinctions—between music and theatre in the first instance and between painting and theatre in the second—are displaced by the illusion that the barriers between the arts are in the process of crumbling . . . and that the arts

themselves are at last sliding towards some kind of final, implosive, hugely desir-able synthesis. Whereas in fact the individual arts have never been more explicitly concerned with the conventions that constitute their respective essences.[64]

The assumption that clear and unequivocal essential characteristics separate both art from life and one art from another is key to Fried's argument. Such arguments as Lessing's, Greenberg's, and Fried's tend to polarize discussion into either-or debates—art is possessed of either pictoriality or theatricality—indeed, these binary oppositions are characteristic of modernism in general. There is a fixation on absolute and exclusive contrast. Questions of value, as of definition, are arrived at by the privileging of the pictorial over the theatrical—works that display a high degree of "pictoriality" are by definition better than those that display "theatricality." I have suggested, following Mitchell and Barthes, that inter-disciplinary study needs to do more than simply address issues across a polarized divide. What a study of hybridity can show us is that gray areas, those that lie be-tween such oppositions—the hyphens—are sites of rich and provocative activity. Indeed, such compound and hybrid sites are more characteristic of the processes of making art in history than are attempts to reduce practice to essentialist oppo-sitions. Hybridity was characteristic of premodern culture (considered in the next chapter), as well as postmodern culture (as we shall explore in the final chap-ter). Attempts at purification and homogeneity are reinforced by, and carried out within, the professionalization of academic disciplines as they form themselves into discrete subjects, from inside specialist branches of knowledge that seek to differentiate practices one from the other.

In Chapter 2, I explore a number of currents that operate as a counter to the highly exclusive theory of modernism as a pursuit of purity and media exclu-sivity. Such ideas emerge more emphatically with the advent of what may be called postmodernist sensibilities, but they were always present within moder-nity. Indeed, my point is that such impulses were very much part of modernity. What happens within postmodernity is the amplification of a preexisting state of affairs. A synthetic impulse can be detected in such apparently diverse figures as Wassily Kandinsky, Marcel Duchamp, and Sergey Eisenstein, the collages of Pablo Picasso and Georges Braque, the aesthetic programs of the Vienna Seces-sion, the Bauhaus, de Stijl, and constructivism, as well as in the work of more recent figures such as Joseph Beuys and John Cage. In these cases it is not just artistic boundaries that are crossed but also the distinctions between art and non-art. Not all of these artists and movements are discussed in what follows, but I hope to show that such impulses toward synthesis have always been more than simply dormant peripheral activities.

TWO "DEEDS OF MUSIC MADE VISIBLE"

WAGNER, THE *GESAMTKUNSTWERK*, AND

THE BIRTH OF THE MODERN

I have been told that Wagner's music is better than it sounds.
—Bill Nye

There is no longer any doubt, today, that the different arts, painting, poetry, music, after having followed their long and glorious courses, have been seized with a sudden malaise that has made them burst their dreary, time-honored traditions.
—Paul Delaroche

The importance of the music and ideas of the German composer Richard Wagner on late nineteenth- and early twentieth-century European culture would be hard to overemphasize.[1] Few musicians have had such a wide-ranging impact on neighboring disciplines. Although Igor Stravinsky and Arnold Schoenberg stand as key figures in the history of twentieth-century music, only John Cage has had such a reverberating effect on the polity of art.

Wagnerism was a mass phenomenon of the cultivated bourgeoisie, affecting all branches of the arts, and it is due almost solely to Wagner that musical metaphor, in discussion of the arts, held a prime and ubiquitous position at the turn of the twentieth century.[2] The reasons for this dominance of music are complex, but in part they are to be found in the relatively modern nature of music itself. Music's practice has no antique precedent; no notes of ancient music survive. If, as was certainly the case from the fifteenth century, the classical arts of the Greeks and Romans formed the foundations of an expressive tradition and offered a set of paradigms by which any judgments of achievement were to be measured, then the notion of modernity must in large part be understood as a challenge to this perceived fixed inheritance. Its institutionalization in the art academies of Europe from the mid-seventeenth century on formed the conventions against which the avant-garde set itself.

In doing this one of the principle concepts of debate was the notion of mimesis, or imitation, and here the modern example of music was paramount. By the nineteenth century music was viewed as a strictly nonillusionistic art form. However, for some ancient thinkers (and some thereafter) music shared, with all the arts, a root in the soil of representation.

As we have already seen, for Aristotle, "epic and tragic poetry, comedy too, dithyrambic poetry, and most music composed for the flute and lyre, can all be described in general terms as forms of imitation or representation."[3] Here music serves the word; its power derives from imitation of poetry or is twinned with it as song (lyric or melic poetry or, once having been sung, elegy or iambus), poetry being almost exclusively performed rather than read until the end of the third century. This imitation aims to represent "men's characters and feelings and actions." Indeed, very little verse was entirely divorced from music, and very little music was without words. The Greek word *mousike* signified the complex "music and poetry." This makes it difficult to use the term *music* to signify both ancient Greek and modern usage. However, although the practical "liberation" of music from words emerges from the fourth century, the philosophical subservience of music to the word was to last until the eighteenth century,[4] finding its apogee in the volte-face of Schopenhauer's idealism, which positioned music less as imitation than as the thing itself: less representation than equivalent. Schopenhauer had postulated that behind ordinary reality lay the ultimate ground of being, what he called the *Urgrund,* and whereas the other arts reproduce this ordinary reality, music uniquely reflects the ground itself.

> Our world is nothing but the phenomenon or appearance of the Ideas . . . in music, since it passes over the Ideas, is also quite independent of the phenomenal world, positively ignores it, and, to a certain extent, could still exist even if there were no world at all, which cannot be said of the other arts. . . . Therefore music is by no means like the other arts, namely a copy of the Ideas, but a *copy of the will itself,* the objectivity of which are the Ideas. For this reason the effect of music is so very

much more powerful and penetrating than is that of the other arts, for these others speak only of the shadows, but music of the essence.[5]

Music is animated by the same force that expresses itself in the phenomenal world, but it is quite autonomous: it is sound set free from all material bounds; it "could still exist even if there were no world at all." Schopenhauer's philosophy had a profound impact on Wagner's practice and theory,[6] even though Wagner had been thinking in a manner sympathetic to Schopenhauer's ideas before this direct influence took place, which was sometime during the autumn of 1854, via the poet Georg Herwegh.

Here I am principally concerned with Wagner's theoretical writings that predate direct contact with Schopenhauer's ideas, the so-called Zurich essays launched in July 1849: *Art and Revolution* (1849), *The Art-Work of the Future* (1849), and *Opera and Drama* (1851). In these works Wagner reappraises the function of art, providing the theoretical basis for artistic synthesis in the Gesamtkunstwerk. These writings display a more equitable relationship among the arts than do his pronouncements made post-Schopenhauer, wherein music becomes the prime mover.[7] The vicissitudes of Wagner's theorizing are not my main concern, although I agree with Bryan Magee that "the later theoretical approach subsumes most of the earlier, rather than replaces it."[8] Nor is my interest the problematic relationship between Wagner's theory and practice. My objective is to explain those aspects of his theorizing that stimulated his admirers from all branches of the arts. It is not surprising, therefore, that those elements of Wagner's thinking that most inspired the emerging avant-garde were artistic synthesis, albeit via the power of music. These ideas were unified in music's paradigmatic role in redirecting the other arts, as they aspired to reach its condition or to join with it. As often happens with followers, Wagner's devotees tended to emphasize those elements of his thinking that were of greatest interest to themselves. To this end Wagner became a cipher, a cause, a magus, a mythmaker and mythical figure who conjured a fusion of artistic ambition. As succeeding generations positioned themselves as *sub specie Wagneri* they were less concerned with chronology, often picking elements of his thinking from disparate sources, often secondhand and frequently only loosely related to the original source of inspiration. The idea of the Gesamtkunstwerk became the leading aesthetic concept around which the Wagnerian movement formed.

Wagner acknowledges Schopenhauer's influence in the 1872 introduction to his theoretical writings:

Only those who have learnt from *Schopenhauer* the true meaning and significance of the *Will,* can thoroughly appreciate the abuse that had resulted from this mixing up of words; he who has enjoyed this unspeakable benefit, however, knows well that

that misused *"Unwillkür"* should really be named *"Der Wille"* (the Will); whilst the term *Willkür* (Choice or Caprice) is here employed to signify the so-called Intellectual or Brain Will, influenced by the guidance of reflection. Since the latter is more concerned with the properties of Knowledge . . . whereas the pure *Will*, as the *"Thing-in-itself"* that comes to consciousness in man, is credited with those true productive qualities.[9]

This maneuver is to an extent inherent in Aristotle's challenge to Platonic exceptions to art—as imitations of imitations—in that art's poetic treatment of universal truths is ultimately closer to truth than are the mere facts of history. Nevertheless, it is with German idealist philosophy that music achieves a special metaphysical status, a position corresponding directly with the will; a mimesis of the spirit, but one that is so close as to be more "presentation" than "representation."[10] Whereas in earlier writings Wagner had argued for full artistic synthesis, after his acceptance of Schopenhauer's characterization of music as the will made audible, he shifted to a form of parallelism; the music becomes a discloser of the inner truth of the drama. The poetry and visual action play a role of equal importance as mediators between the *noumena* (of music and the will) and the *phenomena* (of drama and experience). This is a looser relationship, but a relationship nevertheless; although music enjoys a higher degree of freedom, an integral interweaving of elements remains.

WAGNER'S SYNTHETIC IDEAS

Wagner's effect on a wider European culture is due in part to the German philosophical tradition on which his theory of art is based, little of which was directly known in France, the emergent center of modernist culture. At the hub of this center was the critic and poet Charles Baudelaire, the archetypal modern thinker.[11] His role in relation to Wagner is discussed later, but it is in France that the beaux-arts tradition had been carried on mainly in the name of "littérature" and into which Wagner brought his "art work of the future," a conception driven by the engine of "tone" over "word." Importantly, for Wagner, the art work of the future is soundly based on the art work of the ancient world. As he expresses it in his essay "Art and Revolution" of 1849, written in exile in Zurich (while being sought by the police for the part he played in the Dresden revolt of 1848), "In any serious investigation of the essence of our art of to-day, we cannot make one step forward without being brought face to face with its intimate connection with the *Art of ancient Greece.*"[12]

Here Wagner posits a history where art in its antique state was a unified activity, where dance, music, and poetry all operated under the banner of Drama, and where this tragic drama was a mass religious event: "Such a tragedy-day was a Feast of the God [Apollo]; for here the god spoke clearly and intelligibly forth, and the poet, as his high-priest, stood real and embodied in his art work, led the measure of the dance, raised the voices to a choir, and in ringing words proclaimed the utterances of godlike wisdom."[13]

Tragic drama shows the arts working together as a spiritual guide for public life. The collapse of Greek civilization caused a rift in drama and led to the dissipation and separation of the forces of art into individual disciplines: "Hand-in-hand with the dissolution of the Athenian state, marched the downfall of Tragedy. As the spirit of *Community* split itself along a thousand lines of egoistic cleavage, so was the great united work of Tragedy disintegrated into its individual factors."[14] Only a few months later Wagner elaborated on these ideas in *The Art-Work of the Future*.

For Wagner the inception for this art work of the future was rooted in the soil Ludwig van Beethoven had cultivated in his ninth symphony:

This was the word which Beethoven set as crown upon the forehead of his tone-creation; and the word he cries to men— *"Freude!"* (Rejoice!) With this word he cries to men: *"Breast to breast, ye mortal millions! This one kiss to all the world!"* — And *this Word* will be the language of the *Art-work of the Future*.

The Last Symphony of Beethoven is the redemption of Music from out [of] her own peculiar element into the realm of *universal Art*. It is the human Evangel of the art of the Future. Beyond it no forward step is possible; for upon it the perfect Art-work of the Future alone can follow, the *Universal Drama* to which Beethoven has forged for us the key.

Thus has Music of herself fulfilled what neither of the other severed arts had skill to do. Each of these arts but eked out her own self-centred emptiness by *taking,* and egoistic borrowing; neither, therefore, had the skill to *be herself,* and of herself to weave the girdle wherewith to link the whole. But Tone, in that she *was herself* completely, and moved amid her own unsullied element, attained the force of the most heroic, most loveworthy self-sacrifice,—of mastering, nay of renouncing her own self, to reach out to her sisters the hand of rescue. She thus has kept herself as *heart* that binds both head and limbs in one; and it is not without significance, that it is precisely the art of Tone which has gained so wide extension through all the branches of our modern public life.[15]

He continues, recalling Aristotle's point that art is grounded in mimesis, that because the intervening generations of composers effectively ignored Beethoven's great achievement (here he makes a snide comment at the expense of Felix Mendelssohn), the art of Tone set free from dance and poetry, in its symphonic guise, has become unnecessary to society because it breaks all links with nature. As each of the other arts in the process of separation held onto the measure of nature ("howsoever capriciously"), Tone framed itself according to abstract laws: "To the sculptor, the painter, and the poet, their laws of Art explain the course of Nature . . . to the musician are explained the laws of Harmony and Counterpoint . . . an abstract, scientific system,"[16] and it is this level of abstraction that accounts, for him, for the gap between public comprehension and modern music; it does not affect the "Folk." This characterization makes music, in Wagner's eyes, the most "purely human art" (as civilization was cleaved from nature), yet this individuality is double-edged, for in the hands of great artists it speaks true, but through the "schools" that grow up "round some great master in whom the soul of Music has individualised itself," repetition is likely that does not follow the "world-historical task" of music but stays "an egotistic, self-sufficient art," a form of (bourgeois) entertainment. With Beethoven's last symphony the final decisive development was made. After him there have been only "patched and cobbled harlequin[s]" taking their wares to the music market; art has become commodious.[17] Beethoven produced a situation in which the art work of the future was the next true development, and according to Wagner, those who have not grasped this point hold a false belief in the "possible necessity of [their] own selfish caprice."[18]

The extract just quoted starts with a reference to Word, and as evidenced by Aristotle, music's significance was linked to the word in antiquity. But for Wagner the effect of the word is to be found in its affect; and music was primarily an art of affects, as he wrote in 1851 in "Communication to My Friends" about *Der fliegende Holländer (The Flying Dutchman)*, "I no longer tried intentionally for customary melody, or, in a sense, for Melody at all, but absolutely *let it take its rise* from feeling utterance of the words."[19] In his major theoretical piece of writing, his monumental *Opera and Drama*, published in 1851 just before "Communication to My Friends," Wagner makes it clear that for him the setting of word to music is ultimately a product of the musicality of language itself, the means of expressing feelings. In other words, poetry is a kind of proto-music—verse's measure as rhythm and rhyme as melody.[20] Words are understood as sensual presentation or expression. Music is thus the prime vehicle of emotive communication, containing within it the "*Ur*-tone of all human speech."[21]

Plato, of course, had recognized this power of music in his discussion of the various modes in the third book of *The Republic* inasmuch as music (in the guise of the modes) was a dramatization of the passions. Plato's greatest objection was the change that had taken place in the fifth century B.C., when mousike began to devolve into separate musical and poetic forms. In other words, the word lost its dominance on the tone as new types of instrumental music evolved. As music moved from the rational control of language to a more emotive role, so Plato detected a moral danger. The modes he most objected to were those that deviate from the mimesis of speech.[22] In *The Politics,* in contrast to Plato, Aristotle encouraged instrumental music, focusing on the psychology of listening rather than on words. Imitation (or mimesis) in this context becomes more a matter of "the affinity with the soul" than an affinity with language.[23] Music affects the subject contiguously; it is beyond rational control, speaking to the feelings directly. Yet we must remember that Greek music, particularly the dithyramb (the cult song of Dionysus), does not survive in words, let alone music, before the fifth century. The dithyramb may have been more disposed to tone than word, as some believed, but the view that it was wilder and more intoxicating than the paean can be no more than speculation. For Friedrich Nietzsche the dithyramb is the root and essence of tragedy, developed (here his argument follows Aristotle) from the satyr chorus. Such a chorus was involved with dancing, speech, and music, and its role was to express nature, to proclaim truth.

Such speculative thinking is at the core of Nietzsche's early important arguments on the subject, in his recognition of musical power. It is to his first major publication, *The Birth of Tragedy* of 1872, that we now turn.

OUT OF THE SPIRIT OF MUSIC

This book originally had the longer title *The Birth of Tragedy Out of the Spirit of Music* and was dedicated to Wagner.[24] In it Nietzsche argued against the strict "Apollonian" view of Greek culture, with its "noble simplicity and grandeur," presented by Johann Joachim Winckelmann through a series of publications in the eighteenth century.[25] Instead, Nietzsche stressed a "Dionysiac" interpretation of classical literature and used his discussion of passion and intoxicating aspects to show the reciprocal necessity of both principles:

> Through Apollo and Dionysus, the two art-deities of the Greeks, we come to recognize that in the Greek world there existed a sharp opposition, in origin and aims, between the Apollonian art of sculpture, and the non-plastic, Dionysian, art of music. These two distinct tendencies run parallel to each other, for the most part openly at variance; and they continually incite each other to new and more powerful births, which perpetuate an antagonism, only superficially reconciled by the common term "Art"; till at last, by a metaphysical miracle of the Hellenic will, they appear coupled with each other, and through this coupling eventually generate the art-product, equally Dionysian and Apollonian, of Attic tragedy.[26]

Apollo is the god of the "fair appearance of the inner world of fantasy"; he is the *principium individuationis* (principle of individuation). Dionysus, in contrast, looks in the other direction, to union between man and man and between man and nature. In a statement close to Wagner's reasoning, Nietzsche writes, "Transform Beethoven's 'Hymn to Joy' into a painting . . . then you will be able to appreciate the Dionysian," emphasizing the protean manner in which music is open to pictorial suggestion.[27] In such a state of musical intoxication one is "no longer an artist, [one] has become a work of art."[28] Tragedy is born from the reconciliation of such intoxication with dreams and ecstasies and self-knowledge. For a rebirth of tragedy, Nietzsche looked to Wagner, through the composer's self-knowledge.

The traditional mix of words and music in opera, particularly as manifested in the *stile rappresentativo* (recitative), does not acknowledge the Dionysian nature of music, for it makes of music a servant and of text a master. It is with German music, and specifically with Wagner, that this Dionysian spirit is let loose. But, Nietzsche continues, there are dangers in the direct absorption of such an intoxicating spirit; if, he asks, it was possible to hear the third act of *Tristan und Isolde* without the aid of word or scenery, as purely a "vast symphonic period," would he who thus hears the "heart-chamber of the world-will" not "collapse all at once?"[29] What is needed to intercede is myth, and along with it a more explicit visual dimension, for this reintroduces the Apollonian effect that creates the distance necessary to save us:

> With the immense combined power of the image, the concept, the ethical teaching and the sympathetic emotion—the Apollonian influence uplifts man from orgiastic self-annihilation and deceives him concerning the universality of the Dionysian process into the belief that he is seeing a detached picture of the world (Tristan and Isolde for instance), and that, *through music,* he will be enabled to *see* it with still more essential clearness. What can the healing magic of Apollo not accomplish when it can even excite in us the illusion that the Dionysian is actually in the service of the Apollonian and is capable of enhancing its effects, in fact, that music is essentially the representative art for an Apollonian content?[30]

It is, however, the power of Dionysus that triumphs over Apollo, for in this conception of tragedy music is the leading player; "music is the essential idea of the world, drama is but the reflection of this idea, a detached adumbration of it."[31]

In Nietzsche's selective view, then, Dionysus is the god of music. He tends to ignore the fact the Greeks regarded Apollo as the sole god of music.[32] Dionysus was simply associated with one type of music, the dithyramb. Nevertheless, according to Nietzsche, Apollo provides the "illusion," the "visible middle world" (drama) that is animated and charged with Dionysian sound—music is the force that moves, both literally and metaphorically: "And while music thus compels us to a broader and more intensive vision than usual, and makes us spread out the curtain of the scene before our eyes like a delicate texture, the world of the stage is as infinitely expanded for our spiritualized, introspective eye as it is illumined outwardly from within."[33] Nietzsche's Schopenhauerian view was that music is less mimetic or illusionistic than the plastic arts he associates with Apollo, or indeed the arts of the word: "The muses of the arts of 'appearance' paled before an art which, in its intoxication, spoke the truth."[34]

Why, Nietzsche finally asks, should we so often find the ugly and the unharmonious as vehicles of aesthetic pleasure? The answer is to be found in the tragic experience of heroic suffering: "The joy aroused by the tragic myth has the same origin as the joyful sensation of dissonance in music."[35] Such dissonance, or dissonant content, provokes a higher aesthetic pleasure. Dionysian dissonance, he concludes, is more fundamental to life and truth, to tragedy (the highest achievement of the Greeks), than the Apollonian, which is secondarily focused on "illusions" (mimesis) but which performs the important role of safeguarding individual consciousness against destruction by the overpowering, raw nature of Dionysus.

DISSONANCE

Wagner firmly grasped this issue of dissonance and incorporated it in technical terms into his aesthetic of the "music of the future," as is evident from the outset of the Prelude to *Tristan und Isolde* (completed 1859, first performed 1865) (ex. 2.1, 2.2).

Wagner starts with a small motif (less than a "tune"), an upwardly moving phrase that resolves into dominant seventh chords from diminished seventh chords, since known as "Tristan" chords. These cadences hold open the harmonic texture and suspend the sense of closure that is associated with conventional tonality. Wagner slips from the "Tristan" chord to a seventh chord three times. The "conclusion" of this passage is signified by a repetition, an octave higher, of the cadence of bars 10 and 11 in bars 12 and 13, a further fragment of which follows in bars 14 and 15. We can see the radical nature of this procedure most starkly if we resolve this motif in the way in which harmonic conventions would lead us to expect, so that we conclude with a sense of closure in the key of A minor (ex. 2.3).

This is a procedure of thwarting expectation by suggesting cadential closure but holding it open, so as to develop through a series of motifs rather than the question-and-answer phrases of conventional harmony. These developmental devices become a feature of all Wagner's mature operas. They produce sequential development, progressively increasing the harmonic tension over long periods of music, an apparently seamless succession of motifs. The result is that a feeling of repose or resolution is suspended, providing a harmonic language that fulfills

Nietzsche's Dionysian "intoxication" metaphor, leaving the listener adrift in a sea of harmonic texture without the aid of conventional cadential life rafts.

In technical terms, Wagner employs chords that are harmonically ambiguous, unlike conventional triads. They can lead almost anywhere, to almost any tonality. By relying on such chords Wagner expands the harmonic language of European tonal music. Indeed this ambiguity is extended so far that it threatens to overwhelm the diatonic framework. But despite this threat, resolution finally does take place, albeit at some remove.[36] In other words, Wagner is, despite Nietzsche's special pleading, a mix of the Apollonian, in his formal concerns and ultimately consummate control of structure, and the Dionysian, in his concern with affect and the transmission of powerful feelings and emotional states.[37] Baudelaire recognized the same tension when he described Wagner as a man of order and of passion, with passion as his principal quality.[38]

THE GESAMTKUNSTWERK

Such Wagnerian conceptions of the art work are generated from, to use Nietzsche's phrase, the Dionysian world of the artist's imagination. They are the products of the feelings, or the intuition. Beethoven, for Wagner, was the artist who had shattered the rigid shackles of rationalism (the Apollonian) and restored music to its true role as the vehicle for and articulator of feeling. As Ernest Newman has written, "Beethoven[,] . . . had it not been for Wagner, would probably not have meant as much to us as he does now, or become the fertilising force he is in modern music; and even this fertilisation is effected through Wagner's work rather than along lines in continuation of Beethoven's own."[39] In other words, the romantic Beethoven, the colossus who stands astride the classical (Apollonian) versus romantic (Dionysian) divide, is a post-Wagnerian Beethoven, one whose work is part of a teleology that reaches to Wagner and beyond to the art work of the future. Wagner believed that he had access to Beethoven's heart and could divine, more clearly than Beethoven himself, the romantic strivings of Beethoven's art.

Feeling, as the subconscious creative wellspring of the will, could only be tapped by intuition (the genius), and through this source of life (will), man is related to the whole of nature; genius is entwined with will and nature.[40] The inherently nonrational aspects of Dionysian art—feeling over thought—privileged in this way are part of the wider project of romanticism. Specifically, such reasoning positioned Beethoven as a messiah in the holy land of Germany, the site for the renaissance of culture.

Both Wagner's and Nietzsche's interpretations of classical civilization are out of step with utilitarianism and positivism in Plato and Aristotle. For both these modern thinkers, art is essentially didactic. It is not that philosophical notions

Erster Aufzug.

2.1 Richard Wagner, *Tristan und Isolde*, 1859, Prelude, bars 1–8. Reproduced by kind permission of Peters Edition Limited, London

of truth are applied to art so much as that philosophical truth comes out of art. This is what makes art, in the eyes of both, antithetic to entertainment, which to them comprises conventional opera (French and Italian) and indeed most modern music, except that of Germany. The true course of art can be traced through the apostolic passage from J. S. Bach to Beethoven, and from Beethoven to Wagner, with whom we reach the endpoint.[41] The rebirth of the Dionysian spirit in art presages the rebirth of culture as a whole. As it was with the Greeks, so it shall be with the Germans.

The validity of this teleology is, as we have seen, promulgated through classical roots. According to Nietzsche, Greek tragedy is essentially music: "the essence of tragedy, which can be interpreted only as a manifestation and illustration of Dionysian states, as the visible symbolising of music."[42] Music best conveys the transmission of mood or feelings (*Stimmung*). The effect on the spectators is characterized as "exciting, purifying, and releasing the entire life of a people" and, a little later, "Tragedy sets a sublime symbol, the myth, between the universal au-

cadence I
(bars 2-3)

cadence II
(bars 6-7)

cadence III
(bars 10-11)

2.2 *Tristan und Isolde,* Prelude, harmonic breakdown of the principal cadences from bars 1 to 11

thority of its music and the receptive Dionysian hearer, and produces in him the illusion that music is only the most effective means for the animating, the plastic world of myth."[43] The Apollonian drama provides the means by which the power of the Dionysian music is filtered. The hero is the medium by which spectators are given sight of a higher (metaphysical) existence, but the effect is beyond the individual; it affects all: "Dionysus speaks the language of Apollo; Apollo, however, finally speaks the language of Dionysus; and so the highest goal of tragedy and of art in general is attained."[44]

As Dionysus subsumes Apollo, so music, as the signifying art par excellence, subsumes the other arts in this process of unification. Nietzsche argues that, whereas visual art and poetry invite a contemplative response, the presence of music in tragedy produces a gleam of deeper meaning. "The greatest distinctness of the picture did not suffice us: for it seemed to reveal as well as veil something."[45] The spectator is compelled to see, while at the same time requiring something beyond sight: music. Tragedy, the art work of the future, is not an imitation of nature. Rather, with its agency of myth and the construction and destruction of heroic individuals—the inherent tension of opposites—it offers a prescience of fundamental forces that lie behind the world of appearances. Art, and especially the Gesamtkunstwerk, is important to the modern, alienated individual in bringing them in contact with others, with nature, and with the core (the will) of life itself. The Gesamtkunstwerk is thus the consummate modernist art work: "Man can only be comprehended in conjunction with men in general, with his Surroundings: man divorced from this, above all *the modern man,* must appear *of all things the most incomprehensible."*[46]

What we see in Wagner's notion of the "art-work of the future," or the Gesamtkunstwerk as it is more commonly styled (although Wagner himself rarely used the term), is the "end of art." "The spirit, in its artistic striving for reunion with nature in the art-work, must either look forward with hope to the future, or mournfully practice resignation."[47] It is the terminus, in that it represents a reunification and synthesis of all the individual arts—poetry, visual spectacle and set

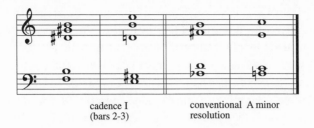

cadence I   conventional A minor
(bars 2-3)   resolution

2.3 *Tristan und Isolde,* Prelude, bars 2 and 3

design (both architectural and painted), dance and music. The trajectory of the separated strands of art practices, which we commonly term "the arts" (the "art-varieties," as Wagner calls them), have come to a point where their independence has provoked a crisis of comprehensibility; they have individually reached their limits, their zenith. In isolation, the severed arts wither. Torn from their root, they cannot reach their potential. The only course of action open to them from this extremity, according to Wagner, is reunification. In this way they can attain maturity.

Wagner describes the nature of these limits in *The Art-Work of the Future:* "In our general survey of the demeanour of each of the three humanistic (*rein menschlich*) arts after its severance from their initial communion, we could not but plainly see that exactly where the one variety touched on the province of the next, where the faculty of the second stepped in to replace the faculty of the first, there did the first one also find its natural bounds."[48] He attempts to clarify the issue by use of a personification: through procreation, man passes through woman "into a third being, the Child," and in this way via the "loving trinity," he finds himself "a widened, filled, and finished whole." So each separate art form can find its fulfillment in union. Willing for *itself,* not for the common art work, by contrast, leaves it "empty and unfree." "It only stays *throughout itself,* when it *thoroughly gives itself away*," as he typically, rather cryptically, puts it.[49] The arts, therefore, must find fulfillment in a third term, the Gesamtkunstwerk—not by mere coexistence, however (as crossdisiplinarity), but in synthesis (as inter-disciplinarity): "He who can only conceive the combination of all the arts into the Artwork as though one meant, for example, that in a picture gallery and amidst a row of statues a romance of Goethe's should be read aloud while a symphony of Beethoven's was being played, such a man does rightly enough to insist upon the *severance* of the arts."[50] Alone the arts can merely "suggest" through the imagi-nation. Only the Gesamtkunstwerk "presents" to the senses, for it addresses the entirety of the human capacity for artistic receptivity, not just one element of it.

The purity of the arts, Wagner explains in *Opera and Drama,* has been misunderstood from Lessing's essay *Laocoön* because, he argues, Lessing takes poetry to be merely the descriptive, literary form of Virgil, not the "dramatic artwork brought about by physical performance" of ancient Greece.[51] For Wagner, as we have seen, there lurks in the heart of poetry the sound of music or, more abstractly, the "tone" of speech in the word ("Ur-tone"). To be pure—that is, in a "natural" state—the mix of mousike must be retrieved, for this is art's root. Purity in this sense is the product of reunification. Art returns to its foundation as tragedy. Here Wagner uses a musical metaphor, the separate arts as "*Klavier*" compared to the Gesamtkunstwerk as orchestra.

Wagner's theory and practice are famously at points incongruous. If the Gesamtkunstwerk aspired to a blending or synthesis of the arts, his later worship of Schopenhauer inevitably made the partnership unstable in music's favor.[52] Indeed, *Tristan und Isolde* (a work that came into being at the time Wagner first encountered Schopenhauer's writings) is a good example of a work where the weight of the music almost completely shatters the "poetry." Perhaps only *Das Rheingold* and *Die Walküre* (the former finished in the same year the latter was begun, 1854) come close to the Gesamtkunstwerk ideal. Nietzsche's *Birth of Tragedy* is in part an attempt by the philosopher to rescue these contradictions, or at least to emphasize the strands of thinking that, if pulled tightly enough, might cover the holes in Wagner's arguments. This is not to suggest that Nietzsche's book is simply about Wagner or that it springs from the composer's aesthetic: the question of influence is complex and can be said to work in both directions. What is important is that for both Wagner and Nietzsche (at least initially) the redemption of modern art was to be sought in antique models, specifically in the idea of tragedy, which is in turn understood as an art form that is rooted in a mix of "art-varieties." "Music/drama" is addressed to both eye and ear: "from the longing of the Ear, incited by her sister Eye, does this language win a new immeasurable power."[53]

BAUDELAIRE

One important consequence of the influence of Wagnerian ideas on modern culture was the effect his ideas and music had on the French poet and critic Charles Baudelaire, who was largely responsible for characterizing modernism. His long essay "The Painter of Modern Life," written in 1859, did more than any other to define and guide the essential character of modernity at the time of its birth.[54] "By 'modernity,'" writes Baudelaire, "I mean the ephemeral, the fugitive, the contingent, the half of art whose other half is the eternal and the immutable."[55] The right mix of these elements, the ephemeral (or *evanescence*) and eternal, results in beauty: "In short, for any 'modernity' to be worthy of one day taking its place as 'antiquity,' it is necessary for the mysterious beauty which human life accidentally puts into it to be distilled from it."[56] Beauty depends as much on the present as it does on the past.

Even though Baudelaire refers to the illustrator and watercolorist Constantin Guys as the archetypal modernist artist, most subsequent histories have alighted on Edouard Manet as the first major modernist artist. Indeed, Baudelaire himself, on the few occasions that he did directly address Manet's work, did so in terms that clearly place Manet at the forefront of modern art. In 1865 Baudelaire wrote to Manet from Belgium, in mildly patronizing terms, about Manet's critical reception: "*They are making fun of you; the jokes* annoy you; they don't do justice to you, etc., etc. Do you think you are the first to be in such a situation? Are you a greater genius than Chateaubriand or Wagner? They made fun of them . . . those men are models, each in his genre, and in a world full of riches, and that you, *you are but the first in the decrepitude of your art*."[57] In equating Manet with Chateaubriand and Wagner, he implies that the powerful effect that these two figures have had on literature and music will soon be matched in art by Manet. However, Baudelaire had, some years earlier, seen Wagner as not just the modernist musician but, through his expressive capacity, as paradigmatic of modernity in general. Wagner could fashion beauty, as Manet could, from a mix of the antique and the modern: "It is true that an ideal ambition presides over all of Wagner's compositions; but if in choice of subject and dramatic method he comes near to antiquity, in his passionate energy of expression he is at the moment the *truest representative of modernity*."[58]

In January 1860, Wagner returned to Paris, having first lived in the city between 1839 and 1842, when he had hoped to establish himself as a composer of the first rank. He had singularly failed, spending most of this time on the breadline, living by "means of wretched tasks," as Baudelaire put it,[59] copying out scores for more successful composers, musicians he regarded as spiritually and aesthetically his inferiors. This time he hoped for a more fortuitous visit, on 25 January conducting the first of three concerts at the Théâtre Italien, where he performed extracts of his major works to date: *Tannhäuser, Lohengrin,* the overture to *Der fliegende Holländer,* and the prelude to *Tristan und Isolde*.[60] But Wagner was little better received on this occasion, his work meeting with a critically hostile reception that was due as much to political motives—anti-German feeling was then running high—as to aesthetic concerns.[61] After these concerts, on 17 February, Baudelaire wrote to Wagner, driven by indignation, to express his gratitude: "I want to be distinguished from all those jackasses" (Wagner's French critics, mainly the young aristocrats of the Jockey Club). Baudelaire said that the German composer had been responsible for giving him "*the greatest musical pleasure I've ever experienced*." He continued, in what is a remarkably frank and effusive letter:

What I felt is beyond description, but if you'll deign not to laugh, I'll try to convey my feelings to you. At first it seemed to me that I knew your music already. . . . It seemed that the music was *my own*. . . . It represents the heights, and it drives the listener on to the heights. In all your works, I've found the solemnity of Nature's great sounds, her great aspects, and the solemnity, too, of the great human passions. One instantly feels swept up and subjugated. One of the strangest pieces, one of those that aroused in me a new musical emotion, is that designed to depict religious ecstasy . . . in hearing it ["The Introduction of the Guests" from *Tannhäuser* and "The Marriage Feast" from *Lohengrin*], I frequently experienced a rather odd emotion, which could be described as the pride and the pleasure [*jouissance*] of comprehension, of allowing myself to be penetrated and invaded—a truly sensual pleasure. . . . Your music is full of something that is both uplifted and uplifting, something that longs to climb higher, something excessive and superlative. To illustrate this, let me use a comparison borrowed from painting. I imagine a vast extent of red spreading before my eyes. If this red represents passion, I see it gradually, through all the shades of red and pink, until it reaches the incandescence of a furnace. It would seem difficult, even impossible, to render something more intensely hot, and yet a final flash traces a whiter furrow on the white that provides its background. That, if you will, is the final cry of a soul that has soared to paroxysms of ecstasy.

I had begun to write a few meditations on the pieces from *Tannhäuser* and *Lohengrin* that we heard, but I recognised the impossibility of saying it all . . . .

I could continue this letter interminably.[62]

A number of points are worthy of comment. As in Wagner's aesthetic theories, word is dependent on, or grows out of, music. Here Baudelaire, the poet and essayist, finds words impotent in the face of Wagner's overpowering (*jouissance*) music: "What I felt is beyond description," "I recognised the impossibility of saying it all," "I could continue this letter interminably." His only possibility for linguistic expression lies in synesthetic analogy or metaphor: "let me use a comparison borrowed from painting." Such synesthesia is central to Baudelaire's poetic aesthetic. He believed that the human mind has an innate tendency to experience, or to understand, one sense phenomenon through the agency of another.[63] This is above all a faculty of evocation, and for Baudelaire, of all the arts, music had the greatest ability in this area. In his poem "La musique" —indeed, in many of the poems that make up the circle *Les fleurs du mal* (The flowers of evil), published in 1857—these metaphorical possibilities are explored. For example, in the first stanza of "La musique":

La musique souvent me prend comme une mer!
Vers ma pâle étoile,
Sous un plafond de brume ou dans un vaste éther,
Je mets à la voile;

Music often takes me like a sea!
Towards my pale star,
Beneath a ceiling of fog or in a vast ether,
I set sail;[64]

Even more explicitly such synesthetic connections can be found in another poem from *Les fleurs du mal,* "Correspondences," a poem that, perhaps more than any other, profoundly affected the direction that the symbolist movement was to take at the end of the nineteenth century. I quote the second stanza.

Comme de longs échos qui de loin se confondent
Dans une ténébreuse et profonde unité,
Vaste comme la nuit et comme la clarté,
Les parfums, les couleurs et les sons se répondent.

Like long-held echoes, blending somewhere else
into one deep and shadowy unison
as limitless as darkness and as day,
the sounds, the scents, the colours correspond.[65]

Such correspondences are often related to pseudoreligious ideas; their importance within the theosophical movement is discussed later on. Baudelaire acknowledged that the mystic Emanuel Swedenborg had given him this idea of resonance between apparently disparate phenomena. Swedenborg had characterized the idea as the theory of correspondences in his *Clavis hieroglypica.*[66] In a discussion of the viability of a universal philosophical language and the significance of Egyptian hieroglyphics, Swedenborg argues that all symbols have three levels of meaning: the natural (material things, science, and history), the spiritual (ideas and the imagination), and the divine (the ultimate reality of God). All material things in this way signify correspondences between the spiritual and the divine. The means to reach the divine was through the facilities of imagination and intuition at the expense of reason. He argues that reason is but one route to truth and that all human faculties are needed to take account of the different levels of reality. Swedenborg's belief in the accessibility of the realm of the spirit, the imminent dawning of a new age, and the importance of imagination and intuition as means of reaching truth all had a great influence on theosophy and other alternative systems of thought.

On a more conventional level the philosopher Pierre Leroux introduced the German idealist tradition to France. Ideas that emanated from the German tradition were of particular importance in the second half of the nineteenth century, especially in France (we have already touched on these ideas in the work of Winckelmann, Schopenhauer, Lessing, and Nietzsche as well as Wagner). This

work helped artists appropriate the art of the past for their present use. The growing awareness of the complex pattern of diverse phases of art, of cultures very
different from modern Europe, loosened the grip of the classical canon as understood through the Renaissance and played an important role in the emergence of
the avant-garde and modernism, which have their roots in this romantic reevaluation.

Leroux was interested in theology and the history of religions and was influenced by such German thinkers as Immanuel Kant, Gottfried von Herder, and
Friedrich Creuzer.[67] In 1831 in "De la poésie de notre époque" (On the poetry of
our time), he postulated that the soul consists of a mix of colors, sounds, movements, and ideas all "vibrating simultaneously." From these vibrations an "accord" emerges that is "life" itself. When life is thus expressed it becomes art and
is manifested in the guise of a symbol: "Poetry, which chooses for its instrument
the word[,] . . . is an accord, as is music, as is painting, as are all the other arts:
so that the fundamental principle of all art is the same, and all the arts get fused
into art, all the poetries into poetry."[68] Here poetry still maintains a place apart
from (above) the other arts. What becomes important for Baudelaire is that while
following such arguments he became convinced that music, not poetry, sat at the
acme. The site of this intermingling is the soul or the imagination or, as E. H.
Gombrich has more prosaically put it, "somewhere in the centre of our minds."[69]
If Gombrich is right that such a possibility for synesthetic experience "springs
from the infinite elasticity of the human mind," that it is, in other words, part of
the human condition, it would explain the ubiquity of music in such equations.[70]
Such synesthetic tendencies need not necessarily be "hard wired" (as is the case
with psychological synesthetes); nearly all of us form associations that might be
described more accurately as cultural or contextual synesthesia. But it may also
be due to the more elementary fact that music, as a nonverbal but formally complex "object," is hard to write about; translation is always fraught with problems
and the need to employ metaphor. This in fact is Baudelaire's point and mission,
and as Margaret Miner has argued in her analysis, his essay "Richard Wagner and
Tannhäuser in Paris" is an attempt to erase the distinction between reading about
Wagner's music and listening to it.[71] Although he may ultimately fail, the attempt
itself can be illuminating, even as rewarding.

Baudelaire's almost literal seduction by Wagner's music, "allowing myself to
be penetrated and invaded—a truly sensual pleasure," showed him in the most
direct terms that the long-affirmed supremacy of poetry had now been conquered
by music. Not only did Wagner's aesthetic subsume the other arts in the process
of synthesis with music in the Gesamtkunstwerk, but the effect of his music itself
was powerful enough to knock the poet off his pedestal.

As we have seen, music, for Wagner, is superior to language because it is not fixed in the particular (French, English, German, and so on) but instead addresses itself to the general, the universal, or, following Schopenhauer, the Will itself. Music is dynamic and thus better able to reflect the changing temperament of the feelings. Above all its power is to be found in its subjectivity, that it speaks directly to the individual imagination, even if that individual finds himself or herself a part of the crowd-folk-chorus.

Baudelaire described imagination as the "Queen of the Faculties." He says, "It is Imagination that first taught man the moral meaning of colour, of contour, of sound and of scent. In the beginning of the world it created analogy and metaphor."[72] Imagination is the soul of correspondences. His aesthetic theories were first drawn from mainstream romanticism, but after 1847, when he met the artist Eugène Delacroix, they harmonized with the painter's ideas and practice. In short Baudelaire argued that gifted artists can tune themselves to detect the hints provided by nature of both the tangible and intangible. Such hints can be found in the evocative power of colors, scents, and sounds. In "The Salon of 1846," he writes, quoting Ernst Hoffmann from Hoffmann's *Kreisleriana:* "It is not only in dreams, or in the mild delirium which precedes sleep, but it is even awakened when I hear music—that perception of an analogy and an intimate connection between colours, sounds and perfumes. It seems to me that all these things were created by one and the same ray of light, and that their combination must result in a wonderful concert of harmony."[73] Imagination thus stands as the key to subjectivity, in waking life and in dreams. Central to Baudelaire's ideas is the essential importance of "musicality," by which he means the expressive use of line and color, comparable with rhythm and tone:

> Harmony is the basis of the theory of colour.
> Melody is unity within colour, or overall colour.
> Melody calls for a cadence; it is a whole, in which every effect contributes to the general effect.
> Thus colour leaves a deep and lasting impression on the mind.
> Most of our young colourists lack melody.
> The right way to know if a picture is melodious is to look at it from far enough away to make it impossible to understand its subject or to distinguish its lines. If it is melodious, it already has a meaning and has already taken its place in your store of memories.[74]

In art, specifically in drawing and painting, such expressive power is to be achieved by abbreviation, deformation, and synthesis. These elements are generated in the mind, not from nature; they are the products of subjectivity and the memory. They similarly prompt the spectator's imagination to translate external life from the mind of the artist as manifested in his or her work. Such effects he detected in archaic "mnemonic" art: "What I mean is an inevitable, synthetic, childlike barbarousness, which is often still to be discerned in a perfected art, such as Mexico, Egypt, or Nineveh, and which comes from a need to see things broadly and to consider them above all in their total effect. It is by no means out of place here to remind my readers that all those painters whose vision is synthesizing and abbreviative have been accused of barbarousness."[75] This interest in and justification for modern art, although it draws on different historical examples, is part of the same impulse as motivated Wagner to revive ancient ("primitive") arts. The corollary of Baudelaire's argument is that such "barbaric" art, through abbreviation, deformation, and synthesis, is in essence musical: it has musicality. Like Wagner and Nietzsche, for Baudelaire the musical therefore lies at the root of the artistic.

Such a synesthetic conception was to find its apotheosis in the work of a Russian composer, one also working under the shadow of Wagner: Aleksandr Nikolayevich Scriabin. Because his work throws a number of these ideas into sharp relief, we shall make a short detour to Russia before returning to Baudelaire and France.

ALEKSANDR SCRIABIN

Scriabin (1872–1915) was one of the first composers in the early twentieth century to pursue the notion of dissonance in music inherited from Wagner. He discarded the concept of absolute tonal stability and so in doing sought to develop an alternative method of coherence and construction that would organize his nondiatonic music. Wagner had achieved coherence through the employment of the leitmotiv and through the ultimate resolution of harmonic tension within a tonal framework. Scriabin sought another route. But like his German predecessor, Scriabin's aesthetic has an important "extramusical" element, and his revolution went far beyond an internal technical recasting of musical elements to embrace the wider perspective of the Gesamtkunstwerk and even to what one of his principal biographers has called "Omni-art" aiming to achieve "all unity" (vse-edonstvo).[76]

Like Baudelaire, Scriabin found support for his aesthetic in mystical ideas, specifically in theosophical sources, and in the movement that the French poet had himself played an important part in establishing, symbolism. Scriabin remained an eclectic thinker who sought justification for his aesthetic in a range of areas while never fully adopting one particular doctrine. The one constant in his ideas throughout their formation is a deep distrust of rationalism. He shared with both Wagner and Baudelaire a sense of validation in the imaginative and subjective drives of creativity, believing that true insight is intuitive. A supreme individualist, Scriabin nevertheless saw nature and imagination as a part of the same spirit and through his art sought contact with the world external to the imagination. Art for him was an action, a process whose aim was to reach out to and affect life. As he described it, the ultimate aim of art was to bring about "oneness," to resolve the parts into the whole.

There are commonalities between Scriabin's thinking and the *Naturphiloso-phen* of the early nineteenth century. Novalis believed in the mystical unity of all things, and figures such as Wackenroder, Jean Paul, Friedrich von Schelling, and Friedrich Hölderlin held to the notion that the idealized transformation of the natural world through art was a form of communion with the divine. The result of the ecstasy and yearning evoked through the creative act could produce an intense sense of personal inadequacy (in extreme cases leading to suicide). Although Scriabin certainly felt much the same, he was confident of his "God-given role." It was to fulfill this role that he employed the idea of the Gesamtkunstwerk.

Two of his earliest guides on this path were, not surprisingly, Schopenhauer, from whom he understood the primacy of subjective consciousness, and Nietzsche, whose *Birth of Tragedy* supported aesthetic synthesis and sensuality and whose later work confirmed Scriabin's belief in the artist as superman. The notion of the evolution of consciousness was also to find a root in theosophical beliefs, but one of his first sustained philosophical encounters was around 1898, when he made two important contacts: the social and intellectual circle surrounding Prince Sergey Nikolayevich Troubetzkoy, who was at the time professor of philosophy at Moscow University, and the ideas and writings of Vladimir Solovyov. Through this he was in turn introduced to the literary salon of Margarita Morozova. There he met many of the leading lights of the Russian symbolist movement, among them Valery Bryusov, Emilli Medtner (brother of the composer Nikolay), who was a close friend of Aleksandr Blok, and Andrey Bely; these last two were connected by family to Solovyov and by inclination to his millenarianism and theology. Typically, Scriabin took from these encounters what he felt was relevant to his art, but he could not really be classed as a follower or member of a group.

Scriabin spent much time traveling abroad and living in Belgium and Switzerland (c. 1904–10). His personal contact with Russian cultural life was reestablished in January 1910, when he moved back to Moscow. Here he attended lectures, concerts, art exhibitions, and literary discussions. Through these activities he became a close friend of Jurgis Baltrusaitis, a leading symbolist poet. And through Baltrusaitis he met other leading poets of the movement, including Konstantine Balmont and Vyacheslav Ivanov. Together with Bryusov, these poets drew their inspiration from Baudelaire, Paul Verlaine, and Stéphane Mallarmé, whose work began to appear in translation in the early 1890s. The mouthpiece for the work of these "decadents" was the journal *World of Art* (*Mir iskusstva*), founded by Sergey Diaghilev in 1898, which harmonized with Scriabin's messianic tone and promotion of the "spiritual." The mix in their work comes not just from French sources but also from the German idealist tradition, especially as filtered through Solovyov's philosophical system. Through the interests of Aleksandr Benois and Diaghilev, the synthesis of art and music in the Gesamtkunstwerks of the Ballet Russes became a focus for the construction of a Russian mythology, whose "answer" to the Germanic language of Wagner's mythic works can be seen in Igor Stravinsky's first score for Diaghilev set to Michel Fokine's choreography, *The Firebird,* which premiered at the Paris Opéra on 25 June 1910.

Solovyov's thought exerted a considerable influence on many young Russian artists toward the turn of the twentieth century, through both his theoretical and poetic writings, although he viewed their work with some skepticism. A notable example is Bely, whose early works, published between 1902 and 1908, were in the form of prose "symphonies" — that is, their synthesizing aesthetic also relies heavily on Wagner's notions, especially in their use of leitmotivs. Bely later spent time in Switzerland under the influence of Rudolph Steiner's anthroposophical theories before returning in 1916 to Russia, where he published his most famous work, the experimental novel *Petersburg.*

Solovyov began as a follower of Ludwig Feuerbach and others and later turned to the idealism of Kant and Schopenhauer, following a course similar to Wagner's.[77] He imagined an ultimate synthesis of the divine and human, earthly and ideal, embodied in part through the figure of Christ. Reality, he argued, could be fully comprehended only on the basis of a synthesis of religion, philosophy, and science (or faith, thought, and experience). Art, in turn, was a microcosm of this unity: "Art must be a real force enlightening and regenerating the entire human world."[78] The role of the artist was therefore theurgic. Like Orpheus, the artist should lead us from the underworld to the light (from death to resurrection).[79] This regeneration was necessary, not just because of the crisis of expression art faced as the classical paradigm began to collapse in the face of modernity and the power of naturalism began to wane, but because such a change could or should bring about a concomitant revolution of social structure. Further, the advent of the new century seemed to signal a new era, one marked by a heightened spirituality in contrast to the positivism of realism.

Solovyov's apocalyptic vision led him to believe that the forces of the Antichrist would threaten civilization from the East. Such a fundamental shake-up of society was indeed about to take place with the Russian Revolution and the First World War, but Scriabin died during the war and never experienced the new social order that followed the revolution. He did nevertheless read Karl Marx or, according to Boris de Schloezer, at least the first part of *Das Kapital,* which he encountered through his socialist friend Georgy Plekhanov.[80] He embraced the economic elements of Marxism but not the concomitant ideology. For Scriabin the spirit had to maintain ultimate independence from environmental or material circumstances, although he agreed with Marx that the collapse of capitalism was inevitable. It was art, Scriabin believed, rather than social or political revolution, that would bring about real change. New ideas would flow from artists, not the proletariat. For him art was a superior form of knowledge, similar to that possessed by mystics, gained by intuition, that bore the seeds of true reality and that could ultimately help humanity progress to a higher plane, to divinity. His view was closer to Solovyov, who argued that the nature of this (spiritual) change was to be found in metaphysical, not materialist principles and that humanity had a potential for attaining spiritual perfection. Such a notion fits well with the idea of music characterized by Schopenhauer (as "eternal truth") and Baudelaire, but it also had another important echo.

Theosophy enjoyed a wide influence at the turn of the twentieth century.[81] Founded in 1875 in New York City by Helena Petrovna Blavatsky (known simply as Madame Blavatsky, 1831–91), assisted by her spiritualist friend Colonel Henry Olcott, theosophy represented a synthesis of pre-Christian and Oriental philosophies (mainly Indian), opposing itself to what it saw as the twin evils of science and theology (specifically Christianity). Blavatsky's two major theosophical texts were *Isis Unveiled* (1877) and *The Secret Doctrine* (1888). In an era when science was threatening long-held beliefs, theosophy's mysticism and antimaterialism made it a natural ally to artists who were turning from naturalism and positivism. Its capacity to subsume an eclectic range of ideas made it the paramount force for resurgence of spiritualism as the new century dawned.

Scriabin first became acquainted with the movement in Paris in 1906, when he subscribed to the theosophical journal *Le lotus bleu*. When he returned to Russia he took the Russian counterpart the *Teosifski zhurnal*.[82] While in Switzerland he read Madame Blavatsky, Annie Besant, and C. W. Leadbeater. These writings impressed him with the grandiose sweep of their synthesis, which matched the scope of symbolist ideas. Indeed, according to Schloezer, Scriabin specifically likened Blavatsky's vision to the "grandeur of Wagner's music dramas."[83]

The principal work he consulted was Blavatsky's *Secret Doctrine*.[84] In this work Blavatsky outlined the belief that all existence was ordered into seven planes, ranging from the most material or physical to the highest, most spiritual (the mahapâranirvânic).[85] There were also seven "root" races, each reflecting a phase in the evolution of spiritual life, so that consciousness and its various levels was characterized on a personal, psychic, and social plane. Music had a privileged place among the arts. As Schopenhauer had argued, music spoke of the thing itself, so, too, theosophists saw music as engendering higher consciousness through its perceived immateriality. In the process of doing this, however, music also brought about "thought-forms," as Annie Besant and C.W. Leadbeater claimed in their book on the subject: "Sound produces form as well as colour . . . every piece of music leaves behind it an impression of this nature, which . . . is clearly visible and intelligible to those who have eyes to see."[86]

Such notions played an important part in Scriabin's development of color-key relationships. Many ideas from theosophy share common ground with Wagner-inspired symbolist thought: a belief in the theurgic function of art, music as the pinnacle of artistic expression, and a conviction for the centrality of the artist in bringing about a new world order. In a way Scriabin is not dissimilar from Wagner, who believed that the Dresden May Day uprising would bring about a new cultural climate more sympathetic to his art. So, too, Scriabin saw political unrest in Russia as helpful to the fulfillment of his aesthetic aims:

> The political revolution in Russia in its present phase [the 1905 revolution] and the change which I want are different. Of course, this revolution, like every other political agitation brings the beginning of my moment closer. I make a mistake in using the word change [*perevorot*]. I do not want the actualization or establishing of anything. I want only endless *élan* of creative activity brought about by my art. This means that before all else I must complete my important composition. . . . My moment has not yet begun. But it approaches. There will be a celebration! Soon![87]

The "important composition" that Scriabin mentions was to be his *Mysterium*—in his eyes the ultimate Gesamtkunstwerk. For like Wagner he believed that the arts could reach their potential only through synthesis or, at the least, through a form of parallelism, a reunification under the banner of music. Music appears to be the engine that propelled the art work, but its impact could be increased in concert with the other arts. Or to express it through a more symbolist route, the "musical element" inherent in all art could in concert be brought out.

The idea for this work had been growing in Scriabin's mind since 1902, but he constantly delayed working on it. In large part this was due to its hugely ambitious character: a vision of apocalyptic ecstasy leading to the end of the material world. In fact, although the *Mysterium* was thought out in some detail and a preliminary work was started, it was never actually begun before his death. Because it was to be the culmination of Scriabin's work, an endpoint, an ultimate synthesis, a transformatory act, it is not so surprising that he never felt quite ready to face it.

Scriabin greatly admired Wagner but had in fact only heard part of the *Ring* cycle. He first heard *Siegfried* in 1902 and *Götterdämmerung* much later, but he never saw a staged performance of *Das Rheingold* and never, according to Schloezer, heard either *Parsifal* or *Tristan und Isolde*. His understanding of Wagner's theories came mainly through magazine articles, but such contact offered him enough to support his burgeoning aesthetic. Given this limited, contact it is not surprising that there are significant differences between the two composers, notably in relation to the role of the audience. Scriabin took issue with Wagner's positioning of his audience:

> The audience, the spectators are separated by the stage instead of being joined with the performers in a single act. I will not have any sort of theatre.
>
> Wagner, with all his genius, could never surmount the theatrical—the stage—never, because he did not understand what was the matter. He did not realise that all the evil in this separation lay in that there was no unity, no genuine experience, but only the representation of experience. The true eradication of the stage can be accomplished in the "Mystery."[88]

Scriabin, in other words, had no qualms about direct contact with the Dionysian as Nietzsche had characterized it: liberation through ecstasy. Indeed, given that the work aimed to end in cosmic transformation, such beliefs as the power of music (art) to provide "the presentment of supreme joy, through which the path through destruction and negation leads," would mean that what is imagined for Nietzsche when the spectator "hears the innermost abyss of things speaking to him" is not for Scriabin imagined but lived, hence his argument that Wagner merely represents.[89]

Scriabin's notion of the spectator may share something in common with the primordial world of the *Volk* evoked in Wagner's reactionary nationalism, despite the cry to "brotherhood," but for Scriabin there were not to be spectators in the usual sense; all were to be participants. Unlike Wagner, who excavated his ideas from Greek culture, Scriabin had a practical model closer to home: the use of the chorus in Russian opera from its foundation in the time of Mikhail Glinka. Glinka had famously chided Western grand opera: "Ah, these choruses! They arrive from God knows where, sing God knows what and make off as they came in . . . ! Padding!"[90] Since the inception of Russian opera the chorus had played a role as a collective dramatis personae—not dissimilar from the Greek chorus. Rather than simply commenting on the unfolding drama, roving about in a more passive role, the Russian chorus was conceived as a participant with as central a place as the soloists. Scriabin's attitude of fuller participation was prefigured (or promoted) by Vyacheslav Ivanov, who had written in 1905: "Wagner-heirophant does not give a choral voice and words to the community. Why not? It has a right to that voice, because it is supposed to be not a crowd of spectators, but an assemblage of orgists. . . . Wagner stopped halfway and did not pronounce the final word. His synthesis of the arts is neither harmonious nor complete."[91] Ivanov had been influenced by both German philosophy and Solovyov's theology; in particular, his focus on ancient myth and art had been fostered by Nietzsche's *Birth of Tragedy.* Ivanov's promotion of community over individualism put him out of step with many symbolists, but his view that it was the artist's task to create myth for the people chimes with the importance of the mythic in Scriabin's aesthetic and with symbolism in general.

Scriabin's *Mysterium* was to extend the "gesamt" qualities of Wagner's art work of the future by involving all senses through the use of colored lights, music, scents, and even tastes.[92] As a synesthete, Scriabin experienced sound as inter-related with colors, images, and ideas, so sound for him was never a priori autono-mous; it was the content of his own psychological experience. His view that the arts required reintegration, as reported to Schloezer, has its origin in the dawn of history rather than in antiquity, as with Wagner. Scriabin believed that humanity had first known only an inchoate Omni-art in which the visual, auditory, and motor sensations were wedded into one aesthetic experience. All organic senses played a part in primordial Omni-art. Indeed, the memory of this Omni-art sur-vived as a dim echo in Greek tragedy, to which Wagner had responded. Only those arts capable of artistic development flourished, those associated with the senses of sight and hearing, which in turn gave birth to the separate branches of art.

Although Wagner's account of ancient history had admitted failings, he did seek some chronicled evidence. Scriabin's view, by contrast, is purely hypotheti-cal. Theosophy offered Scriabin a model of speculation on the spirit of prehistory. Yet for both composers the important point is not so much historical accuracy as justification for their practice. Neither was retracing the past; each was point-ing to the future. Neither attempted to evoke antique practice, nor did they make direct reference to ancient models.

For Scriabin the association of the arts did not follow a preexisting path. Their relationships had to grow spontaneously in the process of composition. He aimed to weave a polyphonic design in which all the arts (poetry, music, visual art, dance) played an equal role, so that ultimately it would be impossible to disen-tangle them. There are even hints, according to Schloezer, that what Scriabin in-tended to bring out was the choreography of making music, the music of poetry, the visual spectacle of enactment: the faint resonances of Omni-art that hover below the surface of the modern separated arts. He hoped to promote not paral-lelism but counterpoint through the voices of commonality—the visual in music, the music in poetry, the poetry in dance—that exist implicitly in each art form.[93]

Not surprisingly, the details of how this was to be achieved remained unspeci-fied. Scriabin spoke of the nature of this magnum opus for the last ten years of his life, and only too aware of the enormity of the task his imagination had set him, he began more and more to resent his busy performance schedule for taking valuable time away from the *Mysterium.* In 1913 he pronounced himself at work on it, but he quickly modified the work in hand so that it became a kind of prolegomena, what he called the *Acte préalable* (Prefatory act). This work, in turn, was unfinished at his death. Before this, around 1900, Scriabin had been working on an opera, but it, too, he abandoned. Its musical fragments were used in other smaller works and some of the text found its way into the verse poem associated with *The Poem of Ecstasy,* op. 54, as its conception was subsumed and surpassed in the *Mysterium.*

The *Acte préalable,* which Scriabin originally conceived as a way of preparing both himself and the public for the *Mysterium*, absorbed so much of the material of the *Mysterium* that it became a palimpsest of the larger, unrealized work.[94] It consists mainly of text, but he made some sketches for the music, fragments of thematic motives and outlined harmonic progression, notated in black, red, blue, and violet pencils, presumably bearing some relation to his wish to include color. They were to take their place on the pages of manuscript made up of seventy staves, forty more than in the scoring of *Prometheus*. The poem on which the *Mysterium* was based exists in two versions, the second showing the divisions for choir and soloists. It has little narrative drive; rather, it is a sequence of sensuous images (fields, mountains, light, sea, death, flames, and angels) that aim to be evocative. It was to open with the following text over a tremolo chord:

Once again the Deathless One bestows
A blessed gift of Love on you;
Once more the Infinite One shows
In the Finite his image true

According to Schloezer, in whose book more of the text is found, the rhythm and rhyme of the words would dictate the music or, rather, the music was to emerge from the musicality of the verse.[95]

The *Acte préalable* is deeply theosophical in imagery. It was conceived as opening with the birth of the universe, from which two opposite principles emerge, personified as male and female (tenor and contralto). It concludes with the reintegration of the many into one, the transfiguration of matter into pure spirit (ascending the planes of existence, as described by Leadbeater).

The language for the text of the *Mysterium* had to go beyond the specific connotations of ordinary words to embody the universal references Scriabin envisaged. If music was, as Scriabin understood it, a universal form of expression, then his text likewise needed to be universal. He believed that human speech had first been inseparable from emotion, part of the world of Omni-art synthesized with expression. Modern languages had become abstract, however, too much part of the expression of rational discourses, like science, that subdued the emotive. He wanted instead to find an urtext, a language at the root of speech, a prelapsarian voice.

When Scriabin was working on the *Mysterium,* popular opinion believed Sanskrit to be the primordial Aryan language. So this was where he turned, hoping that Sanskrit would give him a lingua franca. After some study, however, he decided that, despite its antiquity, Sanskrit was already too highly developed to be closely related to the origins of speech. His only option was to invent his own language, which he began just before his death. The only examples he left are simple abstract notions like "joying" and "loveness." As with Wagner, we see an attempt to transcend the fixity of language, but perhaps the most radical attempt to find a protolanguage was carried out concurrently with Scriabin's by Velemir (Victor) Khlebnikov.

Khlebnikov had moved from the symbolist circle around Ivanov to the circle of artists around Mikhail Larionov. He signed the futurist manifesto "A slap in the face of public taste" and became a leader in the cubo-futurist movement. Khlebnikov argued that language had once expressed everything clearly and directly. To recover this state of language he took the opposite route of Scriabin and the symbolists. Instead of focusing on the emotive aspects of language, Khlebnikov argued for a more rational approach. It was therefore necessary to "distil the language by scientific means to obtain those original meanings and then build on this foundation a universal language." The result would have utopian political ramifications; it would "lead to a cessation of wars because people would understand one another."[96] This idea he called *Zaum,* a term he had taken and differently applied from his fellow futurist poet Alexey Kruchonykh, from the prefix *za,* meaning beyond, and the root *um,* meaning mind. The formalist critic Victor Shklovsky, however, stressed in his definition of *Zaum* the emotive aim of this rational investigation: "the language that is so to speak personal, with words having no definite meaning, but affecting the emotions directly."[97] This is the clearest statement of the power of music over poetry, for, as Baudelaire had detected in Wagner's aesthetic, poetry here becomes a form of protomusic in its attempt to reflect emotional life accurately and with little intercession. It surrenders precision to embrace suggestion.

Other experiments in poetry lead to closer links between it and the visual arts.[98] Nikolay Kublin, a doctor by training, was a major player in prerevolutionary Russian cultural life, although his influence and reputation quickly faded after the revolution. He promoted microtonal music, contributing an article to *Der Blaue Reiter Almanac* on freedom from conventions in music. He also devised a synesthetic alphabet that borrowed both symbolist and theosophical ideas. He associated phonemes with color, which in turn had emotional signification.[99] Nikolay Burlyuk, the futurist poet and brother of the artist David Burlyuk, in his book *Poetic Principles,* also discussed the role of color and the effect of visual presentation on the function of words.[100] Scriabin's interests are thus part of a more general investigation of art's relationships.

Interestingly, Scriabin found support for his synesthetic notions in Sanskrit sources. According to Sourindro Mohun Tagore, Sanskrit authorities have associated "the seven notes . . . respectively . . . with the following colours: black, tawny, gold, white, yellow, purple and green."[101] Not surprisingly, Scriabin imagined the performance of the *Mysterium* taking place in India. Theosophists in London suggested Darjeeling to him, for he wanted to replace Wagner's landscape painter's backdrops and scenery with animate nature itself; the Himalayas, the sunrise and sunset as part of the decor and action. The sights, smells, sounds, and textures of nature were to be integral to the work. Later, he referred more generally to the siting of the work as simply "tropical." To house his magnum opus he initially conceived of a temple situated in a terraced clearing in a forest. The temple was in the form of a hemisphere surrounded by water, creating a sphere in the reflection, and on a scale that made Wagner's architectural projects appear modest. The landscaping and construction would be part of the score and performance, there being no actions or elements outside the rubric of the *Mysterium*. Later his concrete temple disintegrated, replaced by a projection, an ephemeral structure made from pillars of incense and columns and walls of light, the temporal changes of nature and insubstantial architecture providing a counterpoint to the temporally unfolding music. Its lack of material substance provided a more appropriate metaphor for spiritual transcendence.[102]

Scriabin's interest in Indian culture was principally fostered through theosophical tracts, among them Auguste Barth's *Religions de l'Inde,* Edwin Arnold's *Light of India,* Konstantine Balmont's translation of Asvaghosa's *Life of Buddha,* and a number of travel guides. The overriding spirit of the *Mysterium* remains theosophical. In addition to the inclusion of natural elements in the work, the seven races of theosophical dogma were to be reflected in the time cycle of the work (again, exceeding Wagner's ambition): seven days in total, the fifth day corresponding to our own time, after which, presumably, some form of transcendence was to take place, climaxing on the seventh day in "cosmic ecstasy." Serge Koussevitsky, who at one time was to be the conductor, had a refreshingly down-to-earth view, declaring, "We will all go out and have a fine dinner afterwards."[103]

We can gain insight into the extraordinary imagination behind this uncompletable work by looking at Scriabin's fifth symphony, *Prometheus—The Poem of Fire,* op. 60, which he composed between 1908 and 1910, and which was his last completed orchestral score. By no means as ambitious as the *Mysterium,* the work nevertheless sought to synthesize two elements: color and sound (fig. 2.1).

Prometheus is scored for large orchestra, including quadruple woodwind, eight horns, five trumpets, eight trombones and tubas, two harps, a piano, a large percussion section (including celesta), an organ, a wordless chorus, and, to add to this palette of timbre, a *tastiera per luce* (light keyboard: notated on the top line of

2.1 Robert Sterl, *Piano Concerto with Skriabin,* 1910, oil on canvas, 23 x 31.5 cm. State Art Gallery, Dresden. © DACS 2000

the score in conventional music notation) (ex. 2.4). There is no detail in the score as regards how the light is to be projected (on a screen, throughout the concert hall?) or via what precise means it is to be "played"; rather, it confidently assumes that *luce* is as commonplace in this setup as flute or piano. Scriabin planned the first version of this device in consultation with Aleksandr Moser, a photographer and professor of electromechanics at the Moscow School for Higher Technical Training. But there is no evidence that the design of this "instrument" got off the drawing board. Nevertheless, light seems to have been a central conceptual strand of the composition process, even if the form of notation adopted by Scriabin subordinates color to musical convention.[104] The notation for this luce is written on a single stave in two parts (and in three parts for four bars before bar 30) in the treble: one forms the "background," which changes slowly, ten times in all, each change lasting about two minutes. This part moves in whole tones from F♯ (blue) to the midpoint C (red), which divides the octave in half through a tritone, onto the "resolution" in F♯, where the piece concludes on the only true triad of the piece (F♯, A♯, C♯), signifying spirit (in opposition to C=red, which signifies material): the move from F♯ to F♯¹ represents a complete revolution of the cycle of fifths. However, the inclusion of very occasional "passing notes" (B, D♭, E♯)

skews the gradual move through the color circle by introducing colors from diverse parts of the color circle. For although moves between "pitches" maybe only by a notated semitone, as can be seen from the table below, the corresponding color is more distant. This is because the division of color into twelve separate units is a matter of nomenclature rather than physical fact. The mapping of color onto pitch (the chromatic scale) is then neatly achieved, though totally arbitrary. In short, the slow-moving part played by the luce appears to have been conceived to provide an indication of the overall conceptual framework of the piece, which has in practice occasional "wrong notes." Either this, or it is independent, a free counterpoint in light.

The other part of the luce notation, the "foreground," reflects more rapid harmonic progressions and is closely tied to the movement of the music. The relationship is less schematic and specifically appears to follow the course of the so-called mystic chord (C, F♯, B♭, E, A, D)—the harmonic root of the work—as it occurs throughout the piece. It reinforces the particular, as the slower part acts to do something similar to the "deeper structure." In both cases the function of the luce is analogical, offering the same "root" experience in two manifestations; it is therefore cross-disciplinary, as we described it earlier.

The color-pitch correspondences that Scriabin used are arranged in a circle of fifths. Scriabin, however, experienced color-tone relationships not individually but through chordal complexes, and according to some sources, he deduced the full cycle from his spontaneous recognition of C=red, D=yellow, and F♯=blue:

C = Red	F♯ = Bright blue
G = Orange	D♭ = Violet
D = Yellow	A♭ = Purple
A = Green	E♭ = Metallic gray/blue
E = Pale blue	B♭ = Blue-gray
B = Very pale blue	F = Dark red[105]

Such synesthetic correspondences, like theosophical thinking, were common in symbolist circles and indeed have a history that reaches back at least as far as Aristotle: "It is possible that colours may stand in relation to each other in the same manner as concords in music, for the colours which are (to each other) in proportion corresponding with musical concords are those which appear to be most agreeable."[106]

In the early modern era, Isaac Newton offered relationships between the seven colors of the spectrum and the seven notes of a diatonic scale. These ideas were later taken up by Thomas Young, and in turn the color theorists, who influenced the postimpressionists, German physicist Hermann Helmholtz, French chemist

Prométhée.

2.4 Aleksandr Scriabin, *Prometheus—The Poem of Fire,* op. 60, 1908–10, opening. Reproduced by kind permission of Peters Edition Limited, London

Michel-Eugène Chevreul, and American physicist Ogden Rood. An alternative, less scientific rationalist tradition, which ran in parallel, can be seen originating in the subjectivist color theories of Johann Wolfgang von Goethe and culminating in the abstract art of Kandinsky. Goethe writes: "Colour and sound do not admit of being directly compared together in any way, but both are referable to a higher formula, both are derivable, although each for itself from this higher law. They are like two rivers which have taken their source in one and the same mountain, but subsequently pursue their way under totally different regions, so that throughout the whole course of both no two points can be compared."[107] The important point here is Goethe's belief in a common root, and following both symbolist and theosophical views, music, closer to the thing-itself, becomes the route to this root.

Kandinsky, too, believed that color had a fundamental power to affect the human soul, as he famously put it in *Concerning the Spiritual in Art* (1911). Following a discussion of synesthetic reactions, in a metaphor that combines sound, color, and keyboards, he writes, "Color is the keyboard. The eye is the hammer. The soul is the piano, with its many strings. The artist is the hand that purposefully sets the soul vibrating by means of this or that key."[108]

Light keyboards also have a long technical history, the first documented case being Bertrand Castel's *clavecin oculaire,* devised in 1734. With the discovery of electricity, Alexander Rimington breathed new life into the instrument in the late nineteenth century. Between 1837 and 1925 more than three hundred works for "color organs," as they were then known, were published. Moser's tastiera per luce, however, existed only as at most a prototype, and the first performance of *Prometheus,* which took place under Koussevitsky, with Scriabin as pianist, on 2 March 1911, had no accompanying light show. Even when these experiments did not rely on a direct translation of a musical piece into its color equivalent, as some did, they are nearly always based on the same type of subjective synesthetic color-chord relationships as Scriabin's formulation.[109] Despite the convenience of the metaphorical use of colors to evoke tone, we should remember that synesthesia is real for those who experience this type of sensory crossover. The phenomenon of "color hearing," a specific type of synesthesia and one of the more common, has been rigorously investigated, but what emerges from this work is the individualized nature of the experience; agreements over correspondences seem to be little more than coincidences.[110]

Scriabin's motivation behind his concept of the Gesamtkunstwerk, with its acme in the *Mysterium,* was characterized by Leonid Sabanayev in his article on "Prometheus" in Wassily Kandinsky and Franz Marc's *Der Blaue Reiter Almanac* in 1912. Here Sabanayev uses terms very similar to those of Baudelaire in describing the impact of Wagner's music: ecstasy was its aim and all senses were

involved in its means. "We find as much in our contemporary church service—
a descendent of classical mystical ritual—on a smaller scale, the idea of uniting
the arts is preserved. Don't we find there music (singing, sounds of bells), plastic movement (kneeling, ritual of priests action), play of smells (incense), play
of lights (candles, lights), painting? All arts are united here in one harmonious
whole, to attain one goal, religious exaltation."[111] Sabanayev not surprisingly finds
the roots of Scriabin's mystical-religious Gesamtkunstwerk in classical Greek
ritual—the same source as for Wagner. But as we have seen, this is not the justification Scriabin himself sought for "Omni-art." Some commentators, for example, read the title of *Prometheus* (the Greek god who saved the world through
the gift of fire but, having stolen it from Olympus, was punished by Zeus by
being chained to a rock and having his liver repeatedly torn out by an eagle, until
Hercules set him free) as emblematic of Scriabin's view of his artistic role. The
underlying theme of equality with the theme of divinity through imagination and
creativity—the giving of light and spiritual triumph—were for Scriabin grounded
in the emergence of human nature at the moment of creation, an event that is
older than its manifestation in Greek culture and thought in Omni-art, when all
was one.[112]

Prometheus, despite its more modest proportions, is constructed around the
same theosophical concerns as the *Mysterium* was to have been. The piano part
represents microcosmic humanity, and the orchestra represents the cosmos. Pep-
pered throughout are various themes that go by such titles as the Will, Dawn of
Human Consciousness (or Reason), Play of Creative Spirit, and Joy of Life. There
are eleven motifs in all, generated from a relatively limited pitch content. The
tonal core of the work is the so-called mystic chord: C, F♯, B♭, E, A, D (which
forms the key for color changes, the faster section of the light keyboard part).
Emphasizing a quartel arrangement, Sabanayev accounted for it in terms of a
fourth-chord overtone theory, as it relates to the upper partials of the harmonic
series of C. More recent analysis, however, has shown it to be part of a more complex, octatonic structure grouped around tritones: in pitch-class number notation
0, 1, 3, 4, 6, 7, 9, 10 or 1, 2, 4, 5, 7, 8, 10, 11 or 2, 3, 5, 6, 7, 9, 11, 0.

In much the same way that Wagner used dominant and diminished seventh
chords, which hold open the harmonic texture and thus suspend a sense of closure, so Scriabin extended the boundaries of diatonic harmony. In Scriabin's case,
however, the interlocked tritones at the heart of such seventh chords (for example, a dominant seventh chord with a flattened fifth [C, E, F♯, B♭] consists of
two interlocked tritones [C–F♯ and E–B♭]), which are used to generate series of
such chords, and extensions into ninths and eleventh chords produce whole tone
and octatonic scales, operating as new harmonic centers that allow for "modulations."[113] In most of Scriabin's mature works it is no longer appropriate to talk of

melodic lines, for all is subsumed in the harmony. Foreground and background elements are compressed into a single element, developed through motivic fragments. Although his later works have often been regarded as virtually atonal, and therefore without method, his sequentially developed tritone approach, as explained by recent investigations, shows how close he came to developing a dodecaphonic method (the tritone divides the octave into two equal halves—in effect, two hexachords). As the musicologist Ellon Carpenter has pointed out in what is a post-serialist judgment, "Not until Schoenberg with his twelve-tone technique do we find a composer so consistent in his compositional technique . . . and Skriabin comes so close to this twelve-note system that it seems probable he would have taken it as the next logical step."[114] However, as we shall see in Chapter 5, another composer, Josef Matthias Hauer, devised a true dodecaphonic method that uses hexachordal tropes and has more in common with Scriabin than Schoenberg's precompositional row technique.

Before we return briefly to Baudelaire, we should mention one of Scriabin's followers, a composer who took up the challenge of the "extended Gesamtkunstwerk" and technically uses a dodecaphonic method: the little-known musician Nikolay Obukhov. In so doing we are returned to France and to another better known figure with mystic and synesthetic leanings, Olivier Messiaen.

NIKOLAY OBUKHOV

Like Scriabin, Obukhov (1892–1954) was deeply religious. He left Russia in May 1917, on the eve of the Revolution, and traveled for two years through the Crimea before finally settling in Paris in 1919. Having previously been a student at the Saint Petersburg Conservatory with Maximilian Steinberg and N. N. Tcherepnine, he resumed his studies, becoming a pupil of Marcel Orban and Maurice Ravel, with whom he studied orchestration. He set down his theories in his *Traité d'harmonie tonale, atonale et totale* (Paris, 1947), for which Arthur Honegger wrote the foreword. Throughout this period he concentrated on one work, his *La livre de vie* (Book of life, also known under the Russian title *Kniga zhizni*), a work of more than eight hundred pages in short-score with a libretto in Russian, composed in seven chapters (reflecting the six days of creation and the day of rest) and divided into fourteen stages (*étapes*). The last of these stages takes the form of elaborate, composite, fold-out sheets, collaged from cloth and colored paper, stuck, sewn, and clipped together, to form six separate scores. Together they have considerable visual impact, an effect of obvious importance to Obukhov, that transcends the necessity for sonoric organization. The painstaking nature of the manuscript makes the work a visual art object of an obsessive and haunting homemade beauty (ex. 2.5).[115]

Obukhov's interest in Russian symbolist thinking is evident in his early songs ("liturgical poems"), which date from 1913 and are based on, or around, the poems of Balmont, many of which were later incorporated into *La livre de vie*. His aesthetic was driven by the belief that there was a higher reality to which art could reach. He differs from Scriabin, however, in the strength of his commitment to Christianity as a justification for his idealism.

Like Scriabin, Obukhov considered his art a means to an end, not simply an aesthetic product that stood alone, and although he felt that all five senses should be involved in this goal, he regarded music as his greatest ally: "Music enjoys decided advantages which endow it with possibilities of insinuation into the depths of the soul, and the mind, of emotions inaccessible to other arts. This faculty resides in the fact that music is hindered less than any other art in the realisation of its aims by material conditions."[116]

For Obukhov, however, this "advantage" needed to be restated after the sentimentality and chromatic saturation of romantic music. In the modernist drive to reinvent the "language" of music, in the pursuit of notions of purity music had become all system and no heart. He wanted to maintain music's spiritual core. Only the employment of a dodecaphonic method of composition, what he called "absolute harmony," could establish a true equilibrium of mind and spirit. This was, he believed, in accordance with music's origins and would lead humanity to salvation.

Like a number of early dodecaphonic composers, such as Schoenberg and Hauer, Obukhov believed that new harmonic ideas and systems of organization required a corresponding reevaluation of musical notation. The problem was that the conventional system of notation was based on a diatonic foundation, the key of C major. All other keys are to a greater or lesser extent deviations from it. With the growth in chromatic music the number of accidentals grew to a point where it became hard always to discern how they were to be interpreted. Should they be placed before each new note, or only once within a bar? This meant that a system devised in relation to a key with no accidentals (indeed they are only "accidental" to C) was having to contain music that shifted key constantly or was outside a single key system altogether. Such moves away from accepted convention and expectation led to many different notation systems in the twentieth century.[117]

All notational systems constrain as much as they facilitate expression and exactitude. The history of such systems provides an account of the priorities composers place on the elements of music. The most common concern within the Western tradition has been on issues of pitch and duration, placing less stress on the precision of other aspects of performance such as timbre, texture, mode of attack, presentation (the physical presence of the performer before an audience), and areas of the performance that are left to the creative discretion of the per-

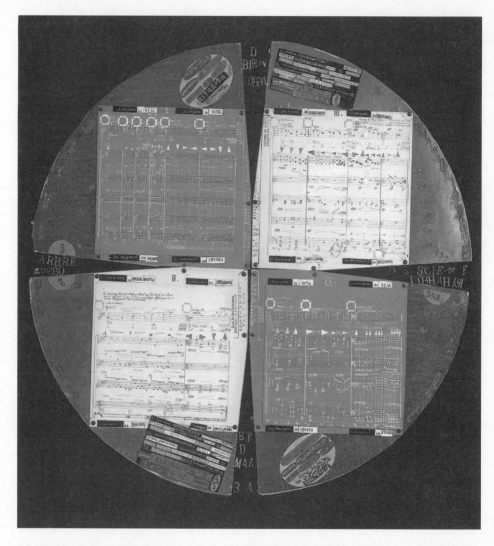

2.5 Nikolay Obukhov, pages from the *Book of Life*. © Musicom. All rights reserved. Reproduced by permission

former. In addition, notation serves a number of functions: it acts as an indication of a composer's intentions for the performer, it allows the composer to control large forces and organize them simultaneously, and it provides a visual record for the analysis and classification of sound. The two poles around which musical notation has tended to circulate are, on one hand, to reduce ambiguity as much as possible, providing a transparent medium to intentions, so that a performer needs

only to "read" rather than interpret (to paraphrase Stravinsky); and, on the other, which has more in common with contemporary theories of language, to see all notation as a priori ambiguous, to a greater or lesser extent, and therefore to regard notation as a catalyst for creativity, giving the performer more creative license with the work. The invention of new musical instruments (including electronics and computers), the increase in chromaticism, changes in the relationship among composer, performer, and audience, increasing interest in the graphic (visual), as opposed to symbolic, character of signs and sonic outcomes — all of these made notation a much more various activity by the late twentieth century than it was at the beginning.

Given that Obukhov took part in the early rumblings of this process (he dates his system from 1915), it is perhaps not so surprising that he came up with a fairly conservative solution. He based his system on equal temperament, divided into two hexachords (adding to Guido d'Arezzo's foundational single hexachord, for example, Ut-re-mi-fa-sol-la [doh-ray-me-fah-sol-lah]).[118] In addition to sol-fa designation, his system designates sharped notes by a "x" (de-re-fe-se-le), rhythmic values by the conventional tails, and various bar-line variations to designate "emotional episodes" and other phases of significance, in a way not dissimilar to Messiaen.[119] The importance of equal temperament, and hence dodecaphony, had mystic significance for Obukhov. The equality of tonal relations between chromatic notes and their disposition, had, he believed, more than a simple metaphorical relationship to spiritual equipoise.

In addition to modified notation, Obukhov also felt the need to supplement the conventional orchestra with new musical instruments in order to realize his aesthetic. The most intriguing of these was to be an instrument he called the "Ether." This was either a type of electronically powered wind machine, in which a large rotating wheel produced a low humming sound, or, theoretically, was inaudible.[120] Its aim was to produce infra- and ultrasonic sounds that ranged from approximately five octaves below to five octaves above human hearing.[121] The effect of such an instrument was likely to be physiological, partly depending on amplitude—some ultrasonic sounds can induce fits in susceptible people, and infrasonic sound is most likely to be felt through slow, loud vibrations, as with the rumble of an earthquake.[122] Given the expanded notion of the Gesamtkunstwerk, such an instrument would be an effective way of extending sensory experience. However, there is no record that it was ever constructed.

A more conventional instrument of his invention he called a "crystal," a keyboard instrument in which hammers were to strike semiglobes of crystal, rather in the manner of a celesta. This also, as far as we know, never made it to the construction stage.

One instrument that was realized was the "croix sonore" or sounding cross,[123] which, together with Michel Billaudot and Pierre Dauvillier, Obukhov devised and constructed in the 1920s and early 1930s.[124] Aptly named, it consisted of a brass cross that acted as an aerial about four feet (1.2 meters) high, surmounting a globe with a flattened bottom, about two feet (60 centimeters) in diameter, which contained the oscillator, which was inscribed with the name of the instrument in both French and Russian (fig. 2.2). The rate of oscillations generated by the valve circuit affected the pitch, which was modified by moving a hand, or hands, closer and further away from the aerial-cross, focusing on the "star" between the

2.2 Nikolay Obukhov's "croix
sonore." Reproduced by permission of McMillan

horizontal and vertical bars.[125] The sounding cross's most immediate precursor
and probable model is the instrument known as the theremin.[126]

Invented by and named after Professor Lev Theremin, a Russian scientist of
French descent, this instrument was demonstrated by Theremin in Europe and the
United States between 1927 and 1928. (It was first called the Etherophone, bearing another link to Obukhov's "Ether.")It would be surprising if Obukhov had
not heard of it. In its basic makeup and means of modulating sound, the theremin
is remarkably similar to the sounding cross; Theremin's original had two electric
circuits, a vertical metal rod, and a horizontal metal loop. The vertical rod controlled pitch with the right hand, in the same way as Obukhov's instrument; the
horizontal loop controlled volume with the left hand. In addition harmonics could
be switched and filtered through another circuit, producing changes in timbre.
In 1929, RCA Victor placed a version of the instrument on the market together
with an electric gramophone on which the provided records could be played to

accompany the melodies produced on the theremin.[127] Like the sounding cross, the theremin is purely melodic and requires the performer to imagine the sound and check it aurally, the movements to modulate volume and pitch in both instruments being almost entirely dependent on muscle memory. The musicologist Percy Scholes has vividly characterized performing on the theremin: "The conditions might be described by the terrifying conception of a violinist with the strings in the air and with no neck or finger board to help him as to the placing of his fingers."[128]

The slightly earlier "ondes musicales" (1928), which, like the theremin, is now more commonly known by the surname of its inventor, Maurice Martenot, also has elements in common with the sounding cross and was on occasions scored in works by Obukhov. The ondes martenot is certainly more musically versatile, as possibly is the theremin, but Obukhov's instrument has greater visual impact. In addition, the mode of varying the pitch with two hands meant that playing the sounding cross often resembled the act of praying, in harmony with Obukhov's beliefs as evidenced in *La livre de vie*. The shape and makeup of the instrument also calls to mind orbs (or regna) as attributes of kings and emperors. The first visual record of such globes surmounted by a cross can be traced back to early Byzantine coins, and by the Middle Ages, most European empires and kingdoms had adopted them as symbols of sovereignty (the orb has been used in England since the reign of Edward the Confessor). In religious paintings orbs signify either the Christ Child as *salvator mundi* or God as the Patriarch, the king of kings.[129] Whether the resonance of this design was used by Obukhov for both regal and religious symbolism I can only speculate,[130] but what is clear is that its visual design and performance were of primary concern within the Gesamtkunstwerk, not merely a result of sonoric function.

The religious symbolism of *La livre de vie* is rather convoluted and hard to fathom; for example, there appear to be four central characters, Christ, Judas, the Dove, and the Dragon, who are incarnated into one spirit called the Blessed One, who in turn is the symbol for humanity. During the course of the work these various characters separate to combat one another, after which, at the climax, they are reunited. Like Scriabin, Obukhov argued that his Gesamtkunstwerk was not simply a spectacle; indeed, like the *Mysterium,* there were to be no spectators. All involved would play a part: "some like priests will take part directly in the action, the others witness it, participating mentally like the faithful in church."[131]

We have seen Sabanayev's use of the analogy of a church service to explain Scriabin's Gesamtkunstwerk, but where the *Mysterium* was largely theosophical, Obukhov's work more closely echoes Christian theology, especially Russian Orthodoxy. He called the work a "sacred action," for which he was merely the trasmitting vessel. At the heart of both works is the notion of transformation, but where Scriabin believed that his work would help bring about a shift from a material to a spiritual plane through dematerialization, Obukhov, seeing the human race on the threshold of perdition, conceived his art more as an act of propitiation.[132] Central to both works is the idea of religious ecstasy, "the final cry of a soul that has soared to paroxysms of ecstasy," as Baudelaire put it in his letter to Wagner. It is music that in large part can achieve this. As the paradigmatic mechanism for transformation or assuagement, its nonmateriality, both metaphorically and (so Scriabin and Obukhov believed) literally, acts as a bridge to the realm of the spirit. The transformation brought about by the Gesamtkunstwerk is paralleled in both the transubstantiation of matter into divine spirit that is at the climax of the Catholic Mass and the less absolute consubstantiation that is central to Orthodoxy. Within the Russian Orthodox Church the importance of music as a central part of the ritual, as a vehicle of communion, is likewise analogous to music's role in both Scriabin and Obukhov's broader aesthetic.

In many ways Obukhov's theology shares characteristics with the movement that had been influential in the decades before his arrival in Paris, the Salon de la Rose + Croix, founded by Joséphin "Sâr" Péladan. Péladan's symbolist sect was characterized by a mix of Wagnerian ideas and occult Catholicism. It was part of a reaction against naturalism and sought to promote an idealism that had its roots in the early seventeenth-century German mystical brotherhood the Rosy Cross, named in honor of the fourteenth-century knight Christian Rosenkreutz. According to his followers, Rosenkreutz had studied with Paracelsus and the sages of Damascus. Building on this foundation the brotherhood aimed to unify all knowledge in preparation for the Last Judgment.[133] Even though Rosenkreutz probably never existed and the whole legend was largely invented by Johan Valentin Andreae, a Lutheran mystic who composed the most famous Rosicrucian text *The Chemical Wedding* (an alchemical allegory), such ideas of synthesis and unification took a hold on the imagination of occultists that lasted for many hundreds of years.

Synthesis and unification is at the heart of Obukhov's aesthetic of the Gesamtkunstwerk, and the image of the cross is central to *La livre de vie*, even in its notation, and especially in sections 8, 9, and 10 of the seventh climatic chapter, which are made from scores in the shape of the cross. For example, section 9 is constructed with the first part at the top, the second at the bottom, third on the left, and fourth on the right, so as one reads it one's eyes make the sign of the cross. The design of the sounding cross stands as a symbol of equilibrium, with the orchestra allied to the four elements: air = woodwind and brass, earth = percussion, fire = strings, and water = keyboards. Obukhov also required the participants to make the sign of the cross as a part of the visual ritual of performance. Like Scriabin, who initially conceived the *Mysterium* as taking place in a circular temple, Obukhov imagined a similar structure with those not directly involved in the performance at its center. One commentator described its staging:

When the "Book of Life" is performed, by which I mean when it is lived, the spectators, the participants will be arranged in spirals, in the interior of a circular and raised scene. The "terrestrial" orchestra will be coiled up around the scene. A dome will contain the "celestial" orchestra. Lighting changes will intervene in the "Sacred Action," a synthesis of cult and orgy (the latter meant symbolically). Such is the ritual where science and religion are married[a ritual in the style of a true Rosicrucian alchemical image].[134]

Theosophists found much in Obukhov's aesthetic that was sympathetic to their own ideas. Part of *La livre de vie* was performed at a theosophical venue (the Salle Adyar) in 1926, but the major performance of parts of this huge work in the form of a symphonic poem, fully orchestrated, under the title *Préface de La livre de vie* (Preface of the book of life), took place on 3 June 1926 at the Paris Opéra, under the baton of Scriabin's one-time patron Serge Koussevitsky.[135] The *Préface* is scored for a large orchestra, including celesta, four harps, two pianos, and male and female choirs, with the text in French rather than Russian, as in *La livre de vie* itself. Obukhov and the musicologist Nicolas Slonimsky played the piano parts. But the audience's reaction did not, surprisingly, match Obukhov's ambitions. During the interval a member of the audience advised Slonimsky that for his own safety he should put up a sign saying, "I am not the composer." A later performance of parts of the *Book of Life* was also staged in Paris on 15 May 1934 and provoked a similar reaction from the critics and audience. A *New York Times* correspondent reported the concert under the headline, "Titters Greet Music of Obouhoff in Paris: Singers' Strange Performance Accompanied by Electrical Instrument, Causes Stir." Because this is one of only a handful of firsthand accounts, the review is worth quoting in full:

A Paris concert audience was stirred, and while it squirmed and tittered, tonight when Nicholas Obouhoff presented parts of his "Book of Life" and hitherto unknown "Annunciation of the Last Judgement," to the accompaniment of the new electric musical instrument, the croix sonore.

Henry Prunieres introduced the concert, warning the audience that it was going to hear chords played on the piano, notes sung by a human voice and sounds drawn from an instrument such as it had never heard before. Even this warning, however, did not prepare the listeners for the sudden "shriek" — there is no other word for it — of Suzanne Balguerie on the opening note of one of Obouhoff's liturgic poems. There was no warning, either, when the singer suddenly began to whistle instead of sing. Some members of the audience thought it was one of their number expostulating in the classic manner and began to cry, "Hush! hush!"

Prunieres had praised the courage of the singers, Mme. Balguerie and Louise Matha, in attempting music so new, and as they produced strange note after strange note many felt that this praise was well merited, if only because their mastery of their effects prevented the audience from tittering more loudly.

In "Annunciation of the Last Judgement" the singers stood together, one gowned in white, the other in red, while Obouhoff and Arthur Scholossberg played two pianos, and Princess Marie Antoinette Aussenac de Broglie, apart and sacramentally gowned in black, blue and orange, drew from the croix sonore notes that throbbed like twenty violins or at times sang like a human voice. In all this, it was the instrument that had the most success. Obuhoff, it is said, dreamed of it long before the invention of the radio made application of the principle possible. He wrote music for it, calling it "the etherphone." Out of it, by moving the hand back and forth, the Princess de Broglie drew an amazing sweetness or the most dreadful note, like the knocking of fate, to give Obouhoff's strange religious music far more power than his two pianos or even the distortions of his singers' voices could produce.[136]

Technically the work is dodecaphonic, with little repetition within a cycle of twelve notes: "I forbid myself any repetition: my harmony is based on twelve notes of which none must be repeated. Repetition produces an impression of force without clarity; it disturbs the harmony, dirties it."[137] The notion of non-repetition is the same for Obukhov as it was for Schoenberg: if notes are repeated too frequently within a cycle of twelve, one returns to a position of atonality (an arbitrary choice). Therefore, to maintain a systematic approach, nonrepetition is essential. The melody line is derived from the harmony as a horizontal unfolding of the twelve-note complexes, producing a conflation of foreground (melodic) and background (harmonic) elements. The voice is rarely "accompanied" in unison (for this would produce a type of repetition), and there is much use of vocal glissandi, producing a nontempered, microtonal contrast to the twelve-note organization. Singers are also requested to change from normal voice to falsetto (often within a single phrase) and to sing with closed mouths, mummer, whistle, wail, and sigh. The feature of glissandos is made more pronounced by the use of the sounding cross, which provides an ideal means for executing them.

The following examples demonstrate a number of these aspects of Obukhov's method. The first shows the block twelve-note harmony, although three chords each have a note doubled, D, D♯, and E, so the rule against repetition is not absolute (ex. 2.6). The second shows how the harmony is "horizontalized" to produce a melodic line—the pedal builds the melodic elements into the final twelve-note chord (ex. 2.7). The third shows the vocal line complementing the "accompaniment," so that it helps complete the twelve-note cycle (but again with limited repetition; ex. 2.8). The final example demonstrates the polyphonic combination of the four main characters, Judas, the Dove, Christ, and the Devil, with the use of vocal glissandi (ex. 2.9).

In many ways such cataclysmic works as the *Mysterium* and *La livre de vie* had to remain unfinished and unperformed, for although they are an answer to the question posed by Wagner in his conception of the art work of the future, it is hard to imagine how to move beyond such messianic conceptions. Driven to this

Christ (extasié) et Judas (inspiré) se prenant par les mains.

2.6 *Book of Life*, music extract 1

Notre Mère (dans une extase joyeuse).

2.7 *Book of Life*, music extract 2

point by deeply held spiritual beliefs — indeed they act as the raison d'être for the formal developments — such utopian visions were doomed to remain unfulfilled. One composer who can be seen to have taken up an aesthetic that has many points of contact with both Russian composers, although with a less messianic conceit, is Olivier Messiaen (1908–92).

OLIVIER MESSIAEN

The word that most accurately conveys Scriabin's and Obukhov's artistic mission also underpins Messiaen's aesthetic: mystical. For all three are concerned with

2.8 *Book of Life*, music extract 3

2.9 *Book of Life*, music extract 4

union with the spirit and with a truth that lies beyond rational understanding. If both Scriabin and Obukhov's vision is cataclysmic, as Wilfrid Mellers has remarked, "it is to the point that the work that sums up the first phase of [Messiaen's] career should have been written in a prison camp, in 1940, that year in which a cataclysm was indeed unleashed."[138] The *Quatuor pour la fin du temps* (Quartet for the end of time) is constructed out of seven movements, paralleling the six days of the creation followed by the day of rest (as in Obukhov's *La livre de vie*), with an epilogue eighth movement, "Louange à l'immortalité de Jésus," which aims to transcend earthly temporality, resolving in eternity. The work is based on the tenth book of Revelation, verses 1–7. Verse 6 contains the theme to Messiaen's piece, the dissolution of time—"that there should be time no longer"—an aesthetic aim, subtly evoked through a variety of rhythmic techniques (such as isorhythmic patterns and nonretrograde rhythm), but in sympathy with both Scriabin's and Obukhov's inflated Gesamtkunstwerks. Messiaen's well-known use of Indian musical devices, such as ragas and talas, are but a more technical referencing of Eastern ideas than Scriabin's. In his *Cinq rechants* of 1948, the text employs an invented language based on Hindu, which recalls Scriabin's earlier experiments.

Messiaen's best-known work is the *Turangalîla-Symphony* of 1948, which was commissioned by the Koussevitsky Foundation—Scriabin's patron and Obukhov's conductor. The work's length (in performance, about seventy-five minutes), opulent scoring, and inclusion of an electronic instrument, the ondes martenot, has points of contact with Obukhov's use of the sounding cross in *La livre de vie. Turangalîla* is also the second in a group of three works based on the Tristan myth, most famously enshrined in the music of Wagner and concerning itself with themes of love, death, and cosmic transcendence.[139] The title of this work is a compound Sanskrit word, *Turanga,* meaning "flowing time," and *Lîla,* signifying the divine play of cosmic action on creation and destruction, and the union of spiritual and physical love. It is one of the first works by Messiaen that makes explicit the erotic nature of transcendental consummation, which is implicit in the polyphony of Obukhov's "Blessed One" and essential to Scriabin's metaphysical ecstasy.

In *Chronochromie* (1959–60), the strophic and antistrophic structure, as Mellers has argued, "is significantly analogous to the chorus of classical Greek tragedy, and the work effects a (Greek) catharsis whereby the wellsprings of being are released in order to be renewed. Messiaen has healed the breaches that Christianity committed us to, reaffirming the validity of the sexual impulse and the identity of the creator with created nature."[140] This aesthetic aim is in tune with both Wagner's and Nietzsche's view of Greek drama's role as prescient for the art work of the future, as well as with the effect of Dionysian jouissance that Baudelaire detected in Wagner's music and others have heard in Scriabin's and Obukhov's spiritual ecstasy.

Perhaps the most celebrated point of contact between Messiaen and these Russians is through the concept of synesthesia, specifically the phenomenon of "color-hearing."[141] In the conversations between Messiaen and Claude Samuel, published under the telling title *Music and Color,* Messiaen explains that for him and, he believes, many other composers, color and music are always linked. Indeed, "those who haven't taken it into consideration have committed a grave error." However, beyond the metaphorical implications of this assertion (as regards timbre or texture), the fact remains that these correspondences are aspects of "an inward reality."[142] This inward reality may be fixed for particular individuals and may also inspire a variegated range of sound combinations (his "modes of limited transposition," for example), but it remains nontransferable to others who do not experience synesthesia or even to those who do and who might experience different twinnings: "When hearing sounds, I see colors in my mind's eye. . . . No matter how much I put in my music—harmonies, sound complexes, and orchestration—listeners hear, but they see nothing."[143] In Messiaen, color-sound relationships are part of the conception if not reception of his works. With Scriabin and Obukhov, devices are employed to make the reception of their works as multifarious as their conception.

In drawing attention to points of contact among Scriabin, Obukhov, and Messiaen I do not intend to establish some kind of scale of influence and originality or to reduce the aesthetic of a magnificent composer like Messiaen to simple precedence. The aesthetic outcomes of these composers are inevitably various. Rather, I wish to stress that the term *music,* as simply referring to sound alone, is too simplistic to cover this aspect of modernist artistic development that they share. The art of all three composers did not seek to dramatize or express so much as it aspired to re-present. Although the Gesamtkunstwerk is not conceptually explicit in Messiaen's aesthetic, his music always carried with it (at least for him) colorful, imaginary visual experiences. It was always more than a sonoric vehicle, more than pure sound in his conception.

For Scriabin and Obukhov the Gesamtkunstwerk manifests the climax of their aesthetic ideas. Music had pushed up against a limit, necessitating an expansion into fields of activity that had traditionally been the preserve of other art forms: poetry, theater, dance, visual presentation, and so on. "The spirit," wrote Wagner, "in its artistic striving for reunion with nature in the art-work, must either look forward with hope to the future, or mournfully practise resignation."[144] They endorsed Wagner's view that in isolation the arts only "suggest" through the imagination.

It is solely the Gesamtkunstwerk that can "present" (or re-present) to the senses, because it addresses the full range of our capacity for artistic receptivity, not just a single element. Rather than a "retreat" into purity, their art instead sought synthesis, a synthesis that could bring about not just artistic regeneration but spiritual transformation. "I recognized in fact that it was precisely at the point at which one of these arts reached impassable frontiers that the sphere of action of the other started, by the intimate union of these two arts [music and poetry] it was possible to express what neither of them could express in isolation," wrote Wagner.[145] The critical point reached by Wagnerian chromaticism and dissonance finds resolution in tritone sequences, octatonic scales, or dodecaphonic methods, in approaches that sought a new musical and artistic language to speak for the art work of the future, a future that these composers believed had arrived in their aesthetic.

Wagner's theories of the art work of the future, and the power of his music, had convinced Baudelaire that music had superseded poetry as the preeminent art. It was under the baton of music that the other arts now had to place themselves. The "impassable frontiers" that had been reached by individual arts as a consequence of modernity, the move to or beyond the limit, is the enterprise of modern art in Wagner's eyes, which required union and synthesis with music in order to survive, combining to become (once again) "the only true art-work." In other words, the Gesamtkunstwerk was the way of containing meaning and excess when, as separate entities in "isolation," the arts were in danger of overstepping themselves, leading "at first to obscurity and confusion, and then to degeneration and corruption of each art individually."[146] This is an act of recuperation. Returning to ancient Greece provides a paradigm for future art.

Music's power was in Wagner's works amplified (literally) through technical innovation: additions to the tuba family (tenor and bass), bass trumpets (or valve trombone), expansion of the horn section (as many as sixteen, regularly eight) and additions to the percussion section (eighteen anvils of three different sizes in *Rheingold*). In Scriabin's *Mysterium* and Obukhov's *Livre de vie* the orchestration is even more monumental, with the addition of electronic instruments and an expansion beyond traditional opera into the realms of multimedia spectacle. This was achieved through the use of color projection, an environmental setting, scents, and gestures. The integration of voice with tone in Wagner's aesthetic is moved in Obukhov beyond conventional vocalization into the realm of cries, mummers, and whistles. Neither Scriabin nor Obukhov was content with a passive audience but required all witnesses to participate. The art form of music, conceived as essentially temporal and nonmaterial, was the vehicle that subsumed the other arts in its mission to transcend time, to achieve spiritual transformation. Instinct and imagination, as opposed to rationality, were the mechanisms by which the artist could access truth, harnessing the power of dreams and interior consciousness over waking external existence. In so doing, conventions had to be overturned. Dissonance, asymmetry, and organic growth, the Dionysian elements, were privileged. Structure was maintained through leitmotiv, and motivic development in general, or dodecaphony, but was not based on conventional diatonic harmonic systems or symmetry.

For Baudelaire, and many who followed him, music's power was in this very ambiguity. It had great effect in communication, but the nature of what was communicated remained mysterious. While Wagner, Scriabin, and Obukhov changed the nature of musical "syntax," heightening ambiguity, Baudelaire's poetry remained syntactically stable, challenging at the level of semantics. Even in Stéphane Mallarmé's work, where the power and preeminence of music is challenged (and this is not the place to pursue Mallarmé's complex aesthetic in any detail) the conception of poetry, in his *Livre*, as once again consummate, is within a notion of the Gesamtkunstwerk that is every bit as ambitious as Scriabin's *Mysterium*, and as accepting of the need to transcend individual art forms.[147] It is interesting to note that both Mallarmé and Obukhov's ultimate artistic aim was to be manifested in a work entitled "Livre"—the idea of a Book as something more than purely words; a metaphor for the heterogeneous nature of art, in contrast to its purist conception. *Mysterium, La livre de vie,* and *Livre* were all unrealizable summas that aspired to transpose life into art, in Mallarmé's case through the synthesis of poetry and music, in Obukhov's through a broader synthetic project.

In Baudelaire's "Correspondances," the power of music is rooted in the belief that the human mind can experience synesthesia. Here a follower of Baudelaire takes this notion from metaphor into simile or equivalence: "A black, E white, I red, U green, O blue; vowels." This is the opening of Arthur Rimbaud's sonnet "Les voyelles" (Vowels, c. 1875).[148] Like Mallarmé, Baudelaire, Scriabin, and Obukhov, Rimbaud drew on a variety of sources in his exploration of "correspondances" between art forms, material and spirit. Some were scientific, but most are esoteric and nonrational in their explanations of these mysterious connections.

For Clement Greenberg, as was described in Chapter 1, modernism is characterized by the "common effort in each of the arts to expand the expressive resources of the medium," and this has the effect of accentuating their differences. He continues: "Only by accepting the example of music and defining each of the other arts solely in the terms of the sense or faculty which perceived its effect and by excluding from each art whatever is intelligible in the terms of any other sense or faculty would the non-musical arts attain the "purity" and self-sufficiency they desired."[149] Such a view does not account for the developments that followed in the wake of Wagner's influence, an influence of considerable reach. As Baudelaire had expressed it, "in his passionate energy of expression he is at the moment the *truest representative of modernity*."[150] This is not a pure modernity but one fashioned from synthesis and unification of the arts. Greenberg conceives of music as simply sound, divorced from its visual, social, and political manifestations as a cultural practice. Acceptance of this broader definition of music as a field, rather than as just sound, allows us to reconceive Bill Nye's perceptive joke, "I have been told that Wagner's music is better than it sounds."[151] It is true that the impact of Wagner's art traveled far beyond its sonic effect.

The art work of the future, reaching toward unity and synthesis, runs in parallel with the notion of artistic purity. It emerges in a related form in the cabarets of the futurists and dadaists immediately before and after the First World War, in the neo-dadaism of American art after the Second World War, and especially in the aesthetic of John Cage, whose impact on the art world is equivalent, if antithetical, to that of Wagner. It is with Cage that our discussion will conclude. But first we should consider another important aspect of the modernist paradigm, perhaps the defining aspect, and consider whether cubism was as free from hybridity as Greenberg and others have suggested. Here we shall be more concerned with the specifics of subject matter, with the use of music not as a structural paradigm so much as an historical practice. We shall consider the relationship of music-making to images and look beyond the surface of the picture to its extravisual dimensions.

THREE

INSTRUMENTS OF DESIRE MUSICAL

MORPHOLOGY IN PICASSO'S CUBISM

The viol, the violet, and the vine.

—Edgar Allan Poe

This art [cubism] will have so many links with music as only an art that
is the opposite of music can have. This will be pure painting.

—Guillaume Apollinaire

In 1958, Clement Greenberg published an article on cubist collage entitled "The
Pasted-Paper Revolution."[1] It is a relatively short but eloquent discussion of the
formal implications of introducing extraneous materials into the heart of painting, creating works that play a "pivotal role in the evolution of modern painting
and sculpture." According to Greenberg, the reason for using such materials is
to provide a dialogue with the actual surface of the work, the picture plane: "the
resistant reality of the flat surface and the forms shown upon it in yielding, ide-
ated depth." Such a dialogue is necessary, Greenberg continues, to prevent the
hermetic, cubist works of Picasso and Braque from reducing to surface pattern.
Pasted papers, along with the use of lettering, are thus "introduced in paintings
whose motifs offered no realistic excuse for their presence."[2]

Subsequent art historical methodology has moved from an almost exclusive concern with textual questions to a more contextual approach. This has encouraged a more explicit interest in issues of content.[3] The modernist, textual approach, characterized by Greenberg among others, has concerned itself with the "language" of art, a dialogue with form and its gradual refinement, through a divestment of external association, to a state of "purity" reached through the act of "self-criticism."[4] The more sociohistorical approach of some recent scholars has tended to look beyond the works themselves to a consideration of the political contexts of production and reception, a broader conception of dialogue. Yet neither of these approaches considers in a sustained way the choice of subject-matter or its link to the role of formal innovation in composition. Specifically, little has been said about the almost ubiquitous presence of music and musical instruments in the work of the cubists. Scrutiny of these works (often addressed to the texts) failed for a long time even to recognize the difference between single- and double-reed wind instruments. In this chapter I consider the work of Pablo Picasso as a focus for analysis of these issues, for, as John Richardson has written, although both Georges Braque and Picasso were very interested in musical subject-matter and Braque's works "may look like Picasso's *Musicians[,]* . . . they are as different in their resonance as woodwind is from brass."[5] In considering Picasso's cubist works we shall be concerned with music as a subject for painting and collage.

With few exceptions, two classes of musical instrument are found in the canvases of the cubists: woodwind and strings. Specifically, there are double-reed instruments, usually members of the shawm family: the tenora, the tiple, or possibly the earlier tarota; the violin; and members of the guitar family: mandolin and guitar.[6] Picasso tended to use string instruments, whereas Braque more often used woodwind instruments. A brief description of the background to both classes of instruments will provide a foil for our primary focus on Picasso and string instruments.

Before considering the use of such instruments in cubist works, we should briefly note their role in the wider historical context of Western painting. To do so, we must map out the *ideal* distinctions, as classically established and handed down from ancient times. The modern categories of *high* and *low* culture, which will be useful to evoke in the work of Picasso, acknowledge, more or less tacitly, these antique terms. Idealism and its sometime twin, mythology, come before history and its somewhat dissolute companion, reality.

History, though it is by no means disconnected from myth, is charismatically unpredictable and elliptical rather than serving as a parabolic example. In the construction and interpretation of history, boundaries are not rigid; they can be denied, subverted, transgressed, ridiculed. Although notions of "high" and "low" can be used to elucidate, musical and artistic activities have a more fluid relationship to them in historical circumstances, as we shall see in the example of the use of the violin and guitar. As a result, the visual representation of musical subjects, texts, and acts of music-making should be thought of as part of a dialogue — implicit rather than voiced — with the oppositions set up in antiquity. What is apposite here in regard to cubist works is that the musical references in Picasso's pictures betray his relish for the ambiguity of such coexisting oppositions.

APOLLONIAN AND DIONYSIAN CONTRASTS

We saw in Chapter 2 how this duality manifested itself in the thinking of Wagner and Nietzsche, in the function of the intoxicating dithyramb. Here our focus is on oppositions between the types of musical instruments themselves. The woodwinds and strings typically characterize opposite sides of a dualistic system in Western modes of representation. In classical mythology, this duality is captured in the myth of the competition between Apollo and Marsyas. There are, of course, various versions of the myths that narrate the origins of music and musical instruments. This myth has roots in the *Homeric Hymns* and is mentioned in the *Oresteia* in the story of the transition of the shrine at Delphi from Gaea to Apollo.

The myth begins by telling how each competitor got his instrument. In the *Homeric Hymns*, Apollo's adoption of the lyre from Hermes is relatively tranquil; in the *Oresteia,* it is more violent. The outcome of the contest, however, is always bloody. The infant Hermes had stolen Apollo's herd of cattle, and using the guts of two slaughtered cows, the shell of a tortoise, and two cow horns, he had constructed a musical toy (the *lura,* or lyre). Satyrs, led by Silenus, tracked Hermes to his cave and reported the crime to Apollo. But the sweet music played by this instrument won Apollo over and saved Hermes from his wrath. According to this version of the myth, music was thus invented and remained in the hands of the gods.[7]

Marsyas's double *aulos* came from Athena, who had fashioned it from stags' bones and played it at a banquet of the gods. Although Athena's music seemed to delight most of the gods, Hera and Aphrodite laughed at her playing. Upset by their ridicule, Athena went to the Phrygian woods and consoled herself by sitting down beside a stream and playing once more. As she played she looked at her reflection in the water and realized that it was the contortions of her face and cheeks that had caused Hera and Aphrodite to laugh. Disgusted, she threw the aulos to the ground. Marsyas came across the discarded instrument. As a creature less than human, let alone divine, he was not concerned with such vanities, and he played the instrument to the delight of local peasants, who proclaimed him equal to Apollo as a musician. This led to the contest between Apollo and Marsyas, in which the winner could inflict on the loser any punishment he pleased. The contest was equal only until Apollo turned the lyre upside down and challenged Marsyas to do the same. Marsyas could not, of course, meet this challenge. Apollo's ruthless revenge was to flay Marsyas alive and nail his skin to a tree near the source of a river that still bears his name.[8] Here, Apollo triumphs with music made of the exact mathematical ratio of string lengths, vanquishing the mortal piper whose music is made of, and exists in, the material (natural) element, air.[9]

Within Christian theology, the oppositions of sacred and profane, or religious and pagan, tended to allocate strings to heaven and woodwinds to the earth.[10] Later, Nietzsche, as we have seen, saw such oppositions in terms of Apollo (civilized) and Dionysus (nature-bound). The continued distinctions between "high" and "low" levels of culture are also predicated on such divisions. Contrasting pairs of musical instruments were, in classical times, the aulos and kithara (or lyre). In the Middle Ages they were the bagpipe and the lute. Comparable modern oppositions are more problematic because of the proliferation of musical styles and genres. It is, therefore, harder to isolate specific instruments, although the broader categories of high and low still pertain in ideological nooks and crannies. It is to these that the work of Picasso makes reference.

Music has been featured in Western painting in many contexts. Within medieval religious painting the most familiar examples are those illustrating the scriptures, including apocalyptic themes, such as the Rex Psalminsta and the Psalm 150, sections 3, "Praise him with the sound of the trumpet: praise him with the psaltery and harp"; 4, "Praise him with the timbrel and dance: praise him with stringed instruments and organs"; and 5, "Praise him upon the loud cymbals: praise him upon the high sounding cymbals." For example, the elders of Revelation are often shown holding vielles (a plucked string instrument) and harps as mentioned in Revelation 14.2, "and I heard the voice of harpers harping with their harps." Medieval sources from the fifteenth century show King David playing psaltery, harp, or, by the end of the century, the *lira da braccio,* an instrument associated with the revival of classical musical practice. Music appears frequently as the attribute of the great poets of classical civilization, especially Homer. In many Renaissance depictions of Apollo's contest with Marsyas (for example, Titian's), and sometimes in his later contest with Pan (whom Apollo also defeated),[11] the lira da braccio signifies noble "mathematical" music as opposed to the lascivious, passionate, and sensual music of the various reed instruments played by his half-human opponents. As Emmanuel Winternitz has written of these mythic contests, they represent "a poetic condensation of the eternal conflict, the antagonism between two musical realms, between strings and wind instruments. . . . It means in the rationalized form of the Greek myth the realm of

3.1 Titian, *The Three Ages of Man,* c. 1512–13, oil on canvas, 90 x 150.7 cm. Duke of Sutherland Collection, on loan to The National Gallery of Scotland

inhibition, of reason, of measure—in the literal Pythagorean sense of measuring strings and intervals, and in the metaphorical sense of *mesure*—as opposed to the realm of blind passion: in short, the antagonism between Apollo and Dionysus."[12] The values thus represented function ideologically to patrol the borders between the realms of high and low cultural expression. Following Pallas Athena, the deformation of the face through blowing was considered unacceptable to those with high social aspirations. This distinction is underlined further in the phallic symbolism of wind instruments in fifteenth-century paintings of lovers such as Titian's *Three Ages of Man* (fig. 3.1).

By the sixteenth century, wind instruments were becoming more acceptable to those in the upper sections of society, although they were still largely played by traveling and professional musicians. It was a considerable time before wind instruments were deemed socially acceptable for domestic performance, the gentler-sounding flutes and recorders being the first to achieve such a status. In seventeenth- and eighteenth-century France, for example, the aristocratic fashion for the pastoral idyll may be seen as the main force behind the development of the musette, a relative of the bagpipe, but with smaller, less awkward and heavy parts. Importantly, the musette replaced the blowpipe—unbecoming in the mouth of a lady—with bellows. Eighteenth-century attempts to foster an antimetropolitan and antiabsolutist sensibility, in order to discover the beauty of a "humble" life of rustic labor, had reason to favor the pipe, especially the flute. Frederick the

Great's accomplishment on the instrument was more than a mere accident of his early musical education.

This brief consideration of the historical and symbolical distinctions of the wind and string families enables us to survey, in a little more detail, the historical context of the two most common instruments found in Picasso's cubist works: the violin and the guitar.

The violin was not invented in the way that the pianoforte was but rather evolved through a long and variegated process. Not until the later sixteenth century did a standardized form of the instrument emerge from the workshops of the Italian makers, principally Amati, Guarneri, and Stradivari, all centered in the northern town of Cremona. One important strand of the violin's generic background can be found in the lira da braccio, an instrument of strong pedigree. But the instrument we now recognize as the violin is most often depicted in images of the century following its standardization as the partner of strolling musicians—that is, among members of the lower classes. Not until the last third of the seventeenth century was it accepted as an instrument of the "civilized" classes, illustrating the change in attitudes concerning the social status of classes of instruments. As David Boyden has written in his history of violin playing: "The violin, in short, was barely respectable from a social point of view, and compared to the lute, viol, or organ (the instrument of the church), it had practically no musical or social prestige at all. It was regarded as the common instrument of dance music with all the attendant disparaging associations, and it was played largely by professionals who earned 'their living by it' and who were regarded socially as servants."[13]

By the eighteenth century, however, the violin had undergone a remarkable volte-face and was instead regarded as the archetypal instrument of the best music from "the European courts to the opera theatres."[14] In this way, the instrument operated across the borders of the cultural divide as both fiddle and violin, but in a complicated fashion. In the eighteenth century, for example, it was not regarded as appropriate for the violin to transgress the divide of gender. As a contemporary diarist, Hester Lynch Piozzi, wrote of a female exponent of the instrument: "Madame Gautherot's wonderful Execution on the Fiddle;—but to say the Critics a Violin is not an instrument for 'Ladies' to manage, very likely! I remember when they said the same Thing of the Pen."[15]

The other principal instrument featured in Picasso's cubist works is the guitar, whose principal antecedent is the lute. For several centuries the lute played a central role in European musical life. It was popular in the Middle Ages, and its demise began only with the rise in popularity of the polyphonic keyboard instruments around the beginning of the seventeenth century. Many factors contributed to the lute's privileged place among musical instruments, but chief among them was its portability, which enabled the lute to play an important part in al fresco concerts and fêtes champêtres, as can be seen in Jan Steen's *Music Making on a Terrace* (c. 1663, London, National Gallery). The lute also lent itself to more spontaneous music-making, and it was appreciated for its rich tone, suited to accompanying the voice, along with its ability to play a number of musical lines at once. With the lute, people could perform polyphonic compositions in which the top line was sung and the others were played. This versatility led to the lute's appearance in numerous *trionfi d'amore* (baroque paintings of music lessons), such as Gerard ter Borch's *Music Lesson* (c. 1675, Cincinnati Art Museum).

In short, the lute was often regarded as an aid to "winning the favors of ladies." Combining the seductive power of the voice (defined as a wind instrument) and the Olympian purity of measured strings, the music of the lutenist could entertain while devotedly expressing ambiguous protestations of love. The lute was so clearly associated with lovers, and so clearly symbolized sex, that sixteenth-century English prostitutes often carried simple lutes with them into public spaces (taverns, for example) as a mark of their trade.

The emblematic literature of the period also equated the structural makeup of the instrument—specifically the bulge of the lute's back—with the physiology of a pregnant woman. By the seventeenth century, *luit,* the Dutch word for the instrument, meant, in the vernacular, the vagina. As Leppert among others has shown, Netherlandish paintings of the seventeenth century that emphasized the presence of a lute often punned on the standard and vulgar uses of the word.[16] The familiar subject of the procuress, in paintings by Gerard van Honthorst and Dirck van Baburen, for example, shows her involved in a transaction accompanied by a young woman playing or holding a lute.

The guitar largely supplanted the music of the lute in the eighteenth century.[17] In its early form, the guitar combined European and Moorish traditions. Because it was easier to tune and play than the lute, the guitar enjoyed great popularity not only as a concert instrument but also, like the violin, as a folk instrument. This was particularly the case in Spain, where the *vihuela*—a guitar-shaped instrument with many strings (usually twelve), almost exclusively associated with the aristocracy—declined in favor and was replaced by the folk guitar, which originally had four strings, then later six.

The guitar was a popular accompaniment to singing, dancing, and wooing and in this way took over the role, as well as the music, of the lute. Like the violin, the guitar crosses the boundaries of cultural divisions. Again, this is particularly the case in Picasso's native country, where, in Eric Bloom's words, the guitar "is not only the possession of blind beggars, but a thoroughly serious instrument with an advanced technique and great possibilities for modern music."[18] In terms of its shape, it obviously does not carry the same connotations as the womblike lute,

3.2 Pablo Picasso, *The Old Guitarist*, 1903, oil on panel, 122.9 x 82.6 cm. The Art Institute of Chicago, Helen Birch Bartlett Memorial Collection. © Succession Picasso / DACS 2000

although other members of the family (which sometimes figure in cubist canvases), the Neapolitan mandolin and mandola, do. Nevertheless, like the violin, its figure-eight shape has long been associated with the female torso, and it thus maintains a potent physiological symbolism.[19]

MUSIC IN PICASSO'S PRECUBIST WORKS

Nearly half of Picasso's works produced between the 1912 and 1914 include musical subjects.[20] Music and musicians are rarely directly evoked in his earlier "blue" and "rose" periods, but music or its evocation are seldom far away in such "minor key" works. Even though musical themes are not common, when they do appear, they are never merely neutral subjects: they are there to imply other symbols.

Picasso's early works with musical subjects fall in two groups. One group represents the artist (musician) or beggar, condemned to an existence on the

3.3 Pablo Picasso, *At the Lapin Agile,* 1904–5, oil on canvas, 99 x 100.3 cm. The Metropolitan Museum of Art, The Walter H. and Leonore Annenberg Collection, Partial Gift of Walter H. and Leonore Annenberg, 1992 (1992.391). © Succession Picasso / DACS 2000

fringes of society, as in, for example, the small conté drawings *Caridad (Charity)* and *The Street Violinist,* both of 1899, and the larger-scale, iconic *Old Guitarist* of 1903 (fig. 3.2). This painting depicts a poor old man, blind and bent, sitting cross-legged, seemingly playing and singing for his own solace. The skeletal fingers of his left hand eloquently and delicately embrace the elongated neck of the instrument. He sits in a simple interior space, the somber tonality largely blue, with yellowish and gray flesh tones. The old man's blindness relates the work to the theme of the five senses. In this case the sense is hearing, evoking also, perhaps, the figure of the poet Homer with his lyre, but here there is no audience except the viewer, for whom the blind musician shows no awareness.[21] The *Hurdy-Gurdy Man* of two years later is similar in mood, despite the warmer hues, as is the earlier version of the 1903 painting *The Old Jew,* in which the subject originally held a mandolin.[22]

At the Lapin Agile—a larger, more elaborate work from 1905, the same year as the *Hurdy-Gurdy Man*—contains a self-portrait (fig. 3.3): Picasso is Harlequin, and Germaine, the woman for whose unrequited love his close friend Jaime Casagemas committed suicide, is Columbine. She may have been a stand-in for Fernande Olivier (who at that time was married to Paul-Emile Percheron but was living with the sculptor Debienne), and, as Richardson has argued, "could not have allowed herself to be *affiché* on the wall of a bohemian cabaret, above all in the company of yet another lover."[23] The psychological isolation of the figures would certainly support this. The Lapin Agile was a tavern situated on the rue des Saules and much frequented by Picasso at this time. This painting was intended to hang in the tavern's interior and was probably painted as security against credit. Interestingly, the interior space of the tavern was presided over on one side by a huge classical sculpture of Apollo with a lyre,[24] whose real-life counterpart was the guitar-playing owner of the Lapin Agile, Frédé, as shown in André Warnod's watercolor of 1909, *Intérieur du Lapin Agile*.[25] The overriding sense of alienation in Picasso's painting is here made more acute by this background figure playing the guitar. The painting renders a community of friends (*bande à Picasso*), a milieu of potential bohemian gaiety, lonely and melancholic. The spirit of the commedia dell'arte characters harks back to Antoine Watteau, among others, but the effect is here more tragic than comic.

A small drawing by Picasso of the same year, *The Violinist,* depicts the musician as a more direct consoler, this time at the bedside of a dying woman. This sentiment echoes the commonplace inscription in Jan Vermeer's 1660s painting *A Lady at the Virginals with a Gentleman Listening:* "Musica letitiae comes medicina doloris."

The other principal group of works of this period with musical connections offers a counterpoint to the sadness and loneliness of the first group. Here the subjects are peasant and country folk at leisure. In these works music signifies the simplicity of a harmonious communal existence, a life so plaintively denied in *At the Lapin Agile*. These pictures, produced in Horta in 1903, depict Catalan peasants listening to a guitarist or dancing the *jota,* as in *Guitarist Playing* and *Practicing the Jota*. The slightly later *Harlequin's Family* (1905) may have been an ironic image dedicated to Picasso's then-mistress Fernande, cruelly chiding her for her inability to have children, but its mood is of familial concord: a doting mother and child with a harlequin happily singing and playing an accordion in the background.

In short, the guitar, the violin, and the evocation of music in general signify two contrasting themes: the solitary bohemian existence of the artist and the struggle for an artistic life, in contrast to the joys of a shared experience of community. The dialectically suggestive contrast between art and folk culture is poignantly distributed.

MUSICAL SUBJECTS IN PICASSO'S CUBISM

I shall look in detail first at two images from the period of synthetic cubism (1912–14) and then one from late analytic or hermetic cubism (1910–11). This more specific study is intended to offer up themes and ideas that are broadly relevant to the body of works on musical subjects Picasso produced throughout these cubist years.

Guitar and Wine Glass

Picasso's collages are dated largely through his use of newspaper fragments. *Guitar and Wine Glass* (513) is probably his first papier collé, containing a fragment of the newspaper *Le Journal,* dated 10 November 1912 (fig. 3.4).[26] The picture consists of a background of brown-and-white flower-patterned wallpaper over which, in the bottom left corner, is stuck the fragment of newspaper. The horizontal placement of this strip of newspaper suggests that it signifies both itself as newspaper and the tabletop on which the still life is "placed." Toward the lower right, on a separate white sheet of drawing paper, is an analytic cubist drawing of a glass. The profile aspect of this image forms a reduced echo of the right-hand side of the guitar's curved body. A black semicircle of paper is stuck over parts of both the newspaper and the drawing of the glass, forming the bottom section of the guitar. The left side of the guitar is composed of a sheet of painted imitation wood-grained paper (a technique passed to Picasso by Braque, whose father and grandfather had been house painters and color merchants. Braque himself had trained as a decorator).[27] The main body of the guitar is defined by a space. The fingerboard is a sheet of blue paper cut into a parallelogram, over which, at the bottom, has been stuck a white paper circle representing the guitar's sound hole. Completing the materials is a fragment of printed sheet music, stuck over the right side of the blue sheet, that signifies the fingerboard.

In formal terms the work is wonderfully balanced and succinct in design. The use of the wallpaper renders the picture plane as a flat surface, which projects the other elements of the still life forward from the surface into the viewer's space. Interestingly, the sound hole, by definition a hollow space, is represented by the lightest tone (white), not, as one might expect, by the absence of light (black).[28] In addition, it is placed physically forward of the other elements of the composition. A cavity thus becomes a form of projection. This reversal is taken further in the later construction *Guitar* (471), where the negative space of the sound hole is replaced with the positive space of a tube. (The possibility of conceiving this in sexual terms as a vaginal-phallic reversal is raised below.) This play on two dimensions is taken further in the drawing of the wine glass. This sketch is a complex analytical image, a paradigm of the cubist analysis of three dimen-

3.4 Pablo Picasso, *Guitar and Wine Glass*, 1912, collage and charcoal, 48 x 36.5 cm. Collection of the The McNay Art Museum, San Antonio, Texas. Bequest of Marion Koogler McNay. © Succession Picasso / DACS 2000

sions showing both the profile and plastic elements of the object, with seemingly arbitrary placement of chiaroscuro. Coming from the earlier phase of analytic cubism, it solves the problems of representing three-dimensional reality on a two-dimensional plane as it is conceived rather than as it might appear through linear perspectival projection. The imitation wood-graining works in this image, as it does in most cubist works, as a signifier of the material make-up of the guitar body or other objects made of wood (for example, the table), but it also plays with the illusionism of conventional mimetic art (it looks like real wood but is just an illusion, a decorator's trick). Simultaneously it points to the alternative reality offered by the world of art; it is real painted wood in a "painted" world; it has more in common (especially in terms of its make-up) with the rest of the image, and indeed other images, than it does with real wood.

The newspaper fragment continues this game, the part-word "Jou" acting as a synecdoche both of "journal" (newspaper) and a range of other words variously implied throughout Picasso's collages, such as "jouer" (to play), "joueur" (a player of a game), "jouailler" (to play a musical instrument badly), and "jouissance" (orgasm). The significance of the last is discussed later but is not unrelated to the earlier discussion of musical instruments' symbolism. The newspaper is both a fragment of reality (a real piece of a particular newspaper—"Journal") and another two-dimensional signifier (signifying newspaper in general—"journal"). The undifferentiated tonal character of the sheets of colored paper, black and blue, also adds to the flatness of the image.

This brings us to the other collage element, the fragment of sheet music, which raises the subject of the role that the represented objects play in terms of a wider textual framework, particularly in relation to music. Picasso has selected a section of a popular song entitled *Sonnet,* composed in 1892 by Marcel Legay to a text by Pierre Ronsard.[29] The performance of such popular songs was a nightly event at the Lapin Agile, where Frédé would provide guitar accompaniment, often with the addition of a violinist. Indeed, as Jeffrey Weiss has shown, Marcel Legay himself had performed at the Lapin Agile during the 1880s and 1890s.[30]

A slightly later collage, *Violin and Sheet-Music (Sonnet)* (519), features the opening title page of the song as well as a fragment of the same wallpaper. This song, an unremarkable but neatly crafted ternary composition, is in the key of E-flat major, in 6/8 time, marked *Andantino grazioso con expressione.* The visible fragment is taken from the end of the piece and consists of a short series of common chords moving to the first chord of a perfect cadence on which the piece resolves (ex. 3.1). At the risk of overanalyzing a relatively simple musical phrase, we can describe it as follows: I (2d inversion), VI (C minor, via a chromatic passing chord: A-flat minor) to I (2d inversion), V7 (with suspended G), which implies a resolution to I, with a passing note of F in the upper part, cut off before it can resolve. The final cadence, which is left out of Picasso's collage, concludes in root position after a final arpeggio flourish. In other words, it is a straightforward chord progression that Picasso has literally cut off at the point of maximum harmonic tension, just before the final point of rest. There is no need to analyze the chord progression in the way that I have done, nor even have the ability to read music, to see that the musical phrase is interrupted, suspended, cut off before it resolves (this could be more or less imputed from the words alone).[31] The text reads "[pen]dant qu'êtes bel[le]" (while you are beautiful), and has been described by Weiss as "a plain and elegiac *vanitas* on love, beauty and fleeting youth."[32]

To you I send this bouquet
Lately plucked by my hand
From these fulgent blooms
Which, if left ungathered at dusk
Would tomorrow have fallen to the ground.
That should show you for sure
That your charms, whilst they blossom now
Will soon wither and, like flowers,
Suddenly perish.
Time moves on my Lady. Alas! Time no,
But we, we take our leave
And soon will lie stretched
Beneath the sward
And the loves of whom we speak
When we are dead shall be no longer new.
So love me. Love me while you are beautiful.[33]

The nonresolution of the music, the fact that it is held open, is appropriate for the whole image, a pasting together of disparate elements.

The guitar operates as an element of still life, placed on a table with a newspaper and a wineglass. It can, therefore, be understood most obviously as a central element of a vanitas, as Weiss describes the song itself. Musical instruments in still-life paintings often carry vanitas significance, symbolizing the passing of time and hence mortality. And as we have seen, guitars are often central props in paintings of lovers, for example in Watteau's *La gamme d'amour* ("The Love Duet," 1715). Thus, the fragment of music and the guitar together mutually reinforce the theme of love (announced explicitly in the text) or, more specifically, transient love and passing beauty leading to death. But this is only one half of one of the oppositions set up in this work. To see its antithesis we need to turn to the newspaper fragment in more detail.

The fragment of *Le Journal* consists of a partial headline that reads "La Bataille S'est Engagé" ("The battle has commenced") and within the rubric of the collage can have a number of possible meanings. As John Richardson has forcefully argued, the most obvious is a reference to cubism itself.[34] At the time this work was made, cubism had been under attack by both municipal and state representatives, in reaction to the shows at the Salon d'Automne and the *Section d'Or* exhibition at the Galérie La Boëtie, from all of which Picasso had deliberately stood apart. Added to this was what Picasso saw as his misrepresentation in André Salmon's "Histoire anecdotique du cubisme" (the first published account of the movement) and the publication of Albert Gleizes and Jean Metzinger's *Du cubisme,* which contributed to more public debate about the nature and dramatis personae of this

3.1 Marcel Legay, *Sonnet*, 1892. Text by Pierre Ronsard

revolutionary art. So the headline may have been intended to announce any of a number of things: that Picasso was entering into battle with municipal and state philistines, or with the other artist associated with the more public face of cubism at the Salon d'Automne and *Section d'Or,* or, according to Jack Flam, with Henri Matisse.[35] Closer to home, the most obvious candidate (according to Richardson) is Braque, who had first used the technique of papier collé and who had returned to Paris from a trip a few days after the date of the newspaper fragment.

Patricia Leighten offers a rather different reason for the choice of headline. Her reading of the work centers on Picasso's interest in anarchistic themes of antimilitarism and antinationalism. She has shown how the fragment relates to a large number of other collages that all seem to engage with the Balkan conflict then raging in central Europe. The phrase "La Bataille S'est Engagé" is edited from the full headline "La Bataille S'est Engagé[e Furieuse sur les Lignes de Tchatldja]" ("The battle is joined at the Tchataldja front"), a dispatch from Constantinople about a specific battle. In Picasso's version, a headline from a war that is well under way is made to signify the first engagement in hostilities. This is indeed the first of Picasso's collages that treats the Balkan theme.[36]

Picasso's love of puns, riddles, and mystification has produced a work, and a series of references, that hold open the possibility of both public and more private resonances. The reasons for Picasso's choice may well be as Richardson states, but this does not affect the object that Picasso has left behind. This work has a number of elements that have resonance aside from intention by virtue of their place in the history of the period of production specifically and in the history of art more generally.

The headline sets up an opposition or conflict within the theme of love created by the music and guitar elements, introducing strife as an important dialectical element. It is a worldview with a long pedigree, found perhaps most eloquently in the cosmology of the Greek thinker Empedocles.[37] He had taught that reality is compounded of the four elements, fire, water, air, and earth, which continually mingle and separate under the influence of the alternately predominating forces of love, the unifier, and strife, the divider. For Empedocles both love and strife are primitive substances on a level with the four elements. Their disposition is cyclical and controlled only by chance and necessity. Although these primitive substances are everlasting, their arrangement is always temporary; there is no stable state. I am not suggesting that Picasso explicitly calls on Empedocles, for such a view of philosophical oppositions has long been associated with the human principles that are the irreconcilable stuff of poetry. Interplay between apparent binary oppositions is part of the content of this collage.

According to Leighten's argument, Picasso rejected patriotic jingoism. He had, as a "vertical invader" (to use a phrase of John Berger's),[38] an ambivalent attitude to French national culture and did not embrace the idea of war with quite the patriotic fervor of some of his cubist colleagues, for example Braque, André Derain, Gleizes, Metzinger, Roger de la Fresnaye, and Fernand Léger. Even Matisse, who was as profoundly pacifistic as Picasso, later tried to enlist,[39] and Apollinaire, who was Italian by birth, applied for French citizenship so that he could volunteer for service, and was assigned to an artillery regiment. Nevertheless, writes Leighten, "Picasso, though from a neutral country, still would have to justify his noncombatant position, given the passionate rhetoric aroused by the threat of a general European war."[40] He can be seen to have done this, in part, through his art, in a work where the subject matter holds in tension the notions of love and strife, and the location—a café or wallpapered interior—reflected the setting where world affairs were discussed and debated. By combining such elements as a mass-circulation French daily, a popular love song, a "Spanish" guitar,[41] and high art (in the form of a cubist drawing of a wineglass), all within the traditional Western genre of the still life or vanitas, he creates a highly charged dialectical and polyphonic image. In short, this work offers a meditation on the fragile pleasures of a civilized peace—wine, women, and song—placed in opposition, compositionally, to news of destruction. The act of making art itself, along with the suggestion of lovemaking ("jouissance") through the musical elements, provides a poignant counterpoint to the belief in an imminent European war.

The drawing of the glass is also a player in this game. Picasso has inserted a drawing from the hermetic stage of analytic cubism. It is perhaps a complex image to comprehend unless one is familiar with the visual codes on which it is based. It appears to be a preliminary sketch for an object that is common in cubist works of the period 1910–14. It describes both the profile and volumetric elements of the object—the circular top, stem, and foot, and the curve of the side and foot—superimposed one on top of the other, with the addition of shading to suggest solidity but rendered in a relatively arbitrary way. Because Picasso was working under the financial security of an exclusive contract with Daniel Kahnweiler, in which every image he could create (except those he regarded as necessary to his artistic development) was a guaranteed sale, Picasso was at liberty to develop a language of representation that expressed a problematic and contradictory experience of modernity in what was a largely private, avant-garde environment. The development of collage was in part an attempt to clarify this emergent, cubist view of reality, to make it more legible.

The notion of realism in this context is complex. One can see a number of strands and definitions working together in opposition to nineteenth-century views of realism. For example, appearance is set against reality in terms of outward illusion versus inner conception. Modernity amplified the view that reality was a compound of elements, not all of which were visible (like inner feelings and

3.5 Pedro de Acosta, *Trompe l'oeil*, 1755, oil on canvas, 92 x 124 cm.
Real Academia de Bellas Artes de San Fernando, Madrid

social or political forces), which we can summarize as conception over perception. Finally, as Greenberg argued, the medium in which representation occurs is radically different from the objects it chooses to represent, a lesson absorbed from Cézanne among others. In cubism this can be seen in the use of both imitation wood effects and real found objects, like newspaper and sheet music, so that reproduction is understood as based more explicitly on a diverse set of conventions, naturalism being but one species. Such a drawing as that of the glass, in Picasso's work, placed within the context of a collage, therefore stands as an emblem of elite fine art practice. But there is a more general point to be made in relation to the still-life tradition.

In the first half of the eighteenth century there was a genre of Spanish still-life painting that operated with the convention of trompe l'oeil. Such paintings often concerned musical subjects, for example Pedro de Acosta's *Trompe l'oeil* of 1755 (fig. 3.5). Acosta belonged to a small group of painters working in cosmopolitan Seville who made popular the type of decorative trompe l'oeil pictures first produced in northern Europe by such artists as Samuel van Hoogstraeten, Norbertus Gysbrechts, Wallerand Vaillant, and Evert Collier in the seventeenth century.[42] As Robert Rosenblum has pointed out, instruments in these paintings were often represented upright or hanging on a wall. Occasionally, open musical scores were also shown fixed to a flat wall.[43] These elements are to be found in the work by Picasso under discussion, but in relation to cubist notions of realism another point should be raised. Trompe l'oeil paintings are illusionistic works par excellence. Indeed, their raison d'être is to fool the eye into believing that the objects depicted are the real thing.

That the cubists should have been so concerned with such still-life elements, or even still life as a subject and a tradition, underlines the point that their conception of realism, though cerebral rather than visible, is nevertheless central to their practice; it is the obverse of such illusionism. That musical instruments figure so highly in such trompe l'oeil works, in the Netherlands in the seventeenth century, in Spain in the eighteenth century, and in the United States in the nineteenth century, is rarely explicitly addressed. One reason for their ubiquity may well be that they invite touch. If reached for, the shock of the deception would provide the trompe l'oeil artist with the ultimate checkmate, as in the tale told by Pliny the Elder of Zeuxis fooling birds with a painting of grapes that they flew down to peck. Even greater was the later deception of the artist himself by Parhassius, with a painting of a curtain that Zeuxis reached to draw aside.[44] But musical instruments are also specific objects whose existence in still lifes is predicated on the fact that, though visible in the work of art, they fulfill their true raison d'être only through the senses of touch and hearing. Both these senses are better represented, according to the cubists and their critics, within the conventions of cubism than within the conventions of trompe l'oeil. Although such still-life paintings often evoke the five senses, only the sense of sight ultimately achieves full evocation.

In the Picasso collage, a fragment of a popular song is juxtaposed with the drawing of the glass. The song is a cultural artifact with a relatively wide circulation and a different audience from the cubist depiction of glass. This implies another form of cultural opposition, but in a form more complex than a simple high-low characterization, for musical notation, like the cubist glass, can be deciphered only by those who know its codes and conventions. This use of musical notation is important in another regard: it draws explicit attention to the use of sign systems, methods of representation that are not dependent on visual equivalence. The use of musical script, a set of signs operating within a system of difference, is, as we have seen, only one among a number of sign systems interacting within this work, one form of nonillusory signification. As with the use of words in the newspaper fragment, musical notes have a nonmimetic relationship to the thing they signify, and this is made even more emphatic by the way Picasso has left both music and words unresolved in terms of their original context and meaning. Although the guitar may be abstract and diagrammatic, the collaged elements (the glass, newspaper, sheet music, wallpaper, even the wood-grained sheet) function both as signifiers of general concept, as particular objects standing for a class of objects within the frame of "art," and as themselves, real objects imported from a world outside the frame.

The use of an abbreviated language of signs, the use of synecdoche, and the conflation of oppositions that are apparent in Picasso's collages have their origins in the analytic cubism of the period 1910–11. The next work considered, *Ma Jolie,* exemplifies the development of an artistic language that is replete with private references but is based on an iconography that is meaningless without its conscious dependence on a set of shared artistic conventions, resonant with history.

Ma Jolie (Woman with a Zither or Guitar)

This work (430) was painted in Paris in the autumn of 1911, although it is possible that Picasso reworked it a little later, as he commonly did at this time to keep abreast of developments within the cubist "syntax" (fig. 3.6). There has also been discussion over its title. An inscription on the stretcher, *Femme à la cithare,* suggests that the instrument depicted is a zither. Kahnweiler's early catalog entries (for the Munich and Vienna exhibitions of 1913 and 1914, respectively) also label it *Frau mit Zither.* However, the German word *Zither* has two meanings, the other of which is cittern, an instrument often known in the eighteenth century as the "English guitar." Kahnweiler probably named the work, and the ambiguity over the German term *Zither* and evidence internal to the work itself has led to equivocation over the instrument's identification. Both the zither and the guitar are plucked string instruments with fret boards and circular sound holes. Both can be played on the knees, and both have folk and art music associations (the zither was highly praised as an instrument of complex musical effects by Franz Liszt, for example). The zither has between thirty and forty-five strings, most of which are open and resonating. The few strings that pass over the fret board are used to play the melody. The cittern, by contrast, usually has nine strings and resembles a lute, but with the guitar's flat back.

The subject matter verges on the indecipherable, thanks to the complexity of the formal language. Yet by working with the few clues that can be gleaned from earlier works, the subject begins to emerge. A human figure, devoid of physiognomic detail, is probably sitting with a music stand to the left and a musical instrument placed on the lap. Six strings are visible over a circular sound hole, which tends to support the instrument's identification as a guitar. Corroborating this identification is that, as far as I am aware, the zither does not occur in any other works by Picasso of this period, whereas the guitar is commonplace. We might detect another clue in the "S"-shaped fragment to the left of the sound hole (a sign for the figure-eight shape of the guitar). As far as our argument is concerned, however, the iconography of the two instruments is not dissimilar. They share many characteristics and historical associations.

The figure and objects are placed, as with *Guitar and Wine Glass,* in an extremely shallow space. The lavish faceting constantly brings the eye back to the

3.6 Pablo Picasso, *Ma Jolie (Woman with a Zither or Guitar)*, 1911–12, oil on canvas, 100 x 65.4 cm. The Museum of Modern Art, Acquired Through the Lillie P. Bliss Bequest. Photograph © 2000 The Museum of Modern Art, New York. © Succession Picasso / DACS 2000

picture plane, and the muted palette of earth colors militates against any effect of aerial perspective. The anti-illusionistic implications of the words at the bottom of the work, which give it its title, and the treble clef and stave, all contribute to the flatness of the picture space in a way that anticipates the later papier collés. The words have a stenciled trompe-l'oeil effect, similar to Braque's contemporary use of lettering. As Greenberg has observed, "These intrusions, by their self-evident, extraneous, and abrupt flatness, stopped the eye at the literal, physical surface of the canvas in the same way the artist's signature did. . . . The surface was now *explicitly* instead of implicitly indicated as a tangible but transparent plane."[45] This is formally correct, but the "extraneous" nature of the use of such words is significant and is taken up again presently.

The inclusion of words that complicate the issue of pictorial space has precedents other than the artist's signature. A specifically Spanish antecedent is found in the work of Francisco de Zurbarán (1598–1664). His early paintings of saints, expressed in sober colors, share the tonality and neutral backgrounds of Picasso's hermetic paintings, and they include the use of lettering as names to identify the saint as part of the image, situated in the same place as *Ma Jolie* (for example, *Saint Apollonia* of 1636 in the Louvre, Paris).[46]

Picasso's subject, a figure playing a plucked string instrument, is related to a number of significant antecedents in the art of the preceding centuries as well as to Picasso's previous work. The most obvious model is in the paintings of the nineteenth-century French artist Jean-Baptiste-Camille Corot (1796–1875). He was a painter of some prestige among the first generation of modern artists, notably Gustave Courbet and Edouard Manet. Picasso's first exposure to Corot's paintings, particularly the twenty-five figure paintings shown in the Salon d'Automne of 1909, greatly affected him. To most people at the time, Corot was known as a painter of landscapes. His individual figure paintings had been produced largely for himself and had seldom been exhibited. According to Richardson, these paintings of women holding mandolins, in particular their studio settings, were a revelation to Picasso. Corot's works entitled *Artist's Studio,* produced mainly between 1866 and 1870, usually depict the musical instrument as silent, not played, alongside the model's contemplation of an easel painting (a landscape by the artist), evoking a melancholic mood through the rapt meditation of art; Braque called them "paintings about painting."[47] In contrast, Corot's earlier pastoral painting the *Concert,* of 1844, and the classical subject work *Homer and the Shepherds* of 1845 both depict music-making in the open air. The *Concert* shows a woman playing a cello—the instrument's shape echoing the pose of her companion—while other figures listen attentively. *Homer and the Shepherds* depicts the blind poet outside a city, playing the lyre and reciting his verse to a group of three youths, his only audience. The blind performer functions much as in Picasso's painting of the *Old Guitarist,* the lack of outward vision compensated by the power of music to provoke the imagination to inner visions. Both convey a mood of rapt attention, suggesting the power of music to transport the listener to another realm. The imagination of the listeners inside the works and the viewers outside are linked through the evocation of music.

The work with the most immediate formal connections with *Ma Jolie* is Corot's

3.7 Jean-Baptiste-Camille Corot, *Gypsy Girl with Mandolin (Portrait of Christine Nilsson)*, 1874, oil on canvas, 80 x 57 cm. Collection of the Museu de Arte, São Paulo Assis Chateaubriand. Photograph Luiz Hossaka

1874 painting *Gypsy Girl with Mandolin (Portrait of Christine Nilsson)*, a work that associates the gypsy, an outsider, with music and romantic reverie (fig. 3.7). To quote Richardson: "Thanks to Corot, Picasso and Braque saw how the presence of a stringed instrument could endow a figure painting with the stasis of a *nature morte*. Corot provided the cubists with their quintessential human subject."[48]

He also provided them with a model for their own tonally subdued palette, a reaction in part, no doubt, against the impressionists. As Rosenblum has pointed out, Picasso was also aware of this subject of the gypsy mandolinist through a series of picture postcards inspired by the popular nineteenth-century opera *Mignon* (1866), by the composer Ambroise Thomas (1811–96).[49] A number of these show the title character playing the mandolin. The romantic nature of the setting and the relaxed pose create a kitsch counterpart to Corot's original paint-

3.8 Jean-Baptiste-Camille Corot, *Young Women of Sparta,* 1868–70, oil on canvas, 41 x 73 cm. Gift of Mrs. Horace Havemeyer, The Brooklyn Museum

ing. Both sources act as a thematic bridge across the high-low cultural border, the crossing of which, as we have seen, was frequently an outcome of Picasso's work.

The relationship, however, goes much deeper than just a formal connection with such artistic precedents. In Corot's less well known painting *Young Women of Sparta* (1868–70), the subject of music is combined with a pose of more explicit sexual allusion (fig. 3.8). The Italian (Neapolitan) mandolin, with its distinctive round back, like its older cousin the lute and unlike the pear-shaped, flat-backed Portuguese version, is placed in the lap of the reclining figure, making clear the sexual symbolism—the womblike swelling of the back, which in the lute had been associated in the seventeenth century with the physiognomy of pregnancy, and the provocatively placed sound hole. Picasso's *Ma Jolie* possesses these same essential features.[50]

Within the formal language of analytic cubism, the conflation of subject elements occurs; that is, the sounding body and the human body are allowed to merge. The use of a restricted palette—earth colors—and faceted planes, within a work that provides few keys to the specificity of objects, makes parts of the human subject and surrounding objects interchangeable. Where does the human figure stop and the guitar and background start? *Ma Jolie* can thus be seen to take the relationship between similar shapes, such as the rhyming of cello and figure in the *Concert* by Corot, to the next stage, so that they become truly interchangeable. The sound hole and fingers (also Picasso's cubist sign for pubic hair) thus take on an explicitly sexual connotation, so that the act of playing a musical instrument (*jouailler*) can also be read as "playing with yourself" or masturbation (*jouir*), consistent with Picasso's predilection for puns. Supporting this reading is that we know on whom the figure in the painting was modeled and what Picasso's relationship to her was. To examine this further we need to return to the painting's title.

"Ma Jolie" refers to a popular song called "Dernière chanson," itself a kind of compound (collaged) composition. The first three verses were written by H. Christine and set to music by a popular music-hall artist, Harry Fragson. Fragson also wrote the words of the refrain, which refer to gypsy musicians (tziganes) recalling both Corot and *Mignon:*

O Manon, ma Jolie, mon coeur te dit bonjour!
Pour nous, les tziganes jouent ma mie
Leur chanson d'amour
Leur chanson d'amour
Et cette mélodie
Me donne le frison
Ecoute la donc
Ecoute la donc
C'est notre première chanson

This he set to the music of a passage from the ballet *Dans les ombres* ("In the Shadows") by Herman Frink, a simple tune in common time in C major.[51] As Rosenblum has shown, the title has a number of ambiguous meanings. First, it seems to function as a mocking evocation of a gallery or museum title plate.[52] Second, by referring to a popular tune that the band at the Cirque Médrano, a cabaret on the rue des Martyrs in Montmartre, was constantly playing, the title sets up an opposition between the difficult language of cubist high art and the more familiar vernacular language of low art. Third, and most significant for the reading I offer above, is the private reference in the title to Picasso's then-lover, commonly known as Marcelle Humbert but also known as Eve Gouel, described by the Italian painter Gino Severini as "a small, spicy girl who looked like a Chinese doll."[53] Picasso Hispanicized her name to Eva (to play against his Adam). It is unclear when their affair started, but by the 12 June 1912 he had declared in a letter to Kahnweiler, "I love [Eva] very much and I will write this in my painting."[54] It appears he had been doing this for some months, for in *Nude Woman* of 1912 he wrote in the groin of the cubist figure "j'aime Eva." It is therefore likely that the words "ma jolie," written on the earlier painting, also refer to Eva. The generalized nature of this pet name helped Picasso to keep his relationship with Eva from his waning love, Fernande. As Richardson has commented, this was

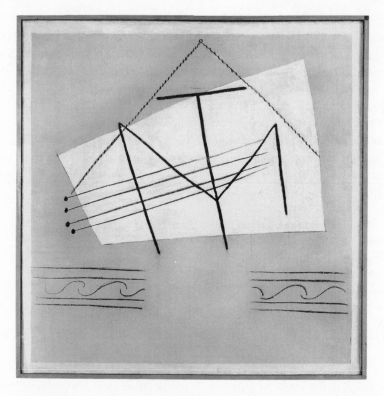

3.9 Pablo Picasso, *Guitar (MT)*, 27 April 1927, oil and charcoal on canvas, 81 x 81 cm. Musée Picasso, Photograph © RMN—J. G. Berizzi. © Succession Picasso / DACS 2000

not unique behavior for Picasso, for when he fell in love with Marie-Thérèse in the late 1920s while married to Olga Koklova and Marie-Thérèse was under the age of consent, he concealed his feelings among other ways by disguised use of her initials. In the work *Guitar* of 1927 he uses "MT" as the body of the instrument that appears to be hung on a wall as a portrait, thus again conflating the body of a guitar with the identity of a lover (fig. 3.9).[55] The only work he gave to Eva was a painting entitled *Guitar* of 1912 (485), which had the words "j'aime Eva" on a gingerbread heart stuck to the bottom of the work (which has since been lost). His relationship with her was cut short by her tragic death from cancer on 14 December 1915.

Ma Jolie typically contains a play on a series of oppositions: public (Mignon) and private (Eva), high culture (Corot) and popular culture (Fragson).

The metamorphic process evident in these examples of analytic cubism achieved further development in synthetic cubism.

3.10 Pablo Picasso, *The Violin (Violin and Fruit)*, 1912–13, charcoal, colored papers, gouache, painted paper collage, 63 x 52 cm. Philadelphia Museum of Art, A. E. Gallatin Collection. © Succession Picasso / DACS 2000

The Violin (Violin and Fruit)

This is one of Picasso's most formally complex works (530; fig. 3.10). As Edward Fry first noted, the newspaper fragments incorporated into this work are from *Le Journal* of 6 and 9 December 1912. In formal terms, this picture is far more hetero-geneous than *Guitar and Wine Glass*. Here the relationship between ground and figure is more ambiguous, the overlap more prevalent. Rosalind Krauss, in her discussion of the formal innovations in this collage, has presented it as paradigmatic of collage in general: "It is the eradication of the original surface, and the reconstitution of it through the figure of its own absence that is the master term of the entire condition of collage as a system of signifiers."[56]

The material elements are newspaper, color illustrations, painted wood-grained paper, black, white, blue, brown, and cream pasted paper, and a considerable amount of overdrawing. Again, the written content of the newspaper is significant. The section in the upper right has the headline cut off so that it reads "... arition" (*apparition*, or appearance). It is a report of a séance, during which one Madame Harmelie made contact with a dead woman, occasioning an utterance, "C'est elle!" (It is she). This sudden appearance of a female presence has obvious parallels with the morphology of musical instruments under discussion. The rest of the newspaper fragments concern contemporary modern life, with a significant absence of political reporting in Picasso's choice. However, two other short items situated near the white plane to the left also invite comment in this context. One reports on the case of a murderess, and the other is an account of a female pugilist.

The images of fruit placed in the bowl have been cut from color illustrations. They form a striking contrast to the rest of the composition, which operates according to non-naturalistic cubist conventions. The way Picasso has cut them out compounds the illusion. They appear to overlap, which adds to the sense of illusionism and gives the appearance of three-dimensional space. In fact, however, they have been slotted together in the manner of a jigsaw, cut to fit next to one another, not stuck on top of each other—a typical move by Picasso to tease systems of representation. But perhaps the most significant illusionistic play is with the simultaneous depiction of two images within one element. In her discussion of this work, Marjorie Perloff has directed attention to the representation of the glass, drawn on a cutout fragment of newspaper that has been stuck over the newspaper fragment on the right, the section that deals with the "appearance."[57] She argues—and once it has been pointed out, it is hard not to see it—that this seemingly typical cubist analysis of a glass, showing the round top, curved and shaded side, and stem and rounded foot, can also be read as a caricature of a figure reading the newspaper on which it is depicted. This figure is not alone, however; it has a companion ("in the shadow"? the edge of the shadowed part of the drawing points to this phrase in the newspaper text). The representation on the blue pasted paper of the central part of the violin, to the left of the glass and or figure can also be understood morphologically, the string representing a twisting torso, the sound holes, arms, and the tail piece, a skirt. The apparent swagger of this figure is pronounced because one of the sound holes is placed further back than the other, creating a sense of depth against the flat picture plane. The sound hole on the right is brought forward to form the rest of the letter U that has been cut from the word "Journal," to produce a compressed form of the word: "jrnal." The reintroduction of the U allows the word to be read as "urnal" (urinal), a typically childish pun, perhaps on the sensationalism of the "gutter" press.

This female figure finds a further echo in the larger body of the violin, the echoed, simplified, figure-eight shape that resembles buttocks or breasts as well as a torso's curves. They are juxtaposed to the newspaper fragment that reports on the murderer and the pugilist, both women of violence. This horizontal axis then reads from right to left: man(?) reading a newspaper stuck onto a fragment of newspaper from which a female figure appears ("It is she"); a swaggering woman formed from the center of the violin, leading via breasts or buttocks to women of violence—from seduction to abuse? The phallic pear and apples (served up in a dish) are also a sexual allusion. It is worth comment, as Perloff has argued, that the word *collage* (pasting) was a slang expression for a couple's living together (stuck together) in an illicit union. The past participle, *collé*, also meant "faked" or "pretended." "The word collage thus becomes itself an emblem of the 'systematic play of difference,' the 'mise en question' of representation that is inherent in its verbal-visual structure."[58]

The possibilities of such a reading—violin (and guitar) as woman, the scroll (or peg box) as head, the fingerboard as neck, and sound box as torso—may first have been suggested to Picasso by an article in the anarchist journal *Arte joven* in 1901, which he coedited with Francisco de Asís Soler in Madrid. Nicolas María López contributed an article entitled "La psicologia de la guitarra" (Psychology of the guitar) to the first issue.[59] In this deeply misogynistic article, López describes the guitar and a woman in terms of each other:

The guitar is the symbol of the popular soul and a symbol of feeling. Perhaps because of this it has the face of a woman. The guitar is feminine grammatically and psychologically. Its peg box is a head, like the adorned women with red and blue ribbons . . . ; its neck is the erect equivalent, rectilinear like the Venus de Milo. The frets are pearl necklaces, sometimes misshapen (because it is Moorish). And the sound box has the arrogant curve of the shoulders, the magic of the hips . . . .

Like a woman, the guitar prostitutes itself easily. It falls in the hands of vice and happily accompanies the raucous songs of an orgy; it becomes intoxicated and its notes, hoarse and out of tune, ring out with the heaviness of the drunkard . . . .

Like a woman it is capricious and difficult. It rebels at first, then it submits like a slave with copious cooing. It refuses to play, frequently goes out of tune in order to make itself more interesting, and when it despairs it jumps up at its player and embraces him with an abundance of harmonies.

It is faithful and affectionate always; it is forgotten easily and is as ungrateful and treacherous as the feminine heart.

It feels every tenderness and when old, when it can no longer sing its joys nor sigh for its loved ones, it puts itself in the hands of a poor blind man and asks him for charity.[60]

What we have seen in Picasso is a much greater subtlety than this crude outline, but a play nevertheless on many of its essentially misogynistic features. The play is part of a complex set of relationships in dialogue with images that not only relate to a tradition of symbolism in Western art but also take such symbols further, so that the objects within the frame stand equally as symbol and referent. They become truly synthetic.

Picasso used a similar set of relationships and devices in a small work he designed to woo his new love, Gabrielle Depeyre, who was twenty-seven when Picasso met her sometime in 1915, after Eva's death. This time he expressed his love, not in large works meant to be sold, but rather in a series of small-scale watercolors and drawings that he intended to be private. One of these, known as *Je t'aime Gaby* and dated 22 February 1916, exemplifies Picasso's elision of instrument and lover (fig. 3.11). It consists of a sheet of black paper on which six cameos are stuck: a photograph of Picasso, one of Gaby, and three still lifes of flowers, sheet music, and guitars in increasing stages of cubist development. The final cameo is an allegorical portrait of Gaby lying naked on a bed, with a putto hovering overhead and lifting a curtain to reveal the figure. Each of these small images bears a different declaration of love on the back, and the three musical still lifes can be read as emblems of the lover and equivalents of the figure, the silent instruments awaiting the hand of the player to awaken the music as the sleeping figure of Gaby awaits the embrace (or look) of the artist. Like the works discussed above, they echo the figure's recumbent position. They find resolution in the final portrait.

Here the genres of still life and portraiture are assimilated. The central decorated proclamation, the title *Je t'aime Gaby,* contains one further conflation in the form of calligraphic lovemaking, used more than once in these works for Gaby: Picasso's name entwined with hers.

Picasso selected musical subjects for a number of reasons. Musical instruments are formally distinct objects; they can be fragmented and still retain their identity. Musical subjects also allowed Picasso to allude to themes that were important to his perception of the role of art as both a public and a private form of expression. In these works music functions as one preexistent sign system among others and as a marker of culture and civilization. Music is a metaphor for the act of making art: sounding or bringing out from silence. By referring to popular entertainment and folk music, Picasso allows himself to slip between the realms of high and low cultural practices. By including certain classes of musical instruments as symbols of both high and low cultural expression, he makes further connections with the

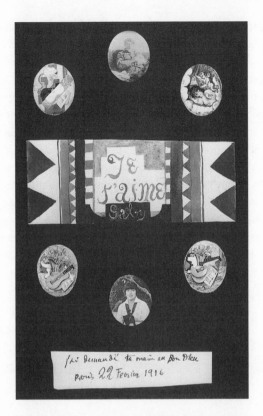

3.11 Pablo Picasso, *Je t'aime Gaby*, 1916, five oval watercolors and two oval photographs, each 4.2 x 3.5 cm, rectangular sheet with text and decorative border, 6.5 x 17.5 cm, rectangular sheet of text, 3 x 13.2 cm. Musée Picasso, Collection William McCarty-Cooper, Photo Martin Bühler (Kunstmuseum Basel). © Succession Picasso / DACS 2000

history of musical symbolism that point to reality beyond the illusionistic. And through the use of the guitar, he evokes his Spanish roots. He is able to fashion equations of physical materials, imbue both representational and metaphorical meanings, and accrue value by association. In particular, his materials conjure musical instruments in the process of metamorphosis into human figures, an objectification from object to subject, which he endows with thoughts of love or lust. This development plays a seminal role in Picasso's later surrealist works, where the sign carries more than one object of interpretation, the result of the many voices of cubism and collage become truly polyphonic.[61]

This fluid shift of artistic styles, from representational images to synthetic cubism, particularly in *Je t'aime Gaby,* shows Picasso's ease with different languages of expression, a facility that is perhaps most evident in his sketchbooks. His eclectic approach is characteristic of his work from the 1920s on, a metamorphic transformation of images that the surrealists saw as a forerunner of their own aesthetic. We might suggest that it demonstrates his fundamental conception of art as a conversation with history; all previous art can be contained in the rubric "Picasso," to put it immodestly. But as Picasso turned to embrace classicism following cubism, the Apollonian and Dionysiac tendencies that are hidden in the musical subjects of this cubist stage emerge more explicitly. As Richardson has so perceptively put it, "Picasso will depict these scenes with godlike indulgence" from the viewpoint of the artist. "It is as if he wanted to prove Plutarch wrong, that 'the great god Pan' was no longer dead, now that Picasso had returned to the classical scene."[62]

FOUR QUASI UNA MUSICA KUPKA AND KLEE, MUSIC, AND THE IDEA OF ABSTRACTION

The poet ranks far below the painter in the representation of visible things, and far below the musician in that of invisible things.
—Leonardo da Vinci

And so gradually the different arts have set forth on the path of saying what they are best able to say, through means that are peculiar to each.

And in spite of, or thanks to this differentiation, the arts as such have never in recent times been closer to one another than in this latest period of spiritual transformation. . . .

. . . With few exceptions and deviations, music has for several centuries been the art that uses its resources not to represent natural appearances, but to express the inner life of the artist and to create a unique life of musical tones.
—Wassily Kandinsky

At the time of the emergence of abstract art, the ubiquitous nature of ut pictura musica depended on the idealist conception of music as employed by Wagner and on symbolist aesthetics that issued from Baudelaire's writings. By this route, ut pictura musica was translated into the more prosaic formalism of Greenberg's theory of modernism. Here music is a paradigm of autonomy, a model for painting because of its "absolute" nature and its "almost complete absorption in the very physical quality of its medium . . . an art of 'pure form.'"[1] The contrary perception of music within notions of a "theatrical" postmodernist sensibility is dependent on a materialist understanding of music, which sees it as a complex discourse, a polyphony of elements that include the sonoric (broadly understood to include noise) but are not sufficiently contained within notions of "pure form." Music squeezes itself out into the realm of the visual between texts and contexts.

In the work of the Czech-born painter František Kupka we can see the move from symbolism to full abstraction. And in the work and ideas of Paul Klee, we see an aesthetic that was born into modernism but cannot simply be contained within it; Klee's understanding and use of ut pictura musica introduce elements that disrupt the purism of modernist thinking.

FRANTIŠEK KUPKA

Kupka (1871–1957) was a product of the Austro-Hungarian Empire and a significant figure in twentieth-century culture. His role in the development of abstract painting is not generally given the attention it deserves, especially since he was probably the first artist to bring abstraction to the attention of the public when his *Amorpha* paintings were exhibited at the Salon d'Automne in 1912.[2] In addition to his paintings Kupka wrote a treatise on his aesthetic — this was not uncommon for an artist of his time — *Tvorení v umeni vytvarném* (Creation in the plastic arts), similar in scope and ambition to Kandinsky's more famous *Über das Geistige in der Kunst* (1911). Kupka worked on this text at various times between roughly 1909 and 1914, but it was published in Czech only in 1923 and as late as 1989 in French, under the title *La création dans les arts plastique*.[3] His ideas have not been widely disseminated, and his work, even with his commentary, often remains caught between metaphor and metamorphosis of natural elements and his intent to capture the immaterial in the material of paint.[4]

Kupka's thinking and art derive from a range of sources, a curious mixture of scientific materialism, idealism, spiritualism, and aestheticism.[5] His beliefs echoed contemporary scientific discoveries about the structure of matter, and his interest in chronographics and chronophotography, and its demonstrations of space-time occurrences, set him apart from artists like Kandinsky who saw the demise of materialism in the dawning of a new spiritual age. (Indeed, one of the remarkable things about Kandinsky's works of the first decades of the century is how his paintings hold the material world in charged tension, dissolving the form of objects—mountains, animals, figures—into abstract patterns. He called this artistic synthesis.[6]) Much of Kupka's thinking was also formed against a background of nineteenth-century theories of *correspondance* (discussed earlier in relation to Baudelaire) and developed through an early exposure to spiritualism. But Kupka does not appear to have felt that his interest in things spiritual was antithetical to concurrent developments in science. Rather, he believed that science was an alternative way of tapping into the essence of things; spiritualism and science were both a part of his essentialism. Kupka is not the only artist who, when he appropriated ideas from diverse sources, was more concerned with what the ideas meant to him than what they signified in their original contexts.

If we review what we know of his early life, we can detect the roots of his diverse aesthetic and go some way toward explaining the importance of music as a powerful agent of meaning in the development of his abstract painting. Kupka had been apprenticed at the age of thirteen to a saddler who initiated him into spiritualism. He later attended the Prague Academy, having first received lessons from the painter Alois Studnicka, who specialized in modern and traditional decorative arts. The abstraction of these decorative arts were to find an echo in Kupka's mature work, further developed through the study of Greek vase painting, which he studied in the Louvre, and Celtic art, studied during his trips to Brittany. He also looked to the purified forms of Islamic art, which he regarded as Platonic in its idealization.[7] During this time as a student he came into contact with the art of the Nazarenes, artists who placed a higher premium on allegory than realism. Nevertheless, his work at the Prague Academy was relatively conservative, and he appears not to have returned to an overt interest in symbolism until the magnet of Vienna attracted him there in the summer of 1892, following his graduation. Here he entered the Vienna Academy to study under August Eisenmenger, a painter of the Nazarene school.

While in Vienna Kupka read widely: philosophy (Plato, Schopenhauer, Nietzsche, and Kant), Eastern religion (especially the *Rig Veda*), chemistry, astronomy, astrology, and alchemy. He became interested in theosophy and made money, as he had in Prague, as a spiritual medium.

In Vienna at this time there was a wider interest in abstract pattern and its significance than elsewhere—ideas that provided a scholarly justification for the interest in ornament Kupka had already developed in Prague. Alois Riegl published his *Stilfragen: Grundlegungen zu einer Geschichte der Ornamentik* (Problems of style: foundations for a history of ornament) in 1893, the year after Kupka moved to Vienna. Riegl proposed that the history of ornament should be understood not as derived from an exclusive focus on the analysis of materials and techniques (as Gottfried Semper had done) but through the study of its internal principles.[8] Form is then transformed by motifs that are purely aesthetic. Wilhelm

Worringer later took up this idea in Vienna in *Abstraktion und Einfühlung* (Abstraction and empathy, 1907), in which he assesses the "urge to abstraction" as a "refuge from appearances."[9]

Kupka became a close friend of Arthur Roessler (1877–1955), who lodged in Kupka's apartment for a short time. Roessler is perhaps best remembered as an art critic of the *Arbeiter-Zeitung* and enthusiastic collector and promoter of Egon Schiele's work, but at the time of his acquaintance with Kupka, he was a student at Vienna University, studying philosophy and art history. In letters to his friend sent later from Paris, Kupka spoke of his belief in the independence of formal elements in painting from subject matter, signing himself "color symphonist." The idea of form as separate from subject was a view held by Eduard Hanslick, the professor of music at Vienna University who, in his book *On the Beautiful in Music* (1854), had proposed a similar formalist aesthetic in his attack on Wagner: that music and musical logic are independent of "extramusical" considerations (including emotion) and are simply "sounding forms set into motion."[10] For Kupka, however, it was music (an "extravisual" consideration) that was to become a subject for painting, not for itself so much as for what it signified.

In 1894, Kupka briefly became a follower of Karl Diefenbach, a Nazarene painter and mystical thinker who promoted meditation, open-air naked exercise, and the importance of the model of music to art (he arranged for piano and violin music to be played while he and his students worked).[11] These were ideas that Kupka was to follow for the rest of his life. He was also aware of the discussions then taking place in certain intellectual circles in Vienna about the nature and limits of language, making conclusions similar to those he later reached about the nature of painting.[12]

After travels to Scandinavia and England, Kupka settled in Paris in the spring of 1895, although he remained in contact with Viennese ideas through his friendship with Roessler and others.[13] In Paris he began to pursue a living as an illustrator while continuing to paint. His paintings were not exhibited at this time. He later wrote in a letter to his Czech friend the poet Josef Machar in April 1905, "It seems unnecessary to paint trees when people see more beautiful ones on the way to the exhibition. I paint, but only concepts . . . syntheses, chords . . . but this I do for myself. I am not anxious to show it."[14] Music, in other words, operates as the signifier of "concepts"; it is the vehicle through which his ideas are synthesized, a metaphor for the unsayable.

His illustrative work was mainly published in the anarchistic and satirical journals *Canard sauvage* and *Assiette au beurre* (to which Juan Gris was a later contributor), under the French version of his name, François. He also illustrated the stories and poems of the American writer beloved of the symbolists, Edgar Allan

Poe. The best known of these is the *Black Idol* (also known as *La révolte* [Defiance] and *La résistance*) of 1900, which illustrates the following stanza from Poe's "Dreamland":

> By a route obscure and lonely,
> Haunted by ill angels only,
> Where an Eidolon, named NIGHT,
> On a black throne reigns upright,
> I have reached these lands but newly,
> From an ultimate dim Thule —
> From a wild weird clime that lieth, sublime,
> Out of SPACE — out of TIME

Space and time are themes that recur in Kupka's abstract works, where, as we shall see, the notion of temporality (earlier developed in his figurative works in relation to photography) becomes wedded to music. In addition, both his illustrations and his painting had one thing in common: the idea that abstract art had to be more than simple pattern-making and had to carry with it the didactic mission of earlier figurative painting; form needed to correspond to the idea. Here he deviates from Hanslick's formalism. His paintings shift from the symbolic expression of ideas (found in his illustrations) to an attempt to reach the form of ideas themselves. At this time he appears to have felt that the two art forms most capable of achieving the form of ideas were architecture and music. We can follow the evolution of these thoughts in more detail through consideration of a sample of works.

While in Vienna, Kupka's interest in theosophy may well have been facilitated through contact with the German journal of the theosophical society, the *Sphynx,* first published in 1886. The image of the sphinx appears in a number of his works, including the now-lost *Quam ad causum sumus* (Why are we here?) and its later variant of 1900, entitled *The Way of Silence* (fig. 4.1). *The Way of Silence* depicts an avenue flanked by a row of sphinxes on each side (resembling the Eidolon in "Defiance"), with a stream of stellar light arching through the sky toward the vanishing point of the avenue, which, because of the angle, remains hidden from the viewer's sight lines. In the middle of the avenue is a small figure, a self-portrait, contemplating the question that is inscribed at the base of the sphinx closest to the picture plane: "Quam ad causum sumus." The need to include words (as a title) is characteristic of symbolism in guiding the viewer toward the subject. Kupka was well aware of this and regarded the relationship between text and image as one of musical counterpoint; illustration was thus "a genre that has its place in the highest spheres of art. The book is the true friend of man, and as long as the proportions sing out, the balances are right, the white of the engravings suggests the

4.1 František Kupka, *The Way of Silence,* c. 1900, pastel on paper, 58.1 x 65 cm. Narodni Galerie, Prague

soprano, sustained by the alto or the bass of the black typescript, then illustration is by no means unworthy of the great artist."[15]

The silence is therefore broken by language. Words are needed to mediate the contemplation. The Egyptian sphinx was an emblematic figure, a symbol of the pharaoh, most often with the head of a man and the body of a lion, a union of intellect and physical force. Within the orthodoxy of theosophy it appears to have had an ambiguous meaning, representing the material world (especially if asleep), but for some theosophists the sphinx represented the mediation on the problems of humanity and the universe, the micro- and macrocosmos.[16] In Kupka's work the sphinx appears to operate as the medium to a higher reality, a reality that is immaterial, to be reached only through nonnaturalistic means.

In an earlier work, *Méditation* (1899), he uses a similar device (fig. 4.2). Here the kneeling, naked figure of Kupka is shown meditating on the reflection of the summit of a mountain shown in the background. We can consider the reflection as a metaphor for the painting itself, an indirect route to a higher reality. The artist kneels before nature in an attempt to perceive beyond the veil of appearance. In his abstract works Kupka attempted to evoke the idea more directly, to make unmediated contact with the realm above the conscious. This was not an easy path to follow. It took great effort to supersede his academic training and his dependence on conventional pictorial means. Throughout the period 1905–10 he gradually gave up his work as an illustrator of journal articles and concentrated on editions of the classics, for example, Aeschylus's *Prometheus* and Aristophanes' *Lysistrata,* and on his painting.[17] In 1905, he moved to Puteaux, near his

4.2 František Kupka, *Meditation,* 1899, charcoal on paperboard, 60.6 x 44.7 cm. Museum of Fine Arts, Ostrava

friends Jacques Villon and Raymond Duchamp-Villion (Kupka and Villion had previously been next-door neighbors on the rue Caulaincourt), and with Villon's brother Marcel and others discussed issues of spiritualism, alchemy, and higher reality, which probably had an impact on Duchamp's work and thinking of this time (see, for example, Duchamp's painting *The Bush,* 1910–11).[18]

Kupka's paintings of the same years began to address more directly two of his overriding concerns: light and movement. In *La baigneuse* of 1907–8, he paints his wife bathing in a pool in Théoule. The natural element of water, and the light reflected by it, animates and absorbs the figure into nature, breaking up contours to provide an overall surface pattern. The dissolving of the figure was carried further in a series of works produced between 1907 and 1909 based on a painting of his stepdaughter Andrée playing in a sunny garden (see fig. 4.4). This painting originated many of the elements that were to be found in his first exhibited abstract painting, *Amorpha, Fugue in Two Colors* (1912). Following this static,

conventional study of his stepdaughter, Kupka produced a series of small drawings in an attempt to find a graphic equivalent of the movement of the figure
and the ball. Alongside these abstracted works Kupka continued to work on less
radical paintings, but these, too, soon mutated into paintings that developed his
division of the picture plane into a series of vertical planes (such as *Planes by
Color* from the earlier studies of *Woman Picking Flowers*). In this way a number
of works emerged that can be divided into two groups: those concerned with the
representation of movement through circular forms and those more directly concerned with surface divisions into a series of vertical planes. I want to consider
two works, one from each group, and explore their relationship to music.

Amorpha, Fugue in Two Colors

This large painting (just over two meters square, or about seven square feet)
was exhibited in 1912 at the Salon d'Automne (fig. 4.3) together with *Amorpha,
chromatique chaude* and alongside works by Matisse (*Nasturtiums* and *Dance*),
Francis Picabia (*Procession*), and cubist paintings by Gleizes, Metzinger, and La
Fresnaye.[19] I do not intend to repeat here a full list of its stylistic precedents, as
this has been done by others.[20] Rather, I wish to explore the ramifications of its
reference to music.

   From the Renaissance to the eighteenth century, one of the striking things
about the "sister arts" of painting and poetry is their common stock of subject
matter, drawn mainly from the classics and the Bible. For various reasons (by no
means restricted to the realm of culture), the shift that we have identified elsewhere from the mimetic theory of art to the expressive theory that largely replaced it, led to the supersession of music over poetry as the analogue for painting. Music often had no subject beyond its formal development as symphony,
concerto, or sonata, and so on. Throughout the romantic era music became more
important, as emphasis was given to form over subject, to expression over imitation. As Baudelaire made clear, it is the imagination (an internal site) that has
the power to create synthesis through expressive correspondence, because it ap-
prehends the interaction among the senses. For Baudelaire and the symbolists,
as well as many early abstract artists, imagination is the site of a priori ideas
manifested through a language of symbols. This thinking was important in regarding color and forms as operating independently of objects or subject matter.
As Baudelaire wrote in his review of the Salon of 1846: "The right way to know
if a picture is melodious is to look at it from far enough away to make it impossible to understand its subject or to distinguish its lines. If it is melodious, it
already has a meaning."[21] This meaning is achieved through the art of composition, which links painting to music through the concept of "melody." These
ideas, which Baudelaire expressed so eloquently in his writings, nevertheless

4.3 František Kupka, *Amorpha, Fugue in Two Colors*, 1912, oil on canvas, 211 x 2210 cm. Narodni Galerie, Prague

started before him and continued to flourish after him. In early romantic think-ing, music's ability to move the listener through harmony and rhythm separated it from literary associations. Furthermore, the central place of rhythm connected it in the eyes of such thinkers with the organizing principle of a universe per-vaded by dynamism and flux: Hans von Bülow later summed up this belief with the aphorism, "In the beginning was rhythm." Novalis had already imagined the liberation of painting from the need to copy nature, speaking of a "visual music" existing as "arabesques, patterns, ornaments."[22] If music, free from rational dis-course and language, can utter the ineffable, why could painting not do the same? As Greenberg put it:

> As the first and most important item upon its agenda, the avant-garde saw the ne-cessity of an escape from ideas, which were infecting the arts with the ideological

struggles of society. Ideas come to mean subject matter in general. (Subject matter as distinguished from content: in the sense that every work of art must have content, but that subject matter is something the artist does or does not have in mind when he is actually at work.) This meant a new and greater emphasis upon form, and it also involved the assertion of the arts as independent vocations, disciplines and crafts, absolutely autonomous, and entitled to respect for their own sakes, and not merely as vessels of communication. It was the signal for a revolt against the dominance of literature, which was subject matter at its most oppressive.[23]

The outcome of this strategy was that the content of painting became its form, the form its content. By shedding its dependence on literature, painting could turn its attention to the issue of its own medium; music thus became "the principal agent of the new confusion of the arts."[24] But this confusion was alleviated, according to Greenberg, when music became a methodological rather than an effectual model. This view, however, as I have argued, is predicated on a view of music simply as sound. It might be helpful, at this stage, to go back a few steps in order to gain a better perspective on the role of music as model in abstract art.

A Question of Artistic Differences It is seldom remarked that there are a number of arts, rather than just one. An exception is in the work of Jean-Luc Nancy. His essay "Why Are There Several Arts and Not Just One?" in his book *The Muses* (1996) is a complex analysis that takes a different direction from mine, but he raises a number of issues that I wish to recontextualize here.[25] Rarely is the plurality of the arts affirmed. Rather, plurality is taken as a given. That plurality is then often a question of classification, which begs the question, What means of classification and what limits? And yet, it is also the case that art is discussed as if there were an essential character shared across, or beneath the arts— "Art," in other words, rather than the "arts." This is a largely romantic notion, and we see it in Kandinsky, for example, writing in 1911, in terms similar to Greenberg but to different ends:

> And so; gradually the different arts have set forth on the path of saying what they are best able to say, through means that are peculiar to each.
> And in spite of, or thanks to, this differentiation, the arts as such have never in recent times been *closer to one another* than in this latest period of spiritual transformation.[26]

The proximity of the arts, despite material differences, is due to "inner necessity," an idea Kandinsky takes from Schopenhauer's *World as Will and Representation,* which locates the essence of art in the soul, or will, relating it directly to the eidos. Subject matter is then the outer clothing of this inner essence. Goethe, another thinker who influenced Kandinsky's theory, put it laconically: "An art attains to supreme heights when its subject is a matter of indifference and the art itself truly absolute, with the subject-matter merely its vehicle."[27] Its "absolute" character places it outside history as a transcendent signifier.

Another way of approaching the question of pluralism within the concept of art is to assume that the essence of an art lies in the sense to which it is addressed. Greenberg, we have seen, defined purity against such a point, so that only "by excluding from each art whatever is intelligible in the terms of any other sense . . . would non-musical arts attain 'purity.' "[28] This is an old argument that Hegel had earlier summed up: "The specific characterization of the senses and of their corresponding material . . . must provide the grounds for the division of the individual arts."[29] But questions remain: Why should art appeal to only one sense? Should it not rather aspire to a type of Gesamtkunstwerk, as Wagner had argued?[30] What of the other senses, smell, taste, and touch, that are poorly served (if at all) by "fine art"? And, perhaps most radically, is our sensory experience in fact so autonomous, or is it rather that our senses always operate in relation to one another (as to an extent the cubists explored)? What happens to the sense of taste when the sense of smell is lost? Do not the senses form a kind of sensory hermeneutic circle, what physiologists call "sensorial integration"? The French filmmaker and theorist Michel Chion has argued along similar lines: "The eye carries information and sensations only some of which can be considered specifically and irreducibly visual (e.g., color); most others are transsensory. Likewise, the ear serves as a vehicle for information and sensations only some of which are specifically auditive (e.g., pitch and intervallic relations), the others being, as in the case of the eye, not specific to this sense." He is at pains to point out that this conception is different at root for correspondence. "In the transsensorial or even metasensorial model, which I am distinguishing from the Baudelarian one, there is no sensory given that is demarcated and isolated from the outset." This is because Chion views the senses as channels, not domains. The visual dimension may be as central to vision as the auditive dimension is to hearing, but, he maintains, these specific elements (if they exist) are in a minority and particularized; a single channel can convey all the senses at once.[31]

At some level synesthesia (or the transsensorial) could be viewed as fundamental to our understanding of the world. I have mentioned Gombrich's discussion of metaphor and substitution (in Chapter 2), but here the notion of correspondence, so important for Baudelaire and the symbolists, and Chion's conception of a metasensorial model, allows a challenge to the purist assumption that the arts as defined by sense are an a priori given. Instead, the situation can be reversed. Art then becomes an important factor in our categorization and conceptual experience of the different senses, so that division becomes a product of reflection through culture rather than a "naturally innocent," prior condition.

Subject matter is then only the material manifestation of a more fundamental reality that all arts share, and abstraction offers the opportunity to contact this more directly, since music's paradigmatic role is its immateriality, its simple concern with form. Similarly, we earlier considered time and space to be insufficient to define the different arts' essential characters. We now add to this the problems of conceiving of the arts as "naturally" addressed to unique senses within paradigms of autonomy, offering the equally logical proposition that the situation can be seen in reverse.

Let us return to Kupka's choice of subject for the painting under discussion. On one level this is music, or at least a musical form. Again I call on Kandinsky's writings to characterize this move to abstraction. In his essay "Content and Form" of 1910–11, he wrote, "This [new] kind of composition will be constructed upon the same basis which is already known to us in embryonic form, only which now will develop into the clarity and complexity of musical 'counterpoint.' "[32] The fugue is the contrapuntal form par excellence, its essential character being the weaving of melodic fragments into a harmonic whole. The minimum number of voices (melodies) a fugue can contain is two. These voices are in flight from each other (the French word for *fugue* means "flight"). A brief characterization would be as follows: the "exposition" contains the initial appearance of these voices. There then tends to follow a development section, based on motifs already heard, called an "episode," which usually produces modulations to other, related keys. At the conclusion there is often a "stretto," where the voices are squeezed together, allowing a return to the original key. To apply this literally to Kupka's painting would lead us to say that it seems to be a two-voiced fugue known as a "double fugue," and it seems to take one of the two most common forms: the two voices appear in harness from the beginning.[33] In this way the red and blue elements form the main thematic counterpoint, with the black background and white discs forming a still harmonic "pedal," perhaps best understood not as a literal translation but as a kind of pictorial fugal analogue.

One of Kupka's friends in 1911 was a noted interpreter of Bach fugues, Walter Morse Rummel. According to a number of sources, the performances he gave inspired Kupka to consider fugues in physical form.[34] The development of the movement of the red and blue ball, from the painting *Girl with a Ball,* and his more general interest in studies of light, color, and motion, found a logical summation in a musical subject (fig. 4.4). Even if it was the case that the title of fugue was arrived at after the fact (as he himself later claimed),[35] this does not detract from the appropriateness in his own mind of musical forms for the task of abstract composition. He said a year after *Amorpha* was exhibited, "I am still groping in the dark, but I believe I can find something between sight and hearing and can produce a fugue in colours as Bach has done in music."[36] He wished to eliminate

4.4 František Kupka, *Girl with a Ball,* 1908,
oil on canvas, 114 x 70 cm. Musée National
d'Art Moderne, Paris

subject matter and replace it with theme,[37] but this is only a minor semantic shift, for the subject-theme remains analogously linked to music, which has become the new subject matter. Even if we consider the word "Amorpha" in the title, this is still the case.

Although in this context "Amorpha" is an invented word,[38] it derives from the root Greek *amorphos,* meaning formless. Related to the original subject of a young girl, it is an appropriately feminine form of the noun *amorphe.* As we have already seen within the idealist tradition, music was paradigmatic precisely because it was conceived as immaterial but formally coherent; it had form but no material substance. Virginia Spate has argued that this word may also derive from theosophical sources, specifically the concept *arupa* (formless), which within theosophical orthodoxy is contrasted with *rupa* (having form).[39] Theosophists were not the only esoteric cult to place a high premium on music as a way of accessing this higher plane of existence. But as Scriabin's work shows, the particular interest of their orthodoxy was that, just as the spiritual realm could be "seen" by the initiated, so could music be "clearly visible and intelligible to those who have eyes to see."[40] Music was a visible art, albeit one invisible to all but the most sensitive souls.

Their view appears to be an emotive one, with music as a phenomenon of emotional ideas manifested as vibrations, which can be detected by the spiritually aware (a medium such as Kupka), not just via the ear but also the eye or mind's eye. In this way it signifies not only musical form without material but the higher consciousness engendered by this superior plane of existence. This theosophical notion is inspired by, but challenges, Darwin's evolutionary theory, for here spirit, rather than "man," is the endpoint, moving slowly from the material and physical to the immaterial and spiritual. Music has an important role, for its spiritual, immaterial nature connects us to this higher plane. For Scriabin, this went even further, for he ascribed to music the ability to help bring about this next "evolutionary" step.

The romantic desire for ut pictura musica needs to be seen as a complex network of affiliations using a range of unitary devices. Abstract artists and theorists dipped into this pool of relationships to service their needs, drawing further analogies from other contemporary sources in the effort to achieve a theoretical grounding for the development of their art, one that contradicted the conventions that had given art meaning and structure since the Renaissance.

Another source of historical justification for such a revolutionary move is located in Greek art and thought. Like Wagner and Nietzsche, Kupka and other Nazarene follower looked to the Greeks. He wrote, "It was in 1911, I created my own uniquely 'abstract' way of painting, Orphism, disregarding all other cultural systems except that of Greece."[41] Although the Platonic conception of music (and the music of the spheres) forms part of this, the other point of contact with Greece is manifested in the name of the movement, Orphism, the christening of which reportedly took place by Apollinaire (an appropriate name in this context!) under this very painting by Kupka.[42] (There is no evidence of this in Apollinaire's writings; it appears to have developed through an oral tradition based on the comments of other critics.)[43] The term *Orphism* is notable for, on one hand, its rather general application to the postcubist avant-garde in general and, on the other, its particular identification with Robert Delaunay in Apollinaire's definition and with Kupka in the criticism of other contemporary writers.[44]

The exact origin of the term is unclear. Gabrielle Buffet, Picabia's wife, claimed that she gave it to Apollinaire, and because she was a musician, this analogy may have been more immediately apparent to her. Orpheus was one of the most celebrated figures of Greek mythology, a musician of such power and sweetness that he could charm wild creatures and move inanimate objects through his song and playing upon the lyre.

There was evidence that an obscure mystical movement known as the Orphists, dating from about 600 B.C., claimed Orpheus as the founder and Dionysus as a central god. Orphism in this guise was important to Nietzsche's account of tragedy (see Chapter 2), especially the notion of "oneness," a primordial unification to be achieved through "mysteries." The Orphist creation myth begins with primeval Kronos (Time) and culminates in Dionysus. The sons of Gaea (Earth), the Titans, were jealous of Dionysus and murdered him by eating. They left his heart, however, from which a new Dionysus was born. Zeus extracted revenge on the Titans by striking them with a lightening bolt, and humanity emerged out of the soot of their bodies. In this way, humanity inherited both the Titans' criminal nature and an affinity with Dionysus, on whom the Titans had fed. Humanity thus stands somewhere between material earth (Gaea) and divine spirit and temporality (Kronos). According to M. S. Silk and J. P. Stern, Nietzsche conflated the original Dionysian myth with the sixth-century Orphic version in his account of tragedy as a vehicle of aesthetic reunification.[45] What is interesting about this mythic account of primeval origins and "oneness" for our discussion is the importance of Time (Kronos) as opposed to material (Gaea), and the association of music with divinity through the figures of Dionysus and Orpheus.

Although I do not claim an explicit connection between this Orphism and Apollinaire or Kupka's version, for an artist such as Kupka, "the problem of the one and the many," the depiction of time via musical analogy, and mystical notions of spiritual oneness, could well have filtered into his (and others') aesthetics through these ideas being refined, modified, and translated in the writings of Schopenhauer, Nietzsche, Blavatsky, and Steiner, all of whom he had read.

The name of the movement and the title of Kupka's painting (Amorpha/ Orphism) also have a close relationship. Apollinaire, however, never explicitly mentioned the relationship between music and painting in any of his published pronouncements, including the definition that appeared in his *Les peintres cubistes* (1913), nor indeed does he name Kupka.[46] But as Spate points out, it was never Apollinaire's practice to offer much in the way of explanation. Perhaps the mere association conjured by the name was enough, but more likely Apollinaire felt as did Kupka, who did not want musical associations to be used as an excuse to dismiss art as a mere "illustration" of music; music stood for more than itself, more than a sonoric and formal art. A letter from Kupka to André Warnod, written sometime after 18 March 1913, makes this clear. Kupka wrote that he was surprised to be linked to Orphism, because he was not clear what the term signified, though he feared it was the opposite of morphism (*uopon*, form).

He explained that his reservations sprang mainly from his wish not to be seen as tied to a specific dogma, especially one that appeared to "have issued from the mind of someone very ill-informed." "I have been obliged to admit to a certain illogicality in giving the title *Amorpha* to my two paintings at the last Salon d'Automne. It was out of place, even despite my intention to go beyond the need to represent a subject. In doing that I was more obliged to remain morphic than if I had been interpreting forms taken from nature."[47]

We can take it that Kupka was suspicious of having his work explained simply in terms of what he took to be, at this time, a rather nebulous concept. In addition, as Jeffrey Weiss has shown, by this time the word *amorpha* had acquired a specific pejorative meaning. A number of critics used it to express distaste for art that derived from the distortion of natural forms, having probably taken the term from this very painting by Kupka.[48] Nevertheless, Kupka clearly wanted to "go beyond the need to represent a subject," and the association of music as a form without an object (Amorpha) served this purpose. The musical title "Orphism" therefore seemed to many critics an appropriate noun to apply to this stage of his work.

For Apollinaire it was important to move from the possibility of a "musicalist" art (one that communicated meaning without literary subject matter) to an exploration of pictorial concerns, formal concerns particular to painting. In his review of the Salon d'Automne of 1913 he argues that this new painting may have the same relationship to traditional mimetic painting as music has to literature, but (and here he follows Lessing) painting is a simultaneous experience whereas music is a successive one.[49] Indeed, Apollinaire echoes Leonardo in the *Paragone* when he says that it is this simultaneity that places the visual arts above the auditory arts in the representation of the essence of life—an idea that is also in debt to the French philosopher Henri Bergson's concept of élan vital.[50]

Piano Keys—Lake, painted in 1909, shares a number of these concerns.

Piano Keys—Lake

Kandinsky's words aptly describe this work, painted in 1909:

> Colour is the keyboard. The eye is the hammer. The soul is the piano, with its many strings.
>
> The artist is the hand that purposefully sets the soul vibrating by means of this or that key.[51]

Piano Keys—Lake forms an important stage in Kupka's development toward abstract painting (fig. 4.5).[52] Unlike *Amorpha,* this work is concerned not with circular and arabesque patterns as a means of articulating movement but with vertical planes. Both are formal investigations of the depiction of movement carried

4.5 František Kupka, *Piano Keys—Lake,* 1909, oil on canvas, 79 x 72 cm. Narodni Galerie, Prague

out simultaneously. This concern with movement, and Kupka's need to find an appropriate mechanism to depict it, should be borne in mind in relation to Apollinaire's points about simultaneity.

The lake appears occasionally in Kupka's earlier work, where it carries considerable symbolic baggage. *The Beginning of Life* (1900), for example, is a curious painting of lotus flowers floating on the surface of a lake (at dawn?) and a hovering fetus in a circle (the circle forms an important element in *Amorpha*);

4.6 František Kupka, *The Other Side,* 1895, oil on
canvas, 46 x 38 cm. Narodni Galerie, Prague

together these images form a rather clumsy combination of Tantric Buddhist and
theosophical ideas in an attempt to symbolize creation.[53] *Méditation* (1899) uses
a lake as a surface for the reflection of aspirations through the image of a mountain, which could be understood in this context, with the kneeling, naked figure
of Kupka, as a symbol of physical transcendence. As Spate has shown, Kupka's
earliest painting on this subject may be *The Other Side* (*L'autre rive*), said to
have been executed in 1895 (fig. 4.6). Although this is a relatively straightforward
study of a lakeshore with trees in the background (somewhat reminiscent of Gustav Klimt's work), its title and its still, empty mood suggest a symbolic element—
perhaps the surface of the reflecting water conceals hidden depths, a not unusual
symbolist subject.[54] Even in *La baigneuse* (Paris) of 1906–7, mentioned earlier in
relation to *Amorpha,* the water's surface acts to dissolve the figure and figurative
element. Of such reflections, Kupka wrote in 1912, "What adorable tricks on the
absolute limits of things."[55]

Piano Keys—Lake shares with other works produced at this time a double title.
Kupka worked on *Planes by Colors—Large Nude* on and off between 1904 and
1910, starting with academic pastel drawings. The titles of the two works indicate
the combination of more abstracted elements with naturalistic sections. In *Piano
Keys—Lake,* naturalism is more disrupted by the introduction of the abstracted

4.7 František Kupka, *Nocturne,* 1911, oil on canvas, 66 x 66 cm. Museum of Modern Art Ludwig Foundation, Vienna

planes, whereas in *Planes by Colors—Large Nude,* the contours of the figure are maintained beneath the screen of colored slabs. This subject found a more radical treatment in the later series of works entitled *Woman Picking Flowers* (1910–11) and *Planes by Color* (1911–12), in which the title stands alone, although the figure is still discernible. Yet these works, though they employ planes of color, do not concern themselves with movement in the manner of *Piano Keys—Lake* and its nonfigurative offspring, such as *Nocturne* (1911, fig 4.7).[56]

At the bottom of the picture Kupka has painted a right hand playing a chord of A major (see fig. 4.5). This chord, while not fundamental in the way that C major could be, is alphabetically primary as "alpha." The effect of this chord appears to reverberate from the keyboard up into the reflections in the water to disrupt the naturalism of the boat and lakeshore, much as a pebble fractures a reflection on water's surface. Spate relates this point to Leonardo, arguing that the relationship between the musical and visual elements can be understood as a form of simultaneism, different mental states corresponding in a single moment, a notion taken up in the fugue of *Amorpha.* This is a reasonable assumption, but we should also note that the movement the eye is obliged to take from foreground to background (bottom to top) is a real temporal event. The use of music, a resonant chord, conflates succession with simultaneity in the viewer's imagination. This links with Bergson's ideas, particularly his argument that we tend to spatialize time intellectually:[57]

Beset by the idea of space we introduce it unwittingly into our feeling of pure succession; we set our states of consciousness side by side in such a way as to perceive
them simultaneously, no longer one in another . . . the succession thus [taking] the
form of a continuous line or chain, the parts of which touch without penetrating one
another. We introduce order . . . by distinguishing [the parts] and then comparing
the places they occupy. . . . [In this way succession] is converted into simultaneity
and is projected into space. . . . We here put our finger on the mistake of those who
regard pure duration as something similar to space. But how can they fail to notice
that, in order to perceive a line as a line, it is necessary to take up a position outside
it, to take account of the void which surrounds it, and consequently to think a space
of three dimensions? If our conscious point A does not yet possess the idea of space
[then] the succession of states through which it passes cannot assume for it the form
of a line; *but its sensations will add themselves dynamically to one another and will
organise themselves, like the successive notes of a tune.* . . . In a word, pure duration
might well be nothing but a succession of qualitative changes, which melt into and
permeate one another, without precise outlines, without the tendency to externalise
themselves in relation to one another, without any affiliation with number: it would
be pure heterogeneity.[58]

This understanding of space has ramifications for Kupka's work, best illustrated
through consideration of another painting he produced around 1912–13.

Solo of a Brown Stroke was first exhibited at the Salon des Indépendants in
Paris in 1913 (fig. 4.8).[59] In his writings of the time Kupka differentiates between
line (*la ligne*) and stroke (*le trait*), arguing that a line acts to divide space, whereas
a stroke forms an ideogram. The painting consists of an art nouveauesque stroke
suspended between two sets of overlapping, curved-sided triangles on the far
right and left of the canvas. On a small study drawing he wrote, "Solo of a brown
sinuous [line], orchestration of spots placed with no motivation, solely to send
off and receive the line."[60] In these terms Kupka has developed in a literal way a
graphic equivalent to melodic and harmonic musical elements that "assume the
form of a line like the successive notes of a tune." This painting fulfills Bergson's
point that "to perceive a line as a line, it is necessary to take up a position outside
it, to take account of the void which surrounds it." It refers to musical forms in
order to provide (or amplify) a temporal structure.

Bergson maintained (as Lessing had), however, that space and time were polarized concepts, although, as Mark Antliff has shown, Bergson allows for the possibility that animals only experience space as nonhomogeneous perceptually, not
conceptually.[61] Real duration was an intuitive inner experience, and therefore time
could be represented only as something that has happened, not something that
is currently taking place (it becomes a record of movement). Nevertheless, there
was an important role for memory. It played a central part in the artistic use of the

4.8 František Kupka, *Solo of a Brown Stroke,* 1912—13, oil on cardboard, 70 x 115 cm. Narodni Galerie, Prague

concept of simultaneity; accumulated experiences became the basis for conceptual knowledge of objects in a constant state of change. "The object [the painting] remains the same . . . ; nevertheless the vision I now have differs from that which I have just had. . . . The truth is that we change without ceasing."[62] George Hamilton sees this in Cézanne, and Kahnweiler saw it in cubism.[63] Kupka also regarded time as central to modernity, but his use of music as analogy and structural reference brings into play a special set of temporal considerations. It allows him to recover felt experience, and his idealist conception of music provides an analogue for temporal spatial perception. In other words, music has direct contact with our raw felt experience of the world, especially in its transcendence over words or concepts. As Antliff has shown, this is also evident in Bergson's theory, in that music can penetrate to the "rhythms of life" and get below the surface to "grasp something that has nothing in common with language."[64]

Time and space are always elements in art; temporal imagination creates narrative contexts in the process of "reading" an image. Although it is possible to "take in at a glance" the overall structure of a painting, its organization in space requires viewers to move their eye across and over its elements.[65] The making of the work also takes place in time, and even though this temporal element can rarely be "read off" from the final image, works such as *Solo* offer the opportunity or illusion that this trace, or "becoming," to use Bergson's term, can be followed. Perhaps the clearest example of this is seen in the mature method and works of the abstract expressionist artist Jackson Pollock, whose painting is a record of such a mark-making process. The philosopher John Dewey makes the same point in the context of a discussion of architecture. The beholder or viewer, he writes, "must create his own experience and his creation must include relations comparable to those which the original producer underwent." He goes on: "They are not the same in any literal sense. But with the perceiver, as with the artists, there must be an ordering of the elements of the whole that is . . . the same as the process of organisation the creator of the work consciously experienced. Without the act of recreation the object is not perceived as a work of art." [66]

In *Piano Keys—Lake,* Kupka conflates the time it takes to "read" the image with the notion of musical time. A number of scholars have shown that our understanding of time underwent radical reassessment in the early twentieth century, in part as a result of Albert Einstein's work. [67] In short, there was a shift from the polarized Euclidean space and time of Lessing to a unified spatial-temporal field. For Lessing, space was a single unitary and infinite container, where art was restricted to the picturing of an instant, a tableau, founded on the mathematics of perspective. Here both space and time are a priori. But Einstein's thinking in the early part of the century suggested the relativistic nature of space and time and the interdependence of these concepts. Time became the fourth dimension of space. This is not the place to pursue this complex phenomenon in detail, but a number of points are worth comment.

Kupka was very much the product of the late nineteenth century, its philosophy, theology, and artistic conventions. But he was also interested in science and in developing an appropriate aesthetic for the experiences of modernity. The painting *Piano Keys—Lake* is a useful example of the tension that existed for a sensitive artist in resolving changes in worldview, a tension expressed by Baudelaire in his definition of modernity as "the ephemeral, the fugitive, the contingent, the half of art whose other half is the eternal and the immutable." [68]

The touch of the hand on the piano keys and the consequent resonance of the chord integrates kinesthetic and sonoric sensations with visual perceptions; [69] indeed, the concept of a chord itself signifies a sounding together, a synthesis, both in these terms and in the more prosaic mixing of abstract and figurative elements. Because the viewer is placed as the pianist, the viewer's perceptions are also positioned as those of the painter.

The inverse occurs in the Italian futurist painter and musician Luigi Russolo's slightly later painting *Music* (1911), in which the keyboard is reversed, showing a performer who imagines, evokes, or performs a more literal translation of music. Perhaps the faces shown in Russolo's painting are those of the audience members, who are swept up in the centrifuge of the musical effect. [70] In this case the painting is a mirror inversion of Kupka's. Russolo places the viewers in the background, the pianist in the midground, and the keyboard in the foreground, whereas Kupka places both the viewers and keyboard in the foreground, and the lake and boat in the mid- and background. Kupka also allows the dissolving of the keyboard to intrude slightly forward of the hand playing the chord, right to the edge of the picture plane, perhaps to suggest that the abstracting effect of the sound on the image originates from the position of the viewer (roughly in line with the position of the viewer's eye level). There is also another interesting resonance with the subject of this painting in a small early work by Marcel Duchamp. *Flirt* (1907) shows Duchamp's awareness of the equation, expressed in Kupka's painting, of the impression, the title, and musicality. *Flirt* depicts a woman seated at a piano with a man at her side. At the bottom of the image is the following inscription: "Flirtation / She—Would you like me to play "On the Blue Waters"? You'll see how well this piano renders the impression suggested by the title. He (witty)—There is nothing strange about that, it's a grand piano." As Arthur Schwarz points out, the French for grand piano, *piano à queue,* puns on *piano aqueux,* which means watery piano. Duchamp has provided a witty comment on Kupka's choice of subject, the boat and water being a standard subject of impressionist painters; the musical element recalls the American painter James Abbott McNeill Whistler's titles for similar subjects.[71]

The notion of tactility (in Kupka's painting the touch of the pianist's hand) and the organization of bodily sensations in general, affected cubist theory through the filter of mathematician Henri Poincaré, as Linda Henderson has shown.[72] Gleizes and Metzinger, in *Du cubisme,* follow Poincaré in the contrast they make between geometric and sensory space, the former associated with Euclidean geometry, the latter with time as the fourth dimension. In this way space becomes relative to sensory faculties. Our knowledge of space is the result of the experience of touch, the tension of muscles, and our physical disposition. In a similar way, Bergson separated intellectual time from psychological time or its felt experience.

The concept of musical time is different from clock time. The psychological effect of tempo, a deliberate lack of meter or recognizable beat, repetition, isorhythms, and other techniques in a piece of music have the effect of providing a prolonged or shortened experience of duration. A composer can compress time or stretch it out, as Schoenberg remarked in relation to his psychological music drama *Erwartung* (composed in the same year as Kupka's *Piano Keys—Lake,* 1909): "The aim is to represent in *slow motion* everything that occurs during a single second of maximum spiritual excitement, stretching it out to half an hour." Adorno put it more laconically, writing, "[*Erwartung*] develops the eternity of the second in four hundred bars."[73]

Kupka's reference to music and his depiction of space are involved in a complex interaction with psychological and felt experience and spiritual aspirations. Music is the vehicle for the extension of painting and the prime metaphor for its goal.

I have mentioned the use of titles to point viewers in the intended direction, often from explicit subject to implicit content. It is also worth noting that the use of musical titles, in such works as these by Kupka, signals a more general reaction, fostered within the aesthetics of romanticism and symbolism, leading away from the positivistic, rationalist description toward suggestion and allegory. Such titles also reemerge as a dominant paradigm within the formalism of painting in the 1950s and 1960s, under the auspices of Greenberg's critical project, often in terms of the more neutral concept of "composition," although here the history of musical association is still part of the resonance of such entitling.[74]

For Kupka it was important to create images, pictorial forms, that suggested a new internal reality for those who took the time to experience them. The process of evolving forms was slow and complex, and in the dialogue set up between him and them he came to feel that their otherness came closer to the realm of "super-consciousness" that music could touch. As Spate has pointed out, he came to refer to his purest works as "silent." Silence need not be the opposite of music. Music is both sound and silence. Within idealism music is immaterial, suggestive rather than declarative, in contact with higher reality, an agent of emotive movement. For Kupka, during the time he was associated with Orphism, music stands at the very least as an analogous bridge from matter to spirit, from earthly sound to the unheard (silent) music of the spheres. Silence is for Nietzsche, too, the highest experience of humans, a realization of the perfect oneness and existence:

> Oh happiness! Oh happiness! Would you sing, O my soul? You lie in the grass. But this is the secret, solemn hour when no shepherd plays his flute.
>
> Take care! Hot noontide sleep upon the fields. Do not sing! Soft! The world is perfect.[75]

As we shall see in the last chapter, this silence finds its apogee in John Cage, for as the early Nietzsche spoke for Wagner, so perhaps the later Nietzsche spoke (silently) for Cage.

PAUL KLEE

The wonderfully diverse and prolific work of the Swiss artist Paul Klee (1879—1940), both graphic and written, is more generally known than that of Kupka. This is also true of his long and committed relationship to music. Like Kupka, but in contrast to Lessing, Klee was interested in the temporal character of plastic expression, as he wrote in 1920:

All becoming is based on movement. In Lessing's *Laocoon,* on which we wasted a certain amount of intellectual effort in our younger days, a good deal of fuss is made about the difference between temporal and spatial art. But on closer scrutiny the fuss turns out to be mere learned foolishness. For space itself is a temporal concept.

When a point turns into movement and line—that takes time.[76]

And in his *Diaries* he had noted earlier, in May 1905, "More and more parallels between music and graphic art force themselves upon my consciousness. Yet no analysis is successful. Certainly both arts are temporal; this could be proved easily."[77] These two quotations conjoin the major productive forces of Klee's aesthetic—music and nature. Temporality is important because it is common to all creativity, that of nature and of art (music). "All becoming is based on movement" reminds us again of Bergson: "Matter and mind, reality has appeared to us as a perpetual becoming."[78]

Klee addresses these issues explicitly in the lecture on modern art he delivered at the opening of an exhibition that included his work at the museum in Jena in 1924. In describing the nature of modern artists' approach to their work, he uses the simile of the tree: the root gathers from the source, which is transformed in the trunk to find fulfillment in the branches (the crown). Throughout this lecture Klee is at pains to point out that understanding and analysis (the purpose of his address) are at odds with the simultaneity of the product of analysis, in this case nature and the visual art work.

> It is not easy to arrive at a conception of a whole which is constructed from parts belonging to different dimensions. And not only nature, but also art, her transformed image, is such a whole . . . .
>
> This is due to the consecutive nature of the only methods available to us for conveying a clear three-dimensional concept of an image in space, and results from deficiencies of a temporal nature in the spoken word.
>
> For with such a medium of expression, we lack the means of discussing in its constituent parts, an image which possesses simultaneously a number of dimensions.

Language is temporal, or more to the point, it is monophonic, it is incapable of conveying "simultaneously a number of dimensions." Although music is also temporal, its more usual state is one of polyphony. Thus music and visual art share the ability to "sound at once": "What the so-called spatial arts have long succeeded in expressing, what even the time-bound art of music has gloriously achieved in the harmonies of polyphony, this phenomenon of many simultaneous dimensions which helps drama to its climax, does not, unfortunately, occur in the world of verbal didactic expression."[79] We shall return to these points, but a further observation is needed first. In addition to polyphony, music and visual art share a concern with rhythm as an element of structure. For Klee, it is these more aesthetic devices that language surrenders in its development of conceptualization. Art (all arts) share such aesthetic concerns, and in the realm of temporality the visual arts could learn a great deal from music.

The notion of simultaneity in reference to Kupka and Bergson has been mentioned, as has Klee's notion of becoming, which is likewise linked to Bergson. It is also likely that Klee was introduced to simultaneity through his interest in the work of another member of Apollinaire's Orphists, Robert Delaunay. But in Klee's case, this concept was related to his already sophisticated understanding of music's explicit polyphonic make-up.

The desire to incorporate notions of simultaneity stems from the perception of modernity as experienced in urban life. It is essentially concerned with interrelationships, not unitary or pure singular experience. It is perhaps a little ironic that Greenberg sees modernism as an expression of modernity addressed to purity, and an attitude of static, detached contemplation. For this is opposite to the experience of many urban dwellers during the "birth of the modern": the flux and flow, the more than purely optical, the embodied and incoherent perception of modern life, the melting of all that was solid. The roots of this view were undoubtedly romantic, but it was certainly given new life by the "new age."[80]

Bergson's remarkable fame and influence on artists (especially at Puteaux) during the early years of the twentieth century are due in large part to the prism through which his philosophy provided a focus, making simultaneous the various strands of modern experience. His understanding of the real as a "fluid continuity," and the difficulty of accurately conveying the nature of this consciousness through the spatialized time of the text, which fixes and kills it, presents a major difficulty for artists working in different media. Placing images side by side, or one on top of another, does not produce simultaneity, only what Bergson regarded as fragmentation, which destroys the unity of space and time.

Delaunay moved on from this more cinematic procedure, which he and others had developed out of cubism and their reading of futurist theory between 1910 and mid-1912, and adopted a more abstract depiction, one that we have seen in Kupka and that we can see in Delaunay's *Fenêtres* series of paintings (1912). Delaunay went on to characterize a more subtle conception of Bergsonian ideas in "La lumière," a text he asked Klee to translate for *Der Sturm* when Klee was visiting Paris in April 1912.[81] In this text and in another related essay ("Réalité, Peinture pure"), Delaunay ironically characterizes the perception of sound (and music) as essentially successive.[82] He argues that only painting can communicate simultaneously, through the use of color and light. This is ironic because, as we have seen, it was largely the example of music that encouraged the development of abstract (what Delaunay calls "pure") painting. Anyone with a good understanding of music, however, or anyone who takes time to reflect on their experience of it, will recognize that although music may consist of temporally successive events, harmony is simultaneous, and polyphony is perceived through memory simultaneously with present events. The understanding of musical structures is possible only because we hear in relation to past events with expectations about future ones. Indeed, this is true of all temporal structures (including speech). The perception of simultaneity requires memory and time to reflect, whether it is manifested in sight or sound.

Klee recognized this. He noted in his diary in July 1917:

> Movement is so fleeting. It has to penetrate into our soul. The formal has to fuse with the *Weltanschauung*.
>
> Simple motion strikes us as banal. The time element must be eliminated. Yesterday and tomorrow as simultaneous. In music, polyphony helped to some extent to satisfy this need . . . . If, in music, the time element could be overcome by retrograde motion that would penetrate consciousness, then a renaissance might still be thinkable.
>
> . . . Polyphonic painting is superior to music in that, here, the time element becomes a spatial element. The notion of simultaneity stands out even more richly. To illustrate the retrograde motion which I am thinking up for music, I remember the mirror image in the window of the moving trolley. Delaunay strove to shift the accent in art onto the time element, after the fashion of a fugue, by choosing formats that could not be encompassed in one glance.[83]

What Klee understood was that whereas in music the conception of the musician dictates the temporal unfolding of the structural elements, within the visual realm the roving eye can take things in at its own pace, and that this is only partly under the control of the artist. This means that visual simultaneity is potentially variable; it is possible to move both "forward" and "backward" (retrograde motion) across the surface of the image. Polyphony allows in music the simultaneous presentation of both melodic and harmonic elements; the latter becomes a consequence of the former. Individual themes blend into the overall formal structure of the piece. It was one thing to decide that these ideas needed to be carried into the practice of his painting; it was much more difficult, however, to actually incorporate them.

Rhythm

It is a commonplace assumption that the concept of rhythm can be applied only metaphorically to the visual arts; for example, in his large study of the classification of the arts, Thomas Munro wrote, "It is confusing to speak of rhythm as something visible in a motionless painting or statue, as is often done in textbooks of 'art principles.' . . . Rhythm occurs here, then, as a *suggested* component in the visual form."[84] If we consider the derivation and original uses of the concept, however, we arrive at a more subtle evaluation.

J. J. Pollitt's seminal study of the critical terminology of ancient Greek criticism, *The Ancient View of Greek Art,* devotes one section to the interpretation of *rhythmos.* Following scholar Eugen Petersen's important essay of 1917, Pollitt supports the derivation of the concept from the root *ern,* meaning "draw," rather than *reo,* meaning "flow," which was its commonly accepted derivation in the eighteenth and nineteenth centuries. Petersen argued that words joined with the suffix *-thmos* appear originally to have signified an active "doing" rather than a more passive "happening"; thus he suggests that *rhythmos* might originally have meant not "a flowing" but rather "a drawing." As Pollitt points out, there is a close connection in many languages between *draw,* meaning a physical action, of traction, and the word *drawing* in a pictorial sense. Thus *rhythmos* meant "drawing" and conveyed the same double meaning in Greek as *draw* and *drawing* do in English. Pollitt believes that this understanding is key to a correct understanding of how ancient Greeks used the concept. The philosopher Arthur Danto has also pondered this issue: "Since it is unlikely that the action of drawing a picture is so described because the draftsman pulls the pencil across the paper . . . the term must refer to something that takes place *between* the artist and the subject, rather than merely on the surface of an inscribed sheet . . . what one might properly call 'drawing power' (or 'attraction'). . . . But there is a darker ideal carried by the etymology of the term, which means 'draw forth' . . . , as if through an act of metaphysical extraction, the [subject] were drawn forth or 'captured by' the paper."[85] And as Klee often made clear, for him drawing was always in part a magical process; the setting of a point in motion to produce a line (a drawing) is the genesis of form.

The move of the meaning of *rhythmos* from something like "form" or "shape" or "pattern" to "repetition" as part of its more familiar modern meaning is an interesting one, and one that resonates with Klee's usage. Petersen argues that *rhythmoi* was originally used to refer to the "positions" of the body in the course of a dance, and that the natural repetition of these positions marked distinct intervals in the music. (This further explains, Pollitt says, the use of such terms as "foot" (*pous*) and "step" (*basis*), "lifting, up-step" (*arsis*), and "placing, downbeat" (*thesis*) as basic elements in music and its poetry (*mousike*)). Pollitt concludes with one further idea based on Petersen's "interesting and compelling" suggestion: "Patterns of composition in Greek sculpture, particularly Early Classical sculpture, were understood as being like [*hremiai*] or 'rests' which the musical theoretician Aristoxenus describes in all movement and sound but particularly in dancing and music. In motion [*hremiai*] were points at which fleeting movements came to a temporary halt, thus enabling a viewer to fasten his vision on a particular position that characterized the movement as a whole."[86]

In short, the concept of rhythm appears to have originally related to drawing and, through usage in relation to dance and music, applied to the "rests" that signify stages of repetition. Such a nuanced account becomes usefully applicable to Klee's investigations of rhythm during his years at the Bauhaus. It allows us to perceive his ideas as more than mere simplistic borrowings from the technical vocabulary of music, although I make no claim that he was conscious of this original meaning.[87] The most important point to emerge from Klee's interest in rhythm is his reclamation of this original meaning from the assumption of its metaphorical application. In other words, rhythm's apparently inappropriate migration from spatial to temporal to spatial art forms, from literal to metaphorical mode and back again, becomes emblematic of the fluid nature of distinctions between art and music in general. Such unstable terms as rhythm, within the lexicon of critical discourses of art, demonstrate relative, not absolute boundaries. They act against, for example, the modernist position of media that are formally distinct—uncontaminated by neighboring art forms. Klee's reinvention of the project of painting in his years at the Bauhaus drew heavily on music theory. In so doing he muddies the picture of art as solely concerned with its own resources.

An example of linear rhythmic development can be seen in Klee's visual experiment with another musical notational device. In music, rhythmic development most often takes place against a background of regular beats. These beats, when arranged into duple or triple patterns, provide points of stress, which result in a meter, most conventionally on the first of each pair of beats [2], or the first and then third beat [4], both of which produce a duple pattern: $\_ - \_ -$, or on the first of every three beats, producing a triple pattern: $\_ - - \_ - -$. Other combinations are derived from either of these two (for example, a five-beat pattern is a combination of duple and triple $\_ - \_ - -$, and so on).

During a performance one of the conductor's tasks is to indicate the meter by visual hand (or baton) movements, where the movement of the hand downward (the downbeat, recalling Pollitt) designates the stressed beat, so that musicians are provided with visual cues to their position within a bar. Klee adopted this custom and in his lecture notes and subsequent works produced a series of images that develop these gestures into graphic signs, which plastically use and elaborate an existing visual musical convention. This can be traced in the series of works of boats and ships, for example, *Departure of the Ships* (1927.140, Berlin), *Four Sail Boats* (1927, fig. 4.9), and *Bustling Harbor* (1927, Bern). *Bustling Harbor* also contains another musical sign that often found its way into Klee's work, the fermata ($\frown$), which designates a pause, a point of rest, the suspension of movement.

4.9 Paul Klee, *Four Sail Boats*, 1927 [1927.142 (e2)], oil on canvas, 18.7 x 58.4 cm. Owner unknown. © DACS 2000

This recalls the point made earlier about the derivation of the concept rhythm: "In motion [*hremiai*] were points at which fleeting movements came to a temporary halt, thus enabling a viewer to fasten his vision on a particular position that characterized the movement as a whole."

A slightly later work, the witty *(Little) Fool in a Trance* of 1929, also extends this use of rhythmical line. This painting takes the viewer's eye for a walk over the surface of the canvas, tying it into a web made from a single circumscribing line that at one point (right leg) describes a partial treble clef. This twisting and turning line enraptures the viewer's eye, echoing the mesmeric trance of the subject, the little fool. A point of rest is fully achieved for the viewer's eye only with, or in, the eye of the fool, which this time recalls the pause sign of music, a literal suspension. As Klee wrote in *Creative Credo*, "There are paths laid out in an art work for the eye to follow as it scans the ground. . . . The image is created from movement, is itself fixed movement and is recorded in movement (eye muscle)."[88]

Klee's works *Rhythmic Landscape with Trees* and *Rose Garden* (fig. 4.10), both produced in the same year as his Jena lecture, 1920, and part of a series of related works, show an interest in the blending of graphic notational conventions with abstracted figural elements.[89] These works share a compositional arrangement of trees and roses as a kind of rhythmic notation, articulated within a network of parallel lines that can be understood as staves. This is not a naive transliteration, since the use of an existing graphic sign system (musical notation), modified into a semiabstract context, where the tree simile, together with the use of parallel lines, locks all the pictorial elements together to provide a rhythmically articulated and integrated visual surface.

Most of these graphic images by Klee arrange their elements successively, but they also contain them within an overall composition, enabling apprehension at a glance (and, therefore, simultaneity). This allows the overall rhythmic arrange-

4.10 Paul Klee, *Rose Garden,* 1920, oil on cardboard, 50 x 43 cm.
Reproduced by permission of the Städtische Galerie im Lenbach-
haus, Munich. © DACS 2000

ment of elements to be seen as at rest, outside the temporal flux, producing works
whose relationship to the concept of rhythm is closer to its original use. Only
when rhythm joins with color, however, does Klee begin to evolve a more integrated polyphonic conception.

Like most artists in a postfauvist environment, Klee believed that color could
become a vehicle of emotive communication independent from mimetic concerns. During his years at the Bauhaus, one of his prime pedagogical interests
was the development of structural formats that could give meaning to independent color expression. One of the lessons Klee had learned from Delaunay was
the importance of simultaneous color contrasts, harmonious and dissonant colors
(such as red and green), and the use of transparency as an element of color control. As Delaunay wrote to Kandinsky in 1912, to explain his color theories, "The
laws I discovered . . . are based on researches into the transparency of colour,
that can be compared with musical tones. This has obliged me to discover the
movement of colours."[90]

Klee's thinking and experimentation progressed slowly, via a wide range of sources. As I said at the outset of this chapter, I do not intend to map all of Klee's massive output, nor even to cover all the points of contact between his visual and written work and music. It will suffice to pick out indicative case-studies. One result of Klee's interest in these ideas about color can be seen in another series of works, one of which forms an interesting contrast to Kupka's large "fugue" painting.

Fugue in Red

In 1921 and 1922, Klee pursued an interest in what he called "fugal" paintings. They have in common a set of compositional elements: a neutral background against which overlapping abstract shapes, diminishing in size as they progress, are placed in progressive layers of tonal saturation through glazing (laid washes of semiopaque color). *Fugue in Red* (1921) demands to be read top to bottom, left to right, as one would read musical notation or text (fig. 4.11).[91] Unlike Kupka's painting, Klee arranges the elements successively, forming parallel but not inter-penetrating themes. Simple fugal devices can be detected in the basic elements of rectangle, triangle, circle, lozenge (jug), and rhomboid (leaf) and their dispo-sition. The pattern in the top left, for example, is repeated in the bottom right sec-tion, but in an inverted form. The square forms are rotated to form rhombuses and other shapes. The temporal element is aided by the overall format, which, as we have remarked, leads the eye to read the unfolding forms in the manner of musical notation. As Klee remarked about Delaunay's choice of formats in his *Fenêtre* paintings, "Delaunay strove to shift the accent in art onto the time element, after the fashion of a fugue, by choosing formats that could not be encompassed in one glance."[92] Such horizontal arrangements encourage the viewer to scan across the image, building relationships among elements as they go. *Fugue in Red* has the same black background as Kupka's painting (acting as a pedal point?), but a less dynamic disposition of elements within the pictorial space. Klee has kept his forms within a shallow space but not, as yet, within a stable structure. Other works in this series, particularly those with subjects derived more directly from nature, such as *Growth of Plants* and the related *Growth of Nocturnal Plants* of the following year (1922), appear more comfortable with fictive pictorial depth. There is an implied movement of the element from bottom to top, out of the dark into the light. The arrangement suits the subject matter, implying the background as dark soil, out and up from which the plants evolve or grow.

With developments that took place a few years later, Klee was able to construct works that more logically contained his temporal and colorist concerns.

The organization of the picture plane, so as to allow development of structural rhythm, was facilitated by the introduction of a grid. The chessboard pattern, as

4.11 Paul Klee, *Fugue in Red*, 1921, watercolor on paper, 24.4 x 31.5 cm. Private collection, Switzerland, inv. no. 718, ref. no. 2660. © DACS 2000

he explained it in the *Pedagogical Sketchbook,* produces movement in two directions, left to right and vice versa, and up and down and vice versa, but this movement had to move beyond black and white alternations into the realm of color, as in the later example *Rhythmical* of 1930, which articulates the grid into triple divisions, through black, gray, and white.[93] Such arrangements articulate beat and meter and phrasing by using *agogic* and *rubato* techniques. These operate to modify the demands of regularity without destroying it, opposing the straightforward mechanism of a regular grid but without developing into true rhythm. It is with a temporal conception of color relationships that Klee produces his most original contribution to color theory.

The Canon of Color Totality Klee was particularly interested in the movement inherent in spectral color interaction, the infinite gradations of tonality that exist across the visual spectrum. Rather than conceiving of this as an abstracted series of fixed and immobile points, he wanted to find a way of representing the continuous fluid movement across tonal values. The solution to this was what he called "The canon of color totality" (fig. 4.12). This is a three-dimensional structure conceived around the two poles of black and white, with a midpoint of gray. The three primaries stand in a dynamic relationship to one another, so that at the point

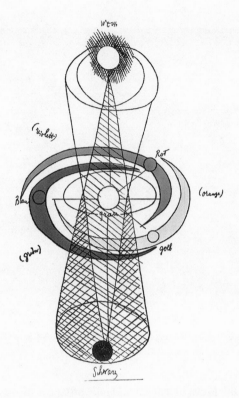

4.12 Paul Klee, *Canon of Color Totality,*
c. 1921. Kunstmuseum, Bern. © DACS 2000

of their nomenclature (red, yellow, blue) they are "louder" (at their loudest) than the secondaries (orange, green, violet), which are formed when the "voices" of the primaries are equally pitched, at a midway point. In other words, as one moves from the primary "red" toward the primary "blue," so the red voice experiences a "decrescendo" and the blue voice experiences a "crescendo" to the midpoint of violet; all other gradations exist as dynamic variants between these points. Tonal saturation occurs as a result of movement toward, or away from, one of the two poles of black or white.

Conceiving color relationships in these terms allowed Klee to quantify and rationalize color in dynamic terms, which in turn allowed him to apply color to the dynamic rhythmical structures of his investigations into form. Objective truth is not the issue. Such an approach was devised for pedagogical reasons, as a practical solution to the disposition of line and color in a nonmimetic role. Like many composers of the early twentieth century, such as Schoenberg, Scriabin, and Hauer, Klee discovered a way of systematizing the formal elements of his art. This allowed him to develop complex structures that exhibit logical internal relationships, in opposition to the systems that had evolved within artistic conventions of figurative depiction. Klee wanted visual art to be more than purely subjective or personal; he wanted to develop or discover rules that produced logical compositions. Atonality in music makes compositional decisions that rest solely on individual choice, unencumbered by diatonic, hierarchical relationships. In order to develop foundational rules and generate larger logical structures, dodecaphonic methods were invented to systematize atonality effectively. Klee strove to do something similar for painting.

Magic Square Pictures

The device of a grid, which locks the disposition of color into the picture plane, allowed Klee to order his interest in color relationships. There is a hint of this procedure in the use of stavelike elements in the paintings of 1920 discussed above. In *Pedagogical Sketchbook,* Klee's discussion of divisional articulation starts with the observation of primitive structural rhythm based on the repetition of the same units, left to right or top to bottom. The top-to-bottom repetition produces the stavelike pattern, and the combination of both produces a grid, with motion in both horizontal and vertical directions.[94] If we see the grid in these terms, rather than as a paradoxical "announcement" of "modern art's will to silence," as Rosalind Krauss has put it, its voice (announces) sound through its reference to music: as an extended stave for the suspension of signs.[95]

Compared to the work of a number of other artists, such as Mondrian, who employed a similar grid device, Klee's grid paintings, dubbed by Will Grohmann "magic squares," are almost always more organic, less strictly regulated.[96] His squares are rarely square, his lines seldom straight. Their wobble induces a sense of movement, bouncing the eye from one square to another, relating it to agogic accent and rubato in music. This arrangement of the picture plane could be used to combine his interest in structural rhythm and color.

It is important to bear in mind that Klee regarded the strict grid as a conceptual and pedagogic model rather than a formal model to be rigorously imposed in the process of visual composition. Through these magic square paintings Klee explored color and tonal permutations, outstanding examples of which are *Alter Klang* (1927) and *Blossoming* (1934).[97] In *New Harmony* of 1936, Klee devised an arrangement of dissonant color relationships (fig. 4.13). Their dissonance derives from their predominantly green and red-yellow mixes, which are noncomplementary colors from opposite sides of the color circle. Further, the painting can be seen to have been composed by a series of transpositions, inversions, and retrograde inversions. As Andrew Kagan has pointed out, there is bilateral inverted symmetry; that is, the right half is an inverted mirror image of the left half. But the

4.13 Paul Klee, *New Harmony,* 1936, oil on canvas, 93.6 x 66.3 cm. Solomon R. Guggenheim Museum, New York. Photograph Robert E. Mates © The Solomon R. Guggenheim Foundation, New York (FN 71.1960). © DACS 2000

painting can also be divided top and bottom and thus seen as four sections, with bottom right a retrograde inversion of top left, and the bottom left a retrograde inversion of top right. Both Kagan and Nancy Perloff have seen such techniques as analogous to the technical procedures of the second Viennese school of Schoenberg, Berg, and especially Webern,[98] but these techniques can also be found in earlier music, such as the first Viennese school, and are particularly highly developed in the earlier polyphonic works of J. S. Bach, such as *The Musical Offering*. This can in part be explained by the persistence of certain musical procedures in Schoenberg's technique, his perception of his method as an extension of previous systems rather than a complete revolution. Such ideas were, as Perloff points out, part of a shared cultural milieu. Therefore, it is not too surprising that Klee, an artist sympathetically and intelligently in tune with music and musical ideas, should seek and exploit such procedures.[99] The notion of variation through retrograde, inversion, and retrograde inversion, is, however, more pervasive in Schoenberg's serialism than in earlier music. Indeed, it is fundamental to the method as a whole. It holds the possibilities of intricate interrelations at both melodic and harmonic levels. As Webern points out in his *The Path to the New Music* (1933), there is a linguistic analogy between this music system and the ancient Latin palindromic square that he terms a "magic square":

SATOR
AREPO
TENET
OPERA
ROTAS[100]

This square can be read vertically, horizontally, and backward (in other words through retrograde, inversion, and retrograde inversion). Questing to find ways of articulating color relationships within abstract designs, Klee's magic square paintings demonstrate a modernist adoption of such structuring devices. Although Klee may not have wholeheartedly embraced all aspects of modern music (see his pen and watercolor *Pianist in Distress—A Satire: Caricature of Modern Music,* 1909), the visual evidence appears to acknowledge its significance as a technical procedure and craft. The music of Schoenberg was performed at the Bauhaus, and according to one ex-pupil, Kurt Kranz, Schoenberg's "method of composing using twelve notes" was demonstrated at a Bauhaus evening early in 1931.[101]

COUNTERPOINT

Andrew Kagan has convincingly shown that, although the magic square paintings gave Klee a way to articulate temporal color relationships in order to develop visual polyphony, Klee needed to develop the notion of transparency in order for one "theme" to be "sounded" with another. Simply laying one color field on top of another obscured the underlying elements; whereas notes sounded together can still be heard as separate elements, one color placed on top of another produces a third, new element, one that does not disclose its constituents. Klee took the first steps toward solving this problem in the early classes he conducted at the Bauhaus. He overlapped shaded rectilinear planes so that the vertical or horizontal lines that made them up let the underlying color field show through. This produced a mix of linear and color elements, but with the color limited to a background role. With his introduction of a screen of colored dots in the 1930s, similar

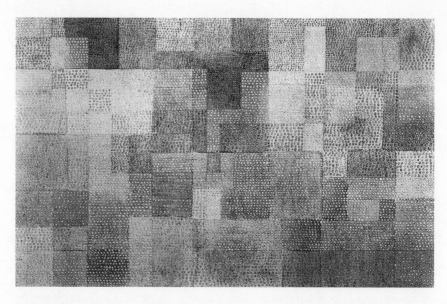

4.14 Paul Klee, *Polyphony,* 1932, oil on canvas, 66.5 x 106 cm. Emanuel Hoffman Foundation, on permanent loan to the Kunstmuseum, Basel. Photograph Öffentliche Kunstsammlung Basel, Martin Bühler. © DACS 2000

to tesserae in mosaics, and wittily called "counter-pointillism" by Kagan, Klee was able to play colors against one another simultaneously.

By 1932, Klee believed he had achieved true pictorial polyphony, in a work of that title, *Polyphony* (fig. 4.14). The ground of this oil painting consists of a colored rectangle theme, mainly in tones of blue and green, which has been overlaid with a separate field of dots in opposing colors. These dots allowed Klee to maintain two truly independent color themes.

Most of Klee's work is, in one way or another, provisional and experimental, a search for answers rather than a statement of achievement. It is also true that he worked on a number of images at the same time. Photographs of his studio show many easels with works in various states of completion, his quest to answer questions that he posed to himself and his students constantly being worked through, following many possible paths. He constantly revisited problems, and his oeuvre does not fit the simple picture of an artist achieving a linear teleological development. Pursuing themes in his work requires the careful observer to move back and forth across Klee's output, seeing what appear to be solutions taken up again and developed in another direction.

Klee's major polyphonic painting is a rare exception to this rule. *Ad Parnassum* is a summa of much of the preceding work and inquiry; it is a statement of

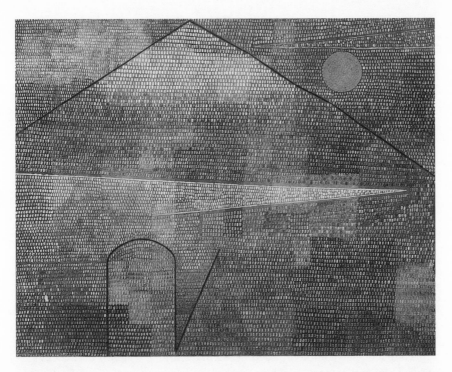

4.15 Paul Klee, *Ad Parnassum,* 1932, oil on canvas, 100 x 125 cm. Kunstmuseum, Bern.
© DACS 2000

achievement (fig. 4.15). It forms a recapitulation of his pedagogic efforts at the Bauhaus, for he finished it shortly after retiring in the spring of 1931, after which he took up a post at the Düsseldorf academy.

Ad Parnassum was executed in much the same way as *Polyphony*. On a white ground, Klee painted a grid of flat squares in a muted casein-based paint. The use of casein (a milk-based medium) produced a subtle, slightly opaque effect, which gave luminosity by allowing the white ground to raise the tonality of the colors. The underlying colors of the grid are, nevertheless, relatively muted tones of olive-green, blue, and violet. In general, the colors move from a fairly muted compass in the bottom left-hand corner, where they are most shadowy and in the blue range, to the top right-hand corner of high intensity in the orange range. Here the brightest part of the work is found in the orange circle, which is a counter-point to the underlying squares but whose circular form is (or can be) generated by rotating a square through a central axis, a square undergoing temporal rota-tional transformation. It is painted over the screen of dots and therefore appears to have been added last in the sequence of the painted layers, forming a literal full stop. The movement of underlying colored squares is in this way diagonal, moving from bottom left to top right, forming "steps" to Parnassus.[102] On top of this subtle modulation of colors Klee added a linear element not found in *Polyphony*.

The linear elements function like musical notation, that is, they operate as signs. They are abstract enough to be equivocal—operating between figuration (a mountain landscape) and "pure" graphic marks (lines and planes). The two principle linear elements are the "mountain," or "pyramid," and the "gateway" and "path"; the pyramid may well have its source in Klee's visit to Egypt in 1928. The first linear element, like a musical phrase mark, arches asymmetrically across the top of the composition, dividing the height of the image along the golden section. The second stands at the bottom left-hand side, the arched gateway opening out on its right side into a path that helps to lead the eye up to the "warm circle." The shape of the gateway is related to Klee's earlier experiments with the gestures employed by conductors in marking the beat and meter of music, in duple time. The downbeat forms a literal counter*point* to the apex of the mountain. There are two other linear sections, but these are more directly related to the color theme. In the center there is a decrescendo sign ($>$) containing a pale yellow screen of dots, which is answered by a crescendo sign ($<$) containing a red screen of dots. Both correlate to the canon of color totality discussed above. Such linear angles are also related to a device commonly used by Klee, the arrow, which is both a demonstration of direction and a symbol of ambition and aspiration, a sign for creativity and striving. "To be impelled towards motion and not to be the motor . . . Revelation: that nothing that has a start can have infinity. Consolation: a bit farther than customary!—than possible?"[103] Here they lead the eye across the surface of the painting.

Finally, over the entire surface of the painting Klee laid down a staccato counterpoint of dots, each individually built up from a series of successive translucent glazes over a white base. This allowed for development of the independent color themes from a common ground.

The title of this work, as Kagan argues, relates to Johann Joseph Fux's (1660–1741) famous Latin treatise on the art of polyphonic writing, the *Gradus ad Parnassum* of 1725. This work was a standard treatise on counterpoint for more than two centuries, and Klee would have known it through his studies in music. But the title most obviously refers to the seat of Apollo and the muses, a site for music, not painting. It was to demonstrate painting's equality to music that Klee strove throughout his life: "Consolation: a bit farther than customary!—than possible?"

For Klee, the process of artistic creation mirrors the processes of nature. To use his own simile, the artist stands as the trunk of the tree, between roots and crown, which are alike. Music was important because it provided a metaphor for abstract temporal development, growth, and aspiration, one that was already culturally saturated and technologically sophisticated. This was realized in his concern with design and color and found its fullest measure in the concept of rhythm, the temporal element of both music and painting.

In an elegant and concise essay, "Art Chronicle: On Paul Klee (1870–1940)," written almost one year to the month after Paul Klee's death in 1940, Clement Greenberg identifies what he sees as Klee's provincial character: his art "grew by intensification, not extension . . . it pretends to no statements in the grand style. . . . [It belongs to] a place comparatively remote from the nervousness and personal uncertainty of the metropolis."[104] It is a provincialism in both geographical and canonical terms. But according to Greenberg, Klee's great achievement was in recognizing this aspect of his art and character, containing it and making of it a virtue: "once he had done these things, he was ready to go home and be himself."

Greenberg then discusses how Klee's works deviate from Renaissance or classical pictorial design. Klee does not produce works to be "taken in at a glance . . . decorative in an architectural sense." Instead, he produces ornamental design on a smaller format. "This is Dutch, German, bourgeois"—although, we might add, this is not necessarily a characteristic of the Dutch artist Piet Mondrian:

> Most pictorial design to which we are accustomed is spatial; that is, the eye travels continuously along a line or passage of color. But in Klee's painting design is almost *temporal* or musical. We seem to be more conscious than is usual in graphic art of something that has to be experienced in terms of succession and simultaneity. . . . Unity of design is realized by relations and harmonies rather than by structural solidity.

Greenberg here admits that even "spatial" design betrays a temporal element in the traveling eye. As we have seen, Klee developed this element by combining a metamorphic model with music's temporal sophistication—"forming" rather than "form." "Form must on no account ever be considered as something to be got over with, as a result, as an end, but rather as genesis, growth, essence."[105] It is this narrative concern, and the way it spills over into some of his more ideographical works, that sets Klee's art up as "perhaps the most literary pictorial art that has ever been attempted." As Greenberg argues, one of the things that makes Klee's art so "provincial" is the tension it demonstrates in its hold on both figurative and abstract elements. Apart from the magic square paintings, Klee's art never really lets go of figurative traces, however reduced they may be. In this regard Klee is unlike Kupka, whose works display a clearer teleology of abstraction. What sets Klee apart from so many other artists labeled modernists, many of whom invoked music as a model, is the provisional and personal nature of his aesthetic production and his profound understanding of the technical side of music.

It is also worth reiterating that Klee's essentially experimental rubric produced an oeuvre that is distinctly unteleologic. In analyzing his ideas it is always necessary to range over his output, comparing works at some chronological remove that nevertheless explore similar motifs and issues. He often explicated problems only to return later and explore them again with fresh insights gained from other investigations. Inversion and retrograde were not merely technical devices for him, they were part of his approach to art. Klee's oeuvre is truly polyphonic in its weaving of ideas forward and backward across its temporal surface. His modesty and imaginative fancy, even whimsy, stand in contrast to the more solemn timbre of figures such as Kandinsky and Mondrian and place him more in tune with the character of many so-called postmodernists.[106]

In the next chapter we consider another figure who is similarly "out of tune," but this time a composer rather than a painter, the Austrian musician Josef Matthias Hauer.

FIVE

"OUT OF TUNE" HAUER'S LEGACY AND
THE AESTHETICS OF MINIMALISM IN
ART AND MUSIC

"Das ist Musik!! Pfui Mozart." —Shouted by a man in the fifth row at a
concert of music by Hauer; he was promptly arrested for "interfering with
a public function and disturbing the peace" (Vienna, 17 February 1933)

In the conventional construction of the canon of musical modernism, the work of
Austrian composer Josef Matthias Hauer (1883–1959) is usually considered little
more than an annotation to discussions of Arnold Schoenberg's development of
serialism (fig. 5.1). Glen Watkins is a good example of this assessment: "The details of the Hauer-Schoenberg confrontation must be seen as little more than a
footnote to the larger issues of an expanding tonal planetary system inevitably
wedded to formal questions that consumed virtually all composers of the time."[1]
In this context Hauer is regarded as producing a somewhat bizarre version of
a dodecaphonic compositional technique in the shadow of his more illustrious
countryman.

The eminent pianist and musicologist Charles Rosen provides another example
of this line of thinking: "By 1913, a composer named Josef Hauer had developed a
technique of composing music that consisted essentially of writing the chromatic
scale over and over again in a different order each time. Schoenberg was obliged

5.1 Josef Matthias Hauer, 1940s

to treat this silly system with the appearance of respect because of its superficial resemblance to the serialism he was to work out later in the early 1920's."[2] The ploy of asperity is not uncommon, especially when driven by the desire to establish primacy of invention, but here it is founded on a number of inaccuracies. If one wished to adopt a similar tone, one could suggest that the idea of "writing the chromatic scale over and over again in a different order each time" is not a totally inaccurate description of Schoenberg's own serial technique nor, for that matter, of the approach of all dodecaphonic composers, by definition. But putting this simplistic portrayal to one side, Rosen's chronology, as well as his description of Hauer's method, is imprecise.

Hauer was brought up about eighty kilometers south of the musical center of Vienna in the town of Wiener Neustadt. From his training as a music teacher he developed an independent interest in composition. He first experimented with conventional formats, if not a conventional tonal style. But he soon developed his thinking within different structures. His first published composition was a re-working of his *Symphony No. 1* (1912), arranged for keyboard and retitled *Nomos in sieben Teilen* in its printed 1918 form. It is, however, a pre-dodecaphonic work where, it is true, traditional harmony is absent, but this makes it no more than atonal. The work employs a wide range of harmonic resources: whole tones, octatonic groups (alternating tones and semitones, or vice versa), diminished seventh chords, bitriadic harmonies (for example, the so-called *Petrushka* chord, a conflation of the major triads of F♯ and C), and all chromatic pitch classes. Importantly, however, there is no system, no worked out and applied technique.

If we are to take the development of Hauer's system from the composition of *Nomos,* op. 19, as Hauer himself would have wished, then we have a date later than the one Rosen states, August 1919 (ex. 5.1). For in this work the so-called nomos (or law), as he rather grandly entitled the rules inherent in his method, first manifests itself in a more systematic form. Yet this work is not a total application of a dodecaphonic method, although it does use its twelve-note sections as articulation for all the major structural sectors. If we are to take the development of a dodecaphonic system from Hauer's first published theoretical writings, *Über die Klangfarbe* (On tone color), we have the slightly earlier date of 1918.

The important point, however, is that such equivocation over issues of priority and chronology have power only if Hauer's system did, indeed, distinguish itself by a "superficial resemblance to the serialism" of Schoenberg. It does not. It is significantly nonserial in Schoenberg's sense, since it is based on paired hexachords in its early "trope" manifestation and on the "continuum" (a web of twelve tetrads; the term follows the usage of Hauer's pupil Victor Sokolowski and is more fully defined later) in its *spiel* guise, rather than on a precompositional note-row. Hauer's approach is conceived in terms of cycles, not rows.

In an article written for the journal *Musikblätter des Ansbruch* on his trope technique in 1924, Hauer draws attention to both his pre-1919 intuitive approach and the distinctive character of his recently discovered method:

> In August 1919 I had the idea of studying my much maligned compositions to see if I could not find in them an outwardly perceptible "practical" law. Until then I had worked largely from instinct. . . . Even earlier it had occurred to me that I dealt extensively with very short phrases . . . and linked them together, thus building up from simple repetition, abbreviation, and extension. . . . I very quickly grasped that *building blocks of all twelve notes of the circle* are real structural elements, the ones that are musically the most fertile.³

Hauer arrived at a dodecaphonic position by placing equal pitches as far apart from each other in time, so as to avoid any one of them functioning as a kind of tonic. As he later wrote, once his approach had been more fully developed, "Equal [*gleiche*] pitches should be separated from one another as far as possible."⁴ The trope technique, first seen in a nascent form in *Nomos,* op. 19, consists

NOMOS.

Josef Hauer, Op. 19.

J. H. 15

Musikaliendruckerei v. Josef Eberle, Wien, VII. Schottenfeldgasse 38.

5.1 J. M. Hauer, *Nomos*, op. 19, 1919, first page. Reprinted by kind permission of the copyright owner © 1976 by Ludwig Doblinger (B. Herzmansky) KG, Vienna–Munich

in the main of the disposition of paired six-note clusters (or "building blocks") of complementary, intervallic relationship to one another, where any one of the first six notes may be used before any of its twinned six notes (for example, 0, 1, 2, 3, 4, 5 : 6, 7, 8, 9, 10, 11). Although the differentiation of the two trope halves remains clear, there is the possibility of building musical forms. If, however, this principle breaks down, as it sometimes does in Hauer's early works, composition returns to an atonal situation with no conscious rules under which to order the musical material. The forty-four possible hexachord pairs thus formed from the 479,001,600 different nonrepetitive combinations of the twelve notes of the chromatic scale (or, more appropriately, 39,916,800 possibilities of cycles), manifest themselves for Hauer as a resource similar to the twenty-four major and minor keys used by composers within the diatonic system (ex. 5.2). It was his familiarity with the forty-four tropes that oriented him in the chromatic universe and that makes his conception different from Schoenberg's more work-by-work, row-by-row approach.⁵ The "correct" selection of the tropes, however, remains an intuitive decision, in much the same way that a "tonal" composer chooses a tonic key. The choice of notes does not originate as a row; rather, it is constituted as "chords" (relationships) from which to make a selection.

Hauer's *Divertimento for Small Orchestra* of 1930, a work that can be regarded as a transition between the trope and spiel techniques, illustrates this point. Here the original two hexachords (trope 18, from the 1948 arrangement) are rotated within themselves, creating variation without the disruption of the relationship between the two hexachords. When all rotations are exhausted, one note is exchanged between them, creating a new trope. This can then be similarly rotated and a new pair of notes exchanged, and so on; the procedure results in forty-nine related cycles. All pitch relationships throughout the piece are therefore generated from the original trope.

The more highly refined spiel procedure starts from any sequence of twelve pitches (which may be derived from a trope) but builds up a web of chords referred to as the "continuum." Once the selection has been made, it can, of course, be described as a row, but it should be clear by now that Hauer's conception of forty-four paired hexachords provides him with a systematization of relationships that is different from Schoenberg's linear approach. In short, he conceived of tonal relationships in a cyclical rather than linear way (ex. 5.3).

This sequence, seen as a twelve-note cycle of repeating pitches, is arranged within the closest possible range: a major seventh. This range of notes is then divided to give four quadrants of semi- and whole-tone note relations (for example, C, C♯, D) (D♯, E, F) (F♯, G, G♯) (A, A♯, B) (ex. 5.4). In order to create a harmonic texture, or continuum, each occurring pitch of the twelve-note cycle is repeated until it is displaced by another note from the same quadrant. This

5.2 J. M. Hauer, *Die Tropen*, 1948

5.3 Twelve-note cycle

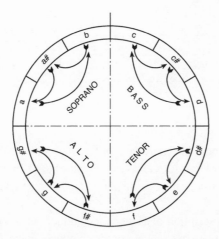

5.4 Quadrants

new note is then repeated in the same way, until the last note of the quadrant is reached; this note then continues until the original is returned to. The whole procedure is then repeated until the continuum is complete. This creates a series of twelve-chords that differ from each other by only a single note (ex. 5.5). This is the harmonic, rhythmic, and melodic basis for all other procedures. Briefly, the rhythm is dependent on the route taken through these twelve tetrads, always starting with the note of the original cycle and ending with the note that connects a step within the quadrant (see example), resulting in crotchets (quarter notes), quavers (eighth notes), triplets, or semiquavers (sixteenth notes), depending on the number of notes used from each tetrad (ex. 5.6). The extractions from the continuum itself may also yield diaphony (contrary motion), paraphony (parallel motion), metaphony (hocket two-part texture), and polyphony (a web of parts referred to as the "melic design," ex. 5.7). The entire continuum can be extended by the procedures of retrograde (backward in performance), which produces a different continuum, and the inversion of the lowest quadrant of the continuum up the octave, and a new course followed through the resulting continuum.

The examples I use here are expressed in Hauer's notational system, a form of

5.5 Complete continuum

5.6 Rhythmic variation

tablature representing a keyboard so that the lines stand as black keys, and the spaces stand as white keys. As well as avoiding the need to notate accidentals, this notation system illustrates the central place equal temperament plays in Hauer's aesthetic (ex. 5.8).

This is a brief description of Hauer's technique, but it should be enough to demonstrate the distinctive character of his approach, in particular how it differs from Schoenberg's better-known serialism.[6]

It is, however, the early trope technique that was developed at the time that Hauer and Schoenberg were in contact, and here Bryan Simms's analysis of Schoenberg's marginal comments on Hauer's article "Sphärenmusik" (published in 1922 in the journal *Melos*) draws out the differences between the two composers' approaches:

> In this commentary, Schoenberg touches upon a major difference between his twelve-tone method and Hauer's. For Hauer, twelve-tone music consisted primarily in a succession of structurally and motivically independent melodic phrases, each of which contained twelve different pitch classes. The harmonies which accompanied these lines did not necessarily pertain to the twelve-tone law, which, as Hauer repeatedly stated, was solely a shaping force of the "melos." For Schoenberg, on the contrary, the method was a unifying device which contributed to intervallic relatedness within both horizontal and vertical dimensions.[7]

Yet, as Robert Weiss has pointed out, in Hauer's opus 19 he used the same technique of discerning between steps and leaps to produce either horizontally connected notes not sounding together or vertically connected notes sounded together.[8] In a letter Hauer sent to Schoenberg following their first meeting, on 10 December 1923, at Schoenberg's flat in Mödling, Hauer attempts to show how

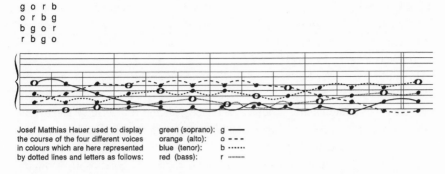

Josef Matthias Hauer used to display the course of the four different voices in colours which are here represented by dotted lines and letters as follows:

green (soprano): g ——
orange (alto): o - - -
blue (tenor): b ┄┄┄┄
red (bass): r ┄┄┄┄

5.7 Melic design

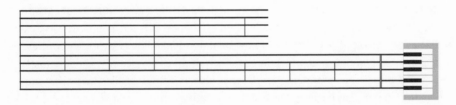

5.8 Keyboard notations

his method can be disposed to unify melodic and harmonic elements.⁹ It should be remembered that Hauer's later development of the spiel technique integrates horizontal, vertical, and rhythmic dimensions, as we have seen, so that what Simms says is applicable only to an aspect of Hauer's early method.

Last, the tone of the Hauer-Schoenberg correspondence could not accurately be described, at this stage, as superficially respectful, as witness a letter that Schoenberg sent to Hauer:

> Please do believe that my wish to reach an understanding with you springs above all from the urge to recognise achievement. . . . [I]n my *Theory of Harmony* I argue against the concept of "atonality" and then continue with an appreciation of you personally: you will realise that I did that for no one's sake but my own, out of my own need to be fair: and this makes the value of my praise objectively even greater.¹⁰

Here Schoenberg hardly seems disrespectful to his younger colleague; on the contrary, he is at pains not to cause offense, having earlier in the same letter suggested that they write a book together. This is apart from his nomination of Hauer, along with his own pupils Albern Berg and Anton Webern, as worthy recipients of the "Relief Fund for German and Austrian Musicians" set up by the American Society of Friends.¹¹ He also proposed to Theodor W. Adorno that a book on musical aesthetics or theory could be compiled giving the historical development of each subject, and should include various views under one heading, "E.g. (e.g.!!!): Schenker, Howard, Mersmann (??), Schönberg, Wiesengrund, Stein, Wellesz (??), Hauer, etc., etc."[12]

In truth, the Hauer-Schoenberg correspondence went through a number of stages driven by the mutual concern (albeit misguided) to establish historical priority, at times antagonistic, at others deeply cordial and respectful.[13] The overall effect was a differentiation of approach between two methods based on very different philosophical assumptions, not the imitation of one method by the other, although it is also true that there are points where the two composers inevitably share concerns.

The fact remains, of course, that it was Schoenberg's system that gained widespread acceptance and development through its use by a large number of canonical twentieth-century composers. Schoenberg's approach and technique was flexible enough to appeal to and accommodate individual musical styles. By contrast, Hauer's later twelve-note procedures tend to produce a voice that is deliberately not individualistic, producing works that always sound similar (the difference existing in details); because the system is relatively binding, it is a matter of following the "law," or nomos. Hauer's system does not, therefore, fit comfortably with the conception of music as a form of individual expression; these later spiel works can more correctly be regarded as "examples" than compositions in the romantic sense.[14] In addition, Hauer consciously set himself against Wagnerian musical developments, preferring the cooler world of classical (both Western and Chinese) or baroque musical models, regarding himself as an interpreter of the dodecaphonic universe rather than a composer expressing his will.

The question of Hauer's historical significance and aesthetic legacy is perhaps most easily assessed through a reconsideration of the nature of this concept of modernism along with those issues that its lineage tends to sideline or silence. I wish to do this by regarding modernism not as a given, unequivocal tradition but rather as a discourse that focuses on a "mainstream" of "aesthetic quality" thought to have been achieved over the century from the 1860s to the 1960s. By so regarding this tradition, I hope to show that what Hauer's work offers is a set of aesthetic issues that lie outside this mainstream, aesthetic priorities that are marginalized within modernism but that may be seen as relating to a set of debates that emerged at the end of this period and initiated a critique of this ideological doctrine. To this end I analyze Hauer's aesthetic in relation to minimalism in both music and the visual arts. It is not my wish to fit Hauer into the canon, for the point is, of course, that all such approaches exclude some figures at the expense of others; indeed, that is their purpose. Rather, I intend to underline the point that by ignoring some figures, one achieves a singular version of historical development, but by considering those often left out of standard accounts we can map alternative and divergent histories or, at the least, uncover examples that present a modernism that is less homogeneous and more internally diverse.

In looking across disciplinary borders, points of common interest may be exposed that single disciplinary methodologies often fail to observe. This is not to claim some historicist connection: I am not trying to extract Hauer from his milieu, for a number of ideas in his work are very much a part of the modernist paradigm. But aspects of his work do make conceptual contact with the critique of canonical modernism manifest in oppositional artistic discourses that emerge in the 1960s. Minimalism marks the first major divergence from the critical dominance of modernist ideology. Although there may not be universal acceptance of this point, at least among contemporary critics, it is true to say that as far as the major theorists of modernism are concerned (Greenberg and Fried), minimalism was (is) seen as the apotheosis of modernist idealism. Perhaps it would be useful, therefore, to continue with a brief map of this terrain.

MUSIC, ART, AND MODERNISM

As we have seen, the most influential characterization of modernism is found in the ideas of the art critic Clement Greenberg.[15] His thesis of modernity in art centers on what he identifies as its investigation of its own means of expression: "in music and the visual arts the medium declares itself as medium."[16] It is this concern that produces "aesthetic value," a view that leads to the complex issue of autonomy, for art progresses, he proposes, by laws internal to itself. Each art focuses on the purity and uniqueness of its own character. None of this is to suppose a break with the past. In fact, historical continuity is one of Greenberg's prime concerns, for this is the culmination of an historical impulse that he first identifies in the philosophical investigations of Immanuel Kant. In terms of music, this can be seen in the crisis in language brought about by the disintegration of tonality as the principle structuring core of Western art music, most often characterized as a "development" from the music and ideas of Richard Wagner. Music, then, in Greenberg's terms, turned to investigate its own language of expression, to rediscover its basic laws, and in the process offered up new musical languages as an alternative to this set of conventions, the most radical of which was Schoenberg's serialism.

One way to understand this development in art and music is to reassess the relationship between "foreground" and "background" events within artistic structures. These two territories are not cognate phenomena in both music and painting, but the shared nomenclature compels analogies in discussions of their changing relationship within modernist debates.

In music, the status of "foreground" elements, such as passing chromatic melody notes, which stand in relation to an implicit triadic harmonic "background," was raised by Schoenberg and others to become absolute entities in their own right. They are developed to a point where foreground motifs take precedence over background structures. As the composer and conductor Pierre Boulez has put it, "Preference [is given] to *melodic* rather than the co-ordinating *harmonic* intervals,"[17] and although this may have been done earlier (in Beethoven and, especially, Wagner), in Schoenberg there is an actual break between harmony and counterpoint, or the vertical and horizontal, in his compositions of mid-1908. The structural role of harmony, in works of this so-called expressionist phase, disappear, and by way of compensation, "motivic work and the tendency to equate the horizontal and the vertical dimensions—in fact the essential elements later codified in the serial method—assume greater responsibility."[18]

Even in an earlier work of Schoenberg's, his 1906 *Chamber Symphony No. 1,* op. 9, the foreground-melodic and background-harmonic elements begin to blur.[19] In this work there is a constant pull against triadic harmony, which in this sense creates "unfunctional" progressions, behind the development of thematically chromatic units that are based on rising fourths or whole tones. Even in the coda the insistent, almost desperate reiteration of the tonic E major triad is pursued by chromatic features that hold the background (harmony) as structurally subordinate to the foreground (melodic) thematic elements (ex. 5.9). Although this relationship is taken further in later atonal works, we can see here an active focus on the musical foreground as triadic harmony begins to lose its structuring role. In short, the relationship between melodic and harmonic elements shades together, despite the framework of E major.

According to Greenberg, painting was the first art to display modernist tendencies and to highlight this foreground-background relationship in a more literal way: an increasing concern with the medium's two-dimensional character. The picture plane (foreground) becomes the point for development, with fictive three-dimensional space (a measurable mid- and background) being replaced, because of its illusory character, by a concern with pictorial space, "one into which one can only look," not "into which one could imagine walking," in Greenberg's words.[20] Greenberg first detects this tendency in the work of Manet. We might briefly consider the example of his *Déjeuner sur l'herbe* of 1863 (fig. 5.2).

If we take the work in purely technical (formal) terms, as we did with Schoenberg's *Chamber Symphony,* we can see Manet exploiting the use of pale grounds, often just off-white, for both luminosity and flatness, because a sense of depth is more difficult to develop over a light ground. In addition, his creation of flattened planes and his use of a strong front lighting, which exaggerates contrasts of light and shade and suppresses half-tone modeling, emphasizes the central group

U. E. 7147   W. Ph. V. 225

5.9 Arnold Schoenberg, *Chamber Symphony No. 1*,
op. 9, 1906, last bars. Reproduced by permission of
Universal, London

of three figures through the compression of the back- and midground against the
picture plane. Thus the stooping woman in the background appears to be projected forward. Manet's painting is as disquieting in relation to its precedents as
were Schoenberg's moves away from tonal fixity.[21]

It is this focus on the picture plane that has commonly been seen to lead to
abstraction. Yet it should be noted that Greenberg is not arguing for abstraction
per se, although he is arguing at a time when abstraction was the locus classicus.

It is interesting to note, therefore, that the concern with foreground structure,

U. E. 7147   W. Ph. V. 225

within this characterization of modernism, is a feature of both music and paint-ing. In the effort to reinvent painting as more than mere illusion, and music as more than conventional tonality, the surface-foreground takes on a central role as the screen against which the tension between convention and modernism is played out.

Once this "development" is established in the case of music, the lineage of composers can be, and often is, established from Wagner through Schoenberg (his conscious inheritor), to Berg, Webern, and on to Pierre Boulez and Milton Babbitt and their extension of serialist principles into the realm of rhythm and dynamics; so-called sérialisme intégrale. In art it is to be found in work ranging

U. E.7147   W. Ph.V. 225

from Manet to Kandinsky and Mondrian to Pollock and Kenneth Nolan, who developed notions of abstraction in relation to pictorial space.

Raymond Williams, in his critique of this canonical view of modernism, has characterized it as an ideology that, in its selective approach, tends to celebrate the self-reflexive text, one in which all other noninternalist approaches are sidelined: "As the author appears in the text, so does the painter in the painting." It is also a theory that, in its concern with formal issues, tends to regard as unimportant (in qualitative terms) all contextual issues. In addition, this view of modernism positions the exile as paradigm, in which self-referentiality and alienation act to "ratify as canonical the works of radical estrangement."[22] Here we should

5.2 Edouard Manet, *Le déjeuner sur l'herbe,* 1863, oil on canvas, 208 x 264.5 cm. Musée d'Orsay, Paris

bear in mind that as a gentile—Hauer was a lapsed Roman Catholic—he could remain in Austria during the Anschluss of the Second World War. However, the National Socialists classed his work as "degenerate" and public performances were banned. In 1938, after the Anschluss, he lost the annual honorarium he had been granted in 1930 by the city of Vienna, along with all the royalties from his works. He did, however, continue to refine his ideas in private. Schoenberg, by contrast, was forced into exile in France, and then to the United States in 1934, where, despite discomforts and his status as a Jewish alien, he had a relatively high public and intellectual profile, accepting a professorship at the University of California in Los Angeles in 1936.

But let us pursue in more detail another important element of the modernist paradigm, "the artist in their art," or, in Greenberg's words, the "personal" character of modernist expression. This provides us with the twin characteristics of formal purity and personal expression, both central to notions of art's progress within the concept of modernism. Although Hauer's work is part of the formal purity, his denial of personal expression is worth exploration.

Schoenberg intended his twelve-note system to supply the basis for a new musical language, to herald a new phase in musical history.²³ Yet, despite the work's revolutionary character, Schoenberg believed that this new era would share with the past a reliance on accepted compositional conventions. All composers, he believed, could shape their own *personal* musical statements. Hauer, too, of course, was part of this impulse to reinvent musical language, but his art was, significantly, one that eschewed the personal. He wished to achieve a non-sensual art. His "objectivity of melody" was brought about by equalizing note-to-note relationships and by destroying "leading-tone tracks" (*geleise*), a tendency for notes to resolve to adjacent tones in some forms of temperament (for example, the seventh to the octave). This explains his emphasis on equal temperament— he contrasts his approach to the romanticism of the nineteenth century and expressionism of the twentieth century: "Absolute objectivity in melody, after all, demands the sacrifice of the personality, for, in realizing a melody in that utter objectivity, the personal element . . . no longer plays a role."²⁴

This objectivity finds its most developed manifestation in the spiel, a form of music-making in which it is hard, if not impossible, to detect an individual voice; all works created by this method sound "Hauer-like." Although the idea of artistic "purity" is very much an aspect of modernist theories, Hauer's notion of a pure music has resonance in minimalist aesthetics. But before we can continue with our discussion of this relationship it is necessary to make a short diversion to explain in more detail this notion of "objectivity" and the philosophical basis of Hauer's aesthetic.

HAUER'S NOTION OF INTERVAL-COLOR

Two texts are principal to an understanding of Hauer's early dodecaphonic approach: *Deutung des Melos: Eine Frage an die Künstler und Denker unsere Zeit* (Interpreting the melos) of 1923, which sets forth the aesthetic basis of his thinking, and *Vom Wesen des Musikalischen* (The essence of musicality) of 1920, which is more musicological in detail. The root assumption of Hauer's thinking is that music is essentially a mental and spiritual event. This is in contrast to its occurrence in the physical world, which constitutes its quantifiable material form. The mental conception of music, if it is to be transmitted from a composer to a listener, must manifest itself in the physical realm, but for Hauer, this process more often than not obscures its "purity," through instrumental noise and other physical events; actual realization moves music from its ideal state. This belief that true music is essentially nonsonoric, existing only for the inner ear, may appear to be radical and, to some, paradoxical. The listener's role is then to reconstitute the musical event in its original mental or spiritual state on receiving its physical manifestation.

Central to an understanding of the formation of Hauer's thinking is his conception of tone-color. This idea is important for a number of reasons. First, it demonstrates one of the ways in which Hauer's approach is antithetical to Schoenberg's,
for it stands in marked contrast to Schoenberg's notion of *Klangfarbenmelodie*.[25]
Second, it is formed through reference to models outside music, specifically the
color theories of Goethe.

The essential musical event for Hauer is not the sounding tone but rather the
interval, not a sonoric unit but a relationship. Each interval has its own "gesture,"
a movement, and this in turn has the character of a "color." The designation of
the intervals is to be based on equal temperament. In *Vom Wesen,* Hauer sur-
veys three methods of generating all twelve pitch classes (C to c′): (1) through
the circle of fifths, based on C, ascending as what he calls "pure" perfect fifths,
(2) through the circle of fourths, based on C, ascending as "pure" perfect fourths,
and (3) through the derivation of the upper partials of the fundamental C. Because
all three methods lead to different representations of the eleven pitch classes, the
approach Hauer favors is that of equal-tempered pitch classes, which tend to reduce "leading-tone tracks" and lead to "objective melody," as I explained above.
Drawing a parallel with Goethe's observation that the complete color spectrum
cannot be seen in nature, Hauer argues that this equal-tempered manifestation is
not found in nature but that it most closely matches the mental or spiritual state of
true music.[26] For this reason he promoted the use of only equal-tempered instruments (piano, organ, and so on, and the voice, which is able to adjust mentally to
provide correct disposition),[27] instruments that reduce the opportunity for interval distortions and later, as we have seen, developed a form of notation in tune
with this reasoning.[28] It is not difficult to see why he rejected Schoenberg's Klangfarbenmelodie as directed to the physical and material, not mental and spiritual,
manifestation of music. He saw Schoenberg as distracted by the sensual effects
of orchestration, part of Schoenberg's inheritance of late romanticism, which, as
I have mentioned, Hauer expressly rejected.

In his appeal to Goethe's theory of colors, the *Farbenlehre,* perhaps the most
consequential notion for Hauer is the importance of the subjectivity of perception; that color is a product of the mind. Goethe opens his study with a discussion
of physiological colors: "We naturally place these colours first, because they belong altogether, or in a great degree, to the *subject*—to the eye itself. They are the
foundation of the whole doctrine, and open to our view the chromatic harmony
on which so much difference of opinion has existed."[29] Similarly, tone-color, according to Hauer, is not rooted in physical sound. The perception of tone-color
is a characteristic of the nature of the ear, and "intuitive hearing" brings this out.
Although this may begin to sound like an idealist conception, it should be pointed

out that, unlike Plato, Hauer believed that the perception of music can be reached only through intuition, not rationality, or if we put it in Kantian terms, the "thing-in-itself" can be perceived through intuitive hearing or auditory perception, not through cognition. In fact, Hauer is anti-idealist in that he rejects the process of rational thinking from perception to idea, in favor of intuition.

For Hauer, then, Western culture since the time of Plato has been too concerned with linguistic and propositional ways of thinking, and this leads further into abstraction, not closer to reality. The correct path to understanding is therefore through intuitive perception. The act of hearing music in its spiritual state connects us with the "melos." The use of this Greek term signals Hauer's need to bypass centuries of cultural convention and bring about a fresh start: a new *Meloskultur*. The use of Goethe's color theory is therefore to be understood as an analogy, because words cannot express the "purely musical," but analogical models can bring us closer contact to the real.

Through cultural habituation, Hauer continues, we are theoretically and musically accustomed to orient ourselves from C (in notation, keyboard layouts, and so on). Following Goethe, who had divided colors into a "plus" side of active and warm character (the yellow and red areas of the color circle) and a "minus" side of passive and cold character (greens and blues), Hauer generated a "plus" side of intervals generated by ascending fifths from C (fifths, major seconds, major sixths, major thirds, major sevenths, and augmented fourths), adding sharps and gravitating upward, and a "minus" side generated by descending fifths from C (fourths, minor seconds, minor thirds, minor sixths, diminished fifths), adding flats and gravitating toward repose by resolving down, "following the falling cadential principle." Goethe's oppositional characterization was, of course, by no means unique, and it is possible that Hauer could have had this characterization reinforced by the work of such physiologists as Ewald Hering, a fellow Viennese who in the 1870s had proposed a Goethe-inspired "opponent-color" scheme.[30]

In Hauer's color-interval circle, C is taken to correspond with white, because C represents the octave and as such is the only "pure" interval in equal temperament. Also, because it has no beats—by which Hauer means that it has no appreciable regular increase or decrease of loudness caused by discrepancies in the vibrations of adjacent notes sounded together—it is taken to be the dividing line between green and yellow, so that Hauer arrives at the following analogies:

	C–c′ = White
C–G = Yellow	C–D♭ = Blue-violet
C–D = Orange	C–A♭ = Ultramarine blue
C–A = Vermilion	C–E♭ = Turquoise blue

C–E = Carmine   C–Bb = Blue-green
C–B = Purple-red   C–F = Vermilion-green
          C–F♯ = Purple-violet
          C–Gb = Black (stands in greatest contrast to C)

Hauer is not suggesting a synesthesia, that one literally sees these colors, for that would be counter to his insistence on the mental and spiritual nature of music; rather, he argues that the *character* of these intervals and colors corresponds, and, of course, that such character is intuitively perceived.

In addition, Hauer gives the character of each associated key by quoting selected passages from Goethe's *Theory of Colors*. The keys are presented in tritone pairs, the minor keys combining the character of the tonic with that of the key signature. For example, G minor would be viewed as possessing the character of G major "broken" or "fractured" (*gebrochen*) by the character of Bb major. I quote his description of the fifth as an example:

The melos of the Fifth
   G: Biedermeier pitch; somewhat blaring as with trumpets (emphasizing the second overtone—beats of the interval of the fifth); somewhat trivial.
   Chamber music in G by the classical composers (popular hymns originally in the Biedermeier pitch now often transposed to E-flat major and presented with military pathos).
   The one which is emphasized when articulating, mostly on the heavy first beat; solemn rhythms.
   In G minor, the colour is fractured by the somewhat awkward B-flat.
   From the *Requiem* of Mozart: *Rex tremendae* . . . "Herr, dess' Allmacht Schrecken zeuget, der sich fromm den Frommen neight, rette mich, Urquell der Gnade!" *Quam Olim Abrahae* . . . "Das Panier des heiligen Michael begleite sie zum ewigen Lichte, welches du verhissen hast Abraham und seinem Geschlechte."
   In the *Symphony in G minor* by Mozart, the sunny, light G is overshadowed by the autumnal, misty B-flat.
   The old Ionian mode.

Goethe says:
   Yellow is the closest colour to light. It comes about through the slightest moderation of light. In its greatest purity, it always bears with it the essence of light and always possesses a cheerful, enchanting quality.

   In this state, it is like a background, be it on clothing, draperies or carpeting. In its totally unmixed state, gold gives us a fresh and better idea of this colour, particularly if we consider the lustre. Thus, as a deep yellow, it produces a splendid and noble effect if it appears on shiny silk (on satin, for example).

Thus, it is in keeping with our experience that yellow would make a thoroughly warm and comfortable impression.

In its purity and its propensity for brightness, this colour is enjoyable and has something cheerful and noble in its entire being. On the other hand, however, it is very sensitive and will create a very unpleasant effect if it is sullied or pulled somewhat to the minus side. Thus, the colour of sulphur, which inclines toward green, has something unpleasant about it.[31]

Hauer employs these examples to help those who do not intuit the nature of the intervals. However, it should be remembered that in atonal music (as Hauer conceived it), only intervals, not keys, play a role.

For Hauer, his thinking had a broader political ramification. He saw modern society as in moral and spiritual decline, initiated by Plato and the dominance of what Hauer calls "language-idealism" (*Sprachenidealismus*). In order to rebuild our culture, we should adopt music ("atonal" music in his terms) as a kind of *Generalbass,* so that social and personal harmony can be achieved through the intuitively perceived melos.[32] "One can say: the Melos (atonal) is the common property of all, the formed language (the one-sided interpretation of the Melos) always that of one side of a people."[33] Such a view of cultural decline and decay is part of the social, intellectual, and moral tension of fin-de-siècle Vienna, caused by the rise of nationalism and democracy within the conglomeration of principalities and kingdoms that made up the Habsburg Empire. Hauer's thinking is echoed in the ideas of other thinkers of his age, notably Rudolph Steiner, the founder of anthroposophy, and the Austrian philosopher Ferdinand Ebner.

THE VIENNESE CONTEXT

Among those few scholars who have engaged with Hauer's ideas, the musicologist John Covach has provided one of the most sympathetic accounts.[34] He has argued that Rudolph Steiner's spiritualist account of Goethe's work particularly chimes with Hauer's ideas, principally Steiner's explanation of Goethe's "super-sensory" perception—the ability to perceive the spiritual content of things— and Hauer's notion of intuitive hearing. Both are accounts that attempt to move beyond scientific methods of verification. In short, Covach identifies four main points of resonance in the work of Hauer and Steiner:

First, though different in certain significant details, Steiner's super-sensory seeing and Hauer's intuitive hearing are generally similar. Second, both call for an act of subjective creation: Steiner's "active" thinking and Hauer's creative hearing. Third, Steiner's "ideal interconnections" and Hauer's intuitively-perceived interval would both appear to lead to a Goethean *Urphaenomen*. And fourth, both men trace the problems with Western thought back to Plato.[35]

If we consider some aspects of the anthroposophical ideas of Steiner and touch on the ideas of other thinkers who worked within this milieu, we can detect a number of resonances with Hauer's concerns and begin to see how Hauer's aesthetic emerged and diverged from the cross-current cosmopolitan, polyphonic voices that composed Viennese modernism.

Unlike many others who were drawn to theosophy, Steiner was a rigorous thinker, well trained in the German philosophical tradition. From his youth he had experienced visions and was at pains to reconcile these experiences with his rational understanding of the world. In his attempt to attune these two experiences, he found it necessary to reject certain rationalist claims such as David Hume's, expressed in *A Treatise of Human Nature* (1739–40), that the human mind can possess no certain knowledge of the world, that we are trapped in isolation from reality. Hume spoke of "perceptions of the mind," continuing the Cartesian tradition of the "veil of appearance," and the division between consciousness and things. Dividing such perceptions into primary "impressions" and derivative "ideas," Hume argued that it is only the appearances in our minds, not those in the external world, of which we can be immediately aware and on which we can base knowledge. In his response to this, Steiner took Kant's argument from the *Critique of Pure Reason* (1781), that although we may never reach the "thing-in-itself" (noumenal), there is no doubt it does exist (phenomenal). We can, however, know only representations of it. Further, Kant argues, our reflection upon objects has a form, or structure, that contributes to our experience, and there are therefore two sources of knowledge: sensibility (objects) and understanding (thought). However, Steiner saw Kant's procedure as limited within the constraints of a kind of materialism and sought to carry this thinking a stage further, into the realm of the spirit. For, he argued from his own experience, the spirit world is real, as real in fact as the perceptible world. And those fortunate to have "seen" it (in visions, through a form of supersensory seeing) had precisely the ability to access things-in-themselves. They had, in effect, bridged the phenomenal and noumenal worlds.[36] This is not dissimilar to Hauer's view that music is (re)created in the mind of the listener.

During his studies at the Technical University in Vienna, under Ernst Haeckel, Steiner found himself unable to accept the then-current materialist and mechanical scientific theories he was taught. They left no space for the realities, as he saw them, of spirit, and it is here that Goethe's scientific and philosophical ideas came to his aid. Goethe's anti-Newtonian theory of optics proposed that light acts as the medium between the sensible and supersensible, and Goethian biology proposed the concept of plant metamorphoses, which argues that lower forms evolve into higher forms through the power of spirit. Steiner extrapolated this into the idea that the human race should follow a similar evolutionary path, from the material to the spirit; the process of evolution, or metamorphosis, is evidence for Steiner of the workings of such a spirit.

Although he wrote little that is specific to music, his collected lectures on this subject, *The Inner Nature of Music and the Experience of Tone,* follow this line of reasoning.[37] Taking up Schopenhauer's discussion of music, which had built on Kant's transcendental idealism in arguing that music provides direct contact with the "Will" (Kant's thing-in-itself), Steiner argues that music is the one art that can penetrate the innermost essence of things. Music's archetypal origin is spiritual rather than material or physical ("Devachan" is Steiner's term for the world of high spirituality reached through tone). This, too, was a view shared by Hauer, and Steiner continues in terms sympathetic to Hauer's frame of mind. It is therefore the task of the musician to translate the spirit world into music, to make it physically manifest. Music supplies an analogue of the supersensible as long as we are unable to experience the spirit directly. The origin of music, he suggests, is in our sleep, when our souls inhabit the spiritual world, and this world, importantly for Steiner, is a realm of color, light, and sound, and is the source of art. Although Goethe certainly does not discuss art in such terms, he did suggest that although "colour and sound do not admit of being directly compared together in any way . . . both are referable to a higher formula, both are derivable, although each for itself, from this higher law."[38] Such a law was understood by Steiner to be spiritual in nature. Hauer, in the foreword to *Vom Wesen,* had produced a table of opposites that placed melos, the interval, and the atonal on the side of the "higher law" (or nomos) and rhythmos, noise, and the tonal on the side of convention. Hauer's belief that music is first an intellectual phenomenon isolated from the physical, and then manifested by a musician to express the musical event, is a similar species of reasoning.

Throughout his writings Steiner identifies two primary forces that act as the main enemies of the human race, which he characterizes as "Lucifer" and "Ahriman," personifications of the spirit of pride and materialism.[39] Such spirits were long established within the pantheon of theosophically inspired thought, but with Steiner they have a particularly contemporary resonance.[40] According to Steiner, Lucifer's authority lies in his abilities to tempt us to overestimate our spiritual powers, persuading us that we can transcend our limitations simply through our own efforts, tempting us into spiritual independence from higher spirits. He stands with his long shadow cast over modern art and philosophy. Ahriman counters this from within his realm, the province of technology and modern science. His task is to lead us from a spiritual understanding, to detach humanity from its spiritual destiny, into the (for Steiner) dark realms of materialism. He is paradox personified, a spirit-negating spirit. The unbalancing of materialism and the spirit is destructive, and it was to the resolution of this dualism that anthroposophy aspired.

The ideas of another of Steiner's teachers are worth brief mention. Robert Zimmermann was professor of philosophy at the University of Vienna from 1861 to 1895. He proposed a doctrine of aesthetics in two important publications, *Aesthetik* (1858–65) and *Anthroposophie* (1882), from which Steiner borrowed the term for his own branch of philosophy. Taking formalist ideas from his friend, the musicologist Eduard Hanslick, Zimmermann argued strongly against art as a vehicle of emotion, which he maintained corrupts the formal integrity of classicism in art. In his aesthetic doctrine he sought to subsume all knowledge and application under the banner of art. Hauer's later injunction to reject music as a means of individual expression but to embrace it as a means of spiritual salvation draws implicitly on this view, for he, along with Zimmerman, saw art's purpose as the embodiment of absolute rather than personal values, although the two thinkers would have disagreed on the nature of those values.

I am not proposing a thesis of connection here, reducing the differences between thinkers to simple similarities; rather, I am outlining an image of which Hauer is a part. Placing Hauer's ideas in this Viennese setting allows them to make better sense.

One of the best-known thinkers in this area has no direct point of contact with Hauer but did know Steiner and, for a time, was a close friend of Schoenberg: the artist Wassily Kandinsky. His interest in theosophy is well documented, and his aesthetic is much indebted to Steiner's eschatological vision. Like Steiner, Kandinsky also saw materialism and the spirit as warring forces. In his *Concerning the Spiritual in Art* (1911), he argued along lines very similar to Steiner, proposing that it was now time for the centuries-long reign of materialism—the procedures of science, the economics of greed, and the politics of control—to give way to the flowering of the spirit. Art stands at the junction of these forces; his paintings show this in the dissolving but present forms of the natural world, together with the nonobjective, art's ultimate aim being to bring about purity through the balance of the opposites.

I make no suggestion that Hauer followed the specifics of such beliefs, simply that his theories have in common such a polarized polemic, emerging from a shared set of cultural references. But Covach has shown that Hauer was almost certainly aware of Steiner, most probably in his guise as a leading Goethe scholar and regular public lecturer in Vienna in the period 1907 to 1915. Later, in the 1930s, after the formation of Hauer's aesthetic and Steiner's development of anthroposophy, there is a direct link between Hauer and Steiner. Hauer's student

Hermann Picht published an essay on Hauer in the weekly newsletter of the Anthroposophical Society *Das Goetheanum* of 10 December 1933. In this article, Picht claims that Hauer's music developed along lines parallel to Steiner's teachings in eurythmy. And as Covach reports in his discussions with the composer's son, Bruno Hauer, there were even attempts to recruit Hauer to the cause of eurythmy, although he declined, not wanting to be a "camp composer."[41]

Hauer's thinking was fostered in this ferment of Viennese intellectual debate, in attempts to come to terms with the apparent irreconcilability of new ideas with old. In one way or another all the major figures of this time and place exhibit this tension in their thinking. What is important about Hauer is just how he sought to deal with this duplicity, for in seeing the particular we can more easily detect the many currents that make up the counterpoint of modernity, some of which linger, some of which fade. Hauer's ideas faded only to reappear later, as the whole project of modernism itself was reassessed.

I mentioned above that Hauer rejected the notion of language as central to full understanding. This placed him in opposition to Ebner and marked the end of what had been to that point a collaborative relationship. Before we turn to discuss this association in more detail, it is worth remembering that Hauer's disquiet with language emerged in the context of general discussions of the role and limits of language in culture in fin-de-siècle Vienna, many of which centered around the critiques of culture and language conducted by Karl Kraus, Fritz Mauthner, and Hugo von Hofmannsthal, among others. Here the most well known and influential thinker was Ludwig Wittgenstein.

In the *Tractatus Logico-Philosophicus* (1922), Wittgenstein attempted to define the limits of the intelligible, not by discursive or sequential argument, but by a series of seven propositions, designed to map the limits of linguistic expression: "Whereof we cannot speak, thereof we must be silent."[42] We shall see this potency of silence developed in the aesthetics of John Cage in the next chapter, but its importance for Wittgenstein lies in the fact that, for him, ethical and aesthetic matters lie outside the world. The limits of language are the limits of the world, and therefore nothing can be said about them: "There are indeed, things that cannot be put into words. They *make themselves manifest*. They are what is mystical."[43] All we can do is to "show" them rather than "say" them. Art should therefore not depict or express subjective intention but show that which is inexpressible in words: "How words are understood is not told by words alone." Hauer's distrust of language and his promotion of melos is rooted in a similar assumption—namely, that art is a mission. Both Hauer and Wittgenstein attempt to separate the spheres of reason from fantasy, "upon which the Viennese critique of society in the early decades of this century was based."[44] But it was specifically against the ideas of Ebner that Hauer formed his promotion of melos over logos.

There are not only intellectual points of contact between the work of Hauer and Ebner but also striking parallels in the trajectories of their lives. We have considered the shadow cast over Hauer's life and ideas by the more illustrious figure of Schoenberg. It is similarly the case that Ebner's contribution to intellectual history has been eclipsed by the work of another, better-known thinker, the philosopher Martin Buber (1878–1965).[45]

Like Hauer, Ebner was born in Wiener Neustadt, and the two were fellow pupils at the local teacher training institute. Hauer studied piano, organ, cello, voice, and music theory. Ebner was also a keen musician. Although he did not specialize in music as a student, he enjoyed playing Bach and Mozart on the piano. Even though Ebner and Hauer lived near each other, attended the same institute, and shared an interest in music, they did not become friends until 1904, following a chance meeting on a train while both were returning from a teacher-training certificate examination. They must have soon discovered that their studies and interests gave them much in common. Back in Wiener Neustadt their friendship and discussions developed at the Café Lehn, where Hauer came to dominate the talk and, according to Walter Szmolyan, a "Hauer circle" soon emerged.[46]

Jørgen Jensen has explored the mutual impact these two had on each other's developing ideas.[47] He has shown that in the first instance Hauer provided Ebner with a series of aesthetic notions, developing out of the practice of Hauer's music, that caused Ebner to question certain base assumptions of his thinking. Later the roles were to be reversed, as Ebner's philosophy honed Hauer's theoretical writings, especially the first version of *Über die Klangfarbe* (On tone color) in 1918, in which Hauer explicitly acknowledges the influence of his friend's thinking.

By 1916, Ebner had discovered the "I-Thou" relation, which resulted in his book *Das Wort und die Geistigen Realitäten* and was to form the core of his philosophy. From this Buber was to develop his more famous dialogical thinking. Ebner proposed that the word mediates between the subject and the other, between man and God. In fact God's existence is imputed through the existence of language. God created man's capacity for speaking, a relationship that is dialogic. However, as William Johnston argues in his book *The Austrian Mind,* Ebner's pneumatological arguments are circular: "what Ebner offers is not reasoning but exhortation."[48] In this regard Ebner and Hauer theorize in similar ways. One of the major commonalities in the thinking of Hauer and Ebner at this time is the view that sound is the medium for communicating from spirit through realization to spirit once again. But in Hauer this sound is the melos, a move from the mental conception of music to its physical realization. In Ebner the sound is the word, or speech, that communicates between I and Thou. He emphasized speech over written language, favoring the vitality of face-to-face communication. It is in the difference between media (music and speech), however, that the two ultimately part company. By the mid-1920s their close friendship had dissolved. We have seen that for Hauer, music (or melos) is closer to the nature of the spirit (in his *Deutung des Melos*). The word is for him but a part of the realization of melos, and in his eyes, the excessive concern with language had led away from the path of true understanding. With the discovery of his dodecaphonic method he had found, he believed, an *objective* basis for creation, one that transcended the solitude of subjectivity through connection with the true realm of the spirit.

The spiel theory is notable in how it controls all the musical perimeters of the composition process, so much so that it is no longer really appropriate to call its manipulation composition in the traditional sense. Rather, such pieces are arrived at through the disposition of musical elements: a game with existing musical elements. Such a technique certainly gives less amplitude to the subjective element of creation, and as we shall see as we turn to consider the minimalist aesthetic, in this way it has commonalities with this later strand of artistic thinking.

In short, I am arguing that Hauer was part of the tendency of his time and place to think in terms of antitheses. The members of the Vienna Circle, for example, positioned themselves as positivists, materialists, defenders of hard knowledge and scientific method, in opposition to the intuitive view of understanding such as Steiner's, who saw spiritual perception as the true root of knowledge. What is important about Hauer is not so much the general point, that his thinking was a species of this binarism, but rather the specific detail of his aesthetic and its points of contact with late modernist thinking and practice, to which we now turn.

DEVELOPMENTS TO "WORK-AS-PROCESS"

The Belgian musicologist and composer Wim Mertens has made a notable contribution to discussions of the development from dodecaphony to minimal music. In his book *American Minimal Music,* utilizing the ideas of Adorno, Gilles Deleuze, and Jean-François Lyotard, he argues that the significance of composers concerned with the minimalist aesthetic—composers such as La Monte Young, Terry Riley, Steve Reich, and Philip Glass—rests, in part, in the concept of the work-as-process.[49] By this I take him to mean music that does not entail a *direct* relationship between form and idea, where, through the process of composition, the musical idea is allowed to work *itself* out. As Mertens puts it, "Nothing is being expressed [in the music]: it stands only for itself."[50] This view regards the work-as-process as embodying the consummate unity of form and content. It stands, therefore, like Hauer's aesthetic, in opposition to the view of music as the vehicle of a composer's subjective, personal, or individual expression. Mertens traces the development of this idea from Schoenberg through Webern and Karlheinz Stockhausen to John Cage:

Initially, the increased expressive potential that atonality gave the composer caused the unity of the work to decrease, and set in motion an eventual disintegration in which the specific and the general, parts and whole, became irreconcilable. And this increase in expressive potential demanded an increase in structural organisation. And although dodecaphony consolidated the subjective dynamics it could not bring about a real reconciliation: the form/content duality remained intact. The twelve-tone technique brought about an equalisation of the musical content.[51]

This is a familiar argument, but because Mertens equates dodecaphony, at its inception, solely with Schoenberg, his assessment of historical developments is missing a link. Hauer's music and ideas represent in part the obverse of this modernist coin. Mertens quotes Adorno: "Music becomes the result [with twelve-note developments] of a process that determines the music without revealing itself."[52] This is notoriously the case with Schoenberg, where it is extremely difficult, if not impossible, to recognize the employed row, relying solely on an auditory response; it is textually, rather than sonically, detectable. Hauer's method, even in its earlier stages, was intentionally different from this. He stressed, for example, that the recognition of the movement from one trope to another should be audible, as in a sense of "modulation." This is heightened in the spiel theory, where the construction of the continuum stresses the movement from notes of the original cycle through to the note in the tetrad that connects to the next cycle note (the so-called exit note). This results in the procedure making itself audible, for as we have seen, each tetrad differs from it neighbor by only one note. The difference therefore stands out audibly.

Mertens continues that it was through Webern's adoption and development of Schoenberg's method that "maximum determination of the material is achieved, which results in *non-sensual* relationships." In other words, Webern's works "produce their form simply through the unfolding of the material."[53] This he regards as a stage further toward the work-as-process, developed from Schoenberg's serialism, yet Hauer preempted this in both his theory and his practice. As I discussed above, nonsensual musical relationships are central to his method, and the spiel works are produced via a process that dictates all musical parameters; pitch, rhythm, and form. In this way Hauer's approach is even more simply the result of "process" than is Webern's.

The next stage in Mertens's argument is taken by Stockhausen, principally in the notion of "moment" or "now" form. Here there is no exposition, development, and recapitulation, but an open work is conceived with no definitive beginning or ending. Although it is true that Hauer's spiel works do not produce an "open work" in this sense, the circular conception of the continuum does allow for a temporal unfolding in the nature of a *perpetuum mobile,* a conclusion that returns us to our starting point. A direct result of Hauer's procedure for setting up a continuum means that the first tetrad can directly follow the last one. In this way, it relates to a minimal aesthetic. As Steve Reich has written:

> John Cage has used processes and has certainly accepted the result, but the processes he used were compositional ones that could not be heard when the piece was performed. The process of using the *I-Ching* or imperfections in a sheet of paper to determine musical parameters can't be heard when listening to music composed that way. The compositional processes and the sounding music have no audible connection. Similarly in serial music, the series itself is seldom audible. (This is the difference between serial [basically European] music and serial [basically American] art, where the perceived series is usually the focal point of the work). . . .
>
> The distinctive thing about musical processes is that they determine all the note-to-note details and the overall form simultaneously. One can't improvise in a musical process—the concepts are mutually exclusive.

I need hardly emphasize, having covered a number of these points above, that although much of this may be true of Schoenberg and serialism, it does not apply in the same way to Hauer; his system is audible, and all "note-to-note details" are accounted for within the rubric of his spiel procedures. Reich goes on: "While performing and listening to gradual musical processes one can participate in a particular liberating and *impersonal* ritual [my emphasis]. Focusing in on the musical process makes possible that shift of attention away from *he* and *she* and *you* and *me* outwards towards *it*."[54] This last paragraph expresses a sentiment with which Hauer would have been in particular sympathy; music as a contemplative agent of communication. As Hauer rather more grandly put it: "Immutable, absolute music is the link with eternity, religion, with spiritual reality. . . . This stands in contrast to the diverse creeds . . . which are mutable and ephemeral elements."[55]

Although Hauer's terms are very much part of the spiritual impulse of much early twentieth-century art, the implied absence of the "personality" mitigates against much of the expressive thrust of modernism: "immutable, absolute music," for which we can read Hauer's music, is "above" the subjective-personal-contingent. For Hauer, then, his music achieved a state of meditation through the manipulation of its materials; the spiel was a form of meditation in its composition as well as in the listening: listening, composing, and performing in this sense focuses away from the individual to something "beyond"—from the I to Thou (Ebner) or "me to it" (Reich).

Reich and Mertens share a perception of John Cage as being in parallel with a minimal aesthetic in the development toward "musical objectivity." In Cage's case this is reached, Mertens contends, through the use of aleatoricism: "Aleatoricism maintains the serialist obsession with objectivity, but from an opposite point of view; objectivity is no longer the result of the total control of sound, but can only be achieved by abandoning control and by putting the act of composing between brackets."[56] It is not the case that chance plays a role in Hauer's aesthetic, far from it, but it is true that both Cage and Hauer aspired to be objective and impersonal in the act of "composing." To this extent both held the *I-Ching* in high regard, and both were drawn to Eastern philosophies, which tend to focus on nature and the natural world—human beings stand in a different relation to the natural world from that of the Western humanist tradition.[57] I do not wish to pursue this issue, for our project lies in a different direction, but I would note that the role of the composer in this context stands apart from many of the assumptions that underpin Western musical aesthetics. As Hauer has put it, "Twelve-note music is not an art in the Classical, Romantic or modern sense, but a cosmic game (Spiel) with twelve tempered semi-tones."[58]

The above account has signaled some of the ways that Hauer's work connects to the developments of the concept of work-as-process, which underpins the aesthetics of musical minimalism. It is now time to turn to a consideration of the roots of this minimalist aesthetic in the plastic arts and to show how an interdisciplinary understanding of these theoretical issues relates Hauer to reactions against modernism, for it is in visual art that the concept of minimalism was first critically employed and developed.

HAUER AND MINIMAL AESTHETICS IN ART AND MUSIC

Schoenberg's music consciously developed out of expressionism. Hauer's did not. Notions of expressionism formed an important predecessor to minimal aesthetics in music and the visual arts. The reigning style of American painting in the early 1950s was abstract expressionism, paintings in which a high degree of gestural spontaneity acts as a trace of the artist in the work. Indeed, the gesture itself becomes the signifier of subjective artistic freedom and expression. This is the artistic context of Clement Greenberg's criticism, and one of its exemplars, as mentioned, was the painter Jackson Pollock. Pollock's drip technique and his method of laying the canvas flat on the floor and painting from all sides signaled the function of painting as an expression of the artist's (inner) psyche or personality. The musical corollary to this is not Cage, as some critics have argued, for the reasons I have explored above and develop in the next chapter.[59] Rather, it is jazz: in brief, a concern with notions of the "primitive," allied to the idea of unconscious, spontaneous invention (such a view often says more about those so influenced than it does of the often complex societies characterized as "primitive"); an improvisatory method and, in the case of painting (and Pollock's work in particular), a reliance on the preeminence of gesture over object; and the method of pouring or dripping paint, which is, like improvisation in jazz, simultaneously composing and performing together; these can be regarded as methodological similarities.

The reaction against this spontaneous form of expression began to emerge in the late 1950s and can first be detected in the work of painters like Barnet Newman and Ad Reinhardt.[60] Newman reverses the approach of Pollock, in that he regards painting as principally an object (rather than a gesture) and, further, as an object that, as far as possible, must stand apart from its creator. For Reinhardt, art was less a form of self-expression, extemporized in the process of composition, than a process to be worked out in detail, precomposed rather than improvised. His late work approaches minimalism, as in his post-1960s canvases with their purity of geometry and near monochrome, smooth, matte surfaces (for example, *Abstract Painting No. 5* (1962, Tate Gallery, London). However, these works can evoke an aura that is in stark contrast to the immediacy of minimalist objects. As the art historian David Anfam has said of Reinhardt, in relation to abstract expressionism, "Critical of its romanticism, he shared its eye for absolutes."[61] Such dissatisfactions with abstract expressionism achieved a definitive break in the 1960s. In the words of Frank Stella: "I had been badly affected by what could be called the romance of Abstract Expressionism . . . the idea of the artist as a terrifically sensitive, ever-changing, ever-ambitious person. . . . I began to feel very strongly about finding . . . something that was stable in a sense, something that wasn't constantly a record of your sensitivity."[62] This search for an alternative aesthetic base is a characteristic swing back from romantic to classical values, and it is worth reminding ourselves that Hauer always regarded Bach and Mozart as his immediate precursors. He is thus overlooking and bypassing the movement of romanticism and its later manifestation, expressionism. Schoenberg, by contrast, was not only the inheritor of Wagnerian romanticism but was also involved in the expressionist movement in painting as well as in music.[63]

I wish to return to reactions against abstract expressionism and, following the useful characterization of musical and visual minimalism by J. W. Bernard, to highlight three principal strands of this emergent minimalist aesthetic, relating them to the work of contemporary artists and composers and then back to the ideas of Hauer. It is, of course, extremely difficult to isolate all defining elements of a style (counterexamples can often be found in the ways creative artists resist conventions), but if we highlight certain strands of the minimalist aesthetic, an interesting comparison can be made for the purposes of analysis. Therefore, the following is not meant to subsume all artists and musicians who have been or might be labeled minimalist. Rather, it is meant to emphasize leading strands or strategies. In the context of a shared impulse to stand apart from tradition these strategies can be characterized as: (1) the avoidance of aleatoricism through the employment of impersonal systems, (2) the emphasis on surface, eschewing detail and complexity, and (3) the concern with disposition rather than composition, a resistance to "development," the making of statements through limited resources, and so on.[64]

There is some debate over the exact relationship between minimalism and modernism, as I mentioned earlier. Some critics have viewed it as a continuation of the project of modernism through its emphasis on formal issues and values, while others see it as a redefinition, through its questioning of the nature of the art object and its apparent refusal to engage with traditional notions of aesthetic interest or value.[65] As we explore the strategies I have outlined above, these issues should become clearer. But whatever the case, the advent of minimalism certainly marks the beginning of a discontent with the paradigm of modernism as an art of personal statement through the expressive use of media.

The Avoidance of Aleatoricism

All art involves choices. Even the employment of chance involves choice and preference, and as the composer Mauricio Kagel has often remarked, each realization is the death of chance. And yet, total control is not achievable, for the act of reception, as well as performance, engages a world beyond the control of the artist or composer. All art, therefore, sits on a line between these two (theoretical) extremes. Those artists associated with minimalism aspired to control, against the spontaneous, improvisatory, and more automatist approach of their immediate predecessors. Creation became a question of limiting, rather than eliminating, chance. But within minimalist aesthetics, because the material itself is simplified and the formal constraints to which it is subjected are considerable, the end results remain focused within a relatively narrow range of possibilities. If we take an example from each medium, music and art, it will be easier to compare these strategies with Hauer.

Terry Riley's *In C* of 1964 is an early classic of minimalism; an exuberant, basal work that stood as a small emblem of the alternative 1960s sensibilities to that of the Vietnam War, riots, and assassinations.[66] In a way this is not dissimilar to the refuge Hauer sought in his musical universe from the political turmoil of Austrian society in the aftermath of the Habsburg Empire and the horrors of two world wars. Such art is, therefore, political in the sense of attempting to disengage from the specific social circumstances of the artist rather than aspiring to intervention.

The very title of Riley's piece sets it in opposition to Schoenbergian atonal and serial music in its declaration of the most elemental of key signatures. We should resist simply calling it "tonal," however, since there is little impression of harmonic progress or motion, no real sense of long-term tonal goals. The tonal resources of the piece consist of simple musical phrases derived from the tonic

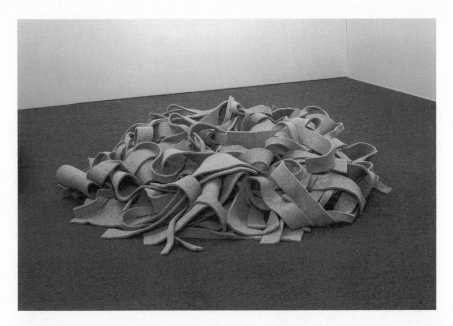

5.3 Robert Morris, *Untitled (felt)*, 1967–68, 254 pieces of felt. Reproduced by permission of the National Gallery of Ottawa, Canada, purchased 1968. © ARS, New York, and DACS, London 2000

chord and scale of C, with only very sparing use of F♯ and B♭. A basic beat in regular quavers is set up in octaves (the two highest Cs on the piano keyboard) and a pedal point, which continues throughout the work. The first phrase, an ascending major third (C–E), establishes the tonal core. From this point the piece unfolds in a gradually spreading canonic texture, almost exclusively diatonic, producing a succession of major and minor triads. It manifests limited improvisational freedom; the number of players, instrumentation, and exact timing of each of the fifty-three figures on a single page that make up the piece are left unspecified. However, the sequence of the fifty-three sections is fixed, the dynamic level is a steady forte, and no performer is allowed to play as a soloist. Further, the performers are directed to remain aware of their fellows, to listen creatively to the others so that all parts can "chime" together. This produces a degree of formal control on a completely determined stock of musical fragments that, nevertheless, allows the performers to become fellow composers. The element of chance is, therefore, reduced, but not eliminated.

In 1967–68, the artist Robert Morris produced *Untitled,* a work that has commonalities with Riley's aesthetic (fig. 5.3).[67] Morris had been a student of Ann Halprin when La Monte Young and Riley were composing works for her performances in the late 1950s and early 1960s. As with Riley's *In C,* this work by Morris presents a formal context that is to some degree variable, a set of instances, rather than a set of formal relations among different constituents, as the specific relations between the various elements are subject to change. When the work is transported from one viewing situation to another, as with different performances of *In C,* the specific formal relations inevitably undergo transformation. Therefore, the spectators or listeners experience a different range of connections at each manifestation, performance, or installation. Again, as with *In C,* Morris's *Untitled* is limited in material—264 pieces of tan felt, one centimeter thick— and to one process, cutting. The work is simply the result of applying the process of cutting to the material. That the strips are of different lengths and widths and that the disposition is variable, like Riley's work, produces control within a fixed material circumstance, which allows for creative input on the part of the installer of the work, as it does for the performers of *In C.* Morris is here concerned more overtly with process than object (what he terms "anti-form"); the siting of the work results from the performance of dropping the felt on the floor. In this way there is a gesture in the direction of Pollock and his technique of dripping paint onto canvas on the floor. In common with paint, the felt has pliancy, a quality not normally associated with sculpture.

Hauer too often allowed another person to arrange the twelve pitches from which he then worked. This is not dissimilar to the casting of the yarrow stalks in the *I Ching.* For Hauer, the choice of "melic" motif or "trope" is the starting point, and one that (like key) is open to choice. "The musical imagination must be at work in conjunction with the system."[68] But from this point on there are peculiarities in the tropes or continuum that must be observed if the method is to retain its structuring role. For example, as I earlier described, within the continuum, the relationship between "cycle" and "exit" notes has to be followed: what we can call the "flux potential," the movement through the tetrads following cycle and exit notes (although, even here, there is the possibility of limited choice). Performing a monophonic extraction from the continuum one can, on occasion, choose to use crotchets (first type), quavers (second type), triplets (third type), or semiquavers (fourth type). In the fifth, mixed type, the flux potential itself would determine the rhythmical structure by providing a certain number of notes to be played between the cycle and exit note, thus giving the range of rhythmical values (crotchets, quaver, triplets, or semiquavers). This produces variety, but without choice. Choice is possible only in the third and fourth types: in the third type the composer can select which of the two axial notes to take, and in the fourth type, the composer can choose which note to play first. In this way, the continuum acts to limit the material and determines the note-to-note relations while allowing constrained choice.

The impulse to limit human input and will is in part an effort to allow art objects relative autonomy, and although this is a more profound impulse in minimalism than in Hauer, both aspire to restrict contingency to allow voice to the more universal. Ultimately, within minimalism, this can lead to profound alienation, which is far from Hauer's intention. His art is more spiritually driven; relative autonomy should lead the subject to the infinite, not the void. This distinction is historically grounded, and we should be aware of it in our comparisons so as not to misconceive the ultimate aims of differing artists, despite commonalties of method.

The Emphasis on Surface

In minimal art, the emphasis on surface is partly aimed at avoiding the centrality of personality. Many of these artists and musicians felt that existential angst and vertiginous gestural flow had become too overt, too excessive, too exclusively the raison d'être of art. Let us consider an early work by the artist Frank Stella, *Six Mile Bottom* of 1960 (fig. 5.4). Stella is unusual in giving his works allusive titles. The titles are, however, always employed sardonically, stressing the lack, rather than the presence, of evocative content beyond the mute surface.

In the works he produced between 1958 and 1960, Stella wanted to create abstract paintings that eliminated the illusion of space, even the space into which the eye alone can travel (to recall Greenberg). In doing this he also, like most minimalist artists, eliminated the use of color as an important expressive element, by first using black, which he considered a noncolor, and then silver aluminum paint, as in *Six Mile Bottom*. The use of varied color inevitably leads to spatial alignment, so aluminum paint was chosen partly for its role in reducing spatial relationships: "The aluminum surface has a quality of repelling the eye in the sense that you could not penetrate it very well. It was a kind of surface that wouldn't give in and would have less soft, landscape-like or naturalistic space in it. I felt it had the character of being slightly more abstract."[69] The regulated surface pattern of this work was arrived at by following the form of the edge of the canvas. The width of the strip was determined by the width of the housepainter's brush used, a tool and technique that Stella felt complemented the design. In this way form dictated content; the chosen formal boundary establishes the system, which unfolds to produce the complete work. The use of a notched canvas draws attention to the procedure, the system of construction. The spectator's eye is required to move smoothly across the surface. There is no background, all is foreground without interiority: "illusionistic space [is forced] out of the painting at a constant rate using a regulated pattern."[70] The eye is given no point of repose except at the limits of the work and, importantly, in the center, the hole, a vortex, a site of real space. The subject of the work could therefore be seen as a dialogue between the

5.4 Frank Stella, *Six Mile Bottom,* 1960, metallic paint
on canvas, 300 x 182 cm. Tate Gallery, London. © ARS,
New York, and DACS, London 2000

idea of surface and (real) depth and between the idea of sculpture and painting. Because the structure directly echoes the shape of the canvas, the painting becomes an objet trouvé. The use of deep stretcher bars pushes the work away from the wall into the viewer's space, away from the notion of painting as an opening onto an imaginary space as it becomes an opaque surface occupying real space.

In the early work of both Steve Reich and Philip Glass, there is concern with melodic rather than harmonic manipulation, with horizontal rather than vertical development. Reich's *Piano Phase,* composed for two pianos in 1967, consists of the same ostinato played in slightly different tempi, so that the second player moves further ahead of the first. It shows a concern with "live" performance in place of the tape-loop phased works, such as *It's Gonna Rain* and *Come Out,* both 1965. *Come Out* is more overtly political in content, like Reich's *Different Trains* of 1988, which contrasts his memories of family trips by train (between 1939 and 1942) with the experiences of European Jews taking trains to their deaths during

5.10 Philip Glass, *Two Pages*, 1969, beginning and end. Reproduced by permission of Chester Music, Ltd. (license no. PL240899)

the same years. *Come Out* originated in a statement from Daniel Hamm, one of the so-called Harlem Six, convicted of murdering a Jewish woman shopowner in the Bronx. The Harlem Six had been beaten after their arrest, and in the taped description of his treatment, Hamm explains that, in order to be transferred from the police station to hospital, his injuries needed to be visible, so he squeezed on a bruise on his leg to "let some of the bruise blood come out to show them." This work is trenchant in its use of repetition and sacrifices overt musicality for the sake of its polemical point.

The return to less "extramusical" issues is evident in *Piano Phase,* which was Reich's attempt to arrest what he felt was in danger of becoming the "gimmick" element of phasing and apply it to a broader musical context. It is, nevertheless, a fairly rudimentary work that lacks any harmonic complications. The first melodic pattern, for example, from which the others are derived, consists of twelve notes but uses only five pitches presented in ascending order: E, F♯, B, C♯, and D.[71] Similarly, Glass's composition *Two Pages* of 1969 consists of highly reduced melodic material, again of only five pitches, G, C, D, E♭, and F, and one rhythmic value, quavers (ex. 5.10). In this piece the formal boundaries, akin to Stella's *Six Mile Bottom,* determine the start and finish of the work. The form confines the content, the work being precisely two pages long. Even in these composers' later works, which have more textural and harmonic complexity, the concern is predominantly with simple chords and clear open harmonies, together with highly limited instrumentation, resulting in limited harmonic depth with little or no sense of hierarchy or complex textual relationships. This produces an effect of musical surface, but not necessarily a simple experience. We should also note that, as Stella used manufactured paint, so the aural, and sometimes textual, impression of much musical minimalism is likewise "premanufactured," a quasi-industrial process of familiar musical units "bolted" together. The feeling of surface is also invoked through the constant pulse and repetition of much minimalist music, which sets up a screen of expectation while placing in the foreground only limited change, giving a sense of "flatness"—continuity in time as the music "unfolds," as there is continuity in space with minimal art.

Within the sound world of the spiel works there are, as I have discussed, limited opportunities for rhythmic development (from crochets to semiquavers), which produces a sense of unfolding. Within the three possible categories of "extraction"—monophonic, complementary monophonic (diaphonic, paraphonic, metaphonic), and polyphonic—there is thus a constant pulse, usually marked at a crotchet equaling 72 to 80, and rhythmic flow. This can be demonstrated by a couple of examples, though what I have to say is applicable to almost all the spiel works. The *Zwölftonspiel* of April 1947 uses a triple meter manifested exclusively in semiquavers. It employs six transpositions of the original cycle, within a pitch range of C below middle C to C♯ above. In Hauer's notation it produces an extremely unified visual statement (ex. 5.11). The *Zwölftonspiel* of 3 February 1954 (in conventional notation) is again in triple meter, manifested in semiquavers and crochets, this time monophonic from a polyphonic extraction (ex. 5.12). It has the same mezzoforte dynamic and pulse. This is common to all zwölftonspiel, for Hauer said that they should be "not too fast, not too slow, not too loud, not too soft; well tempered, well intoned!"[72] The pitch range of this work is from F (two below middle C) to D♭ (three above middle C). These two examples— and I could choose many others—are not markedly different from the constant or simple rhythm, steady dynamic, and limited pitch material of much of Reich's or Glass's early music, and they present a similar image on the page. Such works display a shallow sense of texture and, like the work of Reich and Glass, have limited instrumental means, often keyboard. For Hauer, however, this has to do with the central importance of equal temperament in creating nonsensual note relations. In addition, the processes of following the specific ramifications of the employed system mean that the final work is preordained in the chosen material. No further development is possible without repetition of that which has already been stated. The aural effect of many of these spiel works is similar. If this is seen

Josef Matthias Hauer
Zwölftonspiel für Cembalo

April 1947

mit einem Zwölftonzyklus von Victor Sokolowski

computertypesetting of the twelve tone notation by Robert Michael Weiss ©1999

5.11 J. M. Hauer, *Zwölftonspiel*, April 1947

Zwölftonspiel

mit einer Reihe von Geoffry Kimpton

(3. Februar 1954)

Josef Matthias Hauer (1883 - 1959)

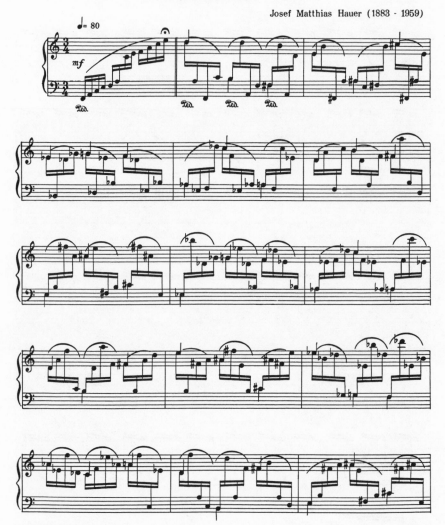

D.16.083

5.12 J. M. Hauer, *Zwölftonspiel,* 3 February 1954, first page. Reprinted by kind permission of the copyright owner © 1979 by Ludwig Doblinger (B. Herzmansky) KG, Vienna–Munich

as a correlate to the "premanufactured" element of the minimalist aesthetic, a characteristic of the employed system, then it would be inappropriate to judge it by the standards of musical analysis that have grown up to deal with the intricate structures of post-Schoenbergian music. Viewed from this perspective it inevitably falls short. If instead we see it in the context of minimalism, this lack of "deep structure" is a positive aesthetic corollary. Stuckenschmidt relates a conversation he had with Hauer in 1955 in which Hauer is reported to have said that such spiel works were not music: "music had died long ago. [They were] a game with mathematics. But if everyone would only learn to read, hear and write it, there would be no more problems."[73] Although this may be deeply optimistic and utopian, it is fundamentally opposed to the idea that a composer expresses things of behalf of others; Hauer, contrarily, is not speaking for us.

The Disposition over Composition

The focus on the concept of disposition over composition in minimalist aesthetics is driven by a desire to achieve a more direct communication with the viewer or listener, to supersede the traditional concept of composition as a process of relating parts. This traditional approach was widely identified by the American avant-garde of the 1960s as a problem produced by the legacy of a now outmoded European phase of modernism, however selective such an identification may have been. In the context of minimalist aesthetics, disposition is taken to mean to put in order, or adapt, and implies a preconceived notion of the whole. This is opposed to composition, which can be taken as the adjustment of parts where the finished product is not preconceived; the artist or composer makes "creative" decisions and choices as the process unfolds. In other words, within a minimalist aesthetic we can, for the purposes of discussion, characterize a disposition as dictated by the materials, whereas composition dictates to, or challenges, the materials. This has other aesthetic ramifications, of course. One important consequence is that works so conceived tend to be more limited in complexity and length, but this, too, is viewed as a positive creative corollary. We can see this approach in the work of the sculptor Carl Andre. *Equivalent VIII* is part of the series *Equivalent I–VIII* of 1966, in which the same number of fire bricks, 120, are placed to form each of the eight larger sculptural groups, all of which are only two bricks high but which vary in all other dimensions (fig. 5.5). There is no challenge to materials here. The original rectangular form of the bricks is merely extended or reflected horizontally: it is this element of "flatness," a concern with sculptural mass, not volume, that connects them to the issue of surface. There is little or no surface interest here; the work operates much as Stella's *Six Mile Bottom* to carry the eye to the edges, the form that defines the mass. Further, the placing of the work directly on the gallery floor obviates the pedestal (both literally and

5.5 Carl Andre, *Equivalent VIII*, 1966, firebricks 127 (h) x 686 (w) x 229.2 (l). Tate Gallery, London. © Carl Andre /VAGA, New York / DACS, London 2000

symbolically) as a device to hold sculpture aloof from the realm of the everyday. Andre did not even make the bricks; they are industrially produced. He merely disposes or arranges them. The art historian Leo Steinberg has risen to the challenge of such works and sought to reclaim some species of expressive effect: "its object quality, its blankness and secrecy, its impersonal or industrial look, its simplicity and tendency to project a stark minimum of decisions, its radiance and power and scale—these become recognisable as a kind of content—expressive, communicative, and eloquent in their own way."[74]

Before concluding this chapter, I wish to make a brief mention of Robert Morris's notion of "gestalt" in relation to certain types of minimalist work. His aim in such an approach is to present "unitary forms," that is, works that do not require a viewer to move around them to grasp the whole. Here sculpture approaches the condition of painting in that painting is often concerned with a fixed spectator in relation to the depiction, in the sense of one "look"—most obviously the case in single-point linear perspective.

In 1965, Morris exhibited *Untitled,* a work that consists of nine L-shaped beams that, although they are identical, are perceived as different through their varied disposition in the gallery space (upended, on their side, tilted, and so on). The effect is heightened, according to Morris, by "the strength of the constant, known shape, the gestalt," against which the manifestation of the pieces, in different arrangements, is always being compared.[75] It is the large size of such works that produces this "presence"; the human figure acts as a constant in terms of scale. Morris's piece can be compared to the sequential work of Andre and others, in that many of these works demonstrate a methodical working out of all the possibilities encompassed by a governing system. However, the theoretical underpinning of all this work, whether concerned with one object or a series, is found in the fact that composition is subservient to disposition.

Context is important. Such works require a specific environment in which to function: the gallery. Bricks become sculpture only in a gallery space, a space for "art." The space becomes a type of pictorial field; it confers form and artistic meaning upon them. Their "objectness" and the viewer's response can function only in such a conventional environment. Thus, the gallery is not a "neutral" space but one that confers meaning and deserves attention.

This should be borne in mind in considering the attempts of such artists to direct the viewer's attention away from the process and toward the object itself. Such an act is not objective in the neutral sense but is rather determined by an alternative ideology. In minimalist music the same can be said of the listener. As I quoted above in relation to Reich: "While performing and listening to gradual musical processes one can participate in a particular liberating and *impersonal* ritual [my emphasis]. Focusing in on the musical process makes possible that shift of attention away from *he* and *she* and *you* and *me* outwards towards *it*."[76] In this way the minimalist composer also focuses on the "wholeness" of the piece. The gradual accretion of the musical material, simple units expanded in musical time, requires, so Glass argues, a different type of engagement:

> When it becomes apparent that nothing "happens" in the usual sense, but that, instead, the gradual accretion of musical materials can and does serve as the basis of the listener's attention, then he can perhaps discover another mode of listening—one in which neither memory nor anticipation (the usual psychological devices of programmatic music whether Baroque, Classical, Romantic or Modernistic) have a place in sustaining the texture, quality or reality of the musical experience. It is hoped that one would be able to perceive the music as a dramatic structure, pure medium "of sound."[77]

Hauer, too, constructed his music out of a set of musical materials, the forty-four tropes. In this sense we can see the act of composition as a problem-solving venture that depends on the proper selection of tropes for its success. The composer manipulates the musical materials. It is a "game," or spiel, operating within a clear set of rules. In such works there is consequently a sense of gestalt, of wholeness. The musical possibilities inherent in the chosen trope or cycle are there in embryo; they are simply worked through in the disposition. The role of the "composer" is to bring about the sounding of these inherent possibilities. It is conceivable, and perhaps in Hauer's eyes desirable, that one trained in his aesthetic could work out the musical relations in the mind with no need to manifest them physically, creating simply a music of the intellect, an art that is truly conceptual. In relation to ancient musical practice, what he presumably took to be oral musical cultures—he refers to ancient Egypt and Mesopotamia—he wrote, "I believe, at this time music has not been written down at all."[78] He later said of the zwölftonspiel: "Putting together a *zwölftonspiel* is child's play, once one has learned the twelve-note notation; playing it properly—reproducing it—is not easy; but *listening* to it is hard, requiring education!"[79]

HAUER'S LEGACY

In a similar way to that of minimalist artists, Hauer's work highlights how the experiences of a work of art may be mediated. Greenberg was extremely critical of minimalism, arguing that it failed to secure aesthetic interest, remaining an idea "and not enough anything else."[80] He saw it as a renunciation of the values that sustain aesthetic quality. This may, in part, be true, for there is renunciation of certain notions that underlie ideas of modernism in minimalist works, and I include aspects of Hauer's work in this, in that they run against the grain of many established patterns of interpretation. Hauer has often fallen victim to assessments of his work that are unaware of the appropriate terms of reference and therefore compare his method unfavorably, for example, with Schoenberg's (as Rosen did in the opening quotation). Hauer is dismissed as an inferior serialist or as "unexpressive," unconcerned with dramatic musical structure, and so on. What I am suggesting is that in order to assess such work properly, we must construct appropriate contexts of inquiry. These should include, not just historical context, but also the artists' and musicians' intentions.

I have offered one such context. Although much of Hauer's thought can be accounted for in terms of the paradigm of modernism, its deviations from this set of criteria must be understood in terms of the unique project Hauer set himself. His approach has conceptual contact with the aesthetics of minimalism; the idea of the work-as-process, the denial of the central importance of self-expression, the reduction of textual density and the increased focus on surface or sonic foreground, the use of preexisting materials, the emphasis on disposition over composition, and so on. Herbert Eimert, the electronic music innovator and outspoken promoter of the avant-garde, has put it thus:

> The cloak of mystical abstruseness, which characterizes poets, philosophers, and eastern philosophies as well as the author under discussion [Jefim Golyscheff], surrounds Hauer's unexciting, static, twelve-note music. His music is consciously antihistorical, intentionally primitive, and, despite the absolute atonality, almost always sonorous. In its meditative character, it avoids subjective differentiations and logically turns to the objective, impersonal set of twelve tempered tones. . . . In the development of new music, Hauer stands as the typical outsider and individualist. In accordance with the trends towards true objectivity, this twelve-note music can be appraised as the first (almost premature) undifferentiated attempt at reshaping of the materials of music.[81]

Eimert's turn of phrase is certainly not mine; I have not described Hauer as "antihistorical." Rather, Hauer was concerned with classical values in an expressionist era. He was not "primitive" but strove for simplification and clarity rather than serialist intellectualism. He was not objective in the usual sense but was object-oriented. I concur, however, with the thrust of much of Eimert's assessment, if not with his tone. My project has been to offer a way of assessing Hauer's legacy by demonstrating its points of contact with a minimalist aesthetic. It is true that Hauer has been linked to more contemporary classical aesthetics, such as de Stijl, for example, and I agree that many of these points of contact are suggestive.[82] My concern has been, however, to link Hauer's ideas to musical consequences and ramifications through an interdisciplinary approach. I am aware that more could be said about the cultural and social context of these ideas. But my task here has been to lay out a set of textual and conceptual issues with which any future contextual work on this relatively little-known composer will need to engage, and which offers a view of modern artists' work that adds complexity to the act of historical writing and critique. In reshaping the materials of music, Hauer's ideas and practice may have been "premature," but they were so in ways that prefigure much that is central to the aesthetics of minimalism.

SIX A CHORUS OF VOICES SEEING MUSIC IN CAGE AND FLUXUS, THE BIRTH OF THE POSTMODERN

How sweet the moonlight sleeps upon this bank!
Here will we sit, and let the sounds of music
Creep in our ears; soft stillness and the night
Become the touches of sweet harmony.
—William Shakespeare

The greatest events—they are not our noisiest but our stillest hours. The world revolves, not around the inventors of new noises, but around the inventors of new values; it revolves *inaudibly*.
—Friedrich Nietzsche

In this final chapter I return to Barthes's characterization of interdisciplinarity, discussed in Chapter 1:

What is new and which affects the idea of the work comes not necessarily from the internal recasting of each of these disciplines, but rather from their encounter in re-lation to an object which traditionally is the province of none of them. It is indeed as though the *interdisciplinarity* which is today held up as a prime value in research cannot be accomplished by the simple confrontation of specialist branches of knowledge. Interdisciplinarity is not the calm of an easy security; it begins *effectively* . . . when the solidarity of the old disciplines breaks down . . . in the interests of a new object and a new language.[1]

Here I wish to place this set of ideas in a historical context through a particular case-study, providing an introduction and context for the work, or more accurately texts, of a notoriously definition-defying group of artists who were centered around the Lithuanian George Maciunas (1931–78). This loose coalition was at various times in the artists' individual careers happy to operate under the banner of Fluxus. The title itself signals the ambiguous and deliberately elusive nature of the activities and ideas of this group.

The concept *flux* is to be understood not just as a noun but also as a verb and an adjective, and, as the standard dictionary definition has it, "a continuing succession of changes."[2] The group's work raises fundamental issues about the nature of the art object and the boundaries of academic study, ranging as these artists do over both temporal and spatial arts. However, as Kristine Stiles has argued, the ontology of Fluxus is essentially performative.[3] Through the inheritance of the work and ideas of John Cage (fig. 6.1) and the Fluxus aesthetic, the performance, or concert occasion, is to be viewed as a complex *field* of activities—visual, textual, and sonorous—one that, among other things, understands the concept of music as a *discourse*. That is, the performance exists as a conceptual constellation, orbiting sound but including the scaffolding that is necessary for the sound to exist (instruments, institutions, traditions, conventions, and so on). This view, which stands diametrically opposed to modernist references to music as a paradigm of autonomy, introduces the concept of music to evaluation on a number of levels, both performatively and textually, not the least of which is the visual.

Music is to be understood as an umbrella under which Fluxus presented many of their ideas within this ontology. Music is performative in the sense Michael Kirby has identified.[4] That is, music is not a theatrical performance in the common sense, for in performance a musician is not playing someone else as an actor might; rather, musicians "play" as themselves. So, too, did Fluxus artists perform or play as themselves, and hence what they performed can be seen as "music." It is only by being aware of the slips and slides between media that the work of Fluxus comes to have meaning: "One key assumption of Fluxus works is that there are close analogies among things."[5] In this way we have returned to the idea that we saw in relation to Wagner that has its roots in the perception that Greek tragedy assumed that the arts work together in concert as a guide for life. Only later did the arts divide and stand apart. Fluxus reintegrated artistic practice in a

6.1 John Cage preparing a piano (before 1950). Courtesy of the John Cage Trust

way that healed this perceived split or, at the very least, failed to recognize that art forms are exclusive.

To understand this aesthetic effectively, we need to develop the concept of *intermedia*. This is to take up a methodological framework first suggested by Dick Higgins, who was a member of, and theorist for, Fluxus. *Intermedia* can be defined as the conceptual ground between media or traditional art disciplines; as the gaps between, rather than the centers of, fields of practice; as an examination of the conditions under which epistemological distinctions function. Andreas Huyssen has suggested that Theodor Adorno's concept of *Verfransung* is close to this notion of intermedia but carries with it a greater sense of dissolution and aesthetic entropy; it suggests not a unity of the arts but differentiation.[6] This entropy became part of the postmodern condition, in which hybrid forms of art and culture often manifested themselves in technologically complex ways antithetical to the Fluxus "low-tech" aesthetic. Nevertheless, even if Fluxus is a historical moment now past, the adoption of an interdisciplinary approach, in the same sense as intermedia (or Verfransung), is an essential academic tool, especially in a post-modern context, for it allows us to see and hear beyond the boundaries set up by the academy.[7] It offers a methodology that is willing to consider the fields that operate between and through disciplines, not in terms of a spurious unity of the arts, but in terms of an analogical or dialectical relationship.

Much of this will remind us of the concept of the Gesamtkunstwerk as discussed in Chapter 2, but it is important that we here register the fundamental difference between this idea in its Fluxus, as opposed to its Wagnerian, manifestation. Whereas the nineteenth-century aim was an integration or merging of the arts under the banner of music, Fluxus was concerned with the ground between media, that which media already have in common, the locus of flux, which is often conceived through the rubric of music. It is, therefore, a less totalizing impulse; a micro-, not a macroview. In contrast, the Gesamtkunstwerk moves toward synthesis away from autonomy. As we have seen, there was a constant struggle in twentieth-century art between these two mutually exclusive dynamics that ebb and flow in the currents of modernism. My contention in this chapter is that synthesis plays a particularly significant role in the emergence of postmodernism.

In Chapter 1, I briefly considered Michael Fried's 1967 article "Art and Objecthood," in which he argues that any art form that refuses to distinguish between art and nonart, or between one art form and another, is labeled "theater." Such works lie, for Fried, outside the application of the concept of quality because they lie outside the true concept of art. In Fried's eyes this is no less than a fight for survival, to keep art aloof from the everyday, to stop it becoming merely an "object" (objecthood being the condition of nonart). The works that most obviously stand on this boundary are "readymades." They lay no claim to essential "artness"; they are understood as art merely by the process of recontextualization. It is precisely this emphasis on context, as opposed to text, that is central to the aesthetic of John Cage and Fluxus. The texts are often minimal and fixed, but they are understood in dialogue with their ambience, which is by nature temporal and hence constantly subject to change, in a state of flux. This is why music is such an appropriate label or metaphor, as it is the art form par excellence of time and dynamic change.

In the last chapter minimalism was considered as work that evokes the readymade (premanufactured) but is never simply "found." Because it is always in some sense constructed, much of the work sits in the space between painting-sculpture-readymade. This helps to explain the difficulty of situating it as an exemplar of modernism or postmodernism. It is in these terms that Fried explicitly rejects it in his essay.

I begin by placing the developments toward this radical conception in context, by reminding us of the way in which the definition of what is to be taken as "music" expanded from Schoenberg through Russolo to Cage and beyond in Fluxus. As the "object" of music has been redefined, so the visual emerges for consideration. Music's silent partner has always been the visual; what emanates from the Fluxus aesthetic is the symbiosis of this coexistence. Fluxus shows that "interdisciplinarity is not the calm of an easy security; it begins *effectively* . . . when the solidarity of the old disciplines breaks down . . . in the interests of a new object and a new language."[8]

THE SOUND OF SILENCE: 4'33"

Absence has always been an important presence in art. As Stéphane Mallarmé expressed it, "The intellectual armature of the poem conceals itself, is present — and acts — in the blank space which separates the stanzas and in the white of the paper: a pregnant silence no less wonderful to compose than the verse itself." But the most infamous occurrence of an aesthetic absence was on 29 August 1952 at the Maverick Concert Hall in Woodstock, New York, when David Tudor came on stage to perform a new work by John Cage. It was a work in which nothing happened. To be precise, nothing happened for four minutes and thirty-three seconds. To be even more precise, no sound was intentionally made by the performer for the duration of the three-movement work entitled *4' 33"*, the time-frame being arrived at aleatorically by the composer.[9] This work is central to an understanding of Cage's aesthetic, and was always regarded by him as his most important work: "I always think of it before I write the next piece."[10]

But let us *look* more closely at this work (and I choose my words carefully). Conceived within the conventions of Western art music, Cage's piece seems to deny the very raison d'être of music itself: sound. Or does it? On one level, as is relatively well known, there is no absolute silence. Even in an anechoic chamber, as Cage discovered, one is assailed by the sounds of one's body: the high-pitched impulses of the functioning of the nervous system and the low-pitched drone of the circulation of the blood.[11] Outside such a device we are even more constantly bombarded by the sounds of civilization and nature. These noises are generally regarded as interruptions to music, but Cage interrupted his "music" to let such sound through. In this instance, at Woodstock, the sounds were the wind and rain outside the concert hall and the bewildered mutterings of the audience within it. The piece itself acted as a prism that refracted these noises as sound, as music from the outside, the culmination of Cage's quest for the art of the nonintentioned. But how was this "silence" achieved?

Tudor came on stage, sat at the piano, and made as if to play, but instead simply raised and lowered the keyboard cover at the beginning of each of the three movements, used a different piano pedal in each movement, and timed himself with a stopwatch. For the rest of the piece, Tudor remained relatively motionless and silent.[12] This was his interpretation of the composer's score, the first unpublished version of which consisted of blank paired staves with the timing added (30″, 2′23″, 1′40″), a relatively conventional notational form, except that the staves contained no notes, or, for that matter, rests. There are, however, a number of different notational realizations of the work. The second version, a birthday gift for Irwin Kremen in 1953, was presented in proportional notation (1 page = 7 inches = 56 seconds), a form that Cage had especially developed for his works around this time to help solve the problems of complex timing. In his 1951 work *Music of Changes,* for example, the duration of notes is in space equal to time (for example, one quaver = 2.5 centimeters), but in *4′33″* there are no notes, just duration. Kremen's version was not published until July 1967 in the journal *Source.* Both this and the lost first version of the score consist of notations that equate textual space with time, requiring page turning during the performance, which adds to the theatricality of the performance by heightening the ritual of presentation. However, the first published form of the work, in 1960, is in the nature of a text (ex. 6.1). This consists of the three movements, each indicated by a Roman numeral, with simply the word "TACET" written under each.[13] This is the best-known version and the one most used by subsequent performers, although it has recomposed timings for each of the movements (33″, 2′40″, 1′20″).

This time change does not produce an irregularity as it might first appear, for in his notes to this published score, after describing Tudor's first performance, Cage writes: "However, the work may be performed by any instrumentalist or combination of instrumentalists and last any length of time." The important points, for Cage, are that the silent time frame is arrived at aleatorically and that the three-movement form is maintained.[14] Interestingly, the published score consists of a written, textual instruction, an archetypal example of the "methodological field" (*text*) that Barthes discusses. It is an instruction employing a conventional Italian musical expression, thus attaching it firmly to music custom, which makes its avant-garde impact even greater. Whereas the first two versions of the score will not elicit any sound in the mind of the musical performer (who might otherwise sound the notation internally), in the third version the word "TACET," a signifier of silence, will internally "sound" as it is read.

Paradoxically, this final version implies a sound through its employment of language rather than "silent" graphics. In contrast, the language used in Fluxus textual scores, discussed below, was prosaic and straightforward. A linguistic instruction thus produces not sound but simply a visual transformation, a performance action. But in *4′33″* as Cage conceives it, the textual element is almost always present. There is, of course, no technical reason for it; if a performer can

I

TACET

II

TACET

III

TACET

NOTE: The title of this work is the total length in minutes and seconds of its performance. At Woodstock, N.Y., August 29, 1952, the title was 4' 33" and the three parts were 33", 2' 40", and 1' 20". It was performed by David Tudor, pianist, who indicated the beginnings of parts by closing, the endings by opening, the keyboard lid. However, the work may be performed by any instrumentalist or combination of instrumentalists and last any length of time.

FOR IRWIN KREMEN JOHN CAGE

6.1 John Cage, *4'33''*, 1952. Edition Peters no. 6777a © 1960 by Henmar Press, Inc., New York. Reproduced by permission of Peters Edition Limited, London

memorize the solo part of a Rachmaninoff concerto, for example, he or she can memorize the timings of *4'33"* with no difficulty. The text is there solely for its visual impact, as a point of focus for the performer and audience, demonstrating the visual as a constituent of all performance ritual.

Given this centralization of the visual elements of the performance of *4'33"*, it is significant that the origins of the work are in part derived from the visual field: the all-white paintings Cage's friend Robert Rauschenberg produced in 1949. As Cage himself noted, these paintings are no more empty or blank than his own piece was silent, for they act as environmental surfaces, on which motes of ambient dust or shadows may settle.[15] They are a *field* of focus for the spaces they occupy. The frame acts for the painting as the "concert occasion" acts for the "music," as a point of elision between art and nonart, text and context. These paintings gave him, he said, "permission" to compose a silent work.[16] The silence is also a critique of modernist terms of aesthetic engagement. The view that art requires a detached aesthetically emotive response, one that for visual art is divorced from any other sense, "purely" visual and self-sufficient, is parodied in Cage's silence, which is anything but pure. If modernist criticism requires silent contemplation in the presence of the art work, suppressing any elements outside the medium, *4'33"* shows that no such pure state is possible, no such absolute silence exists, such suppression ultimately fails.

It is worth highlighting two issues that arise as consequences of the performance of *4'33"*. First, the piece allowed the audience to recognize its role in producing this noise and the potential for hearing such sounds as music: the audience members were the composers as well as the listeners, the literal embodiment of the music. Second, because the piece gave the audience members nothing to listen to from the performer, they were made even more aware of the spectacle, the "theater," the visual nature of musical performance. In short, as the audience shifted to listen to something that was not there (the conventional sound of music), they watched something that was: the ritual of performance. This involved the performer and his limited actions—page-turning, pedaling (in the first version), consulting the stopwatch, sitting still, and so on—the concert hall itself, the object of the piano, each other, and so on, and then (but I do not wish to imply a sequence), the audience members recognized themselves as the producers of the "cultural" sound.[17] Sight (and site), sound, performance, and audience are thus shown as inextricably linked and interdependent. To recall Fried's objections, such a work cannot be seen as modernist, for it makes no attempt to transcend the contingencies of the viewer's or listener's time and place. It is "literalist," encountered as part of, or actually made up of, the everyday context. But, we should add, this "everydayness" is filtered through the conventions of music and art within the frame of the concert hall.

Yet we also need to see Cage's piece as a work that is not just about absence but also about presence. In this way *4′33″* is a Gesamtkunstwerk, but one that is in many ways antithetical to Wagner's. For here there is a concern with silence over amplification, and thus coexistence over synthesis. "Music" does not sublimate the other arts, volume does not drown out the other arts' voices. Rather, through Cage's silence, the other arts can be seen to be a part of the discourse of music. The textual (score), visual, and theatrical elements are already part of the fabric of music, here exposed as parts in the chorus of voices that make up the concept "Music." The difficulty some might have in seeing this work by Cage as music is precisely that the sound acts as a conduit through which we can observe the other elements of musical discourse.

CAGE: FROM TONE TO NOISE

To make sense of this radical departure into the realm in which music encompasses all sound and the act of performing is a theatrical event, we need briefly to review the history of modernist music-making that fed into Cage's aesthetic. In many ways, Wagner was the foil for most early twentieth-century music. In purely formal terms, it was commonly seen that he had pushed diatonic composition to an extreme, where tonality, as an underlying structural principle, began to dissolve. More prosaically, he was also responsible for creating, or developing, many of the production aspects of musical spectacle. As Edward Dent writes in his book *Opera,* "We owe it to Wagner that the auditorium is darkened as a matter of course during a performance, that the doors are shut and latecomers made to wait outside . . . that a soft prelude is heard in silence, and that applause is reserved for the end of an act." And later in the same book, "It is entirely to Wagner's initiative that we owe the modern developments of stage machinery."[18] Wagner has also been credited with being a founder of that most theatrical aspect of orchestral performance, the star conductor. So in dramatic musical terms, as well as the more formal development of music, Wagner's influence was an inevitable point of debate for those who followed him.[19]

As Adorno, among others, saw it, there were, at this point, two main avenues along which music could technically progress.[20] One was retrogressive and culminated in a form of neoclassicism. The paradigm of this trend was, for Adorno, Igor Stravinsky. Alternatively one could follow the logic of this Wagnerian impulse into the untrodden field of atonality. Arnold Schoenberg, the hero of this "atonal" revolution, consciously took on the mantle of Wagnerian musical language, arguing that dissonance was a correlative of consonance rather than a peripheral element of musical language or, more crudely, harmony's opposite. The distinction was a matter of degree, not kind: "They are no more opposite than two and ten are opposite, as the frequency of numbers indeed show: and the expressions 'consonance' and 'dissonance,' which signify an antithesis, are false." He went on, "It all simply depends on the growing ability of the analyzing ear to familiarize itself with the remote overtones, thereby expanding the conception of what is euphonious, suitable for art, so that it embraces the whole natural phenomenon." Concluding this theme in his book *Theory of Harmony,* he states, "what today is remote can tomorrow be close at hand; it is all a matter of whether one can get closer. And the evolution of music has followed this course: it has drawn into the stock of artistic resources more and more of the harmonic possibilities inherent in the tone." [21]

Through the abolition of a strict tonal center, Schoenberg slowly felt his way to the formation of the twelve-note or serial technique in 1923, with the fifth of the *Five Pieces for Piano*. Such an approach to composition (founded on the chromatic rather than diatonic scale) did not recognize tonal chord relations or, inasmuch as it did, subsumed them within a metamusical language that offered an alternative conceptual framework. Notions of what constituted euphony were thus expanded; all tones became equal and available to the composer.

After he immigrated to the United States in 1933, Schoenberg took up the post of professor of music at the University of California at Los Angeles. Teaching a variety of students, he took on the young John Cage as a private student between 1935 and 1937, on the condition that Cage dedicate himself to music. Cage's student works during this time show an interest, not in the use of the serial (twelve-note) techniques of his teacher, but rather in the use of *ostinato* (repetition) and serial fragments, as in his first published piano piece, *Two Pieces for Piano* (1935).[22] His percussion works *Quartet* (1935) and *Trio* (1936) concentrate on rhythmic motifs and are similarly idiosyncratic.[23] With this focus on rhythm and renunciation of harmony, together with the use of repetition and stress on timbre, Cage's early compositions favor unpitched sounds over Schoenberg's raison d'être, the tone. By so moving away from Schoenberg's preoccupations, Cage laid the foundation for much avant-garde art that was to follow.

In 1937, soon after the composition of his first percussion pieces, Cage wrote a lecture called "The Future of Music: Credo," which, significantly, opens with the following declaration: "Wherever we are, what we hear is mostly noise. When we ignore it, it disturbs us. When we listen to it, we find it fascinating. The sound of a truck at fifty miles per hour. Static between radio stations. Rain. We want to capture and control these sounds, to use them not as sound effects but as musical instruments."[24] This declaration expands on his teacher's notion of euphony in music, but here it is a matter not just of all available tones but rather of all available sounds: noise.

Cage's preoccupation was a fundamental questioning of the resources of music.

The range of accepted sounds within the convention of Western art music, even given Schoenberg's expansion of euphony, had remained confined within a relatively small compass. Until the development of electronic sound generators, the instruments of the orchestra, within their classes of woodwind, brass, strings, and percussion, had undergone little beyond superficial development (such as changes to key layout and modifications of valves). The issue was not how to increase the range of timbres but rather how to organize this finite set of sound. Why this set of sounds should be privileged to the exclusion of all others was of little or no concern. This foregrounding of musical form and harmonic invention kept timbre, rhythm, and principally the development of new musical instruments in the background. Cage's development away from this convention was anticipated, however, by a figure from outside the mainstream of art music: not a schooled musician but an artist, the Italian futurist Luigi Russolo (1885–1947).

Russolo proclaimed, "I am not a musician, I have therefore no acoustical predilections, nor any works to defend." With the publication of his manifesto "The Art of Noises" in 1913, he set up an agenda that echoes in Cage's *Credo*.[25] Russolo argued that music had separated from the world of the musician. It stood distinct and independent of life, "a fantastic world superimposed on the real one." Music thus held apart from the world addressed itself instead to "purity, limpidity and sweetness of sound." But the ear is not satisfied with such "gentle harmonies," Russolo argues. Our ears (and here he brings to mind Schoenberg's statements) become accustomed to the familiar and seek out new "acoustic emotions." "Modern music . . . struggl[es] in vain to create new ranges of tone." He proposes instead that "this limited circle of pure sounds must be broken, and the infinite variety of 'noise-sound' conquered." He suggests, as Cage might have, that "we find far more enjoyment in the combination of the noises of trams, backfiring motors, carriages and bawling crowds than in rehearing, for example, the 'Eroica' or the 'Pastoral.'"[26] This carte blanche rejection of past conventions and institutions was part of the modernizing impulse of the futurist aesthetic in general, but for Russolo this rejection of the musical past required the invention of new instrumental resources, the "intonarumori," noise-intoning machines he built to play his "noise" music (fig. 6.2). Despite his intentions to seek ways of joining art to the world of noise through such devices and the music he wrote for them (ex. 6.2), Russolo developed an aesthetic that worked in parallel to the sound-noise world around him rather than one that welded the two. Russolo wished to avoid imitation, preferring that the musicians' sensibilities should become attuned and develop a form of composition liberated from convention. Nevertheless, he maintained in this way the separateness from the "outside" world for which he had chastised orthodox musicians in his writings.[27]

It is only with Cage that this project is taken to its logical conclusion: any sound

6.2 Luigi Russolo and Ugo Piati with *Intonarumori*. *Poesia* (Milan: Edizioni Futuriste, 1916)

can be used as music. More important, there need not even be any intention to compose music for there to *be* music. Cage's *4'33"* shows the willingness or opportunity to attune our hearing to all aural phenomena. In other words, music no longer requires an author, performer, or intentional organization, just someone willing to listen.[28] Consequently, the project Cage's teacher Schoenberg set up, to conflate the concepts of consonance and dissonance, Cage expanded to the dissolution of a distinction between dissonance and noise. Cage concluded that it was meaningless to think of a border between sound and musical sound, for all sound had become musical sound.

In spite of his theoretical assertion to "let sounds be themselves," Cage's practice pursued a strategy of what we might call aestheticism. I mean by this that he adopted a formalist conception of autonomy, where the associative aspects of sound were placed to one side, if not disregarded; "music" becomes a concept into which *all* sound is placed. To put it another way, there is no sound outside music. His work *Variations IV* of 1963, from the *Variation* series composed between 1958 and 1967, illustrates this. The score for this work is a prime example of extreme indeterminacy (ex. 6.3). It consists of a series of transparencies containing seven dots and two small circles. This arrangement is to be randomly superimposed on a ground plan of the chosen performance area, which in turn gives a spatial indication of where sounds arise. Lines are traced from one of the circles to the seven points, and the second circle becomes operative only if one

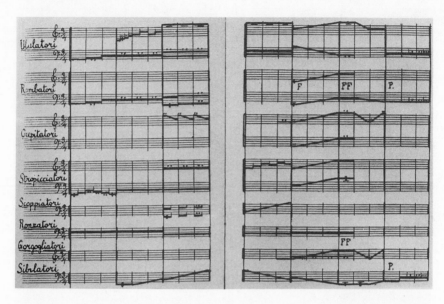

6.2 Luigi Russolo, "Wakefulness of a City," 1914, network of noises. *Poesia* (Milan: Edizioni Futuriste, 1916)

(or more) of the lines touches it. The nature of the music depends on the sound sources found in the chosen site. The score is therefore a description of a situation, a site, not of the sound itself. Cage and David Tudor first performed the piece on 12 January 1964 in the Feigen-Palmer Gallery in Los Angeles.

Central to this score is the importance of space, not only in the location of sounds, but also as a determinant of the type of sound. The work is rarely performed, but a recording was made based on selections from the first performance, which lasted from 7:00 P.M. to 11:00 P.M. This realization made great use of prerecorded sounds and radio. Although the visual element of the performance is missing in the recording, the use of musical materials is worth comment.

In this recorded realization of *Variations IV,* the original context of the prerecorded and broadcast sounds is destroyed so that they can be heard in a "purposeless" way, just as sound. Thus the intention is to produce a collage of sounds that stand apart from their accustomed context. The recording of *Variations IV* uses a melange of sound sources, among them passages from Franz Schubert's fifth symphony, Beethoven's third symphony, Maurice Ravel's *Bolero,* Tchaikovsky's *Nutcracker Suite* ("The Dance of the Sugar Plum Fairy"), Niccolò Paganini's *Capriccios,* European and American folk and popular music, live street and traffic noises, church and telephone bells, radio noise and broadcasts (both music and speech), a typewriter (and, interestingly, a fragment of Erik Satie's *Parade,* the

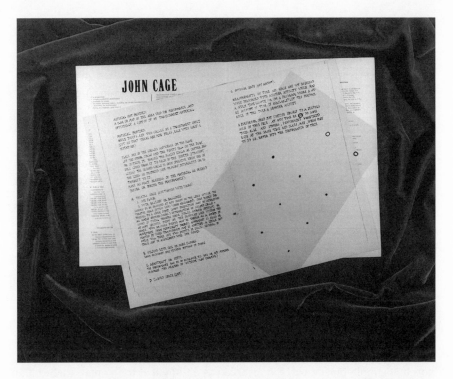

6.3 John Cage, *Variations IV*, 1963. This sheet should be "cut so that there are nine pieces each with only 1 notation." Edition Peters no. 6798 © 1963 by Henmar Press, Inc., New York. Reproduced by permission of Peters Edition Limited, London

first musical work to include a typewriter as a "musical instrument"), audience (ambient) noises (from the bar), and much more. The score does not produce a fixed musical object, in the sense of its internal relations being constant, except with this recording of the work (which Cage called a variation on *Variations IV*).[29] The combinations of elements and the elements themselves will be different with each realization. As the name suggests, this work is variable. It is, therefore, not so much an object as it is an "occasion for experience."[30] The formal relations of tonal and rhythmic elements in a Schubert symphony (or any other prerecorded musical source) have been stripped of their original function and purpose, yet they fulfill Cage's musical purpose. The polyphony of the work is the result of the clash of different sound etiquettes. Fragments are juxtaposed, and some are repeated at intervals, giving a sense of formal continuity. For example, the Schubert is accompanied by, or accompanies, a monologue on the disintegration of a marriage (the counterpoint to this discussion takes place later with a dialogue on "good clean lovers"), along with flamenco guitar, Scottish bagpipe music,

Chicago jazz, the Swingle Singers, symphonic chorus, waltzes and other dance music, babies crying, women laughing and screaming, white noise, and feedback. All these elements are woven together to tease diversity and opposition into a cooperative scheme: the scheme of the composer.

By using such a wide range of sound sources, this "minestrone masterpiece of modern music"[31] creates an "information overload," and can be related to Cage's friend Marshall McLuhan's vision of the world as a global village, but one that does not have the effect of "homogenizing the village quarters."[32] Rather the effect is of pluralism. This is in marked contrast to the Fluxus concern with the singular, as we shall see. But within Cage's aesthetic there is a tension between the "sound in itself," cut off from its original context, and the listening subject. For this Zen notion, that it is simply the role of the artist to alert his or her audience to the beauties of everyday life—art must not be separate from life—places "meaninglessness" and the accidental as central, for the unwilled creative process best "imitates nature in her manner of operation." However, this aestheticization of "life" does not take into account the more prosaic fact that no sounds heard by human beings are ever heard outside society and culture. Experience, memory, and the endemic are ignored in the emphasis on "absolute" sound.[33]

We can regard nature not as separate but coexistent. The real of nature is always the "real," in the way that it is always framed by our humanity. Similarly, art need not, in a simple binary way, be regarded as antithetical to the real. Rather, the two concepts can be seen as conceptually interrelated, dialectically adherent. If we start from the phenomenological assumption that there is a position that is not mine (that is, yours), then Cage's art can be seen to allow contact with the "other" in ways that aspire not to effect, or translate, the fundamental nature of the other through such contact. Even though there is no position outside culture (no unmediated contact with nature), all art will always be in concert with other art, for this is the conceptual frame of its meaning; Cage's music is music by virtue of its place in a cultural continuum, as part of history. Art and aesthetic perception are principal mechanisms by which we see nature.[34] We understand our environment through culture and history. This is not to suggest that there is no distinction between art and nonart, between art and nature, even in the work of Cage, for that would be ultimately to collapse conceptual distinctions and render them inoperable. Rather, the difference between these terms is, in a post-Cagian art world, an issue of contexts, not of autonomous intrinsic meaning. Such conceptions of aesthetic experience as Cage's (open to us as imaginatively participating perceivers) focus on the importance of aesthetic experience as an end, not a means to some further end. Post-Cagian art thus offers a rich conception of the metaphorical implications of creativity—the locus of things and their interpretation.

Like other modernists, Cage proclaimed, perhaps ironically, the importance of the aesthetic in a century where culture was (is) increasingly mediated, socially and politically. As Andreas Huyssen has written, this impulse is the classic modernism of Adorno's "negative dialectic," and Greenberg's conception was an attempt to "save the dignity and autonomy of the art work" from the pressures of political control and the control of the market.[35] This, it should be remembered, was at the time of Hitler's rise to power and then the rise of Stalin and the Cold War and the development of commercial mass culture in the West. However, engagement with the aesthetic in this context need not be viewed as a passive activity, one that is merely "disinterested" in a modernist sense. On the contrary, the act of engagement can be self-reflexive. One becomes, within a post-Cagian (postmodern) sensibility, as much aware of the process of looking and listening as one is aware of the thing looked at or listened to. In other words, one is not just taken out of "context" by aesthetic engagement or contemplation but, through awareness of the act of engagement, reintroduced to the contexts of engagement when the work is understood as a text. In Barthes's terms this process occurs because the text "asks of the reader [viewer or listener] a practical collaboration."[36]

This act of "practical collaboration" is discussed in more detail when we come to consider the place of the audience in the work of Fluxus. We can view Cage, then, as sitting on the border of this "great divide" between the modern and the postmodern, between absolutism and pluralism. Cage brought extramusical sounds (noise) into the fold of music; he made music *represent* more. But for music to be *music* it has to divest sound of association, so that it *represents* the intentions of the composer as culture, not nature.[37] If it does not do this, it is *just* noise; it *is*. Too close an association with the world will return sound-noise to the extramusical. This strategy is precisely what theories of postmodernism attack: the separation of the aesthetic from the sociopolitical world of actual subjects who listen and look. As we have seen, Cage's work wonderfully conjures this difficulty, that representation is diametrically opposed to "sounds in themselves," although he never resolved it.

Even given the problems Cage's ideas raise in practice, his aesthetic poses major difficulties for those who aspire to be "post-Cage." For where does a composer go next in an anarchistic environment in which all sound is available to the musician and the sonic universe is set free?

As I suggested earlier, Fluxus had a microview of artistic practice. The group was concerned not with epic projects but with a rigorous reconsideration of music's sonic materials. They were not so much sonic pluralists, as Cage was, as sonic purists, but not in an essentialist sense. George Brecht used the term "event" to describe the smallest unit of a "situation." It is the event that defines the parameters of a Fluxus musical act. However, the group did also consider the broader frame in which music signifies, through the exploration of the territory of musical practice and performance itself. This involved, among other things, the investigation of the objects of music making. It is not always clear where one of these strategies ends and another begins, for this is in the nature of "flux." But if the diverse activities that make up Fluxus can be characterized, then the concept of an "aesthetics of negation" comes close. For music, this meant the ontological exploration of the borders of the concept of "music" and the spaces between it and the other arts—in short, what can and cannot be considered an act of music.

THE BORDERLINE OF SOUND

One of the starting points in exploring the sonic nature of music was what George Brecht, a prime mover in Fluxus circles, called *incidental* music. This is an onto-logical interrogation through indirect address, not by focusing on the thing itself. This should not be confused with Cage's interest in aleatoric procedures, for in *incidental* music sound is the by-product of action. This differs from conventional performance, where sound is the result of purposeful musical action, and from performances of Cage's work, where sound can be the result of accidental action. An example is Brecht's *Incidental Music* of 1961. This work consists of five pieces for piano, "any number playable successively or simultaneously, in any order and combination, with one another and with other pieces." The fourth piece is scored thus:

> Three dried peas or beans are dropped, one after another, onto the keyboard. Each such seed remaining on the keyboard is attached to the keys nearest it with a single piece of pressure-sensitive tape.

Such a prosaic textual description in the role of a score is typical of Fluxus notations. It needs to be seen both in contrast to traditional notation and against the sometimes hermetic experimental systems devised by other musicians of the avant-garde. Standing to the side of these conventions, it draws attention to the concept of notation itself, reminding us that notation is not simply a transparent vehicle of description or direction but an acquired and culturally mediated system. Fluxus "notation" aims at accessibility through simplicity of description; there is no requirement for acquiring technical language or jargon. However, such a score describes a series of actions; it does not describe or stand for the music in a conventional sense. The "music," or sound, that results from these actions is ancillary to the score. It takes a large number of words to describe even a simple conventional musical perimeter; the scores used by Fluxus artists almost always provide instructions (they are not descriptive) for setting up a situation in which the consequent actions are to be *seen* as music: "The score is the agent that engages the reader-performer in the theater of the act."³⁸ This they share with Cage, as the examples of *4'33"* and *Variations IV* make clear.

However, many such text-scores (or event-scores, as they are also known)— those that are concerned with simple situations—are performable in the mind, as a thought; they do not a priori require physical performance or actual sounding. This is also, of course, the case with more conventional scores (at least for the trained musician), and, as Hauer's example attests, it is even something desired by some composers to achieve a pure musical experience. The difference is that in conventional scoring the re-creation of sound is the intended outcome. In text-scores the intention is the creation of a situation (mental or actual) in which music takes place. A large part of the impact of such scores comes from the imaginative work in conceiving the appropriate situation; they are consulted in advance rather than used as a guide during performance. The active creation of the event by the performer or reader can, therefore, be private or public, and in their challenge to authorial power the scores meet Marcel Duchamp's claim that the creative act "is not performed by the artist alone; the spectator brings the work in contact with the external world"; or we might add, their own internal world (external to that of the composer).³⁹ In this sense the scores are also *incidental*. They clearly stand apart from the realization of the sound of the music, and in so doing they draw attention to the conventional structures and syntax of notation, reminding us that notation is a semiotic of sound, part of the field of music, an element of "music."

But back to our beans. In describing how he performed this piece, Brecht defines the notion of incidence:

> What you're trying to do is to attach the beans to the keys with nothing else in mind— or that is the way I perform it. So that any sound is incidental. It's neither intentional or unintentional. It has absolutely nothing to do with the thing whether you play an A or C, or a C and a C sharp while you're attaching the beans. The important thing is that you are attaching the beans to the keys with the tape.⁴⁰

This concept of incidence finds an important place in the work of La Monte Young, another member of Fluxus. His *Piano Piece for David Tudor No. 2* (1960) can be seen as a comment on Cage's *4'33"*. The instructions require Tudor to concern himself with silence—by performing the same action as was used in the Cage piece to designate the "end" of each of the three movements—raising and lowering the keyboard cover—but here, specifically, without audible sound. By suppressing sound, the score promotes the visual:

> Open the keyboard cover without making, from the operation, any sound that is audible to you. Try as many times as you like. The piece is over when you succeed or when you decide to stop trying. It is not necessary to explain to the audience. Simply do what you do and, when the piece is over, indicate it in the customary way.

The piece is therefore a series of visual, if not aural, actions, and is concluded by the conventional "theatrical" signifier of closure, the bow. From the audience's point of view this piece could well sound the same, whether or not the performer "succeeds," because what is heard by the performer may, in any case, be inaudible to the audience. It does, nevertheless, require focus and a level of skill and concentration from the performer as well as attentiveness from the audience, but not as in conventional music; skill at moving the piano cover silently is a skill, but a different one from that associated with the dexterity required in performing a Chopin étude.

This action focused on "silence" is taken to another level by Young's infamous "butterfly piece," *Composition No. 5,* of 1960. The sound in this work is performed by the butterfly or butterflies themselves and draws attention to the fact that, although in *Piece for David Tudor No. 2* the sound might be audible only to the performer and not to the audience, here no one present, neither the "performer" who releases the butterflies nor the audience, can hear the sound of the nonhuman "instrument." But the overwhelming effect would again be visual; I say "would" because I know of no performance by Young or anyone else to date. An insect recognized as of great beauty, often understood as a symbol of transformation in art, is here the instrument itself. Its flight acts as a visual metaphor for the absent melody, or inaudible sound; Young is reported to have said to his colleague Tony Conrad, "Isn't it wonderful if someone listens to something he is ordinarily supposed to look at?"[41]

Turn a butterfly (or any number of butterflies) loose in the performance area.

When the composition is over, be sure to allow the butterfly to fly away outside.

The composition may be any length but if an unlimited amount of time is available, the doors and windows may be opened before the butterfly is turned loose and the composition may be considered finished when the butterfly flies away.[42]

Writing of this piece, Young raises the issue of audibility as a prerequisite for music: "I felt certain the butterfly made sounds, not only with the motion of its wings but also with the functioning of its body . . . and unless one was going to dictate how loud or soft the sounds had to be before they could be allowed into the realm of music . . . the butterfly piece was music."[43] This work raises problems of boundaries not just between sound and music, or sight and sound, but also between culture and nature. Is the human ear, or, perhaps more important, are the limits of amplification technology, to define music? Can a music exist outside our species in nature (such as whale or bird "song")? Young's approach also lays itself open to claims of anthropomorphism, for music *is* a human construct, *not* a natural phenomenon. But if music is just sound, then sounds are just as much a part of nature as of culture, as Cage argued. Consider this statement on a "performance" of *4'33"*:

> I have spent many pleasant hours in the woods conducting performances of my silent piece, transcription, that is, for an audience of myself, since they were much longer than the popular length which I have had published. At one performance, I passed the first movement by attempting the identification of a mushroom which remained successfully unidentified. The second movement was extremely dramatic, beginning with the sounds of a buck and a doe leaping up to within ten feet of my rocky podium. The expressivity of this movement was not only dramatic but unusually sad from my point of view, for the animals were frightened simply because I was a human being. However, they left hesitatingly and fittingly within the structure of the work. The third movement was a return to the theme of the first, but with all those profound, so-well-known alterations of world feeling associated by German tradition with the A-B-A.[44]

The use of nature in such works draws attention to how culture always frames nature; natural sounds are placed between bar-lines.[45] As discussed earlier, there is no unmediated encounter with nature; it is the human agent (the audience, Cage himself) who perceives such a context as music. The work of art is completed by the spectator.[46] In a series of interviews conducted in 1967–68, Richard Kostelanetz asked Cage, "If you say that music is random sound experience, then why do you compose music?"[47] Cage first replied that it was problematic to ask the question "why?" for to do so is to disconnect yourself from your environment rather than to identify with it. It supposes a value judgment, a focus on one thing at the expense of another, and this is, of course, antithetical to his avowed intent to be "unwilled." His second, more prosaic answer was simply that, as we will recall, he had promised Schoenberg that he would devote himself to music. In other words, rather than feeling constrained by his promise to lead his life as a musician, he expanded the definition of "musician" to include all the work he did.

Later in the interview, he said that, given his time over again, he would not choose to be a musician but would perhaps instead be a mycologist. However, he stressed that he would not want to get rid of art but rather to aspire to identify it with life. The role of the artist is then simply to be a listener.[48] This strategy was shared by Joseph Beuys, a sometime member of the European arm of Fluxus, in his conception of the noun *artist* as one that is applicable to all: "The essence of man is captured in the description 'artist.'"[49] Such a view requires us to consider ourselves producers, as opposed to just consumers, in relation to our world and our ways of living; living itself becomes defined as a creative act. "All the future

6.4 La Monte Young, *Composition No. 7*, 1960

social changes which have to be wrought, of course I mean improvements, can only be based on the definition of humanity as creative, or able. Because only that contains the definition of human freedom."[50] Beuys often stressed that artists should seek to frame appropriate questions rather than seek answers, for this is, in his view, more participatory, less paternalistic. Cage shared this approach, which seeks to conceive of art as discursive, requiring consideration of fields of practice rather than preordained, "natural" demarcations.

To return to La Monte Young and his "butterfly piece," there is, apart from the issue of audibility, the associated issue of temporally fixing a sound so that it can exist long enough to be heard in the first place. For a sound to be contemplated, it has to be arrested or temporally suspended. Here two other important elements of the Fluxus aesthetic emerge: suspension and repetition. Suspension can be seen in another of the series of Young's 1960 compositions, *No. 7* (ex. 6.4). The scoring of this piece, unlike the text-scores considered above, follows conventional Western notation. A specific pitch relationship is designated, the perfect fifth. The image of the score has its visual impact and surprise through this extremely reduced and rudimentary statement. This notation system is precise in terms of pitch (within a range of twelve semitones per octave) but much less precise in terms of the disposition of pitches in time. The use of the treble clef gives the pitches a precise reference point (G above middle C), but because there is no tempo or metronome marking, the time element is equivocal. The two semibreves and the open tie suggest a long duration but in themselves are completely dependent on tempo. Young has added a brief written statement, although this again is contingent. Both forms of instruction, therefore, contain an element of ambiguity that places the interpretative onus on the performer. But this work stresses the act of listening as well as performing.

The aural effect is not, as we might expect, necessarily a simple sound. Here a simple action produces a complex sound. For as the sustained sound interacts with environmental space, the focus on the temporal nature of music is offset and replaced by the occupation of space, a transgression from the borders of the aural to the borders of the visual. In addition, a sound of certain volume — the dynamic is also not specified — can become almost palpable and corporeal when the body is vibrated by its air pressure waves. The physical nature of this environment (the site) can have a profound effect on the reception of the sound. This issue is, of course, central to the science of acoustics and has occupied a range of musicians over many centuries. I offer two examples.

In composing certain organ works for specific instruments in particular locations, J. S. Bach was well aware of the acoustic and its effect on the reception of his music. His use of silences and articulation show cognizance of the effects of specific spaces and sites on his audience. Composing for instruments that were part of the interior of churches requires, from the sensitive composer, an awareness of such spatial characteristics in order for the musical detail not to be lost in a reverberating acoustic.

A more circumscribed response to acoustics can been seen (and heard) in Monteverdi's magnificent *Vespro della Beata Vergine* of 1610. This work makes full and dramatic use of a specific architectural environment, Saint Mark's Basilica in Venice, through its deployment of choral and instrumental forces in various sites throughout the building. Rather than distracting from the musical aspect, the unique acoustic of Saint Mark's provides, in the words of John Eliot Gardiner, a space in which "there is perfect clarity within its long reverberation, with no unevenness of decay nor loss of detail: distance seems not to attenuate the various sounds . . . an architectural setting where the inherently theatrical dimensions of the music can be fully realised and where the richness of both eye and ear can be satisfied."[51] Space has, in this way, often been part of the aesthetic parameters composers have had to take into account.[52] Cage was keen to highlight and exploit the role of site in many of his works. It draws attention to the conventions of the concert hall, in much the same way, for example, that site-specific sculpture does for the gallery. This spatial element in music is accentuated by the listener's ability to focus attention. Shifts of concentration transform the experience of the sound from one moment to the next. This is exaggerated in the case of monotonous sounds: the sound is suspended, but the context is constantly moving. Further, movement in space changes the listener's perception of the character of the sound. This is perhaps more easily imagined in relation to repetition.

(*Arabic Numeral—any integer*) *for Henry Flint* of 1960, or as it is more commonly known, *X for Henry Flint,* is one of Young's best-known works. It requires the performer to play an unspecified sound, or group of sounds, in a regular one- or two-second pulse for as long as the performer wishes—Young's own performance consisted of about six hundred beats on a frying pan. This monosonic approach is antithetical to Cage's polysonic method, although the results may be similar in the emphasis they create on processes of listening. As Cage said, "[Young] is able either through the repetition of a single sound or through the continued performance of a single sound for a period like twenty minutes, to bring about that after, say, five minutes, I discover that what I have all along been thinking was the same thing is not the same thing at all, but full of variety. I find his work remarkable almost in the same sense that *the change in experience of seeing* is when you look through a microscope. You see that there is something other than what you thought was there." [53] As Cage had shown that "silence" is in fact constituted by sounds on which there is normally no focus, so Young uncovers the variety that exists a priori in any act of listening, even in the case of the seemingly monotonous. As Barthes has written, "Hearing is a physiological phenomenon; listening is a psychological act." [54] This moves us from the acoustic fact to the subject's interpretation, from the sound to the audience.

Outside the work of Fluxus, composers associated with so-called minimal music have been most concerned with repetition, as we saw in Chapter 5. Young himself is often included in this group, along with Terry Riley and the now better-known composers Philip Glass and Steve Reich. Glass has written of his own 1970s work *Music in Changing Parts,* in ways echoing Barthes: "Psychoacoustical phenomena are part of the content of the music—overtones, undertones, different tones. These are things you hear—there is no doubt that you are hearing them—even though they may not actually be played." [55] But few works by Glass or Reich are as extreme in their use of repetition as Young's *X for Henry Flint.* One of the best-known performances of this work is that performed by Brian Eno (formerly of the British rock group Roxy Music), around 1967. In this instance Eno played the piece by bringing his forearm down on large clusters of notes, trying to strike the same cluster of notes each time, for an hour (approximately thirty-six hundred times). He later explained:

> Now, until one becomes accustomed to this fifty-odd note cluster, the resultant sound was fairly boring. But after that first ten minutes, it became progressively more absorbing. This was reflected in the rate at which the people left the room—those who didn't leave within ten minutes stayed for the whole performance. One began to notice the most minute variations from one crash to the next. The subtraction of one

note by the right elbow missing its top key was immediately and dramatically obvious. The slight variation of timing became major compositional changes, and the constant changes within the odd beat frequencies being formed by all the discords began to develop into melodic lines. This was, for me, a new use of the error principle and led me to codify a little law that has since informed much of my work—"Repetition is a form of change."[56]

Eno employed an analogy based on his experience of such music—in fact based on the experience of hearing Reich's *It's Gonna Rain,* where that phrase is repeated over and over again on several tape players set at different speeds, so the loops gradually shift in and out of phase. The analogy comes from an essay by Warren McCulloch, "What the Frog's Eye Tells the Frog's Brain." In Eno's words, "A frog's eyes don't work like ours. . . . a frog fixes its eyes on a scene and leaves them there. It stops seeing all the static parts of the environment, which become invisible, but as soon as one element moves [usually its next potential meal!] . . . it is in very high contrast to the rest of the environment. . . . I realised that what happens with the Reich piece is that our ears behave like a frog's eyes. . . . The creative operation is listening."[57]

It is significant that the analogy is one based on sight, for it draws attention to the role of reception, a perceptual field that compels the audience to confront and perhaps revise the borders between the physiological and psychological.[58] Although these works may be formally simple, such notions of repetition or suspension demonstrate that, because of the influence of external factors (both physical and psychological, in the environment and in the listener), the effect, the sonic experience, is neither repetitious nor singular. Further, such a fixated concern fails to possess its subject, for the variety in music so produced means that even such seemingly "static" music evades capture.

From the mid-1960s on, Young developed and extended his concerns with suspension and drones in his ensemble the Theatre of Eternal Music, which forms the counter to the Theatre of the Singular Event (his term for his Fluxus-concept stage). More recent manifestations have included a twenty-three-piece group, the Theatre of Eternal Music Big Band (making links with Young's early jazz training), as well as the Theatre of Eternal Music String and Brass Ensembles.[59] The original Theatre of Eternal Music consisted of, in various permutations and instrumental groupings, first wholly acoustic and later electronic: Young, sopranino; his wife, Marian Zazeela (a painter and light artist), vocal drone; Angus McLise, percussion; Tony Conrad (mathematician and a producer of "minimal" films), bowed guitar and violin; John Cale (later member of Velvet Underground), viola; and occasionally Terry Riley and Robert Morris, who had designed a bowed gong for Young's use. For much of this time Young was developing his ideas within the framework of a series of related works, known under the collective title *The Tortoise, His Dreams and Journeys* (which in 1993 he still regarded as ongoing—although dormant for nearly twenty years). The title signals the metaphor (again based in nature, a constant referent in Young's aesthetic) for a slowly evolving piece with, theoretically, no beginning or end; the work would ideally comprise sections performed every day, lasting a lifetime, with the silences between performances as part of the work. The earlier, extended-duration works, such as *Trio for Strings* of 1958, were conventionally notated. His more recent Eternal Music works comprise improvisation within a context of algorithmic harmonic rules, which determine which pitches can be played together and their melodic sequence. The rules are often developed by oral instructions from Young in rehearsal. In addition, Young conceived of the spaces and time between performance of such works as part of them. The extended duration of works takes place both within and without the concert frame—a post-Cagian conception that allows Young to bracket the works with silence, a "silence" that links his sound world to the constant (eternal) ambient "music" of the outside world.

Zazeela's light-environment *The Ornamental Lightyears Tracery* (as opposed to her sculptures and environments) became an integral part of the Theatre of Eternal Music performances, along with *The Magenta Lights,* environments designed for performances of Young's other ongoing work, *The Well-Tuned Piano* (1964–1973–1981–present), a work of more than six hours' duration. She works with the projection of colored slides and mobiles to produce sites of sympathy for the performance of the music.[60] Their role is in part to aid perception and focus in works that operate outside the time frame of most other music. However, the subtlety of projected color and shadow of such environmental light works requires experience over a long time to appreciate their essential nuances, as does Young's music. Young and Zazeela's light and sound works share concerns with organized tuning systems based on natural harmonics, mathematics, and space, as well as enhanced attention spans. Their six-year-long commission from the Dia Art Foundation resulted in a continuous *Dream House* presentation (1979–85), which was set in the six-story Harrison Street building in New York and featured a number of sound and light–interrelated environments (Young's "magic chord"— in ascending order, E, F, A, B♭, D, E, G, A—and Zazeela's *Still Light*), exhibitions, performances, research facilities, and archives. Their joint work *Dream House: Seven Years of Sound and Light* opened at the MELA Foundation in 1993 and remains on view there.

Part of this project of extended-duration sound works is Young's *Drift Studies* (1966). Here he is concerned with that most elementary of sonic phenomena, the sine wave, which has only one frequency component; all other sound wave forms are multiple. This work makes explicit the role of an active audience, though in this case not just in the processes of listening but in physical activity, too. When a continuous frequency is generated in an enclosed environment, it divides the air into high- and low-pressure zones. The sound is louder in the high-pressure zones and softer in the low-pressure areas; in this way, the space (the room) becomes the musical instrument. Because of the simple composition of the sine wave, the pattern of high- and low-pressure areas becomes easy for an audience to locate as they move through the space, inside the instrument, so to speak. Therefore a passive listener, one unwilling to engage by moving through the space, experiences a single monotonous sound, but the active listener creates an individual piece through physical motion. Variety is generated out of what is formally the most fundamental of sounds. The sculptural, three-dimensional aspect of music therefore becomes significant. One is allowed, in such spatially conceived music, to chart a course around and through the music in one's own time, much as one looks at a static work of visual art, which can be similarly affected by environmental context. This work makes explicit the spatial character of music. We have moved from the conception of music as temporally distinct from the visual arts, a position we saw questioned in the ideas of Klee in Chapter 4, to a conception that addresses the spatial links or common ground between music and visual phenomena, and it is from here that we move to a consideration of the "objectness" of music.

MUSICAL PRACTICE, PERFORMANCE, AND OBJECTS

Fluxus research did not concern itself just with the reconsideration of the sonic materials of music and how there might be mutual ground in the perception of music and visual phenomena. As Young's compositions begin to suggest, the context of sound in a wider sense became just as much a focus as the sound itself. For "music," as I have argued, is not just sounds; it is also performances (realizations), objects and bodies, technologies, texts, and institutions. In short, music is discourse. As Cage's *4'33"* drew attention to the visual aspect of musical performance—by evacuating "music," sight/site rushed in to fill the "vacuum"—so Fluxus took up and developed the ritual around music, which Wagner had played no small part in establishing. Although it is true that all musical performance is intrinsically a discourse, a multimedia ritual (obviously so in opera, ballet, rock concerts, and so on), it is less explicitly the case with concert music. Western musical culture has devised performance rituals that attempt to isolate text from context and minimize the visual and the aurally incidental. In addition, physical expression is minimized, except that required actually to perform the sound, and here gesture is conventionally contained so as not to suggest a spillover into theater. The sounds encrypted in the score are amplified and empowered to silence sight, movement, and audience, who are set apart by the stage.

Young was interested in the audience as a social situation. I mentioned earlier that Wagner was responsible for promoting a darkened listening environment. Another of Young's 1960s "compositions," *No. 4,* similarly has the auditorium darkened, but when the lights are turned on again the audience may (or may not) be told "that their actions have been the performance." As in *4'33"*, the ambient sound is the music, and attention is drawn to the context and site of performance. The theatrical act of lowering the lights prepares the audience for a visual spectacle, but it does not provide one (there is nothing to see). In addition, it focuses listening, even though nothing follows but the audience's actions and sounds. The music slips out of the gap between expectation (lights go out) and realization (lights come up). The work dramatizes the implicit dialogue between sight and sound. *No. 6* of this series reverses the performer-audience relationship, again in relation to sight, by having the performer *observe* the audience:

> The performers (any number) sit on the stage watching and listening to the audience in the same way the audience usually looks at and listens to the performers. If in the auditorium, the performers should be seated in rows on chairs or benches; but if in a bar, for instance, the performers might have tables on stage and be drinking as is the audience.

Optional: A poster in the vicinity of the stage reading:

COMPOSITION 1960 NO.6

by La Monte Young

admission

(price)

> and tickets, sold at stairways leading to stage from audience, admitting members of the audience who wish to join the performers on stage and watch the remainder of the audience.

A performance may be of any duration.

Such an approach reverses the idea of audience as passive spectators in the most direct way. It makes sight (gaze) the sole communicative act. Thus the visual element of musical performance is made conspicuous, for it is all there is. It also underlines the socialized nature of witnessing a musical performance.

Another musical convention that Wagner was instrumental in promoting, the role of the star conductor, was similarly appraised by George Maciunas in his *Solo for Conductor* of 1965. This work focuses on the gesture of recognition, performed by a conductor, to acknowledge the conductor's authorship of a performance, at the start and finish of a work, except here such acknowledgment is the content of the work: the bow is the start and the rising up its conclusion.

The "body" of the piece consists of small inconsequential or incidental activities concerned with the floor (for example, picking up specks of dirt) or with the conductor's shoes (for instance, tying a shoelace). Conductors communicate during a performance silently by visual gesture, a mixture of code (designating beats and cues) and expression, with their back to the audience. Their final "public" gesture (as they turn to face the audience and acknowledge applause) is here sidetracked by the mundane (their shoes or the floor) in the process of acknowledging the profound (their [nonexistent] interpretation).

The orchestra was also evaluated. Brecht, in his *Symphony No. 1,* for example, required the "Fluxus Symphony Orchestra" to play through life-size cutouts of a photograph of another orchestra, as one might pose for a photograph behind an "end of the pier" cutout: "Performers may hold instruments in the conventional way and attempt to play an old favourite." Both of these works highlight the visual element of performance. The conductor's elaborate gestures are reduced to a parody of acknowledgment, and the orchestra's disposition and presence is masked by a visual representation of an absent group of professionals. The visual presentation, in this case, can get in the way of performing the music (an old favorite); the visual thus usurps the sonoric.

Perhaps the most disruptive intervention made by Fluxus artists on the conventional symphony orchestra is Nam June Paik's *Suite for Transistor Radio* (1963). Here the allemande of the suite is to take place between the first and second movements of Beethoven's *Symphony No. 5.* The performer is instructed to play the radio "not very loudly," just as the second movement begins, either directly or, if diffident, by remote control. Here the aleatoric element would probably produce a telling clash of musical languages. It also, in a Cagian vein, introduces outside sound into the heart of a highly controlled musical environment and conflates disparate musical spaces. In all of these works there is an explicit dialogue and investigation among those elements implicit in Cage's *4'33":* sight, site, and sound.

In a more elemental vein, Fluxus performances also added the elements of (visible) fire and water to the use of (invisible) wind in the production of orchestral sound. In the second of Young's *Composition 1960,* the performer is instructed simply to build a small fire in front of the audience: "In the event that the performance is broadcast, the microphone may be brought up close to the fire." Here a largely visual phenomenon generates the sound and involves other senses in the warmth and smell of combustion. In a gentle way this recalls the use of pyrotechnics employed by Jimi Hendrix in his ritual sacrificial guitar-burning stage antics.[61]

George Brecht was particularly interested in the use of water as a musical element. This develops the fact that water as an element is present but suppressed in an orchestral context. As Cage put it: "Even a conventional piece played by a

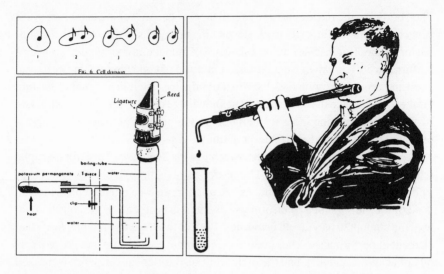

6.3 Slide from George Brecht's chemistry of music lecture, 1969. *Studio International* 192 (November–December 1976), 261

conventional symphony orchestra (is a theatrical activity): the horn player, for example, from time to time empties the spit out of his horn. And this frequently engages my attention more than the melodies."[62] Brecht reverses this process in his *Water Yam* (1963) version of *Drip Music,* in which water is poured from a ladder back into the bell of a tuba or French horn.[63] Brecht's *Chemistry of Music* (1967) brings these two elements, fire and water, together. The performance started with music borrowed from Walter de Maria, a tape of sounds that modulate from drumming to crickets chirping (a move from culture to nature). Then Brecht, dressed in a white lab coat, delivered a visual lecture with slides, a number of which involved water and musical instruments in bizarre experiments (fig. 6.3). To a number of these images he attached fireworks: "in the slide where there's a man playing a flute, I attach a firework that makes a whistling sound. I attach that to the place on the screen where the embouchure of the flute is, and set it off, so that there's fire and a whistling sound." Brecht also employed a series of pseudoscientific diagrams. Conventionally, scientific diagrams privilege explanations over the representation of actual appearance, but Brecht's operate within these conventions while also denying simple explication. In addition to these "diagrams" he used a slide of one of Katsushika Hokusai's *Thirty-six Views of Mount Fuji* (c. 1820–29): "For almost every slide there is a firework that goes with it. And for the final one—Mount Fuji—there's a little rocket set into two wire rings on the top that shoots up into the sky."[64] Brecht had been a scientist and was interested in putting what seem to be disparate areas into a common field (creating puns:

the aperture of a clarinet and a volcano, moving from earth science to art and back again, woodwind instruments involved in chemical experiments, volcanoes becoming musical instruments, and so on). If the essence of chemistry is the investigation of the changes brought about in and by the elements, then Brecht's work is a germane metaphor for Fluxus's approach to the concept of music in general.

The apogee of the idea of water as a sublimated musical element is probably Nam June Paik's *Physical Music* (or the *Fluxus Champion Contest,* 1962). Here water produces sound at the same time that the piece parodies the idea of the athletic virtuosity of the male performer.

> Performers gather around a large tub or bucket on stage. All piss into the bucket. As each pisses, he sings his national anthem. When any contestant stops pissing, he stops singing. The last performer left singing is the champion.

Due to the international make-up of Fluxus as a "movement," the antinationalistic dimension of this act has particular resonance.[65] The issue of virtuosity is also evident in Brecht's *Concerto for Clarinet* (1966), which has the important subtitle "nearby," for the clarinet is suspended from a string tied to its central point of balance, so that it maintains a horizontal position about fifteen centimeters (six inches) above the performer's mouth. The virtuosity lies in the performer's ability to play the instrument—with no hands!—by jumping or contriving to swing the reed end into the mouth. The act of performance, the physical action and visceral nature of engagement, is accentuated in works such as these, so that the body becomes both sight and site of musical action.[66] Music is thus seen as a complex of elements, a field or discourse, and the relationship between these elements of sound and vision is opened up to analysis and attention. The critique of virtuosity through the unconventional use of musical instruments brings us to focus on Fluxus's exploration of the objects of music making.

Paik's collaboration with the cellist Charlotte Moorman provides the most vivid example. As Michael Nyman has written, "Moorman's cello has surpassed any other instrument, in any era, in the number of uses it has been put to."[67] For example, it was frozen in a block of ice and then brought back to life by Moorman's bowing the ice, wearing the ice away through friction, until she finally reached the strings. The physical action eventually achieved sound. Together they also explored the issue of sex and music. As Paik has said, sex is underdeveloped as an element of musical discourse, in contrast to literature or the visual arts. This interest manifested itself most notably in his *Opera Sextronique* of 1967 (fig. 6.4), which Moorman performed topless. This critique of clothing as a style of visual presentation in relation to performance (why dress in black?) resulted in Paik's and Moorman's arrest and their detention for a night, on the grounds that the piece

6.4 *World Journal Tribune*, New York, Friday, 10 February 1967, page 21

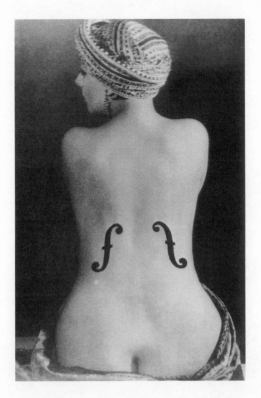

6.5 Man Ray, *Le violon d'Ingres*, 1924, black-and-white photograph, 15 x 11.1 cm. Centre Georges Pompidou, Musée national d'art moderne, Paris. © Man Ray Tust/ADAGP, Paris, and DACS, London 2000

was "an act which openly outrage[d] public decency."⁶⁸ An interesting variation on this theme was their performance of Cage's work *26'1.1499 for a String Player* in the Cafe á Go-Go in New York in 1965. This involved Paik, naked from the waist up, being "played" between Moorman's legs as a human cello (holding the string taut over his back). This work neatly inverts the art historical tradition of stringed instruments' iconic reference to women's bodies—the classic modern example being Man Ray's *Le violon d'Ingres* of 1924—and brings home the corporeal nature of all tactile engagement in musical performance and of its grounding in the body; the musical object becomes a subject (fig. 6.5).⁶⁹

Paik's "decorated" piano, *Klavier Intégral* (1958–63), similarly focuses on the musical instrument as object by rendering that object, in this case the piano, virtually unplayable and turning it into a sculptural body (the decoration puns on

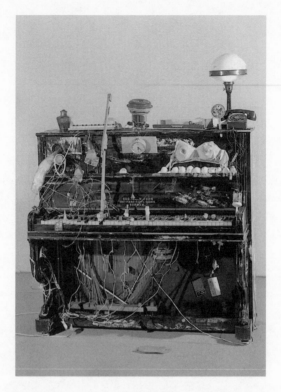

6.6 Nam June Paik, *Klavier Intégral*, 1958–63, prepared with different everyday objects, 36 x 140 x 65
cm. Museum of Modern Art Ludwig Foundation
Vienna, formerly Hahn Collection, Cologne

the notion of body by including clothing: a bra, so no toplessness here!). It could
be considered a joke at the expense of Cage's invention of the prepared piano,
in which objects are introduced in between and onto the strings so as to modify
the sound (fig. 6.6).[70] Brecht also "decorated" a piano (*Piano Piece,* 1962), but
here it is an event-as-object. The score says "a vase of flowers on(to) a piano,"
so a vase of flowers is either placed on a piano or simply observed on one.[71] In
either case the act draws attention to an urbane domestic action, the silent piano
as an item of furniture, a table, a mute object displaying a primarily decorative
function. His score of *Solo for Violin, Viola, Cello, or Contrabass* (1962) simply
states, "polishing." Here again a piece of musical "housekeeping" is the sole objective of the work. The piece can be viewed as an ironic comment on the idea
of the virtuoso as "shining" performer, although no technical skill is required.
Further, the sounds so produced are as much a consequence of the material and

form of the instrument as are the sounds it produces when conventionally played. Young's *Piano Piece for David Tudor No. 1* (1960), the first of three (*No. 2* was the piano-lid piece), also concerns itself with the care of musical instruments. A bale of hay and a bucket of water are offered as feed to that "workhorse" of the virtuoso and composer, the piano. Such approaches to the instruments of music can obviously be seen to fetishize them as much as they parody the notion of the romantic virtuoso.[72]

The counterpoint to this loving and nourishing approach is found in a number of works of a destructive nature. The frustration inherent in the acquisition of skill or experience when learning a musical instrument is dramatized as the obverse of the attachment performers feel for their instruments. Maciunas's *Solo for Violin for Sylvano Bussoti* (1962) consists of twenty instructions to the performer, from the simple inversion of "hold bow to shoulders and bow with violin" (parodying Paganini's demonic presence and performance technique), to the psychological release of biting, drilling, and throwing the instrument or parts of it at the audience.[73] Paik wrote two works of a more destructive nature for violin in the early 1960s. *Violin with String* can be seen as a poetic, if violent, re-presentation of Paul Klee's famous reference to drawing as "taking a line for a walk."[74] Here, however, the "line" is attached to a violin, which is taken for a walk by being dragged behind the performer "on the street"—the violin reflecting Klee's interest in music as a structuring device for visual composition, the "line" adding a fifth string to the normal four of the violin. Paik's *One for Violin Solo* (1961) embraces this violent impulse more laconically. The violin, held by the neck, is to be raised very slowly above the head of the performer. When the top of the arc is reached it is to be brought down with full force onto a hard object. This might again bring to mind Jimi Hendrix's and the Who's Pete Townshend's destruction of their guitars as the high point of their theatrical stage acts, conflating destruction and creation, as well as answering Tristan Tzara's call in the dadaist text *Unpretentious Proclamations* (1919): "Musicians smash your *blind* instruments on the stage," an entreaty that demonstrates frustration with visual absence.[75] It is an attack on the music of the past in a futurist vein ("We will destroy the museums, libraries, academies of every kind"), and has a modernist ring about it in its forward-looking optimism.[76] But as Douglas Kahn has pointed out, the recuperative power of high capitalism in an age of postmodernist ideology restored one of Hendrix's smashed guitars, from 1967, from broken junk back to the status of prized possession, when it was sold in 1991 at Sotheby's in New York for an amazing $45,600.[77]

A more explicit connection with the cultic environment of rock music may be found in Robin Page's 1962 Fluxus work *Block Guitar Piece,* which required the performer to use the feet rather than the hands to produce sound. The performer is to kick the instrument offstage, out of the concert hall, around the block (hence the title), back into the hall, and back onto the stage, having taken it for a "walk." This recalls Paik and Klee, and a similar fate of another guitar in Luis Buñuel's film *L'age d'or* (1930). Such approaches make instruments more than mere transmitters of music; through these works, the instruments become sculptural objects, points of fixation and fetish.[78]

PERCEIVING SOUND

For Fluxus, the concert occasion is a complex field of activities, opening it to critique on a number of levels. Through Cage's works, the audience literally takes center stage; its members not only form a central part of the hermeneutic circle but are often also responsible for the sound of the music. This expansion of the notion of music leads to a focus on music's other constituent elements, principally the visual (the act and body of performance, the objects of music, its sites, its texts). We are best placed to comprehend the visual aspect of music if we adopt an interdisciplinary methodology. If we regard music as only that which is exclusively heard, we ignore music as an occasion that incorporates an integral visual dimension; our definition is limited. Contrarily, to acknowledge that music consists of a visual interrelation between sound and sight (as the aesthetic of Cage and Fluxus compels us to do) is to contextualize our understanding; music is placed. Through this, music acquires much of its conventional intelligibility. Indeed, musicology and art history show the interdependence of texts and nonverbal modes of expression in the creation of meaning. Meanings emerge from the interplay between art and music and words; it is negotiated in the form of a duet (or chorus), not immanent in the form of a solo. Only with the advent of modern technologies of reproduction was music released from its contexts of site and sight. But even here the employment of videos, DVDs, and sleeve-design and notes accompanies the sound with vision, providing a sight and context, and through playback systems (such as personal stereos), provides a potentially numberless series of sites for consumption, sites unimaginable and out of the control of the composer.[79] On occasion, this technology can even liberate the mind's eye to construct pictures or allow us to follow a score (a text, visual notation), but images of some kind are always present and are conventionally determined or rejected. In a post-Cagian musical universe, all sounds and time events can be viewed through a musician's eyes and ears (defining "musician" in the broadest sense), and the interpretative onus is placed on us as audience. Within such an aesthetic, the traditional boundaries among disciplines are no longer hermetic: things are, quite literally, in flux.

A multitude of avant-garde musicians and artists outside the purview of Fluxus have created and performed a wide range of experiments, many based on new technologies—too many simply to list here, let alone study in any detail. My intent has been to draw out a number of themes and consequences, but it is true that many of these experiments take up or develop the aesthetic concerns we have been discussing, concerns that have been developed by a post-Cagian sensibility. As a coda, I mention one by way of illustration.

The 1965 work *Music for Solo Performer* by Alvin Lucier (b. 1931) is a locus for several of these thematic strands. It centers around the inner imaginings of sound, specifically the neurophysiology of the performer. For some of the musicians we have discussed, Hauer for example, this is the most appropriate and "pure" site of the musical. In Lucier's work the soloist's head is wired with electrodes that pick up alpha brainwave activity. This "setting up" is seen as an overture to the work and is carried out in full view of the audience. In this way the performer literally becomes the *corps sonore,* the musical instrument. These alpha brainwaves are processed through filters and amplified through groups of loudspeakers that are placed near percussion instruments that resonate in sympathy to the projected sound waves. The essential point in this work is that alpha waves are produced only during nonvisual brain activity. The output is thus controlled by the performer's opening and closing the eyes—the act of opening them to make visual contact with the environment, the site and audience, in this case produces silence.

To comprehend such works we must be active and broadly based in our references, willing to transgress boundaries. We should, perhaps, open our eyes to hear more clearly. Only by doing this can we, again in Dick Higgin's words, enjoy "concerts of everyday living."[80]

PREFACE

1. The phrase comes from the title of Peter Kivy's *Music Alone,* itself a quotation from the first chapter of Hanslick's classic formalist work, *Vom
musicalisch-Schönen* [1854], 7th ed., trans. G. Cohen as *The Beautiful in
Music,* 1891 (reprint, Indianapolis, 1957).

2. C. Greenberg, "Modernist Painting," *Art and Literature* (Spring 1965),
193–201.

CHAPTER 1: *UT PICTURA MUSICA*

1. The title phrase "ut pictura musica" comes from an article of that title
written by the essayist and critic Louis Viardot in the inaugural issue of
the *Gazette des Beaux-Arts* published in Paris in January 1859. In it he
argues that medium is to become the primary concern of artists, content
becoming secondary. The title was also used by A. Kagan in the essay "Ut
Pictura Musica to 1860" in his *Absolute Art* (New York, 1995), 73–99,
and as "ut musica poesis" as a subsection of chapter 4 of M. H. Abrams,
The Mirror and the Lamp (Oxford, 1953), 88. All of which, of course, derive from the Horatian simile *ut pictura poesis* (see Horace, *Ars Poetica,*
361: translated as "On the Art of Poetry," in *Aris-totle/Horace/Longinus:*

Classical Literary Criticism, trans. T. S. Dorsch (Harmondsworth, 1965; reprint, Harmondsworth, 1986), 91: "A poem is like a painting."

The word museum (*mouseion*) originally signified a temple of the Muses, a school of arts and learning, but it now tends to be used to refer to a house of visual exhibits.

2. Plato, *Republic* 3.3.401, trans. D. Lee (Harmondsworth, 1955; reprint, Harmondsworth, 1979), 162.

3. See Aristotle, "Poetry as Imitation," in *Aristotle/Horace/Longinus,* trans. Dorsch, 31.

4. See E. H. Gombrich, *Leonardo da Vinci* (London, 1989), 1–4.

5. See M. H. Abrams, "Art-as-Such: The Sociology of Modern Aesthetics," in Abrams, *Doing Things with Texts: Essays in Criticism and Critical Theory,* ed. M. Fischer (New York, 1989). For more on the history of the term *art,* see R. Williams, *Keywords* (Glasgow, 1976).

6. Abbé Jean-Baptiste Dubos, *Critical Reflections on Poetry, Painting and Music,* trans. T. Nugent (London, 1748), 360–61.

7. W. J. T. Mitchell, *Iconology: Image, Text, Ideology* (Chicago, 1986). See also Mitchell's "practical companion" to this volume, *Picture Theory* (Chicago, 1994).

8. Mitchell, *Iconology,* 104.

9. Lessing's work has been translated with notes and introduction by E. A. McCormick as *Laocoön: An Essay on the Limits of Painting and Poetry* (Baltimore, 1984).

10. On its discovery, *Laocoön* lacked a right arm; the elder son's right hand and younger son's were also missing. For a summary of the restorations of the statue, see F. Haskell and N. Penny, *Taste and the Antique* (New Haven and London, 1981), 246–47.

11. "Clamores horrendos ad sidera tollit" (*Laocoön,* chap. 4, 23).

12. M. Mendelssohn, *Gesammelte Schriften,* Jubiläumsausgabe, ed. F. Bamberger et al., 17 vols. (Stuttgart, 1971). For the translation of Mendelssohn's writings from which I quote, see D. O. Dahlstrom, ed., *Philosophical Writings,* Cambridge Texts in the History of Philosophy (Cambridge, 1997).

13. *Laocoön,* preface, 5.

14. Dahlstrom, ed., *Philosophical Writings,* 177–78.

15. See J. Neubauer, *The Emancipation of Music from Language* (New Haven and London, 1986), 136. This text also includes a more detailed discussion of eighteenth-century musical aesthetics in general.

16. A. Smith, "Of the Imitative Arts," in his *Essays on Philosophical Subjects* (London, 1795), 133–79.

17. *Laocoön,* chap. 2, 14.

18. This idea later informed the aesthetics of Scriabin; see Chapter 2, below.

19. *Partisan Review* 7, no. 4 (July–August 1940), 296–310.

20. *Laocoön,* chap. 16, 78.

21. Lessing explains in the preface to *Laocoön* that "by 'painting' I mean the visual arts in general; further, I do not promise that, under the name of poetry, I shall not devote some consideration also to those other arts in which the method of presentation is progressive in time" (6).

22. Preface to *Laocoön,* 5.

23. Mitchell, *Iconology,* chap. 5, points out that Lessing's connections between gender and genre had a powerful precedent in the aesthetics of Edmund Burke.

24. *Laocoön,* chap. 18, 91.

25. First published in the *Journal of Aesthetic Education* 18 (1984), 5–13, and reprinted as chapter 2 of J. Levinson, *Music, Art, and Metaphysics: Essays in Philosophical Aesthetics* (Ithaca, N.Y., 1990), 26–36. Nicholas Cook has also investigated similar issues in his book *Analysing Musical Multimedia* (Oxford, 1998). His argument has many points of contact with mine, although the main thrust of his account is specific in addressing what he defines as musical multimedia (film, video, opera, and so on).

26. Levinson, *Music, Art, and Metaphysics,* 30.

27. See R. Kostelanetz, ed., *Scenarios: Scripts to Perform* (New York, 1980), 194.

28. Cage never voted in an American election, although I was told in conversation with Andrew Culver (Cage's musical assistant) that he came close, through disgust at George Bush's administration toward the end of his life. Cage's politics can best be described as anarchist.

29. T. W. Adorno, *In Search of Wagner* (London, 1985), 113; first published as *Versuch über Wagner* (London, 1952). The Wagner quotation is drawn from *Opera and Drama,* trans. W. A. Ellis, vol. 2 of *Richard Wagner's Prose Works,* 8 vols. (London, 1896; reprint, Lincoln, Nebr., 1995), 356n, henceforth cited as *RWPW,* with volume and page numbers.

30. More recently, a free Musicircus was put on at the Barbican Centre in London on Saturday, 24 October 1998, between 3:00–4:15 P.M. and 6:30–7:45 P.M., arranged by Stephen Montague, as part of the Barbican's concert series "American Pioneers: Innovators, Rule Breakers and Iconoclasts." Like event held in 1982 as part of the Almeida Festival to celebrate Cage's seventieth birthday, the sequence of sound and silence for each individual group was determined by chance operations (*I Ching* and dice). The resultant grid informed each group when and when not to perform. The Barbican Musicircus included: the soprano Allison Bell wandering among the audience performing Cage's *Aria* and *Fontana Mix: Song 47;* Hugh Davies performing Cage's *Branches* on amplified plant materials; COMA (Contemporary Music-making for Amateurs) Voices performing various works by Cage, Christian Wolff, Earl Brown, and Stephen Montague; Ensemble Bash, performing works by Cage, Wolff, and Peter Garland; Irish folk fiddlers; Emma Diamond (ex. Cunningham Co.), dancer; Heather Edwards singing on a trapeze above pianist Yoko Ono, performing various works by Cage; Stefan Szczulkun performance artist; and many others. The general atmosphere was of a music fair, a peripatetic audience promenading and sampling various musical wares, lots of smiles and playing children, including my then four-year-old daughter, who was captivated by both the swinging soprano and the opportunity to slide down banisters.

31. "Opera and Drama," *RWPW,* 2:121.

32. "The Art-Work of the Future," *RWPW,* 1:100.

33. Ibid., 111.

34. Ibid., 100.

35. See M. Fried, "Art and Objecthood," *Artforum* (Summer 1967), reprinted in C. Harrison and P. Wood, eds., *Art in Theory, 1900–1990: An Anthology of Changing Ideas* (Oxford, 1992), 822–34. Stella and Fried's work is more fully discussed in Chapter 5, below.

36. See G. Watkins, *Pyramids at the Louvre: Music, Culture, and Collage from Stravinsky to the Postmodernists* (Cambridge, Mass., 1994).

37. See the essay of this title in her *The Originality of the Avant-Garde and Other Modernist Myths* (Boston, 1985), 276–90.

38. Levinson, *Music, Art, and Metaphysics,* 33.

39. As the score explains: "This work was commissioned by Hans Otte on behalf of the Bremen Radio for the Festival of Contemporary Music of May 1966 and was first performed on that occasion." There is also a recording of the piece (obviously lacking the visual dimension) on the album *Magnificathy* (Wergo, Wer 60054-50).

40. In a letter, Neuhaus is at pains to point out, "I have never made sound sculpture . . . and my place works are not a form of music, ambient or otherwise." He differs from other practitioners in these fields in the emphasis he places on "sound continuums which are unchanging and without beginning or end." Most important, in his work, "sound is not the work. Here sound is the material with which I transform the perception of space" (Neuhaus to author, 26 March 2000).

41. Max Neuhaus, *Sound Works,* vol. 1: *Inscriptions* (Ostfildern-Stuttgart, 1994), 42.

42. The relationship between Christo and Neuhaus is an interesting one. Christo, however, tends to be more concerned with mass, not volume, whereas Neuhaus is usually more concerned with sonic and spatial volume, not mass.

43. Irving Babbitt, *The New Laokoon: An Essay on the Confusion of the Arts* (London, 1910).

44. Ibid., x.

45. Ibid., 171.

46. Ibid., 174–75 (my emphasis).

47. Ibid., 185.

48. C. Greenberg, "Towards a Newer Laocoon," *Partisan Review* 7, no. 4 (July–August 1940), 296–310.

49. Ibid., 296.

50. Ibid., 297.

51. Ibid., 304.

52. See W. Pater, *The Renaissance: Studies in Art and Poetry* (London, 1873; reprint, London, 1928), particularly the essay "The School of Giorgione," 128–49.

53. Greenberg, "Towards a Newer Laocoon," 304.

54. Pater, *Renaissance,* 128.

55. Ibid., 135.

56. Ibid., 135–36.

57. Greenberg, "Towards a Newer Laocoon," 305.

58. Ibid., 307.

59. For a more detailed discussion of this point, see W. Steiner, *The Colors of Rhetoric* (Chicago, 1982).

60. For a discussion of postmodernism in relation to the academy, see chapter 1 of Steven Connor, *Postmodernist Culture: An Introduction to Theories of the Contemporary,* 2d ed. (Oxford, 1997).

61. "History of Art and the Undergraduate Syllabus: Is It a Discipline and How Should We Teach It?" in F. Borzello and A. L. Rees, eds., *The New Art History* (London, 1986), 147-56, 149.

62. R. Barthes, *Image-Music-Text,* selected and trans. S. Heath (Glasgow, 1982), 155-64.

63. Ibid., 155.

64. Fried, "Art and Objecthood," 831.

CHAPTER 2: "DEEDS OF MUSIC MADE VISIBLE"

1. The title quotation is taken from Wagner's essay "On the Name 'Musicdrama'" of 1872, reprinted in *Actors and Singers,* trans. W. A. Ellis, from vol. 5 of *Richard Wagner's Prose Works,* 8 vols. (London, 1896; reprint, Lincoln, Nebr., 1995), henceforth cited as *RWPW,* with volume and page numbers. In his discussion of nomenclature Wagner writes: "Herr W. H. Riehl, as he somewhere has said, loses sight and hearing at my operas, for with some he hears, with others sees: how shall one name so inaudible, invisible a thing? I should almost have felt disposed to take my stand on its visiblity, and abide by 'show-play,' as I would gladly have called my dramas *deeds of music brought to sight*" (303). I prefer the translation "deeds of music made visible" ("ersichtlich gewordene Thaten der Musik") to Ellis's "brought to sight."

2. See D. C. Large and W. Weber, eds., *Wagnerism in European Culture and Politics* (Ithaca, N.Y., 1984), and J. Horowitz, *Wagner Nights: An American History* (Berkeley, Calif., 1994).

3. See Aristotle, "Poetry as Imitation," in *Aristotle/Horace/Longinus: Classical Literary Criticism,* trans. T. S. Dorsch (Harmondsworth, 1965; reprint, Harmondsworth, 1986), 31.

4. See J. Neubauer's excellent *Emancipation of Music from Language: Departure from Mimesis in Eighteenth-Century Aesthetics* (New Haven and London, 1986).

5. A. Schopenhauer, *The World as Will and Representation* [1818; 2d ed., 1844], trans. E. F. J. Payne (London, 1969), vol. 1, bk. 3, sec. 38. The idea that music reflects the thing-itself is foreshadowed in the writings of Wilhelm Wackenroder. See his *Reveries Concerning Art,* which Schopenhauer read in 1806.

6. See Jack M. Stein, *Richard Wagner and the Synthesis of the Arts* (Detroit, Mich., 1960), 113-17.

7. See his essays "Music of the Future" (1861), "Beethoven" (1870), and "The Destiny of Opera" (1871).

8. B. Magee, *The Philosophy of Schopenhauer,* rev. ed. (Oxford, 1997), 377.

9. Taken from the 1872 introduction to vols. 3 and 4 of his *Gesammelte Schriften,* reprinted in *RWPW,* 1:26.

10. This is part of an attempt to reconcile Schopenhauer's equation of music with the "Will," and Wagner's earlier Gesamtkunstwerk theories. This later argument can be summarized thus: music operates outside the laws of logic and causality, this is why

it speaks of the thing-itself. But because these laws bind humans, the word needs to work hand in hand with music to act as a mediator. The drama can then in turn affect the viewer so profoundly that they are transported into a receptive condition for the supralogical revelations of the music. For more on this see Wagner's essay "Music of the Future" (1861).

11. Schopenhauer's *The World as Will and Idea* was translated into French in 1886, although Théodule Ribot's book *La philosophie de Schopenhauer* (Paris, 1874) had made known the German philosopher's ideas by the mid-1870s. The impact of German idealism on French thinking was first philosophically filtered through the eclecticism of Victor Cousin; see F. Will, *Flumen Historicum: Victor Cousin's Aesthetic and Its Sources* (Chapel Hill, N.C., 1965). We shall see a similar usurping of the "word" by "tone" in the aesthetic of Hauer in Chapter 5, below.

12. The Dresden revolt of 1848–49 was an attempt at German unification that Wagner, as a nationalist, fully supported. It was violently suppressed by the Prussian government. Wagner first fled to Weimar, then to Zurich, later to Paris, and then back to Zurich. The following year, 1850, found him again in Paris, hoping to get his work produced before returning to Switzerland later in the year. He remained in Switzerland until 1859. Wagner quoted in "Art and Revolution," in *Art-Work of the Future, RWPW*, 1:32.

13. Ibid., 33.

14. Ibid., 35.

15. Ibid., 126–27.

16. Ibid., 129.

17. There is a striking similarity between this phrase of Wagner's and one of Oswald Spengler's invectives in his conservative response to the modern world, published under the title *The Decline of the West* (first published in German, Munich, 1918; trans. C. F. Atkinson, London, 1926). In this work Spengler laments developments in the arts after Manet and Wagner, whom he regards as producing the "last step" in the "great tradition": "We go through all the exhibitions, the concerts, the theatres, and find only industrious cobblers and noisy fools, who delight in producing something for the market" (quotation taken from Harrison and Wood, eds., *Art in Theory*, 229).

18. Wagner, *Art-Work of the Future, RWPW*, 1:131.

19. Ibid., 372.

20. See especially part 3, "The Arts of Poetry and Tone in the Drama of the Future," in *Opera and Drama* (*RWPW*, vol. 2).

21. Ibid., 307.

22. See "Education: The First Stage," 1.d, and "The Myth of Er," 11.3.

23. See especially 8.5–7 (1339a11–1342b17).

24. The best critical account of this work is to be found in M. S. Silk and J. P. Stern, *Nietzsche on Tragedy* (Cambridge, 1981; reprint, Cambridge, 1995).

25. See, for example, Winckelmann's *Reflections on the Painting and Sculpture of the Greeks* (1755), trans. H. Fuseli (London, 1765), and *The History of Ancient Art* (1764); excerpts in D. Irwin, ed., *Winckelmann, Writings on Art* (London, 1972).

26. F. Nietzsche, *The Birth of Tragedy*, trans. C. Fadiman (New York, 1927; reprint, New York, 1995), 1 (sec. 1).

27. This was of course a challenge later taken up by Gustav Klimt, as part of the Gesamtkunstwerk that was the 1902 Vienna Secession exhibition (including Max Klinger's Beethoven statue and Gustav Mahler's wind-band arrangement of the "Ode to Joy").

28. Nietzsche, *Birth of Tragedy*, 3 and 4 (sec. 1). This conception relates to Schopenhauer's understanding of aesthetic experience where "perceiver and perceived become one."

29. Ibid., 77 and 78 (sec. 21).

30. Ibid., 79 (sec. 21).

31. Ibid., 80 (sec. 21).

32. For a further discussion of Apollonian myth, see Chapter 3, below.

33. Nietzsche, *Birth of Tragedy*, 79.

34. Ibid., 12 (sec. 4).

35. Ibid., 90 (sec. 24).

36. This suspension of resolution goes on for more than four hours in *Tristan;* resolution is achieved only at the end, when Isolde joins Tristan in death.

37. For a useful summary of debates about music and emotion, one that characterizes my position, see N. Cook, *Analysing Musical Multimedia* (Oxford, 1998), 86–97.

38. See Baudelaire's essay "Richard Wagner and Tannhäuser in Paris," in J. Mayne, trans., *The Painter of Modern Life and Other Essays* (London, 1964), sec. 4, 137.

39. E. Newman, *Wagner as Man and Artist* (New York, 1924; reprint, New York, 1989), 218.

40. Nietzsche in a letter to Rohde dated 9 December 1868: "Wagner, as I know him from his music, his poetry, his aesthetic, not least from that fortunate meeting with him, is the flesh-and-blood illustration of what Schopenhauer calls a genius." Quotation taken from Silk and Stern, *Nietzsche on Tragedy*, 29.

41. See Nietzsche, *Birth of Tragedy*, 72 (sec. 19).

42. Ibid., 50 (sec. 14). Aristotle, however, does not give music priority in this way. In chapter 6 of the *Poetics*, the essential aspects of tragedy are listed under six headings: *muthos* (plot), *ethe* (characterisation), *dianoia* (the rational thought of characters), *lexis* (verbal expression), *melopiia* (song, melody and words of the lyrics), and finally *opsis* (the visual dimension).

43. Nietzsche, *Birth of Tragedy*, 77 (sec. 21).

44. Ibid., 81 (sec. 21).

45. Ibid., 88 (sec. 24).

46. *RWPW*, 2:168–69.

47. Quotation taken from Newman, *Wagner as Man and Artist*, 187.

48. *RWPW*, 1:149.

49. Ibid., 150.

50. See ibid., 121.

51. G. Lessing, *Laocoön: An Essay upon the Limits of Poetry and Painting* [1766], trans. E. A. McCormick (Baltimore, 1984). Wagner's discussion of Lessing was no doubt due in part to his significance as a critic of the French classical school, in that he argued

that German literature should turn from the narrow French model and look instead to the example of Shakespeare and English writers. Shakespeare was part of an equation Wagner's aesthetic aspired to reflect: Shakespeare + Beethoven = Wagner.

52. See Stein, *Wagner and Synthesis of the Arts,* 150–55.

53. *Opera and Drama,* in *RWPW,* 2:322. Wagner is here talking about the power of speech possessed by the orchestra, its ability to speak the "unspeakable." This language of feeling and the rational language of the Word are heard and understood through the ear, but the part played by the eye and the similarly "unspeakable" language of gesture is also important: "Eye and Ear must mutually assure each other of a higher-pitched message, before they can transmit it convincingly to the Feelings" (381).

54. See title essay in Mayne, trans., *Painter of Modern Life,* 1–40.

55. Ibid., 13.

56. Ibid., 13–14.

57. *Correspondances de Baudelaire,* vol. 2 (Paris, 1973), 496–97; quotation taken from J. H. Rubin, *Manet's Silence and the Poetics of Bouquets* (London, 1994), 103.

58. "Wagner and Tannhäuser in Paris," in Mayne, trans., *Painter of Modern Life,* sec. 4, 137 (my emphasis).

59. Ibid., sec. 1, 111.

60. The concerts were repeated on 1 and 8 February. Present were such distinguished figures as Giacomo Meyerbeer, Daniel Auber, Charles Gounod, Champfleury, and Baudelaire. The following year, 1861, performances of *Tannhäuser* were given at the Opéra in Paris on 13, 18, and 24 March, with a special arrangement of the Venusberg music, the so-called Paris "bacchanal." See also Stein, *Wagner and Synthesis of the Arts,* for information about Wagner's previous time in Paris.

As regards *Tannhäuser,* it is interesting to note that around the same time in England, both William Morris and Algernon Swinburne in poetry, and Edward Burne-Jones in painting, were drawing on the Tannhäuser legend. In Swinburne (*Poems and Ballads,* 1866) and Burne-Jones (*Laus Veneris,* 1873–75) in particular, music is understood as the vehicle of sensuality. The undoing of the knights' masculinity as they enter the Venusberg (the domain of femininity) is facilitated by music; see S. Fagence, "Representations of Music in the Art of Burne-Jones," *Apollo* (May 1998), 9–14.

61. Wagner had been supported by Princess Pauline Metternich, wife of the Austrian ambassador in Paris and a woman distrusted in certain court circles, as a mediator between the French and Austrians. Although Wagner alighted on Meyerbeer as a scapegoat, blaming the hostile reviews on Meyerbeer's influence on the press, the French-settled German composer was not in fact present at the performances of the opera, and had indeed written in his diary about *Tannhäuser:* "in any case a remarkable and talented work," whose reception was "the result of intrigues and not of real judgement"; see H. Becker, ed., *Giacomo Meyerbeer: Briefwechsel und Tagebücher* (Berlin, 1960), quoted in B. Millington, *Wagner* (London, 1984), 70.

62. See R. Lloyd, ed. and trans., *Selected Letters of Charles Baudelaire* (Chicago, 1986), 145–46. A slightly modified translation can be found in Lacoue-Labarthe, *Musica*

Ficta (Figures of Wagner), trans. F. McCarren (Palo Alto, Calif., 1994), 1–3 (originally published in French in 1991).

63. William Hazlitt (1778–1830) had expressed a similar idea in his essay on "gusto," a quality that arises "where the impression made on one sense excites by affinity those of another"; see Howe, ed., *The Complete Works of William Hazlitt,* 21 vols. (London, 1930–34), 4:78.

64. Translation from M. Miner, *Resonant Gaps: Between Baudelaire and Wagner* (Athens, Ga., 1995), 10–11.

65. Translation from R. Howard, *Les Fleurs du Mal: The Complete Text of the Flowers of Evil* (London, 1892), 15.

66. Translated as *A Spiritual Key* and first published in London in 1784.

67. See Herder's *Ideen zur Philosophie der Geschichte der Menscheit* (Ideas on the philosophy of human history), 1784–87; Kant's *Critique of Judgment,* 1790 (especially the discussion of allegorical associations); and Creuzer's *Symbolik und Mythologie der alten Völker, besonders der Griechen,* 1810–12.

68. Quotation taken from H. Dorra, *Symbolist Art Theories* (Berkeley, Calif., 1994), 8.

69. See *Meditations on a Hobby Horse* (London, 1963; 3d ed., London, 1978), 14.

70. Ibid.

71. Miner, *Resonant Gaps,* 2.

72. Baudelaire, "The Salon of 1851," in J. Mayne, ed. and trans., *Art in Paris, 1845–1862: Salons and Other Exhibitions* (Oxford, 1965), 156.

73. Baudelaire, "The Salon of 1846," in Mayne, ed. and trans., *Art in Paris,* 51. In this novel Hoffmann famously described his hero, Johannes Kreisler, as "a little man in a coat the colour of C sharp minor with an E major-coloured collar."

74. Ibid., 50.

75. See "Painter of Modern Life," in Mayne, trans., *Painter of Modern Life,* sec. 5, 15.

76. See Boris de Schloezer, *Scriabin: Artist and Mystic,* trans. N. Slonimsky (Oxford, 1987), first published in part in 1923. This work, though by no means disinterested in its subject nor accurate in all regards, is nevertheless an extremely important primary source. Like another subject of this book, John Cage, Scriabin preferred conversation as a way of expressing his aesthetic, and this presents its own difficulties of consistency and reflection. Schloezer's more academic approach helped to order and characterize the nature of Scriabin's thinking, making his book a fascinating mix of analysis and empathy.

77. Wagner's essay *The Art-Work of the Future* had been dedicated to Feuerbach.

78. Quotation taken from M. Brown, "Scriabin and Russian *Mystic* Symbolism," *Nineteenth-Century Music* 3 (1979), 44.

79. See his poem "Tri podviga" (Three exploits), first published in 1882.

80. Schloezer, *Scriabin,* 66.

81. The ideas of Rudolph Steiner, whose philosophical system was an offshoot of theosophy, are treated in the discussion of Hauer in Chapter 5, below. Steiner was also influenced by Wagner's concept of the Gesamtkunstwerk in his belief that drama

could act as a route to religious understanding. The best and most entertaining account of the history of theosophy and other related occult ideas is P. Washington, *Madame Blavatsky's Baboon: Theosophy and the Emergence of the Western Guru* (London, 1993).

82. For a detailed account of the impact of theosophy in Russia, see M. Carlson, *"No Religion Higher Than Truth": A History of the Theosophical Movement in Russia, 1875–1922* (Princeton, N.J., 1993).

83. Schloezer, *Scriabin,* 68.

84. Published by the London Theosophical Publishing Company in two volumes. The Theosophical Society published a third volume in 1897.

85. For a characterization of this term, see C. Leadbeater, *Man Visible and Invisible* (Adyar, 1959).

86. A. Besant and C. W. Leadbeater, *Thought-Forms* (London, 1925; reprint, London, 1980), 67.

87. Letter to Margarita Morozova, 1906; see F. Bowers, *Scriabin: A Biography of the Russian Composer, 1871–1915,* 2 vols. (Tokyo, 1969), 2:49.

88. Quotation taken from Brown, "Scriabin and Russian Mystic Symbolism," 50.

89. See Nietzsche, *Birth of Tragedy,* 77 (sec. 21).

90. Quotation taken from G. Hindley, *The Larousse Encyclopedia of Music* (reprint, London, 1979), 346.

91. *Zolotoe Runo/La toison d'or* (Moscow, 1905), 5–6.

92. It is interesting to note that Wagner's sensitivity extended to an appreciation of other senses. His rooms in Briennerstrasse in Munich were draped in satin and silks; materials he also preferred to wear, the feel of which he found conducive to thinking, together with the smell of his favorite scent, attar of roses, which he had sent direct from Paris.

93. Schloezer, *Scriabin,* 177–290.

94. There have been two attempts to reconstruct or finish the *Acte préalable,* one by the French composer Manfred Kelkel. The most complete, however, is by the Russian composer Alexander Nemtin (1936–99). From the 1970s, Nemtin devoted all his creative efforts to this task. He searched Scriabin's other works for material originally planned for the *Acte préalable.* The first collation resulted in Part 1, premiered by Kyrill Kondrashin in 1973 under the title "Universe" (BMG-Melodiya 74321 594772). Nemtin later compiled further scores, and the third part, "Transfiguration," was premiered in Berlin by Vladimir Ashkenazy in 1996. The complete reconstruction of the *Acte préalable* has since been recorded by Ashkenazy on Decca (466-329-2) with three movements: "Universe," "Mankind," and "Transformation."

95. Ibid., 291–306.

96. Quotation taken from V. Markov, *Russian Futurism: A History* (London, 1969), 302.

97. Ibid., 284.

98. One of the most radical was by the futurist Vasilisk Gnedov, who was notorious for his *Poem of the End,* which consisted of no words but rather a gesture; a single, sharp circular movement of the arm. This work has points of contact with Cage in as much

as a "suppressed" aspect of poetry (the body and physical presentation) is promoted over its central and conventional defining character, word.

99. "What Is the Word?" in *Charters and Declarations of Russian Futurists* (Moscow, 1914). His associations are: G = yellow-black (selfishness), K = black (hate), Kh = gray (fear), R = red (sensuality), S = blue (spirit), Z = green (transformation), and Zh = yellow (intelligence).

100. Markov, *Russian Futurism,* 176.

101. S. M. Tagore, *Universal History of Music* (Calcutta, 1896).

102. See Schloezer, *Scriabin,* 264–65.

103. Quoted after F. Bowers, *The New Scriabin: Enigma and Answers* (London, 1974), 72.

104. We know Scriabin's color and notated pitch relations through an annotated score to which the composer also attached a table of colors (acquired by the Bibliothèque Nationale de France in 1978, cat. no. Rés. Vma 228).

105. See K. Peacock, "Synaesthetic Perception: Alexander Scriabin's Color Hearing," *Music Perception* 2, no. 4 (Summer 1985), 483–505.

106. Quoted by C. L. Eastlake in J. Goethe, *Theory of Colour* (Boston, 1978), 418.

107. Ibid., 298–99, para. 748.

108. K. C. Lindsay and P. Vergo, eds., *Kandinsky: Complete Writings on Art,* 2 vols. (London, 1982), 1:161.

109. For more on this see J. Gage, *Colour and Culture* (London, 1993). Another source for Scriabin may well have been Rimsky-Korsakov's synesthetic associations, which are, however, apart from "D," completely different from Scriabin's. They discussed this in 1907. It should be noted that, as with Scriabin's color sound associations, there is some disagreement over details. This could be due to the arbitrary nature of such associations between individuals, which was compounded by the relatively imprecise scholarship in early investigations. In Rimsky-Korsakov's case such associations were often described as (again arranged as a circle of fifths):

C = White	F sharp = Grayish green
G = Brownish gray	D flat = Dusky, warm
D = Yellow	A flat = Grayish violet
A = Clear rose	E flat = Dark bluish gray
E = Blue (sapphire)	B flat = none
B = Dark blue (shot with gray)	F = Green

110. See L. E. Marks, *The Unity of the Senses: Interrelations Among the Modalities* (New York, 1978).

111. L. Sabaneev, "Prometheus," in W. Kandinsky and F. Marc, *Der Blaue Reiter Almanac* (reprint, New York, 1974), 129–30.

112. Nietzsche, as we have seen, felt that the Apollonian image had concealed the Dionysian primordial unity. On the title page of his *Birth of Tragedy Out of the Spirit of Music* (1872), the philosopher had represented Prometheus, unbound and triumphant over the eagle, a triumph of will and art over the bonds of a restrictive society.

113. For a more detailed analysis of Scriabin's technique, see V. Dernova, *Garmoniya Skryabina* (Leningrad, 1968), translated by R. J. Guenther as "Varvara Dernova's Gar-

moniia Skriabina: A Translation and Critical Commentary" (Ph.D. diss., Catholic University, 1979). See also G. McQuere, ed., *Russian Theoretical Thought in Music* (Ann Arbor, Mich., 1983), especially the chapter on Dernova by R. J. Guenther, 170–213. A useful summary can be found in Bowers, *New Scriabin*, 146–71. Also of note is J. Reise, "Late Skriabin: Some Principles Behind the Style," *Nineteenth-Century Music* 3 (1983), 220–31.

114. Quotation taken from Bowers, *New Scriabin*, 171.

115. The manuscript is held in the special collection of the music department at the Bibliothèque Nationale de France in Paris under the number Miss. 15226.

116. Quotation taken from M. Orban, "Nicolas Obouhow: Un musicien mystique," *La revue musicale* 16 (1935), 100–108, quotation on 102.

117. Other examples are given in Chapters 5 and 6, below. For Schoenberg's solution to the problem, see his *Style and Idea* (London, 1984), 354–62. The Russian composer and painter Jefim Golysheff simultaneously invented a new notational system based on "x"s for sharps, but as he was then (1915) living in Berlin, it is likely that both Russian musicians derived their approaches from an earlier Russian model.

118. Guido d'Arezzo (c. 995–1050) introduced the movable doh system in the eleventh century. The names he used are taken from a Latin hymn for the Feast of Saint John the Baptist of four centuries before, in which each line begins one note higher than the last—a theological circumstance that would not have been lost on Obukhov.

119. Obukhov's explanation of his notational system can be found in the score to *Préface du La livre de vie* held in the special collection of the music department at the Bibliothèque Nationale de France in Paris. There was also a volume of standard works published by Durand in Paris in 1947 using this notation, among them works by Chopin, Beethoven, Schumann, Liszt, Debussy, Ravel, and, interestingly, Messiaen (a prelude).

120. See Hugh Davis, "Croix sonore," in *The New Grove's Dictionary of Musical Instruments*, 3 vols. (London, 1984), 1:516.

121. See Orban, "Nicolas Obouhow," 104.

122. A more recent example is the "Sensurround" system devised for the 1974 film *Earthquake*, which employed low-frequency pulses and deliberately unsteady camera work, aiming to recreate the sensation of being in an earthquake. There have also been experiments (unsuccessful) in "smell-o-vision," not to mention Aldous Huxley's vision of the "feelies" in *Brave New World*.

123. In Russian, "zvuchashchui krest."

124. A prototype was apparently demonstrated in Paris in 1926, and the final version was presented in 1934; see Hugh Davis's entry on this instrument in *New Grove's Dictionary of Musical Instruments*, 1:515–16.

125. See E. Ludwig, "La croix sonore," *La revue musicale* 16 (1935), 96–99.

126. I thank Hugh Davis for his conversations about Obukhov's instruments.

127. The theremin can be heard in the soundtrack to Alfred Hitchcock's film *Spellbound* (1945) and in the recording of the Beach Boys' hit "Good Vibrations" (1967).

128. *The Oxford Companion to Music*, 10th ed. (Oxford, 1972), 321.

129. For example, Andrea Mantegna's *Holy Family with St. John* (c. 1500), National Gallery, London (NG 5641), and the Florentine painting *God the Father* (c. 1420–50), National Gallery, London (NG 3627).

130. See note 132, below.

131. Boris de Schloezer, "Nicolas Obukhoff," *La revue musicale* 1, pt. 3 (1921), 38–56, quotation on 54.

132. Sabaneev ascribes a political purpose to the work— "the restoration to the throne of the last Russian Emperor, who is supposed to be alive and well, but in hiding"; see "Obukhov," *Musical Times,* 1 October 1927. I have been unable to find any corroboration for this view except the symbolism of the Sounding Cross.

133. See F. Yates, *The Rosicrucian Enlightenment* (London, 1986).

134. Quoted after Orban, "Nicolas Obouhow," 107. Larry Sitsky, *Music of the Repressed Russian Avant-Garde, 1900–1929* (Westport, Conn., 1994), 257, ascribes the design of this temple to the artist Natalia Goncharova. Sitsky's work also contains a useful alphabetical list of Obukhov's manuscripts.

135. Sitsky, *Music,* 259, also mentions French Radio broadcast extracts from *La livre de vie* and that a film was made by Germaine Dulas on the subject, which had limited distribution in France and Italy in 1935.

136. *New York Times,* 16 May 1934, 23.

137. Quotation taken from Schloezer, "Nicolas Obukhoff," 47.

138. W. Mellers, "Mysticism and Theology," in P. Hill, ed., *The Messiaen Companion* (London, 1995), 223.

139. The first is the song cycle *Harawi* of 1945 and the third the *Cinq rechants* of 1948.

140. Mellers, "Mysticism and Theology," 231.

141. It is interesting to note that the Swiss artist Charles Blanc-Gatti (1890–1966), a friend of Messiaen, styled himself a "Musicalist," building, he believed, on the achievements of Kupka (see Chapter 4, below). In his work he attempted to translate musical compositions into visual images (especially the music of Bach and Stravinsky). Messiaen owned Blanc-Gatti's canvas *Brilliance [Rutilance];* see T. D. Schlee and D. Kämper, eds., *Olivier Messiaen: La cité céleste—Das himmlische Jerusalem; Über Leben und Werk des französischen Komponisten* (Cologne, 1998), 167.

142. See Olivier Messiaen, *Music and Color: Conversations with Claude Samuel,* trans. E. T. Glasow (Portland, Oreg., 1994), originally published in French in 1986, 42, 40.

143. Ibid., 249.

144. Wagner quoted in Newman, *Wagner as Man and Artist,* 187.

145. Wagner, "Letter on Music," quoted in Baudelaire's essay "Wagner and Tannhäuser in Paris," in Mayne, trans., *Painter of Modern Life,* sec. 4, 121.

146. Ibid.

147. See, for example, D. Reynolds's discussion of this project in *Symbolist Aesthetics and Early Abstract Art* (Cambridge, 1995), in particular 86–88.

148. Compare with Kublin's phoneme-color associations (see note 99, above). For a more detailed discussion, see E. Starkie, *Arthur Rimbaud* (London, 1973), and C. Lévi-Strauss, *Look, Listen, Read* (New York, 1997), 129–41.

149. C. Greenberg, "Towards a Newer Laocoon," *Partisan Review* 7, no. 4 (July–August 1940), sec. 4.
150. "Wagner and Tannhäuser in Paris," in Mayne, trans., *Painter of Modern Life,* sec. 4, 137 (my emphasis).
151. Bill Nye (Edgar Wilson Nye), American humorist (1850–96). Misattributed on a Bayreuth postcard to Mark Twain. It is, in fact, quoted by Twain in his *Autobiography:* see *Mark Twain's Autobiography,* with an introduction by A. B. Paine, 2 vols. (New York, 1924), 1:338.

CHAPTER 3: INSTRUMENTS OF DESIRE

1. C. Greenberg, "The Paper-Pasted Revolution," *Art News* 57 (1958), 46–49, 60–61.
2. Ibid., 47.
3. See P. Leighten, principally *Re-Ordering the Universe: Picasso and Anarchism, 1897–1914* (Princeton, N.J., 1989), and D. Cottingham, "What the Papers Say: Politics and Ideology in Picasso's Collages of 1912," *Art Journal* 47, no. 4 (Winter 1988), 350–59. R. Rosenberg, "Picasso and the Typography of Cubism," in R. Penrose and J. Golding, eds., *Picasso: 1881–1973* (London, 1973), is perhaps the first study to literally read the text elements of the collages.
4. As Patricia Leighten among others has suggested, this approach itself should be seen in the social context of its birth and development (e.g., McCarthyism, the Cold War) and was motivated by the intention to escape ideology and wrest art free from political control or manipulation.
5. See J. Richardson, *A Life of Picasso,* vol. 2: *1907–1917: The Painter of Modern Life* (London, 1996), 150.
6. See S. Buettner, "Catalonia and the Early Musical Subjects of Braque and Picasso," in M. Pointon, P. Binski, and S. Shaw-Miller, eds., *Image-Music-Text,* special issue of *Art History* 19, no. 1 (March 1996), 112. See also L. Kachur's earlier article "Picasso, Popular Music, and Collage Cubism (1911–1912)," *Burlington Magazine* 135, no. 1081 (April 1993), 252–60.
7. For an entertaining modern retelling of this tale, see Tony Harrison's play *The Trackers of Oxyrhynchus* (London, 1990).
8. Apollo went on to win a second contest, this time against Pan (see note 11, below). This account is based on R. Graves, *Greek Myths,* 2 vols. (London, 1955). See also Ovid, *Metamorphoses,* trans. M. M. Innes (Harmondsworth, 1955); Pindar, *The Odes,* trans. C. M. Bowra (Harmondsworth, 1969); and Hesiod and Theognis, *Theogony, Works and Days, Elegies,* trans. D. Wender (Harmondsworth, 1973).
9. For Aristotle's discussion of the detrimental effects of the aulos, see *The Politics* 1341a17, trans. T. A. Sinclair (reprint, Harmondsworth, 1987), 469–70.
10. The British *Quarterly Review* explained this point to its readers in its July 1871 issue (145–47): "most pagan gods are supposed to be delighted with the noise produced by yelling, clapping and banging gongs about." It concluded by quoting Charles Darwin, explaining that music was used by early humans "for the sake of charming the opposite sex."

11. Some versions of the myth (see note 8, above) suggest that, following Pan's invention of the reed flute, Hermes had copied it and bartered it to Apollo. Pan had pursued the chaste Syrinx to the River Ladon, where she had metamorphosed into a reed to escape Pan's intended rape. In his attempt to locate her, Pan had cut reeds at random, which he later fashioned into the panpipe, having been inspired by the sound of the wind blowing across the open ends of the reeds' hollow stems. As R. Leppert, *Art and the Committed Eye: Cultural Functions of Imagery* (Boulder, Colo., 1996), points out: "Music is thereby accounted for as the twin result of violence against woman and *as* woman in another disembodied form. To avoid a sexual assult, she becomes music, through at the expense of her body" (225).

12. E. Winternitz, *Musical Instruments and Their Symbolism in Western Art* (London, 1967), 152.

13. D. Boyden, *The History of Violin Playing from Its Origins to 1761 and Its Relationship to the Violin and Violin Music* (Oxford, 1964), 4.

14. R. Leppert, *Music and Image: Domesticity, Ideology, and Socio-Cultural Formation in Eighteenth-Century England* (Cambridge, 1988), 168.

15. Ibid.

16. See R. Leppert, *The Theme of Music in Flemish Paintings of the Seventeenth Century* (Munich, 1977).

17. See J. Tyler, *The Early Guitar: A History and Handbook* (Oxford, 1980).

18. *Grove's Dictionary of Music and Musicians,* 5th ed., 9 vols. (London, 1954), 3:848.

19. The reason for this similarity in shape is largely because they share a common ancestor in the viol (in fact, the words *viol* and *vihuela* mean the same).

20. See P. Daix and J. Rosselet, *Picasso: The Cubist Years, 1907–1916: A Catalogue Raisonné of the Paintings and Related Works* (London, 1979).

21. The other works in this series are *The Blind Man's Meal* (1903), representing touch, as the figure feels for a crust of bread and jug of wine; *The Blind Beggar* (1903), representing sight by portraying its opposite; *The Ascetic* (1903), representing taste, again the sense in reverse as an old man looks at an empty plate. This may also be the theme of the painting *The Old Jew,* for here the young boy who acts as the old man's eyes is eati

22. See [...] *sso,* vol. 1: *1881–1906* (London, 1991), 279.

23. Ibi[...]

24. Th[...] culptures: a *Crucifixion* by Wasley and a plaster relief fro[...]s *Life of Picasso* cites him as "Walsey," he is probabl[...]rn in Paris in 1800 and killed at Verdun on 22 March 191[...]ups of religious subjects at the Salon from 1906 to 191[...]*nary of Western Sculptors in Bronze* (Woodbridge, En[...]

25. W[...]rked on the fringes of the Montmartre group. He is perhaps best known for his caricatures of futurist painting (specifically the depiction of movement) that accompanied the French publication of the "Manifesto of Futurist Painters" in *Comoedia* on 18 May 1910; see M. W. Martin, *Futurist Art and Theory, 1909–1915* (Oxford, 1968), facing 46. The watercolor is reproduced in G. Severini,

The Life of a Painter: The Autobiography of Gino Severini (Princeton, N.J., 1995), trans. J. Franchina from *La vita di un pittore* (Milan, 1983).

26. This work is cataloged no. 513 in Daix and Rosselet, *Picasso: Cubist Years*. Henceforth, all works are identified according to Daix and Rosselet's numbering.

27. It is solely the inclusion of this imitation wood-grained sheet that warrants discussion of the work in Greenberg's, "Paper-Pasted Revolution."

28. Picasso may also be making fun of the impressionists by constructing an equation: absence of light = absence of color.

29. Published in Paris by L. Bathlot-Joubert, Editeurs de Musique, 39, rue de l'Echiquier, 1892.

30. See J. Weiss, "Picasso, Collage and the Music Hall," in K. Varnedoe and A. Gopnik, eds., *Modern Art and Popular Culture* (London, 1990), 86.

31. Picasso never studied music, unlike Braque, although he was exposed to a great deal of it, especially in his formative years. His paternal grandfather played double bass in the Málaga opera orchestra, he was a good friend of the Catalan composer Enric Morera, and he met other important musicians during his years in Barcelona. His interest in Spanish music (and the Spanish guitar) may well have blossomed more in exile. See also Buettner, "Catalonia and Early Musical Subjects."

32. Weiss, "Picasso, Collage and the Music Hall," 87.

33. "Je vous envoye un bouquet que ma main / Vient de trier de ces fleurs épanies / Qui ne les eust à ce vespre cueillies, / Cheutes à terre elles fussent demain / Cela vous soit un exemple certain / Que vos beautez bien que fleuries / En peu de temps seront flétries / Et comme fleurs periront tout soudain / Le temps s'en va ma Dame Las! le temps non, / Mais nous nous en allons, / Et tost seront estendus sous la lame / Et des amours des quelles nous parlons / Quand serons morts ne sera plus nouvelles / Donc aimez moi aimez moi cependant qu'êtes belle." My thanks to Catharine Walston and Lindsey for help with the translation.

34. See J. Richardson, *A Life of Picasso,* vol. 2: *1907–1917: The Painter of Modern Life* (London, 1996), 250–52.

35. See L. Zelevansky, ed., *Picasso and Braque: A Symposium* (New York, 1992), 153.

36. For a more extended discussion of the Balkan works, see Leighten, *Re-Ordering the Universe*.

37. As well as being a philosopher, Empedocles is perhaps best known as a scientist, having used experimentation in medicine and been responsible for demonstrating the existence of air. His opposition between love and strife is mentioned in Spenser's *Faerie Queene,* 4.10. He is supposed to have met his death by plunging into the crater of Etna; see Matthew Arnold's dramatic poem "Empedocles on Etna" of 1852 and John Milton, *Paradise Lost,* 3.471. In his *History of Western Philosophy* (reprint, London, 1980), Bertrand Russell quotes another poet: "Great Empedocles, that ardent soul, / Leapt into Etna, and was roasted whole" (71).

38. See J. Berger, *The Success and Failure of Picasso* (London, 1965).

39. See Richardson, *Life of Picasso,* 2:349.

40. Leighten, *Re-Ordering the Universe,* 130.

41. As Tyler, *Early Guitar,* 15, notes, most writers agree that the guitar originated in

Iberia. This establishes the same pedigree for the guitar as Leighten notes for Picasso's use of Iberian images in *Re-Ordering the Universe,* 79–81.

42. See the Museo del Prado exhibition catalog by A. E. Pérez Sánchez, *Pintura española de bodegones y floreros de 1600 a Goya* (Madrid, 1983).

43. See R. Rosenblum, "The Spanishness of Picasso's Still Lifes," in J. Brown, ed., *Picasso and the Spanish Tradition* (New Haven and London, 1996), 61–93, especially 79.

44. See Pliny the Elder, *Historia naturalis* 35.10.65–66, trans. K. Jex-Blake and E. Sellers, *The Elder Pliny's Chapters on the History of Art* (London, 1896). The significant point, in relation to Parhassius and his painting of *Prometheus Bound,* is that such an overriding concern with mimesis at the expense of imagination (the mind) is both morally and aesthetically unacceptable. Art should involve more than simply the eye (or the aim of fooling the eye); it must also engage (but not trick) the mind.

45. Greenberg, "Paper-Pasted Revolution," 47–48.

46. Such a reference places Picasso's work within the tradition of great Spanish art. Richardson does not mention Zurbarán in relation to lettering, but he does point out that the Spanish master's works were shown in an exhibition of ancient art in Barcelona's Palace of Fine Arts in the autumn of 1902—a show that, together with works by El Greco and Catalan Romanesque and Gothic art, was "hailed with patriotic fervour." Richardson, *Life of Picasso,* 1:246.

47. See Richardson, *Life of Picasso,* 2:149.

48. Ibid.

49. See R. Rosenblum, "Cubism as Pop Art," in Varnedoe and Gopnik, eds., *Modern Art and Popular Culture,* 117.

50. For a more recent example of a musical instrument's sexual symbolism, see Louis de Bernière's marvelous and hugely popular novel *Captain Corelli's Mandolin* (London, 1998), especially chap. 42, "How Like a Woman Is a Mandolin."

51. See Weiss, "Picasso, Collage and the Music Hall," 86.

52. See Rosenblum, "Cubism as Pop Art," 117.

53. Severini, *Life of a Painter,* 95.

54. See J. Cousins and P. Daix, "Documentary Chronology," in W. Rubin, ed., *Picasso and Braque: Pioneering Cubism* (New York, 1989), 395. See also the painting *Violin "Jolie Eva"* (1912) in the Staatsgalerie, Stuttgart.

55. See Richardson, *Life of Picasso,* 2:223.

56. R. Krauss, *The Originality of the Avant-Garde and Other Modernist Myths* (Boston, 1988), 37.

57. See M. Perloff, *The Futurist Moment: Avant-Garde, Avant Guerre, and the Language of Rupture* (Chicago, 1986), 42–79. In her more recent book, *The Picasso Papers* (London, 1998), Rosalind E. Krauss calls this a "silly" reading, supporting this accusation by pointing out that this type of schematized representation of a glass had become "utterly standardised throughout this run of collages" (249*n38*). Such fixity with style misses the joke: in *this* context, against *this* newspaper fragment, the glass *can* be seen as a figure.

58. Perloff, *Futurist Moment,* 50.

59. This article was first noted in Richardson, *Life of Picasso,* 1:186.
60. Nicolás Maria Lopez, "Psicologia de la guitarra," *Arte Joven* 1, no. 1 (1901), n.p. Jacqueline Cockburn helped in the translation of these passages.
61. See J. Golding, "Picasso and Surrealism," in R. Penrose and J. Golding, eds., *Pablo Picasso, 1881–1973* (reprint, Ware, Hertfordshire, 1989), 77–121. Of particular interest is his discussion of Picasso's drawing *Nude with Guitar Player* (1914), which he sees as a protosurrealist work, for here the figure and instrument are conflated so that the player is in effect playing the nude woman.
62. Richardson, *Life of Picasso,* 2:433.

CHAPTER 4: *QUASI UNA MUSICA*

1. C. Greenberg, "Towards a Newer Laocoon," *Partisan Review* 7, no. 4 (July–August 1940), 296–310, quotation on 304.
2. The dating of works in this series have recently been reevaluated; see A. Swartz, "A Redating of Kupka's *Amorpha, Fugue in Two Colors II,*" *Bulletin of the Cleveland Museum of Art* 80, no. 8 (1994), 327—51.
3. Published in Paris by Editions Cercle d'Art, 1989. The Prague edition was published by Editions Mánes in 1923. An English translation *Creation in the Plastic Arts* is due to be published by Artists' Bookworks and Liverpool University Press, translated by Edmund Jephcott.
4. These natural elements were often expressed in art nouveau–derived devices. The art nouveau artist Alphonse Mucha was a close neighbor and friend of Kupka when Kupka lived in Montmartre.
5. Kupka was very interested in electric light and its effects on color. He also attended courses on the physical and life sciences at the Sorbonne in 1905, resuming his studies of biology in 1910 after his marriage to Eugénie Straub.
6. See K. C. Lindsay and P. Vergo, eds., *Kandinsky: Complete Writings on Art,* 2 vols. (London, 1982), 1:53.
7. See interview with Kupka in *Koh-i-Noor* 41 (Prague, 1933).
8. See Semper's *Der Stil in der technischen und tektonischen Künsten; oder, Praktische Ästhetik* (Style in the technical and structural arts, or practical aesthetics), 2 vols. (Munich, 1860, 1863).
9. W. Worringer, *Abstraktion und Einfühlung,* trans. M. Bullock as *Abstraction and Empathy: A Contribution to the Psychology of Style* (New York, 1953), 16.
10. The philosophy of Suzanne K. Langer, who studied in Vienna in the 1920s, develops such formalist ideas.
11. Karl Diefenbach, *Ein Beitrag zur Geschichte der Zeitgenössichen Kunstpflege* (Vienna, 1895).
12. One of the most important contributions to linguistic skepticism was to be found in the work of Kupka's compatriot Fritz Mauthner; see his *Beiträge zu einer Kritik der Sprache* (Leipzig, 1901–3), where he argues that verbalization destroys the uniqueness of thought. He exhorts thinkers to the condition of silence.

13. He exhibited with the Vienna Secessionists in 1900, 1901, 1903, and 1908.

14. Quotation taken from Meda Mladek, "Central European Influences," in *František Kupka, 1871–1957: A Retrospective* (New York, 1975), 35. This is also the main source of biographical information.

15. Quotation taken from Serge Fauchereau, *Kupka* (Barcelona, 1989), 11.

16. See Robert Welsh, "Sacred Geometry: French Symbolism and Early Abstraction," in M. Tuchman, C. Freeman, and C. Blotkamp, eds., *The Spiritual in Art: Abstract Painting, 1890–1985* (New York, 1986), 63–87.

17. As noted in Chapter 2, above, both Scriabin and Nietzsche employed the subject of Prometheus in his unbound state to represent the triumph of the will and art over the restrictions of society.

18. According to one source, Duchamp was also responsible for drawing Alfred Barr's attention to Kupka's work, when Barr was organizing the *Cubism and Abstract Art* exhibition for MoMA in 1936; see Fauchereau, *Kupka,* 26.

19. *Amorpha, Fugue in Two Colors,* oil on canvas, 211 × 220 cm, signed bottom right, title bottom left, *Fugue à deux couleurs,* National Gallery in Prague, Modern Art Collection, The Trade Fair Palace (NG 0 5942).

20. See V. Spate, *Orphism: The Evolution of Non-Figurative Painting in Paris, 1910–1914* (Oxford, 1979), and *František Kupka, 1871–1957.*

21. Taken from J. Mayne, ed. and trans., *Art in Paris, 1845–1862: Salons and Other Exhibitions Reviewed by Charles Baudelaire,* 2d ed. (Oxford, 1981), 50.

22. Quotation taken from A. K. Wiedmann, *Romantic Roots in Modern Art, Romanticism and Expressionism: A Study in Comparative Aesthetics* (Surrey, 1979), 73.

23. Greenberg, "Towards a Newer Laocoon," 301.

24. Ibid., 304.

25. J.-L. Nancy, *Les muses* (Paris, 1994), trans. P. Kamuf as *The Muses* (Stanford, Calif., 1996).

26. Kandinsky, "Concerning the Spiritual in Art" [section 4, "The Pyramid"], in Lindsay and Vergo, eds., *Kandinsky: Complete Writings on Art,* 1:127–61 (emphasis added).

27. From a letter by Goethe of 1815; quotation taken from A. Kagan, *Absolute Art* (New York, 1995), 89.

28. See the discussion in Chapter 1, above; this quotation taken from Greenberg, "Towards a Newer Laocoon," 304.

29. Hegel, *Aesthetics: Lectures on Fine Arts,* trans. T. M. Knox, vol. 2 (Oxford, 1975), 621.

30. As Nancy, *Muses,* puts it (following Kant's tripartition into "*word, deportment,* and *tone*" [the arts of *speech,* the *figurative* arts, and the art of the *play of sensations*]): "For Kant declares: 'It is only by the combination of these three kinds of expression that communication can be complete' without asking himself about the privilege that thereby remains conferred upon language. In all good logic, Kant should then be surprised by the absence of a unique art, one which would correspond to perfect communication" (8).

31. See M. Chion, *Audio-Vision: Sounds on Screen,* trans. C. Gorbmann, foreword by W. Murch (New York, 1994), 137. The title of this book draws attention to the fact

that a film is not seen and heard; rather, we hear-see it. Throughout this work Chion develops a technical vocabulary and methodology that points up the interdependence of the audio and visual.

32. See Lindsay and Vergo, eds., *Kandinsky: Complete Writings on Art,* 1:90.

33. The other common form of a double fugue has the voices entering separately, with each voice treated individually followed by their interweaving.

34. He later wrote (1926–27), in one of many autobiographical texts, "Yes fugues, where the sounds evolve like veritable physical entities, intertwine, come and go"; quotation taken from *František Kupka, 1871–1957,* 184.

35. Ibid.

36. In the article by W. Warshawsky, "Orphism, Latest of the Painting Cults," *New York Times,* 19 October 1913, 4.

37. *František Kupka, 1871–1957,* 184.

38. Although it is a botanical name for a North American deciduous shrub with long spiked clusters of flowers!

39. See Spate, *Orphism,* 131.

40. A. Besant and C. Leadbeater, *Thought-Forms* (London, 1901), 82, trans. into French as *Les formes-pensées* (Paris, 1905).

41. Interview in *Svetozor,* Prague, 1 September 1936, 19. It should also be pointed out that Kupka used the term "Orphism" to describe his own art in a way that was more general than Apollinaire's use.

42. Spate, *Orphism,* 77.

43. See N. Beauduin, "Exposition F. Kupka," *La vie des lettres et des arts* 18, no. 3 (Paris, 1924); E. Siblik, *František Kupka* (Prague, 1929; first Czech ed., 1928); and K. Teige, "Orfismus," *Red* 2, no. 5 (Prague, 1929).

44. See A. Pierre, *Frank Kupka in White and Black* (Liverpool, 1998), 32–56. This book also includes a fascinating discussion of the impact on Kupka of Henry Valensi's (1883–1960) ideas on music and painting, although their development in the period around 1924 puts them outside the scope of my discussion of Kupka's earliest abstract canvases.

45. For more on the sixth-century Orphists, see E. R. Dodds, *The Greeks and the Irrational* (Berkeley, Calif., 1951); W. K. C. Guthrie, *The Greeks and Their Gods* (London, 1950); and M. S. Silk and J. P. Stern, *Nietzsche on Tragedy* (Cambridge, 1981; reprint, Cambridge, 1995), in particular 175–78, which I have drawn on in my own account.

46. Although Kupka's name did appear in the printer's proofs of *Les peintres cubistes* under the heading of "Scientific Cubism"; see, for example, the copy later owned by Tristan Tzara, now in the Bibliothèque Nationale de France, Paris.

47. The letter, along with a number of others, was first published in A. Pierre, "De l'orphisme à astraction-création: La réception de l'oeuvre de Kupka dans l'entre-deux guerres," *Bulletin de la Société de l'Histoire de l'Art français* (1995–96), 263–66, trans. by E. Jephcott in Pierre, *Frank Kupka in White and Black,* 58–62.

48. See the discussion of the parodic "Manifesto of the Amorphist School," in J. Weiss,

The Popular Culture of Modern Art: Picasso, Duchamp, and Avant-Gardism (New Haven and London, 1994), 85–87.

49. "Le Salon d'Automne," *Soirées de Paris* 15 (December 1913), 49.

50. Kupka first read Bergson around 1904.

51. Kandinsky, "Concerning the Spiritual in Art" [1911], in Lindsay and Vergo, eds., *Kandinsky: Complete Writings on Art,* 1:161.

52. Oil on canvas, 79 × 72 cm, signed bottom left, National Gallery in Prague, Modern Art Collection, The Trade Fair Palace (NG 0 3790).

53. This imagery is not without precedent. The expression of an evolutionist theory of all life deriving from a few simple elements through a gradual process of transformation was common to theosophy but also to a number of artists and poets in Vienna associated with art nouveau during the time Kupka was a student there, for example, the poet Arno Holz in *Ver sacrum* 1, no. 11 (Vienna, 1898): "Seven billion years before my birth I was an iris / Beneath my shimmering roots revolved another star / On its dark waters swam my blue gigantic bloom" (2).

54. In the work of such artists as Whistler and Kupka's compatriots Antonín Hudecek (see *Moon Landscape,* 1899, Prague) and Jan Preisler (see *Black Lake,* 1903–4, Prague).

55. Quotation taken from *František Kupka, 1871–1957,* 107.

56. The depiction of movement in the horizontal plane relates to Kupka's interest in Eadweard Muybridge's photographic studies of movement and the Praxinoscope method; see his drawing *The Horsemen,* dated by Mladek, "Central European Influences," to 1909–10, by Spate, *Orphism,* to 1907–8, and by Vachtova earlier still to 1900–1902.

57. As Fry has shown, André Salmon had hoped that Bergson would provide the preface to the catalog of the *Section d'Or* (in which Kupka's work was shown). This never happened; see E. Fry, *Cubism* (London, 1966), 67.

58. H. Bergson, *Time and Free Will: An Essay on the Immediate Data of Consciousness* [1886], trans. F. L. Pogson (London, 1971), 101–5; quotation taken from J. McClain, "Time in the Visual Arts: Lessing and Modern Criticism," *Journal of Aesthetics and Art Criticism* 43 (1985), 41–58 (emphasis added).

59. *Solo of a Brown Stroke,* oil on canvas, 70 × 115 cm, marked bottom left, "Le solo d'un trait brun, 1912–13, Kupka" (NG 0 3825).

60. This drawing is held in MoMA's study collection.

61. See M. Antliff, *Inventing Bergson: Cultural Politics and the Parisian Avant-Garde* (Princeton, N.J., 1993), 47.

62. Bergson quoted from G. Hamilton, "Cézanne, Bergson and the Image of Time," *College Art Journal* 16 (1956), 11.

63. See D. Kahnweiler, *The Rise of Cubism* [1915] (New York, 1949).

64. H. Bergson, "Laughter" [1900], in W. Sypher, ed. and trans., *Comedy* (Baltimore, 1956), 61–190; quotation here taken from Antliff, *Inventing Bergson,* 66, who makes the additional point that Bergson also believed in the division of the arts (their diversity) on the basis of particular senses.

65. This follows a similar argument to that of John Dewey, whose *Art as Experience* (New

York, 1934) argues that the distinction between the spatial and temporal arts is misguided, because art is a matter of perception and perception is never instantaneous.

66. Dewey, *Art as Experience,* 220.

67. See S. Kern, *The Culture of Time and Space, 1880–1918* (Cambridge, Mass., 1983), and M. Capek, *The Philosophical Impact of Contemporary Physics* (New York, 1961). I have also drawn on McClain, "Time in the Visual Arts."

68. See "The Painter of Modern Life," in J. Mayne, ed. and trans., *The Painter of Modern Life and Other Essays* (London, 1964), sec. 4, 13.

69. Paul Laporte makes a similar point in relation to cubist simultaneity in his essays "The Space-Time Concept in the Work of Picasso," *Magazine of Art* 41 (1948), 26–32, and "Cubism and Science," *Journal of Aesthetics and Art Criticism* 7 (1949), 243–56.

70. Russolo later wrote that these figures symbolize the feelings awakened by the music, embodied in the various facial expressions; see the journal *Poesia* (December 1920).

71. *Flirt,* pen-and-ink wash and blue pencil on paper, 31.5 × 45 cm (collection Margheita Masullo, Naples); original drawing lost (no. 101 in A. Schwarz, *The Complete Works of Marcel Duchamp* [New York, 1969]). See also J. C. Welchman, *Invisible Colors: A Visual History of Titles* (New Haven and London, 1997), and Schwarz, *Complete Works of Marcel Duchamp,* 399.

    "Flirt / Elle—Voulez vous que je vous joue "Sur les Flots Bleus"; Vous verrez comme ce piano rend bien l'impression qui se dégage du titre? / Lui (spirituel)—Ça n'a rien d'étonnant Mademoiselle, c'est un piano . . . aqueux."

72. See L. Henderson, *The Fourth Dimension and Non-Euclidean Geometry in Modern Art* (Princeton, N.J., 1983).

73. Quotation taken from C. Butler, *Early Modernism: Literature, Music, and Painting in Europe, 1900–1916* (Oxford, 1994), 114. See also A. Schoenberg, *Style and Idea,* ed. E. Stein (London, 1975), and T. W. Adorno, *The Philosophy of New Music* (London, 1973), 30.

74. For a discussion of the function of titles within modern art, see Welchman, *Invisible Colors.*

75. F. Nietzsche, *Thus Spoke Zarathustra,* "At Noontide," trans. R. J. Hollingdale (Harmondsworth, 1961; reprint, Harmondsworth, 1978), 288.

76. See the "Creative Credo," in *Notebooks,* vol. 1: *The Thinking Eye,* ed. J. Spiller, trans. H. Norden (London, 1961), 78, orig. publ. as "Schöpferische Konfession," in *Paul Klee: Das Bildnerische Denken,* ed. J. Spiller (Stuttgart, 1956), pagination the same in German and English editions.

77. *The Diaries of Paul Klee, 1898–1918,* ed. and intro. Felix Klee, trans. B. Schneider, R. Y. Zachary, and M. Knight (Berkeley, Calif., 1964), entry 640.

78. H. Bergson, *Creative Evolution,* trans. A. Mitchell (New York, 1911; orig. publ. Paris, 1907); quoted here from C. Harrison and P. Wood, eds., *Art in Theory, 1900–1990: An Anthology of Changing Ideas* (Oxford, 1992), 142.

79. All quotations taken from *Paul Klee on Modern Art,* trans. P. Findlay, intro. H. Read (London, 1948, reprint, London, 1979), 15–17.

80. The phrase "new age" was a commonplace in the late nineteenth and early twentieth

centuries, as Norbet Lynton has pointed out in his article of the same name, "The New Age: Primal and Mystic Nights," in *Towards a New Art: Essays on the Background to Abstract Art, 1910–20* (London, 1980), in particular 221.

81. See H. B. Chipp, ed., *Theories of Modern Art* (Berkeley, Calif., 1968), 319. Klee had first come across Delaunay's painting at the Munich *Blaue Reiter* exhibition late in 1911.

82. See Harrison and Wood, eds., *Art in Theory,* 152–54.

83. Klee, *Diaries,* entry 1081.

84. T. Munro, *The Arts and Their Interelations* (Cleveland, 1969), 398.

85. Arthur C. Danto, "Oskar Kokoschka," *Nation,* 27 September 1986, reprinted in *Encounters and Reflections: Art in the Historical Present* (Berkeley, Calif., 1997), 63–64.

86. See J. J. Pollitt, *The Ancient View of Greek Art: Criticism, History, and Terminology* (New Haven and London, 1974), 218–28 (quotation on 225), and E. Petersen, "Rhythmus," *Abhandlungen der Kön. Gesellschaft der Wissenschaften zu Göttingen, Phil.-Hist. Klass,* n.f., 16 (1917), 1–104. This definition is also very close to that offered by Suzanne Langer in her book *Problems of Art* (London, 1957), chapter 4 in particular. Langer draws a close analogy between function and rhythm rather than simply with time. A rhythmic pattern arises, she argues, whenever the completion of one distinct event appears as the beginning of another. She gives the example of a pendulum, which creates a rhythm as "a functional involvement of successive events." This is the same example offered by Pollitt: "When a pendulum is depicted [in a painting] in a completely vertical position, we do not ascribe movement to it in our minds, but when it is depicted at the far left or far right point of its swing, at the point where it momentarily stops before changing direction (the *hremiai*), we naturally think of it as being in motion" (*Ancient View of Greek Art,* 140n7).

See also Klee's discussion of pendulum movement in *Thinking* Eye, 386–92.

87. Although it should be pointed out that he had a deep love of the Greek classics, which according to his biographer Werner Haftmann, "he read in the original nearly every evening before going to sleep"; see Haftmann, *The Mind and Work of Paul Klee* (London, 1967), 23.

88. Reprinted in *Thinking Eye.*

89. *Rhythmic Landscape with Trees,* 1920.41, oil on cardboard, 47.5 × 29.5 cm; *Rose Garden,* 1920.44, oil on cardboard, 50 × 43 cm.

90. Quotation taken from J. Gage, "Psychological Background to Colour," in *Towards a New Art: Essays on the Background to Abstract Art, 1910–20* (London, 1980), 27.

91. *Fugue in Red,* 1921.69, watercolor on paper, 24.3 × 37.2 cm. Felix Klee, Bern.

92. See esp. *Les fenêtres sur la ville (1'ère partie, "1"ères contrastes simultanées)* of 1912–13. Klee, *Diaries,* entry 1081.

93. For an extended discussion of this painting and supposed relationships with Schoenberg's dodecaphonic method, see K. Porter Aichele, "Paul Klee's '*Rhythmisches*': A Recapitulation of the Bauhaus Years," *Zeitschrift für Kunstgeschichte* (1994), 75—89. This article also consider's Klee's ideas on color in relation to Ostwald's theories of color harmony.

94. Klee, *Pedagogical Sketchbook,* 1.6 (London, 1953; reprint, 1981; orig. publ. 1925), 22.

95. See R. Krauss, "Grids," in *The Originality of the Avant-Garde and Other Modernist Myths* (Boston, 1986), 9, and W. J. T. Mitchell, *Picture Theory* (Chicago, 1994), 215-16.

96. See W. Grohmann, *Paul Klee* (New York, 1985), 72.

97. See A. Kagan, *Paul Klee: Art and Music* (Ithaca, N.Y., 1983), 67-74, for a discussion of *Alter Klang* that relates it to Leonardo's *Saint John the Baptist.*

98. Ibid., 74-77; N. Perloff, "Klee and Webern: Speculations on Modernist Theories of Composition," *Musical Quarterly* 69 (1983), 180-208. As Perloff points out, it is an interesting coincidence that Webern referred to the construction of his twelve-note rows as "magic squares" (204).

99. He was a good friend of Paul Hindemith, a champion of modern music, although an outspoken opponent of Schoenberg's serialism.

100. A. Webern, *The Path to the New Music,* ed. W. Reich (Vienna, 1960), trans. L. Black (London, 1963). See also Webern's *Concerto,* op. 24, where he attempts to construct the serial relationships modeled on this magic square. Perloff, "Klee and Webern," 205-7, discusses this in some detail.

101. See E. Neumann, ed., *Bauhaus und Bauhäusler: Erinnerungen und Bekenntnisse* (Cologne, 1985), 342. According to Felix Klee, *Klee et la musique* (Paris, 1985), 165, his father met Schoenberg in Munich, Düsseldorf, and possibly at the Bauhaus (indeed, Schoenberg was a named Friend of the Bauhaus, but there is no supporting evidence in the primary literature mentioning a visit).

102. Kagan relates this work, and Klee's interest in polyphony in general, to the text written by Johann Josef Fux, *Gradus ad Parnassum* (1725).

103. Klee, *Pedagogical Sketchbook,* 54.

104. Originally published in *Partisan Review* (May–June 1941), reproduced in C. Greenberg, *The Collected Essays and Criticism,* ed. J. O'Brian, vol. 1 (Chicago, 1993), 65-73 (from which all quotations are taken). Klee died in Orselina sanatorium on 29 June 1940, following five years of suffering from the rare skin disease scleroderma, in which the skin becomes immobilized, like a carapace.

105. Klee, *Notebooks,* vol. 2: *The Nature of Nature,* ed. J. Spiller, trans. H. Norden (London, 1973), 269.

106. For a discussion of this characterization, see M. A. Cheetham, *The Rhetoric of Purity: Essentialist Theory and the Advent of Abstract Painting* (Cambridge, 1991), in particular the postscript, 139-51.

CHAPTER 5: **"OUT OF TUNE"**

1. G. Watkins, *Soundings: Music in the Twentieth Century* (London, 1988), 339.

2. C. Rosen, *Schoenberg* (Glasgow, 1976), 68.

3. J. M. Hauer, "Die Tropen," *Musikblätter des Ansbruchs* (1924), 18-20.

4. J. M. Hauer, *Zwölftontechnik* (Vienna, 1926), 10.

5. In his short study of Hauer, H. H. Stuckenschmidt makes the following observation:

"During [our] long conversations [I] got to know Hauer both as a musician and as a person with an unusually accurate ear. . . . He played some pieces including twelve-note melodies at his grand piano; then he whistled about a dozen of such atonal sequences. The intonation was precise and the notes followed each other astonishingly quickly without any one being repeated before the other eleven had been whistled." H. H. Stuckenschmidt, *Germany and Central Europe,* vol. 2 of *Twentieth Century Composers,* ed. A. Kallin and N. Nabokov (London, 1970), 75. This ability must have been a consequence of Hauer's conception of the tropes. Symmetrical hexachords produce relationships that are easier to hear; asymmetrical hexachords are harder to hear.

6. For a more detailed account, see R. M. Weiss, "Musiktheorie als Wissenschaftstheorie: Musikalische Beispiele für eine 'Metatheorie,'" in F. G. Wallner and B. Agnese, *Von der Einheit des Wissens zur Vielfalt der Wissensformen: Erkenntnis in Philosophie, Wissenschaft und Kunst,* Philosophica, no. 14 (Vienna, 1997), 137–56.

7. B. R. Simms, "Who First Composed Twelve-Tone Music, Schoenberg or Hauer?" *Journal of the Arnold Schoenberg Institute* 10, no. 2 (1987), 109–33, quotation on 124.

8. In conversation with the author.

9. Simms, "Twelve-Tone Music," 127–28.

10. See E. Stein, *Arnold Schoenberg: Letters* (London, 1964; reprint, London, 1987, trans. E. Wilkins and E. Kaiser), no. 78, 103–5. The passage from the *Theory of Harmony* (3d ed.) reads as follows: "and as certain as it is that among the atonalists there are many who could more appropriately occupy themselves with something really atonal, rather than with the manufacture of bad compositions. . . . (Excepted here is the Viennese, Josef Hauer. His theories are profound and original, even where I find them extravagant. His compositions betray creative talent, even where they seem to me more like 'examples' than compositions. But his attitude, his courage and self-sacrifice, make him in every way worthy of respect.)" Quoted from "Appendix," author's footnote from p. 407, on 432–34, *Theory of Harmony,* trans. R. E. Carter (London, 1978), based on 1922 edition, first published as *Harmonielehre* in 1911.

11. The fund was set up to provide financial aid to musicians suffering hardships as a result of postwar conditions, inflation being then rife in Austria and Germany. See Stein, ed., *Schoenberg,* no. 62, 87–88. In November 1923, Hauer received 350,000 Kronen (obtained from the exchange of only five dollars!). Hauer wrote back immediately to Schoenberg to express his thanks and to pass on his condolences over the recent death of Schoenberg's wife, Mathilde.

12. Ibid., no. 121, 145–46. There were also suggestions for a conference to compare views and even collaboration, to disseminate their positions, over a school of dodecaphonic music and a book, both of which, however, came to nothing.

13. See Simms, "Twelve-Tone Music," and H. Kirchmeyer, "Schönberg und Hauer," *Neue Zeitschrift für Musik* 77 (1966), 258–63.

14. See Schoenberg's comments at note 10, above.

15. See C. Greenberg, "Modernist Painting," first published in *Arts Yearbook* 1 (New York, 1961), reprinted with slight revisions in *Art and Literature* 4 (Spring 1965), 193–201. Quoted reference from further reprint (based on latter) in C. Harrison and

P. Wood, eds., *Art in Theory, 1900–1990: An Anthology of Changing Ideas* (Oxford, 1992), 754–60.

16. C. Greenberg, "Beginnings of Modernism," in M. Chefdor, R. Quinones, and A. Wachtel, eds., *Modernism: Challenges and Perspectives* (Urbana, Ill., 1986), 20.

17. Boulez, "Schoenberg the Unloved?" in *Orientations* (London, 1986), 327 (first published in French, 1981).

18. Oliver Neighbour's discussion of Schoenberg's songs from "Das Buch der hängenden Gärten" of early 1908, in *The New Grove: Second Viennese School* (London, 1983), 39.

19. Completed in July 1906.

20. C. Greenberg, "Modernist Paintings," in Harrison and Wood, eds., *Art in Theory,* 758.

21. For a contextual reading of the painting that relates this disquiet to a crisis in allegory, see M. Pointon, *Naked Authority: The Body in Western Painting, 1830–1908* (Cambridge, 1990), chap. 6, 113–34.

22. R. Williams, "When Was Modernism?" *New Left Review* 175 (May–June 1989), 48–52. Quoted from a reprint in F. Frascina and J. Harris, eds., *Art in Modern Culture: An Anthology of Critical Texts* (London, 1992), 26.

23. See Schoenberg's article "Composition with Twelve Tones (1) and (2)" [1941], in *Style and Idea: Selected Writings of Arnold Schoenberg,* ed. L. Stein and trans. L. Black (London, 1975; revised, 1984).

24. J. M. Hauer, *Vom Wesen des Musikalischen* (The essence of musicality) [1920] (reprint, Berlin, 1966, by Robert Lienau), quoted from reprint, 30.

25. "Tone-colour melody," which can be defined as the juxtaposition of different instruments in succession to produce a melody of tone color. See also "Anton Webern: *Klangfarbenmelodie*" [1951], in *Style and Idea,* ed. Stein, trans. Black.

26. See C. L. Eastlake's 1840 translation of Goethe, *Theory of Colours* (reprint, Cambridge, Mass., 1970; 4th printing, Boston, 1978), paras. 814 and 815, 320.

27. Although in a letter of 21 January 1924 Hauer declared "that he wished to renounce the 'icy wastelands' of pure atonal composition for the 'friendly green valleys' of orchestral music." Simms "Twelve-Tone Music," 128.

28. However, it is worth pointing out that in some later works, such as his opera *Salambo,* op. 60 (1929), Hauer happily uses orchestral color. As Weiss has pointed out, the whole opera is based on a single twelve-note cycle: b, f, g♯, c♯, g, a / d♯, f♯, c, a♯, d, e. To maintain its identity but to generate more than twelve tetrads, Hauer systematically permutates the sequence within the halves of the trope: f, g♯, c♯, g, a, b, / f♯, c, a♯, d, e, d♯, then g♯, c♯, g, a, b, f, / c, a♯, d, e, d♯, f♯, and so on. "More complex patterns of permutation occur as well, but always systematically based on minimal alterations of the original structure, an anticipation . . . found again only decades later in *American minimal music.*" See the sleeve notes for the recording of this opera on the Orfeo label by R. M. Weiss.

29. Goethe, *Theory of Colours,* 1.

30. See E. Hering, *Die Lehre vom Lichtsinne* (Veinna, 1878), 110: "Every simple colour has a simple colour, every mixed colour a mixed colour as its opposite."

31. Hauer, *Vom Wesen des Musikalischen* (1966 reprint), 35.

32. The term was used by Goethe quoted after Kandinsky and Marc's *Blaue Reiter Almanac* (1912). Kandinsky placed the following as a preface to Hartmann's article "Anarchy in Music": "Painting has long since lacked any knowledge of *Generalbass,* there is a lack of any established, recognised theory, such as exists in music" (Klaus Lankheit's edition [New York, 1974], 113).
33. *Deutung des Melos* (Vienna, 1921), 64 (translation by J. Covach).
34. See J. Covach, "The Music and Theories of Josef Matthias Hauer" (Ph.D. diss., University of Michigan, 1990).
35. Ibid., 93.
36. This reminds us of Swedenborg (whose ideas were also known to Schoenberg). He, like Steiner after him, had claimed access to a higher realm of reality (see Chapter 2 of this volume), a realm outside time and space, but Kant, who knew his ideas (see Kant's *Dreams of a Spirit-Seer,* 1766) attacked Swedenborg's claims to supersensory perception. Kant maintained that we can never know the thing-in-itself, Swedenborg believed that he, at least, could. See E. Cassirer, *Kant's Life and Thought* (1918).
37. R. Steiner, *The Inner Nature of Music and the Experience of Tone,* published by the Anthroposophical Press (New York, 1983).
38. Goethe, *Theory of Colours,* 298–99.
39. See, for example, R. Steiner, *The Influence of Lucifer and Ahriman*, trans. D. S. Osmond (London, 1954), although there are many other references to these forces throughout Steiner's oeuvre.
40. Within Zoroastrian religion there is the existence of two predominate spirits: Ahura-Mazda (Ormazd), the wise one, the spirit of light and good, and Ahriman, the spirit of darkness and evil. The conflict between these two centers on man, who was created as a free agent by Ormazd.
41. See Covach, "Music and Theories of Hauer," 103.
42. L. Wittgenstein, *Tractatus Logico-Philosophicus* (Vienna, 1922), prop. 7.
43. Ibid., 6.522.
44. A. Janik and S. Toulmin, *Wittgenstein's Vienna* (New York, 1973), 197.
45. For a discussion of this relationship, see R. Horwitz, "Ferdinand Ebner as a Source of Martin Buber's Dialogic Thought in *I and Thou,*" in H. Gordon and J. Bloch, eds., *Martin Buber: A Centenary Volume* (New York, 1984), 121–38.
46. See W. Szmolyan, *Josef Matthias Hauer* (Vienna, 1965), 14.
47. J. Jensen, "Ferdinand Ebner und Josef Matthias Hauer," in W. Methlagl et al., eds., *Untersuchungen zum "Brenner"* (Salzburg, 1981), 242–72.
48. W. Johnson, *The Austrian Mind: An Intellectual and Social History, 1848–1938* (Berkeley, Calif., 1972; reprint, Berkeley, Calif., 1983), 219.
49. W. Mertens, *American Minimal Music,* trans. J. Hautekiet, preface by M. Nyman (London, 1983).
50. Ibid., 88.
51. Ibid., 96.
52. Ibid., 97, quoted after T. W. Adorno, *Philosophy of Modern Music* (first published 1948, English translation, 1973).

53. Mertens, *American Minimal Music,* 100 (my emphasis).
54. All Reich quotations are taken from his *Writings About Music* (New York, 1974), 10–11.
55. Quoted after R. S. Gustafson, "The Theories of Josef Mattias [sic] Hauer" (Ph.D. diss., Michigan State University, 1977), 186. All quotataios in English from Hauer's principal writings are taken from Gustafson's translations.
56. Mertens, *American Minimal Music,* 104.
57. The *I-Ching* was, according to Hauer's son Bruno, the last book in his father's possession after he gave away his library (conversation with author, 1984). In addition, some followers of Hauer have drawn relationships between his forty-four tropes and the sixty-four hexagrams of the *I-Ching.*
58. Hauer, preface to *Zwölftonspiel—Neujahr, 1947* (Vienna, 1962).
59. See J. W. Bernard, "The Minimalist Aesthetic in the Plastic Arts and Music," *Perspectives of New Music* 31, no. 1 (Winter 1993), 91. Although I deviate from Bernard on this issue, I have found his characterization of minimalism useful, and it informs the following discussion.
60. It is not my intention to pursue the issue of chronology in general, any more than it is to provide a detailed definition of minimalism in the abstract. I am more concerned to imply such issues through the discussion of examples. For perhaps the best analysis of the origins of minimalism in all the arts, see E. Strickland, *Minimalism: Origins* (Bloomington, Ind., 1993).
61. D. Anfam, *Abstract Expressionism* (London, 1990), 67.
62. Statement made in 1966 quoted after W. Rubin, "Frank Stella," in E. A. Carmean, Jr., ed., *The Great Decade of American Abstraction: Modernist Art 1960–1970* (Houston, Tex., 1974), 102.
63. See J. Kallir, *Arnold Schoenberg's Vienna* (New York, 1984); see also Kandinsky's essay on Schoenberg the painter in K. Lindsay and P. Vergo, eds., *Kandinsky: Complete Writings on Art,* 1:221–22.
64. These are reformulations of distinctions made in Bernard, "Minimalist Aesthetic."
65. See, e.g., Hal Foster's essay "The Crux of Minimalism," in H. Singerman, ed., *Individuals: A Selected History of Contemporary Art, 1945–1986* (New York, 1986).
66. The work was first recorded four years later by Columbia Masterworks in 1968.
67. It is interesting to note that, just as many works by minimalist artists at this time are titled "Untitled" and consequently known by date, so it is the case that Hauer's zwölftonspiele are designated chronologically.
68. Hauer, *Vom Melos zur Pauke* (From melos to kettledrum) (Vienna, 1925), 14 (see Gustafson, "Theories of Hauer," 126, for English translation).
69. See F. Stella, "Pratt Institute Lecture" (1960), in R. Rosenblum, *Frank Stella* (Harmondsworth, 1971), 57.
70. Ibid. (see also Harrison and Wood, eds., *Art in Theory,* 806).
71. For a detailed anaysis of this work, see Epstein, "Pattern Structure and Process in Steve Reich's *Piano Phase,*" *Musical Quarterly* 72 (1986), 494–502.
72. Quoted after the Doblinger catalog of Hauer's music (Vienna, n.d.), 5.

73. See Stuckenschmidt, *Germany and Central Europe,* 79.

74. L. Steinberg, "Reflections on the State of Criticism," *Artforum* (March 1972), 42–43, reprinted in *Other Criteria* (London, 1972), 61–98, extract reprinted in Harrison and Woods, eds., *Art in Theory,* 948–53.

75. Quoted in M. Fried, "Art and Objecthood," *Artforum* (Summer 1967), reprinted in Harrison and Wood, eds., *Art in Theory,* 825.

76. Reich, *Writings About Music,* 10–11.

77. Glass quoted in Mertens, *American Minimal Music,* 79.

78. Hauer, *Deutung des Melos,* 24.

79. Manifesto of March 1956.

80. C. Greenberg, "The Recentness of Sculpture," in G. Battcock, ed., *Minimal Art: A Critical Anthology* (London, 1969), 183.

81. H. Eimert, "Hauer," in F. Blume, ed., *Die Musik in Geschichte und Gegenwart,* 14 vols. (Kassel, 1949–68).

82. D. Bogner, "Musik und bildende Kunst in Wien," in K. v. Maur, ed., *Vom Klang der Bilder: die Musik in der Kunst des 20. Jahrhunderts* (Munich, 1985), 346–53, esp. 351.

CHAPTER 6: A CHORUS OF VOICES

1. R. Barthes, *Image-Music-Text,* selected and trans. S. Heath (Glasgow, 1982), 155.

2. The term *Fluxus* was first coined by George Maciunas in 1961 as the title for a proposed magazine but was soon adopted to describe a range of activities associated with those artists who shared Maciunas's vision. In his *Manifesto* of 1963 (held in the Gilbert and Lila Silverman Fluxus Collection, New York), Maciunas used part of the dictionary definition of *flux* in describing his ideas. He used seven subdefinitions but concentrated on three main concepts: "purge," "flow," and "fuse." "Purge" was intended as purging the "world of dead art" and "Europeanism," "flow" was understood as promoting "a revolutionary flood and tide of art" ("living art, anti-art and non art reality"), and "fuse" was seen as fusing "the cadres of cultural, social and political revolutionaries into united front and action."

3. On "performative," see K. Stiles, "Between Water and Stone," in J. Jenkins, ed., *In the Spirit of Fluxus* (New York, 1993), 65, adopting J. L. Austin's term to refer to a class of expressions that are not descriptive and have no truth value but rather do something (for example, I promise . . .). The meaning resides in the act of performance; see Austin, *How To Do Things with Words* (Cambridge, Mass., 1975).

   The exhibition for which this was the catalog toured from February 1993 to January 1995, opening in Minneapolis and closing in Barcelona.

4. M. Kirby, "The New Theatre," *Tulane Drama Review* 10, no. 2 (Winter 1965), 25–26. Here Kirby distinguishes between what he calls "matrixed" and "non-matrixed" performance. This essay is reprinted in M. Kirby, *Art of Time: Essays on the Avant-Garde* (New York, 1969), 75–102.

5. D. Higgins, "Some Thoughts on the Context of Fluxus," in *Horizons: The Poetics and Theory of Intermedia* (Carbondale, Ill., 1984). See also his "Statement on Intermedia"

in *Dé-Coll/age* 6 (July 1967), and "Intermedia" in *foew&ombwhnw* (New York, 1969). Since starting to use the term *intermedia,* Higgins has discovered that Samuel Taylor Coleridge first used the word in about 1812; see Higgins, *Some Poetry Intermedia,* poster, 1976.

6. A. Huyssen, "Back to the Future: Fluxus in Context," in Jenkins, ed., *In the Spirit of Fluxus,* 149–50; see also T. W. Adorno, "Kunst und die Kunste," in *Ohne Leitbild: Parva Aesthetica* (Frankfurt, 1967), 158–82.

7. In this sense it is to be viewed as a strength, both politically and academically. See M. Pointon, "History of Art and the Undergraduate Syllabus: Is It a Discipline and How Should We Teach It?" in F. Borzello and A. L. Rees, eds., *The New Art History* (London, 1986), 147–56.

8. Barthes, *Image-Music-Text,* 155.

9. Cage applied chance operations to determine the length of each movement. He employed a deck of homemade cards on which were written durations. His more usual chance procedures, however, employed the *I Ching.*

10. Quotation taken from S. Montague, "Significant Silences of a Musical Anarchist," *Classical Music,* 22 May 1982, reprinted in *Conversing with Cage,* comp. R. Kostelanetz (London, 1989), 66.

11. Cage experienced Harvard University's anechoic chamber, an environment as soundproof and free from reverberation as was technologically possible, sometime in the mid-1940s. For his recollection of this event, see *Silence* (London, 1968), 8, 13, 23, 51, 168.

12. See W. Fetterman, *John Cage's Theatre Pieces: Notations and Performances* (Amsterdam, 1996), 74. This book discusses Cage's scores in detail. The videotaped performance of 1990 can give us a flavor of Tudor's performance approach. Fetterman describes it thus: "Here, one can see very graceful, rounded gestures in details such as starting the watch, closing the keyboard cover, as well as Tudor's close attention between reading the score and checking the stop-watch. Except for turning the pages [a further realization of the score], Tudor has his hands folded in his lap during the three movements, his back erect, his expression very serious and concentrated" (76).

13. Ibid., 72–79, for a discussion the scores of all four versions of the work.

14. Ibid., 80. In addition, Cage notes that whatever the duration of the piece it would still be called *4′33″*—whatever the length of silence, such a silence, is a Cagian silence.

15. Cage, *Silence,* 103.

16. See R. Kostelanetz, ed., *Conversing with Cage* (London, 1988), 188.

17. For a more recent discussion of embodiment in performance, an essay that provides a useful summary of a small but growing "body" of research on the intimate links between musical sound and the bodily movement involved in its production, see E. Clarke and J. Davidson, "The Body in Performance," in W. Thomas, ed., *Composition-Performance-Reception: Studies in the Creative Process in Music* (Aldershot, 1998), 74–92.

18. E. J. Dent, quotation taken from B. Magee, *Aspects of Wagner* (London, 1972), 84–85.

19. Either explicitly, in the case of Schoenberg, or implicitly, in the case of Fluxus, through the establishment and consequent questioning of conventions.

20. See T. W. Adorno, *The Philosophy of Modern Music* [1948], trans. A. G. Mitchell and W. V. Bloomster (London, 1973).

21. A. Schoenberg, *Theory of Harmony,* trans. R. E. Carter (based on 3d ed., 1922) (London, 1983), 21 (first published as *Harmonielehre,* Vienna, 1911).

22. It should be noted that Schoenberg did not teach his twelve-note method. Rather, books such as *Preliminary Exercises in Counterpoint* (London, 1963), *Fundamentals of Musical Composition* (London, 1967), and *Structural Functions of Harmony* (1954; reprinted and revised by L. Stein, London, 1983) (all of which are taken from his UCLA classes) demonstrate that he was keen to establish in his students a thorough grounding in conventional fundamentals. Similarly, he never looked at any of Cage's compositions. Therefore Cage's independent approach should not be considered too surprising.

23. Edgar Varese (1885–1965) had composed his *Ionisation* between 1929 and 1931 for thirteen percussion players, and Amadeo Roldan composed his *Ritmicas* in 1930. Cage may have heard the use of percussion instruments from different cultures (especially Balinese gamelan), but solo percussion pieces were rare at this time. The *Trio* marks the first appearance of Cage's invention of the "water-gong," created to allow swimmers to hear his music underwater.

24. Cage, *Silence,* 3.

25. L. Russolo, "The Art of Noises," in U. Apollonio, ed., *Futurist Manifestos* (London, 1973), 88.

26. Ibid., 76. We can detect elements of Russolo's connection to more orthodox musical practices in his notation system. In the score to his *Wakefulness of a City* (1914) we find a miswritten 3/4 time signature, bar lines, and use of treble and bass clefs, all meaningless in the face of a graphic notation of noise in approximate time and pitch. Nevertheless, it is appropriate that he should invent machines to create his music, given the futurists' obsession with machinery. As regards Cage's position to music of the past, he had no such absolute rejection, but I mention him in relation to this quotation because he did have a strong dislike of Beethoven.

27. Russolo's legacy allowed musicians like Edgar Varese to allude to extramusical sounds without becoming too referential; see O. Mattis, "Varese's Multimedia Conception of Deserts," *Musical Quarterly* 76, no. 4 (Winter 1992), 557–83. This article not only discusses Varese's interest in electronic sound generation, but also his conception of a Gesamtkunstwerk with lights and projections and music of epic proportions: this sense of scale tends to relate Varese to a more nineteenth-century aesthetic, despite his interests in electronic instrumental technology and his friendship with Cage in the early 1950s. His Gesamtkunstwerk has more in common with Wagner than with Fluxus.

28. Here again we can make reference to Barthes; see "The Death of the Author," in *Image-Music-Text,* 142–48.

29. *Variations IV,* in the Everest recording (S-3132) or (M-6132); J. Cage, *For the Birds: John Cage in Conversation with Daniel Charles* (London, 1981), 133 (first published as *Pour les oiseaux,* 1976).

30. Cage, *Silence,* 31.

31. Quoted from E. Salzman's review of the work in *Stereo Review,* May 1969. However, it should be remembered that a different realization of the score could lead to a much less complex and dense sound experience.

32. See M. McLuhan, "Radio: The Tribal Drum," in his *Understanding Media: The Extensions of Man* (London, 1967), 326.

33. For a discussion of this tension between the meaning of sound and its phenomenality, see F. Dyson, "The Ear That Would Hear Sounds in Themselves: John Cage, 1935–1965," in D. Kahn and G. Whitehead, eds., *Wireless Imagination: Sound Radio and the Avant-Garde* (Cambridge, Mass., 1992), 373–408. See also my own "Towards a Hermeneutics of Music," in S. Miller, ed., *The Last Post: Music After Modernism* (Manchester, 1993), 5–26, for a detailed discussion of the history of the idealist philosophical tradition, which positioned music as apart from the world and regarded "absolute" music as paradigmatic.

34. We are reminded here of the philosopher John Dewey. In *Art as Experience* (New York, 1934), he argued that there is cohesion between aesthetic experience and experience in general; they are not fundamentally or necessarily opposed.

35. A. Huyssen, *After the Great Divide: Modernism, Mass Culture and Postmodernism* (London, 1986), ix.

36. Barthes, "Death of the Author," 162–63.

37. My use of the concept "representation" should not be confused here with the more restricted use associated with mimesis, as discussed by P. Kivy in *Sound and Semblance: Reflections on Musical Representation* (Ithaca, N.Y., 1984; reprint, Ithaca, N.Y., 1991). Rather, I use it in the literal sense of "to stand for something else."

38. Stiles, "Between Water and Stone," 66.

39. M. Duchamp, "The Creative Act," in G. Battcock, ed., *The New Art* (New York, 1966), 25.

40. M. Nyman, "George Brecht: Interview," *Studio International* 192, no. 984 (November–December 1976), 257.

41. Quotation taken from E. Strickland, *Minimalism: Origins* (Bloomington, Ind., 1993), 140. Butterfly imagery appears in a number of works by Young. In relation to this specific piece, as Mitchell Clark has shown, within *qin* aesthetics, notations (*shoushitu,* or pictures of hand postures) showing the correct hand position for harmonics (*fan,* meaning "to float"), the image of a butterfly in flight is depicted with the legend *fendi fu hua shi* ("the posture of a white butterfly floating among flowers"). See M. Clark, "Zephyrs: Some Correspondences Between Bai Juyi's *Qin* and La Monte Young's *Composition 1960 #5,*" in W. Duckworth and R. Fleming, eds., *Sound and Light: La Monte Young / Marian Zazeela* (London, 1996), 132–51.

42. Compositions *2, 3, 4, 5, 6, 7, 9, 10, 13,* and *15* are printed in an anthology of art entitled *An Anthology of Chance Operations/ Concept art/ Meaningless work/ Natural disasters/Indeterminacy/Anti-art/Plans of action/Improvisations/Stories/Diagrams/ Poet/ Essays/ Dance constructions/ Compositions/ Mathematics/ Music.* It is (thankfully) referred to simply as *An Anthology,* ed. La Monte Young and Jackson Mac Low, compiled in 1961 (New York, 1963).

43. Quoted after D. Kahn, "The Latest: Fluxus and Music," in Jenkins, ed., *Spirit of*

Fluxus, 106. This was one of the first essays to raise important conceptual issues in relation to Fluxus "musical works." This chapter has reconfigured a number of them, but is more directly concerned with visual implications.

44. J. Cage, "Music Lover's Field Companion," in *Silence,* 276.

45. For a disquisition on this subject, see S. Schama, *Landscape and Memory* (London, 1995).

46. See Duchamp, "The Creative Act," in G. Battcock, ed., *The New Art* (New York, 1966), 23-26.

47. R. Kostelanetz, ed., *John Cage: An Anthology* (New York, 1991), supplemented and reprinted from 1970, 13.

48. Ibid., 14.

49. Quotation taken from S. Nairne, *State of the Art: Ideas and Images in the 1980s* (London, 1987), 93.

50. Ibid., 102.

51. From John Eliot Gardiner's essay on the *Vespers* in the booklet accompanying the Deutsche Grammophon recording (429 565-2/4) in Saint Mark's (1990), 15. This recording was sponsored by ICI under the surprisingly Cagian banner "Challenging Frontiers Through Music."

52. Apart from the issue of "acoustic space," there is also the issue of "notational space." Notational space can be considered as the vertical element of scores that shows the temporal coincidence of different musical timbres and pitches. As Robert Morgan put it in "Musical Time/Musical Space," in W. J. T. Mitchell, ed., *The Language of Images* (Chicago, 1980), 259-70: "Thus many of the surface aspects of musical scores are immediately apparent from the visual format of the score" (269).

53. *Conversing with Cage,* 203 (my emphasis).

54. R. Barthes, *The Responsibility of Forms,* trans. R. Howard (Berkeley, Calif., 1985), 245. He continues, "It is possible to describe the physical conditions of hearing (its mechanisms) by recourse to acoustics and to the physiology of the ear: but listening cannot be defined only by its object or, one might say, by its goal" (245-46). He differentiates three types of listening: (1) *alert,* the awareness of sound; (2) *deciphering,* the recognition of aural "signs," "I listen the way I read, i.e. according to certain code"; and (3) the awareness not of what is said or emitted, but who speaks, or emits. This last type is the birth of the intersubjective space, "where 'I am listening' also means 'listen to me'; what it seizes upon . . . is the general 'signify' no longer conceivable without the determination of the unconscious."

55. Glass quoted in H. Sayre, *The Object of Performance* (Chicago, 1992), 114.

56. E. Tamm, *Brian Eno: His Music and the Vertical Color of Sound* (Boston, 1989), 25.

57. Ibid., 24.

58. For Barthes there is a relationship or affinity between the gaze and music, in that both derive not from the sign but from signification. Later he suggests (quoting Jacques Lacan, *Seminaire XI*), and rather appropriately for our frog, that the direct, imperious gaze's effect is "to arrest movement and to kill life"; see "Right in the Eyes," in *Responsibility of Forms,* 237-42.

59. The first performance of this group in the United Kingdom took place at the Barbican

Hall in London, as part of the *American Pioneers* series of concerts. They performed *The Melodic Version* (1984) of Young's *First Blossom of Spring* from *The Four Dreams of China* (1962). This is one of a series of works that uses a process of improvisation within a framework of fixed rules that determine which of the four pitches that make up the work may be sounded together and in what order. The pitches used derive from the "Dream Chords" common to a large number of works by Young (C, F, F♯, G): his *Trio for Strings* (1958), *For Brass* (1957), and *For Strings* (1958), and *The First Dream of The High-Tension Line Stepdown Transformer*. These pitches are represented by the frequency ratios of the triad 12–9–8. For a detailed discussion of Young's harmonic language, see K. Gann, "The Outer Edge of Consonance," in Duckworth and Fleming, eds., *Sound and Light,* 152–90.

60. This approach is part of a long history of synesthetic and color-sound experimentation, from Louis Bertrand Castel's ocular harpsichord in the eighteenth century to Scriabin's interest in light, sound, and smell in the early twentieth century to contemporary light shows as part of rock concerts or in dance clubs. For these early experiments, see L. B. Castel, "Difficultés sur le claveçin oculaire avec leur réponses," *Mercure de France* (March 1726), n.p.; and J. Zilczer, " 'Color-Music': Synaesthesia and Nineteenth-Century Sources for Abstract Art," *Artibus & Historiae* 16 (1987), 101–126. See also J. Gage, *Colour and Culture* (London, 1993), chap. 13. For a discussion of Zazeela's work, see her essays and those of other authors in Duckworth and Fleming, eds., *Sound and Light.*

61. In fact, Young did perform the work by burning a cheap violin stuffed with matches and drenched in lighter fluid, as a work within Richard Maxfield's *Dromenon* (which continued unabated); see Strickland, *Minimalism: Origins,* 138.

62. M. Kirby and R. Schechner, "An Interview with John Cage," *Tulane Drama Review* 10, no. 2 (Winter 1965), 50.

63. This might remind us of the use of water in Max Neuhaus's *Water Whistle* piece of 1971–74, where whistles placed underwater produced sound by having water pumped through them; see Chapter 1, above.

64. Nyman, "George Brecht: Interview," 26.

65. For example, as already mentioned, Maciunas was Lithuanian, Paik was born in Korea but lives in Germany and America, La Monte Young is American, and Robin Page was born in Canada and has lived in England and Germany. Fluxus mainly operated on the German-American nexus, but its "membership" extended across Europe, Asia, and North America.

This work also brings to my mind my grandfather's description of a lavatory as a "poor man's piano," and James Joyce in *Ulysses,* who describes the strange music of the chamber pot as it is filled, "Diddle iddle addle addle oodle oodle hiss." Its resonance with Duchamp's *Fountain* should also be noted.

66. L. Kramer, *Music as Cultural Practice, 1800–1900* (Berkeley, Calif., 1990), makes a similar point in relation to nineteenth-century bravura performances: "What the audience sees is a theatrical icon of the inspired musician; what it hears is a highly charged extension of the performer's touch, breath, rhythm: the body electric, in Walt

Whitman's phrase. Hence the cultivation of certain physical peculiarites (Liszt's long hair, Paganini's emaciated pallor) and hence, too, the many cartoonlike caricatures of musicians like Paganini, Liszt, Berlioz, and Wagner. . . . Robert Schumann recognizes much of this syndrome when he remarks that 'the Viennese, especially, have tried to catch the eagle [Liszt] in every way—through pursuits, snares, pitchforks, and poems. But he must be heard—and also seen: for if Liszt played behind a screen, a great deal of poetry would be lost' " (90–91). See also A. Durant, *Conditions of Music* (London, 1984), chap. 4, and R. Leppert, *The Sight of Sound: Music, Representation, and the History of the Body* (Berkeley, Calif., 1993), and in a somewhat different but equally rich vein, E. Clarke and J. Davidson, "The Body in Performance," in Thomas, ed., *Composition-Performance-Reception,* 74–92. Barthes's essay "The Grain of the Voice," in *Image-Music-Text,* 179–89, discusses the body in relation to the voice. He identifies two types of voicing, "phenotext" (attention to generic detail, phrasing, and so on) and "genotext" (the eroticized voice beyond particular cultural meanings, the voicing of the body in language): "The 'grain' is the body as it sings" (188). He links the decline of the genotext to the increasing professionalization of music making.

67. M. Nyman, *Experimental Music: Cage and Beyond* (London, 1974), 74.

68. See "From Jail to Jungle, 1967–77: The Work of Charlotte Moorman and Nam June Paik," in G. Battcock and R. Nickas, eds., *The Art of Performing: A Critical Anthology* (New York, 1984), 278–88. Moorman's sentence for "indecent exposure" was suspended. Paik was, however, found "not guilty" because the judge regarded the idea of pornographic music as impossible.

69. See Chapter 3, above, in which I argued that in Picasso's cubist paintings of women playing musical instruments, the female "subject" is transformed into, or becomes synonymous with, the musical "object" (the instrument). The expression "Le violon d'Ingres" is a French euphemism for a hobby, in reference to Ingres's favourite pastime of playing the violin. That an image of a nude woman (Man Ray's mistress, Alice Prin, a cabaret singer known as Kiki de Montparnasse) should be so entitled only underlines the idea of "*play*thing," whether Man Ray intended it ironically or not.

It is also worth noting that the soundboard of instruments in the violin family is called the "belly," its upper part the "neck," and the reverse the "back," which is joined to the belly by the "ribs."

70. The early Soviet composer Ilya Sats experimented with modified pianos thirty years earlier than Cage. He used sheets of metal and other objects to change the sound in an attempt to move beyond conventional timbre. Like the Italian futurists, Sats celebrated the world of noise: "Music is the wind, the rustling, and speech, and banging, and crunching, and squalling. That is the symphony of sounds which makes my soul cringe and weep and for which I long for" (1923). Quotation taken from S. Volkov, *St. Petersburg: A Cultural History,* trans. A. W. Bouis (London, 1996), 188.

71. See also S. L. Scholl, "String Quartet Performance as Ritual," *American Journal of Semiotics* 9, no. 1 (1992), 115–28, especially 128 on the symbolic references in the presentation of flowers in a musical context. Brecht's assessment of the string quartet as ritual can be seen in his *String Quartet* (1965), where the four players shake hands

mutually and depart. For a fascinating discussion of the ideological function of the piano (principally within Victorian culture), see R. Leppert, "The Piano, Misogyny, and 'The Kreutzer Sonata,'" chapter 7 of his *Sight of Sound*.

72. It brings to mind Paganini's loving care and laborious preparations before a performance on his prized Guiseppe Antonio Guarneri ("del Gesu") violin.

73. Maciunas also applied this destructive approach to keyboard instruments. He developed the piano's ability to sustain a note (this is what sets it apart from such predecessors as the harpsichord) in his *Piano Piece No. 13 for Nam June Paik* (1964), by requiring the performer to nail down the keys, from the lowest pitched to the highest, using a hammer. It is, of course, the hammer design that is responsible for the piano's sustaining characteristics.

In reference to Paganini, see L. Hunt in the *Tatler,* 23 June 1831, quoted in P. Weiss and R. Taruskin, eds., *Music in the Western World: A History in Documents* (New York, 1984), 340–45.

74. See Klee, *Pedagogical Sketchbook,* section 1.1, trans. S. Moholy-Nagy (London, 1953; first published as *Pädagogisches Skizzenbuch,* Weimar, 1925): "An active line on a walk, moving freely, without goal. A walk for a walk's sake"(16). It can also be regarded as a literal reversal of Young's *Composition 1960 No. 10,* "Draw a straight line and follow it." Paik performed this work by Young at the first Fluxus festival in Wiesbaden, the Fluxus Internationale Festspiele Neuester Musik (Fluxus International Festival of New Music) in 1962. He dipped his head, hands, and necktie in a mixture of ink and tomato juice, then dragged them along the length of a sheet of paper (160 × 14 cm). He entitled it *Zen for Head,* a work that raises issues pertinent to Fluxus and this chapter in that it starts as a composition, is formed as a performance, and ends as an object (a parody of abstract expressionism).

75. As Simon Frith and Howard Horne have argued, the influence of Gustav Metzger's "autodestructive" art on Pete Townshend (he lectured at Ealing Art College while Townshend was a student) might have been a post-hoc justification of a spontaneous act, but Metzger's influence may have been more direct in the use of acoustic feedback, "when the very discovery of new noise always carried with it the threat (which the group couldn't control) of the destruction of the PA system." Townshend's art school background, under the tutelage of Roy Ascott, therefore allowed him to view his musical activities in terms of performance art. Another important visual art strain of influence was that of pop art theory, which denied an aesthetic separation between high and mass art and informed much of the image of the Who. Such an awareness of art history and theory might lead us to suppose that the use of sounds from outside the mainstream of Western music (noise) have something to do with the influence of Cage and Russolo; see S. Frith and H. Horne, *Art into Pop* (London, 1987), esp. 100–101, and C. Small, *Music, Society, Education* (London, 1977; revised 1984), esp. 169–70, for a discussion of the new musical values of the so-called rock revolution.

On Tzara's manifesto, see T. Tzara, "Unpretentious Proclamations," in B. Wright, trans., *Seven Dada Manifestos and Lampisteries* (London, 1977), 16.

76. "The Founding and Manifesto of Futurism" (1909), in U. Apollonio, ed., *Futurist Manifestos* (London, 1973), 22.

77. Kahn, "The Latest: Fluxus and Music," 115.

78. This destructive impulse can be seen as an example of a wider tendency in art of the late 1950s and early 1960s by such artists as Gustav Metzger, Wolf Vostel, Jean Tinguely, John Latham, and Ralph Ortiz and most notably in the work of the Vienna "Actionists" (Gunter Brus, Otto Muhl, Hermann Nitsch, Rudolf Schwarz-kogler, Alfons Schilling, and Adolf Frohner).

79. On sleeve-design, see, for example, N. Cook, "The Domestic *Gesamtkunstwerk,* or Record Sleeves and Reception," in Thomas, ed., in *Composition-Performance-Reception,* 105–17.

80. See D. Higgins, "A Child's History of Fluxus," in his *Horizons: The Poetics and Theory of the Intermedia* (Carbondale, Ill., 1984).

Synthesis of the arts (*continued*)
in Obukhov, 79–80 in Scriabin, 60, 62;
in Wagner, 38–42, 48–50

Teosifski zhurnal (journal): 59
Ter Borch, Gerard: *Music Lesson* (1675),
95
Theosophy: 56, 59–60, 64; Kupka and,
123, 125–26, 138; music in, 59, 133–34;
Obhukov and, 80; Scriabin and, 62–63,
65, 133–34; Steiner and, 184–87
Theremin: 77–78
Time: and space, in Bergson, 139–43; in
Einstein, 142; in Klee, 145–46; in Less-
ing, 142; musical time: 143. *See also*
Simultaneity
Thomas, Ambroise: *Mignon* (1866), 111, 113
Thoreau, Henry David: 12
Titian: *The Three Ages of Man,* 93, *93*
Tragedy, Greek: Messaien and, 84; Nietz-
sche and, 42–44, 47–48; Wagner and,
40, 209
Trompe l'oeil: 106–8; in Picasso, 109
Tudor, David: 212–13, 220, 225, 241
Tzara, Tristan: *Unpretentious Proclama-
tions* (1919), 241

Ut pictura musica, 4, 9, 29, 30–31, 38, 65,
86, 121–22, 124, 128, 130, 133, 209. *See
also* Abstraction

Vermeer, Jan: *A Lady at the Virginals with
a Gentleman Listening* (1660s), 98
Violin: history of, 94; in Picasso, 115–20;
as woman, 117

Wackenroder, Wilhelm: 9, 57
Wagner, Richard: x, xi, 9, 58, 64, 70, 82,
84, 134, 173, 174, 176, 193, 209; *Art
and Revolution* (1849), 38; *Artwork of
the Future* (1849), 38, 39; Baudelaire
on, 50–52, 54; "Communication to My
Friends" (1851), 41; *Der fliegende Holländer,* 41, 51; *Gesamtkunstwerk,* x,
13–14, 38, 45–50, 121; *Götterdämmerung,* 60; *Lohengrin,* 51; *Opera and
Drama* (1851), 38, 41, 49–50; *Parsifal,*

60; performance conventions and, 216,
233–35; *Das Rheingold,* 50, 60; *Sieg-
fried,* 60; *Tannhäuser,* 51; *Tristan and
Isolde,* 43, 44, *46, 48, 49,* 50, 51, 60; *Die
Walküre,* 50
Wagnerism: 36–37
Warnod, André: 135; *Intérieur du Lapin
Agile* (1909), 98
Water, in Fluxus: 235–37, 241
Watteau, Antoine: 98; *La gamme d'amour*
(1715), 102
Webern, Anton: 156, 176, 189–90; *The
Path to the New Music* (1933), 157, 171
Whistler, James Abbott McNeill: 143
Williams, Raymond: 177
Wilson, Robert: *Einstein on the Beach*
(1976), 11
Winckelmann, Johann Joachim: 5, 42, 53
Wind instruments: history of, 92–94
Wittgenstein, Ludwig: *Tractatus logico-
philosophicus* (1922), 187
"Work-as-process": 189–92. *See also*
Minimalism
World of Art (*Mir iskusstva*) (journal):
57–58
Worringer, Wilhelm: *Abstraktion und
Einfühlung* (1907), 124

Young, La Monte: 189, 195; *Compositions*
(1960) *No. 1,* 241, *No. 2,* 235, *No. 4,*
234, *No. 5,* 226–27, *No. 6,* 234, *No. 7,*
228–29, *228; Dream House* (1979–85),
232; *Drift Studies* (1966), 232–33; *Piano
Piece for David Tudor No. 2* (1960),
225–26; *The Tortoise, His Dreams and
Journeys* (ongoing), 232; *Trio for Strings*
(1958), 232; *The Well-Tuned Piano* (ongoing), 232; *X for Henry Flint* (1960),
230–31

Zamarin, Roberto: 22
Zazeela, Marian: 231; *The Magenta
Lights,* 232; *The Ornamental Lightyears
Tracery,* 232
Zimmerman, Robert: 186
Zither: 108. *See also* Guitar
Zurbaràn, Francisco de: *Saint Apollonia*
(1636), 110